A Lexicon of Terror

A Lexicon of Terror

Revised and Updated with a New Epilogue

MARGUERITE FEITLOWITZ

OXFORD
UNIVERSITY PRESS

OXFORD
UNIVERSITY PRESS

Oxford University Press, Inc., publishes works that further
Oxford University's objective of excellence
in research, scholarship, and education.

Oxford New York

Auckland   Cape Town   Dar es Salaam   Hong Kong   Karachi
Kuala Lumpur   Madrid   Melbourne   Mexico City   Nairobi
New Delhi   Shanghai   Taipei   Toronto

With offices in

Argentina   Austria   Brazil   Chile   Czech Republic   France   Greece
Guatemala   Hungary   Italy   Japan Poland   Portugal   Singapore
South Korea   Switzerland   Thailand   Turkey   Ukraine   Vietnam

Published by Oxford University Press, Inc.
198 Madison Avenue, New York, New York 10016

www.oup.com

Oxford is a registered trademark of Oxford University Press

Library of Congress Cataloging-in-Publication Data
Feitlowitz, Marguerite.
A lexicon of terror : Argentina and the legacies of torture / Marguerite Feitlowitz. — Revised and updated, with a
new epilogue.
p.   cm.
Includes bibliographical references and index.
ISBN 978-0-19-974469-5 (pbk. : alk. paper) 1. Argentina—Politics and government—1955–1983.
2. Rhetoric—Political aspects—Argentina—History. 3. Political violence—Argentina—History. 4. Disappeared
persons—Argentina—History. 5. Terrorism—Argentina—History. I. Title.
F2849.2.F373   2011
982.06'3—dc22   2010026120

To All Those Who Watch Over
Human Rights in Argentina
and to the memory of
Rabbi Marshall Meyer
tzaddik

Contents

Preface

THIS IS A BOOK ABOUT THE LANGUAGES OF TERROR—TEXTS AND subtexts, high rhetoric, dialects, and patois. Brutal, sadistic and rapacious, the "Dirty War" junta, which ruled Argentina from 1976 to 1983, was intensely verbal and used language with diabolical skill to confuse, disorient, and terrorize. "We know," said Admiral Massera, the grand orator of the regime, "that in order to repair so much damage we will have to recover the meanings of many misappropriated words." High on his list for idiomatic repair were "rationality," "lucidity," "democracy," "patriotism," "sacrifice," and "honor." From the moment of the coup, there was a constant torrent of speeches, proclamations, and interviews. The barrage was constant and there was no escape. As the commanders talked, some 30,000 suspected "subversives" were kidnapped from the streets, tortured in secret concentration camps, and "disappeared."[1] Victims died during torture, were machine-gunned at the edge of enormous pits, or were thrown, drugged, from airplanes into the sea. These individuals came to be known as "the missing," or *desaparecidos.*

Argentina's democratic transition has been fraught with conflicts over how, when, to what degree, and to what end the workings of the Dirty War should be investigated and disclosed. Even as he was being swept by the voters to the presidency in December 1983, Dr. Raúl Alfonsín was preoccupied by the dangers of a military backlash. So he decided that only those "most responsible" for the last repression could be brought to court. In 1985, the ex-commanders of the regime were publicly tried and convicted of crimes against humanity, in addition to numerous counts of kidnapping, torture, murder, baby stealing, and robbery. Lower-ranking criminals were never charged. They kept their jobs in the military and police, in businesses and civilian institutions. Alfonsín's more conservative Peronist successor, Carlos Saúl Menem, further rolled back the prosecutions. In October 1989, in a gesture that was blatantly unconstitutional, Menem exonerated virtually all senior military officers still facing trial for crimes committed during the dictatorship. And then in April 1990, Menem declared that the convicted ex-commanders of that de facto government would also be pardoned and free "in time for Christmas." On December 29, 1990—against massive, anguished opposition—President Menem not only pardoned, but praised the convicted ex-commanders, who have lived on the fortunes they looted from the national treasury and extorted from the families of *desaparecidos.*

Menem is in many ways a mercurial figure. He has repeatedly asserted that he had the moral authority to enact this pardon because he himself was tortured during the last regime. While it is true that because he is a Peronist, he was arrested and held captive on a boat in Buenos Aires Harbor, his claims to have been tortured have been disputed by other Peronists who shared his imprisonment, and who have said point-blank that on this issue the president is lying.[2] It is well known that as the dictatorship crumbled, some in the departing regime struck alliances with certain powerful Peronists. Many Argentine commentators find here the roots of Menem's pardons.

I came to be involved in this swath of Argentine history through my work as a literary writer and translator. Since the late 1970s, I have focused on the literature of disaster, a term originally applied to the writing of the Shoah. I have long been concerned with how disaster—and the memory and dread of disaster—affects our relationship to language: to narrative form, the making of images, the rhetorical framing of theater. My introduction to Argentina—my initiation, let us say—was through that country's writers, most particularly Griselda Gambaro, whose plays I have translated into English. One of the most important Latin American playwrights of this century, Griselda was forced into exile in 1977 when then de facto president Videla personally banned one of her books. That, of course, was a death threat. Griselda's masterpiece is a play called *Information for Foreigners*, a prophetic work from 1971, which at once foretold and deconstructed the coming era of state terrorism.[3] She kept the manuscript hidden, and then smuggled it out with her when she left. I began translating *Information* in 1985, when Griselda felt it was finally safe for the play to enter the world. The script had its first public performance sixteen years after it was written, in English, in New York City. *Information* was unlike any translation I had ever done. Indispensable to me as I worked was *Nunca Más: The Report of the Argentine National Commission on the Disappeared.*[4] What I most needed from *Nunca Más* was language, for the Dirty War gave rise to a complicated mesh of linguistic codes, codes I had to know in order to decipher the world of the play, and to do a credible translation.

I became obsessed with the nefarious ways in which language can be used, and therein lie the roots of *A Lexicon of Terror*. This book was born of my need to explore firsthand the world that gave rise to Griselda's play. I began, as all writers do, with nagging questions. I spent over six years (1989–96) speaking at length with hundreds of Argentines in many parts of Argentina, Europe, Israel, and North America. Not all of those people are quoted here, but each one contributed to my understanding of their country. The protagonists of this book are survivors of the torture centers and relatives of *desaparecidos*. Each chapter is organized around a core of individuals whom I interviewed repeatedly over the years of my research. The passage of time influenced the tenor and content of these visits and helped determine the book's structure. I recorded every interview, then listened to the tapes and translated them directly into English. To the extent possible, I wanted my readers to have the nuances of every voice that helped me create this narrative. All translations of published testimony and other texts are also mine, unless otherwise noted.

I have sought to explore torture, and the myths and legacies of torture, by examining not just the great, but the subtle rents it leaves in the fabric of human lives and public institutions. The deformations in the Argentine language—beginning with the unprecedented use of "disappear" as a transitive verb—have changed lives in often subtle ways. "What words can you no longer tolerate? What words do you no longer say?" In this way, I gathered entries for a lexicon of terror. Each entry has quotes from interviews I conducted or other testimony given by survivors, to give the reader a sense of how these words were *lived*. Appallingly, many of the expressions originating with torturers in the camps have become part of current slang, a sign of the extent to which the population has internalized that part of Argentine history.

"The past is a predator," goes an Argentine adage. And it's one that many seem to believe. And yet that perception—like so much in Argentina—seems schizophrenic. On the one hand, there is constant vigilance, the certainty of disaster, carnal knowledge of fear. A sense that history never moves on, but circles, raven-like, round and round. And then there is willed amnesia: "The past has nothing more to teach us," says Menem, categorically. Then why not let it be? Why "undo" it with

measures like executive pardons of convicted criminals against humanity? "We must look ahead, with our eyes fixed on the future. Unless we
learn to forget," Menem warns, "we will be turned into a pillar of salt." So
we're brought full circle, with an official—Biblical—warning that the
past is a source of danger.

How do past events get settled in, or banished from, the present? In
response to whose need? Or dictate? Or inability to cope? When history has
been erased, can it be recovered? When known torturers are said to be
heroes, what happens to the minds of those they injured? When the language itself has been tainted, what must we do in order to speak? These are
not abstract inquiries, but, rather, agonizing questions for many of the
people in my book.

The book opens with an Introduction ("The Gentlemen's Coup"),
which provides a context for the Dirty War. It also discusses the way I
worked in Argentina to gather and present testimony from survivors and
eyewitnesses.

The title chapter focuses on the verbal atrocities of the regime. The
terrorist state created two worlds: one public, one clandestine, each with
its own encoded discourse. I draw a straight line from the public pronouncements to clandestine practice, where language became a form of
torture.

"Night and Fog" (Chapter 2) draws for its title on the Nazi concept of
Nacht und Nebel. According to Hitler's famous decree of December 7, 1941,
prisoners in the occupied territories would be transported to Germany
where they would "vanish in the night and fog." This chapter focuses on the
noche y niebla of the Dirty War, or the world of the Argentine concentration camps. *You had to remember that you were human,* I have been told by
several *ex-desaparecidos.* Said Mario Villani, one of the chapter's protagonists, "I got to the point during torture where I'd think to myself, 'This
torturer, this guy torturing me *now,* is a man like me . . . not a martian, not
a cockroach.' . . . I had just one goal—to stay alive until the next day. . . .
But it wasn't just to survive, but to survive *as me.*" Rather than as a mutation of *them.*

"'Life Here Is Normal'" (Chapter 3) focuses on the dynamics of the
Terror within the Jewish community. The Dirty War was the first major
revival of Nazi-derived tactics and rhetoric since World War II. What happened in Argentina—Jew against Jew, instead of Jews together against a
common enemy—is both astounding and complicated. The chapter centers on families victimized both by the terrorist state and by complicit community leadership.

A little-known aspect of the Terror was the decimation of the peasant Agrarian Leagues founded within a progressive branch of the Catholic Church. "The Land Mourneth" (Chapter 4) tells this story through the Tomasella clan of Goya, in the remote northeastern province of Corrientes. Sergio and Anita Tomasella are subsistence farmers; both were imprisoned and exiled; both have siblings murdered by the regime. To this day, they are watched; their letters and calls are frequently intercepted. The first time I visited, both my arrival and departure were vetted by soldiers. I first met Sergio at a human rights tribunal in Buenos Aires. Unshaven, wearing work clothes and heavy mud-clotted boots, he took the stand and spoke in a provincial accent made more intense by several missing teeth. With eloquence instilled by his Jesuit education, he gave testimony that was not only personal but historical, and deeply rooted in a commitment to preserving the earth.

As official rhetoric worked to conquer the mental space of Argentine citizens, in shared physical space a coercive discourse was also brought into play, one that could turn a "normal" setting into a bizarre, and disorienting, theatrical. "The House of the Blind" (Chapter 5) includes a tour of buildings, neighborhoods, and houses that are concrete reminders of the Terror; and covers recent efforts to reclaim those places appropriated by the regime and never returned.

"'The Scilingo Effect': The Past Is a Predator" (Chapter 6) begins with Adolfo Scilingo, a retired navy captain who in March 1995 publicly confessed to participating in two of the "Death Flights." With his own hands, he shoved thirty naked, drugged individuals out of airplanes into the Atlantic Ocean. In Scilingo's wake, five other repressors came forward to give an accounting, though not necessarily to apologize. The protagonists of this chapter are the Steimbergs, who listened as their son's murderer confessed on the radio; Mrs. Scilingo; the torturer known as "Julián the Turk," who also appeared on television; and several of his surviving victims. I also spoke at length with Army Chief Martín Balza, who made an unprecedented institutional apology for the atrocities of the Dirty War.

What never ceases to move and impress me is the tenacity of many Argentines, particularly those who have been severely abused. I am profoundly indebted to the people who have allowed me into their lives, and this book—though dark and vexing—is my tribute to them.

Acknowledgments

FOR MY "INITIATION" INTO THE WORLD OF ARGENTINA, I THANK Griselda Gambaro, whose work, conduct, and friendship are always profoundly inspiring. She, her husband Juan Carlos Distéfano, and indeed her entire household, were a touchstone for the many months I was far away from home.

A Fulbright Research Fellowship in 1990 enabled me to spend most of that year in Argentina, beginning the series of interviews that would form the essence of this work. A Bunting Fellowship at Radcliffe College (1992—93) provided me with a full year's stipend, colleagues who were supportive and challenging in just the right measure, and beautifully tranquil surroundings in which to write. I wish to extend special thanks to the Bunting Institute's Director, Florence C. Ladd, and to all my "sister fellows" of that year, particularly Kiana Davenport, Linda McCarristan, Ellen Rothenberg, Kathleen Weiler, and Norma Wikler. I was fortunate to also receive a Travel Grant from Radcliffe College in 1993, which helped defray research expenses in Israel. A grant from the Marion and Jasper Whiting Foundation covered my research stay in Argentina during 1995. The support of these grants was crucial to the development of this book.

In terms of editors, the fates have smiled most kindly upon me. Frederick Smock published an excerpt from this book in *The American Voice*; for his belief in my work, for the scrupulous care he bestows on every phase of the production of the journal, and for his exquisite courtesy, I am most grateful. Robert and Peggy Boyers of *Salmagundi immediately* offered a home to an early version of "Night and Fog," and got the piece into print almost in the blink of an eye. To Reginald Gibbons, Susan Hahn, and Bob Perlongo of *TriQuarterly*, my thanks for giving my work such a prominent venue.

I wish to express my gratitude to Leonardo Senkman, for helping to guide my research on Jewish issues, for inviting me to be a Visiting Scholar at the Truman Institute at the Hebrew University of Jerusalem in 1993, and for his care in publishing some of my work in Israel and Argentina. The residence he arranged in Jerusalem was transforming in ways that I will always cherish. My thanks as well to Mishkenot Sha'ananim, indeed a "tranquil dwelling," where I wrote looking out on the Western Wall.

In Argentina my debts are many and profound. To everyone at CELS, the Permanent Assembly for Human Rights, Madres de Plaza de Mayo, Madres de Plaza de Mayo-Línea Fundadora, and the Buenos Aires Union of Press Workers (UTPBA), my thanks for providing documents, testimony, and introductions to numerous individuals.

Readers will come to know many of the people who so generously allowed me into their lives. I did other interviews as well, and even if those individuals are not quoted, our conversations nonetheless informed and enriched my work. I should like to mention ex-Captain José Luis D'Andrea Mohr, who, in addition to an interview, gave me special support on the issue of my meeting with "Julián the Turk"; Rev. José Miguez Bonino; journalist Luis Bruschstein; ex-Ambassador to the U.N. Dante Caputo; Laura Conte, psychologist and Mother of the Plaza de Mayo; Rabbi Daniel Fainstein; psychotherapist Eva Giberti; U.S.-based journalist Fernando González; forensic anthropologist Alejandro Incháurregui; María Cristina Lacroix, scholar and aunt of a *desaparecido*; Alicia La Giudice, psychologist specializing in children of *desaparecidos*; psychologist Ana Meyer; Susana P.; Herman Schiller, co-founder Jewish Movement for Human Rights; lawyers María del Carmen Verdú and Daniel Straga; writer and *ex-desaparecida* Inés Vásquez; Ximena Vicario, who as a baby was kidnapped from a concentration camp and eventually restored to her biological grandmother Darwinia Gallicio; lawyer Paul Warszawski; Dr. Marcos Weistein, father of a missing son; and Rabbi Felipe Yafe. In Israel, I was privileged to be hosted for a time by the Jaimovich family, whose daughter Alejandra was murdered at La Perla; I am grateful for their interview and for their bringing me to the Memory Forest dedicated to the *desaparecidos* located between Tel Aviv and Jerusalem. In Israel I was honored to speak with Anita Nirgad, the widow of Ram Nirgad, ex-Ambassador to Argentina; Daniel Rekanati, former Chief Aliya Emissary to Argentina; and Dr. Joel Barromi, former

Consul in Buenos Aires, member of the Israeli delegation to the U.N., and chief of Israel's permanent mission at the International Organizations in Geneva. The subject of these interviews—Israel's contested role in the rescue of Argentine Jews—ultimately exceeded the parameters of this book.

For their gifts of friendship, hospitality, intelligence, and passion for books and human rights, I thank Néstor Restivo and Marcela Fernández Vidal. From the beginning of my research in Buenos Aires, Néstor made available the archives of *Clarín*, where he is a journalist, and provided introductions to a great many sources and individuals. Cristina Fraire's rambling apartment in the heart of the capital is another home-away-from-home; I am always moved and electrified by her photographs, by the intensity she brings to her work, and by her knowledge of every nook and cranny of her beloved city. For their friendship and hospitality I also thank Angélica and "Goro" Gorodischer, and Alejandro Fogel and Shelley Berc.

In the United States, I am pleased to thank Amnesty International, particularly the Northeast Regional Office and its Director Joshua Rubinstein.

This book benefited from the readings of Lee Daniels, Stephen Donatelli, Leo Emilfork, Robert D. and Virginia G. Feitlowitz, Marta Felcman, Cola and Wolf Franzen, Christine Head, Robin F. King, Juan Mandelbaum, and Dr. Saúl Sosnowski.

I am extremely fortunate in my teaching colleagues at Harvard University. I could not ask for more savvy, more entertaining *confrères*. Nancy Sommers, Director of the Expository Writing Program, has been endlessly encouraging and generous about teaching schedules and leaves of absence; a writer herself, she has created an environment that abets the work we do on our books. I am grateful as well to Former Program Director Richard Marius for his energetic support and encouragement.

To my literary agent, Malaga Baldi, my deep thanks for her commitment, patience, and permanent good humor. At Oxford University Press, my thanks go especially to my editor, Gioia Stevens, who solicited this book, and to Stacie Caminos, who saw it through production. For their skilled and generous help in reading page proofs, I am grateful to Laura Weinrib and Alan Presser.

The work on this book was in many ways difficult, and at times devastating. For the sustenance of their love and friendship, I thank Esther Rehavi and Jerome Kellner, Ethan Riegelhaupt, Christine Head, Stephen Donatelli, Cola and Wolf Franzen, Suzi Naiburg, and Jocelyn Tager.

My deepest gratitude goes to my husband, David Anderson. He is always my first and closest reader. He is my heart's companion, *mi compariero de corazón.*

Excerpts from this work while it was in progress appeared chronologically in the following journals and magazines: "A Lexicon of Terror," *The American Voice*, no. 24 (Fall 1991): 57—67; "Dance of Death: Eduardo Pavlosvky's *Paso de dos*," in *The Drama Review: A Journal of Performance Studies* (Summer 1991): 60—73; "Buenos Aires 1990: The First Two Weeks of July," *Exquisite Corpse*, no. 34 (1992): 34—36; "Night and Fog in Argentina," *Salmagundi*, nos. 94—95 (Spring—Summer 1992): 40—74; "A Daughter of the Disappeared," *Women's Review of Books* 10, nos. 10—11 (July 1993): 7—8; "Life Here Is Normal," *TriQuarterly*, no. 89 (Winter 1993–94): 231—260; "Códigos del terror: Argentina y los Legados de la tortura," in *El Legado del autoritarismo*, Leonardo Senkman and Mario Sznajder, eds. (Jerusalem: Truman Institute of the Hebrew University, and Buenos Aires: Grupo Editor Latinoamericano, 1995), 79—94; " 'The Past Is A Predator': The Scilingo Effect in Argentina," *American Voice*, no. 40 (1996): 110—11; and "Le passé est un prédateur: L'effet Scilingo en Argentine," *Les Temps Modernes* (October—November 1996): 66—81.

My thanks to the editors and publishers of the above publications for their permission to reprint.

A Lexicon of Terror

Introduction

The Gentlemen's Coup

In Latin America, we learn early that our lives are worth little.
—Laura Yusem, director, *Paso de dos*;
Buenos Aires, 1990

AUGUST 1990, LATE WINTER IN THE SOUTHERN HEMISPHERE. IT IS thirteen months since Carlos Menem assumed the presidency in July of 1989. "The Age of Impunity" is how many here refer to the present, marked not only by massive corruption but by two executive pardons covering close to 300 enforcers of the Dirty War, one of which will free the convicted ex-commanders.

At the same time, the cultural world of Buenos Aires is torn apart by a play called *Paso de dos*, described by its prominent author as a "love story" between a torturer and his victim, whose complicity takes the form of extreme, though involuntary, sexual pleasure.[1] The play ends with the woman naked, filthy, and dead; her captor stands facing the audience, erect like a statue. In this violent and punishing work are inscribed the perennially charged Argentine themes: torture, complicity, the contamination and rewriting of history. The artists involved insist the play is feminist ("after her death, her voice lives on") and a homage to the *desaparecidos*. Nonetheless, the work draws protest—and a boycott—from the Madres de Plaza de Mayo. Alone among Argentines, these Mothers—Madres of *desaparecidos*—had dared to situate the crisis in public space. After a series of secret meetings in various churches, on April 30, 1977, the founding fourteen women met for their first silent procession in the main square of

Buenos Aires. Over the years their numbers would grow into the hundreds, and the Mothers' white kerchiefs would come to symbolize what was happening in Argentina and be adopted around the world as an accoutrement of solidarity.[2] Mothers I've spoken with are in equal parts enraged by the work's "salaciousness" and mystified by the artists' "betrayal."[3] Sold out for weeks in advance, *Paso de dos* is a constant theme of conversation. Even those who haven't seen it, or who refuse to see it, read and argue about the play with vehemence and passion. As they watch, many in the audience weep, the woman next to me, uncontrollably. But no one leaves. Most nights there are standing ovations. Is this an exercise in masochism? Erotic fascination with repression? Or is it a tribute to the avant-garde for having confronted a taboo?

Survivors have met their torturers on the street, in the subway, in the buildings where they live.

So who in this country is really exploring taboos?

ARGENTINA IS SUPREMELY ENIGMATIC, even—perhaps especially—to Argentines, who routinely describe it as "schizophrenic" and "surreal." In the aftermath of World War II, Argentina was ranked as the eighth wealthiest nation in the world. Its overwhelmingly European population was known for being cultured, sophisticated, and cosmopolitan (most of the Indians long since massacred). Buenos Aires was called "the Paris of South America." The acoustic perfection of the Teatro Colón was a magnet for the finest opera singers in the world. Well into the 1970s, Argentina had the highest literacy rate in Latin America. According to some estimates, at the time of the Dirty War coup, fully 98 percent of those living in the capital were literate. Due to its vast expanses of fertile land, Argentina is one of the few countries that should never need to import food.

Yet for all these endowments Argentina has been consistently self-destructive— economically, politically, socially. Politicians have the habit of consuming not only their enemies, but restive allies as well. The fall of General Juan Domingo Perón is a prime example. The paradoxical leader—revered equally by the extreme left and extreme right—became president in 1946. He was at once a populist and tyrant: a champion of the *descamisados* ("the shirtless ones") and organized labor, an admirer of Hitler and Mussolini, a magnet for progressive Jews and the host to thousands of Nazis after the defeat of the Reich. He made enemies of the oligarchy by nationalizing industries and services, then kept the workers in line with a combination of giveaways and the iron glove.[4] When Perón (an army man) was unseated in 1955, the navy bombed the Presidential Palace, killing hundreds of Peronists who had gathered mournfully in the Plaza de Mayo. From the moment of the General's fall, the Peronist Party was outlawed. Yet from his exile in Madrid Perón continued, for seventeen years, to exert an almost magical political power from behind the scenes. By virtue of his absence he became a mythic presence. When Perón at last returned to once again be president of Argentina in June 1973, tens of thousands of the faithful made a pilgrimage to Ezeiza to meet him. They walked from Buenos Aires, wading through the Matanza River, only to be met by the Party's right-wing "gorillas" with machine guns. It is estimated that at least 200 were killed in the massacre that day: the wounded numbered nearly 500. On the following May Day, Perón himself, from the balcony of the Presidential Palace, abused his leftist followers, calling them "idiots," and "beardless wonders," and yelled at them to leave the Plaza de Mayo. In other words, they were denied—by their patron, no less—a legitimate political space. Virtually every government has begun by undoing the accomplishments of its predecessor.

Argentine history is marked by recurring cycles of bloody rule. Historians date the modern military era from 1930, the year of José Felix "von" Uriburu's violent coup, the first army takeover since 1854. Between 1930 and 1976 there were nine civilian-backed military coups, two other presidents appointed by the army, two blatantly rigged elections, and two terms of highly theatrical, quasi-fascistic Peronism. The average life span of these administrations was two years and ten months; one government in 1943 lasted but two days. That president, Arturo Rawson, had taken the Casa Rosada by force, but he was quickly replaced by another general.

As the eminent military sociologist Alain Rouquié emphasizes in his magisterial volume on Argentina, military dominance in political life derives as much from the weakness of civilian institutions as from the strength of the armed forces. One of the ironies of Argentine history is that in 1930, relatively few officers participated in Uriburu's coup, yet political culture was decidedly militarized from that point on. Over and over the Argentine military has proved that it is notably lacking in both economic savvy and the skills of governance. Yet elected administrations of various stripes have repeatedly sought the shelter of the armed forces. Good relations with the army was the key to staying in power. No president— civilian or military—has managed to stay in office against the wishes of the men in uniform.[5]

For all its sophistication, the deep structures of Argentine society are feudal. The traditional triangle consists of the landowning "oligarchy," the Catholic Church, and the military, which was modeled on the Praetorian

Guard. Changes in social mores notwithstanding, these anachronistic underpinnings have remained, and not just in the far provinces. Argentina has shown discomfort with the essential untidiness of democracy. The impersonal order embodied by the military was seen as more refined than "grasping parties," above "popular demagoguery," less vulnerable to corruption. Given their history, Argentines haven't much faith in their powers of self-government. *Necesitamos una mano dura*, goes the old saying: "We need a strong hand." Political parties, unions, businesses, and interest groups have all made alliances with the military. "Everyone in Argentina wants their own colonel," says Rouquié, implying that, for many years, it was the only way to get anything done.[6]

In the 1960s, a series of coups were backed—some say prepared—by progressive newspapers such as *La Opinión*, whose editor was Jacobo Timerman. Because the army tended to favor an economy based on international capitalism, it was seen by many in the middle and upper classes as better attuned to their interests than parties that favored a more statist economy with an emphasis on nationalist organized labor. In the early 1970s, as unemployment soared and the peso plunged, guerrilla war broke out between armies of the ultra-right and the ultra-left. Kidnappings, executions, and random violence made everyone vulnerable. The upper middle class hired bodyguards; businesses paid both sides for protection. In the midst of this unrest, in July 1974, Perón died and was succeeded by his widow, Isabel ("Isabelita"), who, in spite of her total political incompetence, had served as his vice president. Responding to threats from the militant left, the Peronist government organized death squads under the banner of the Argentine Anti-Communist Alliance, or the Triple A. Coordinated at first by the Federal Police, the Triple A was eventually taken over by José López Rega, the Minister of Social Welfare who would come to be known as President Isabel Perón's "Rasputin," "warlock" (*el brujo*), and power-mad astrologer.[7] It was in 1975, during the presidency of Isabel Perón, that the "eradication" of "subversive elements" was officially decreed.[8] The decree (no. 261) also mobilized the armed forces for non-military, "psychological" operations. The country, though nominally democratic, was essentially occupied and under siege.

The armed left had its roots in Peronism, though some groups also had a Maoist cast. Che Guevara was of course one of their heroes. The largest opposition group was the Montoneros; also active was the Maoist-inflected ERP (People's Revolutionary Army) and two much smaller groups, the FAR (Revolutionary Armed Force) and FAP (People's Armed Force). At their height in 1974–75, these leftist groups totaled no more than

2000 individuals, of whom only 400 had access to arms. Both before and after the coup, the government grossly exaggerated the strength of the insurgent forces. Over the entire decade of the 1970s, the leftist groups carried out a total of 697 assassinations, killing 400 policemen, 143 members of the military, and 54 civilians, mostly industrialists.[9]

"As many people as necessary must die in Argentina so that the country will again be secure," declared General Rafael Videla, in 1975, in what was both a gesture of support for the Triple A and a statement of his own political ambitions.[10] By the end of that year, the armed left had been routed (a reality the authorities hid so they wouldn't have to soften) but economic and political chaos ruled. Inflation had been mounting at a monthly rate of 30 percent, export earnings were down 25 percent, and the deficit had reached a staggering one billion dollars.[11] On March 24, 1976, the confused and feeble "Isabelita" was ousted in a coup that virtually all Argentines welcomed, and Videla became de facto president.

The country was exhausted, and more than anything wanted order. Spruce and well-spoken, the generals were reassuringly calm. "Now we are governed by gentlemen," said Jorge Luis Borges,[12] and from that moment on, the change of government was called "The Gentlemen's Coup." This coup began what came to be called the Dirty War. In a series of lyrical front-page "reflections" published immediately after the coup, Jacobo Timerman (who had been threatened by the far left) cited the "reserve and welcome modesty," of the "new authorities," whom he praised for resist-ing "pompous titles" and "bombastic slogans." The new government, he believed, "would bring Argentina the civilized reparation that it deserved."[13] Congratulatory editorials appeared in the major international dailies. The International Monetary Fund (IMF) and other lending institutions imme-diately responded with major loans. Even Jorge Daniel Paladino, formerly Juan Domingo Peróns personal representative, said, "Properly speaking, it wasn't a coup. The Armed Forces did nothing more than to *accept* the citi-zens' tacit and/or explicit request that they intervene, take charge."[14]

The generals arrived with a plan, called the Process for National Reor-ganization, whose language lent grandeur to an otherwise desperate moment. This was a fight not just for Argentina but, the generals stressed, for "Western, Christian civilization." By meeting its "sacred responsibil-ity" to forever rid the earth of "subversion," Argentina "would join the concert of nations." Argentina was the theater for "World War III," which had to be fought against those whose activities—and thoughts—were deemed "subversive." Intellectual, writer, journalist, trade unionist, psy-chologist, social worker became "categories of guilt." One of the first laws laid down by the junta decreed that workers could be fired without cause and without any right to indemnification. Strikes were forbidden, and the bank accounts of the General Confederation of Labor immediately seized. Labor unions, professional guilds, teachers' associations, even student councils were specifically targeted in new statutes published on the front page of every major daily. The junta was particularly obsessed with the hidden enemy. Suspects were "disappeared" in order to be exposed (and then annihilated) within a network of some 340 secret torture centers and concentration camps. "The only way to identify this occult enemy is through information obtained through torture. 'And for torture to be effective,' they'd tell us, 'it has to be limitless. . . .'" So testified Martín Gras, a lawyer who for two years was imprisoned in an Argentine concentration camp.

The regime was headed by a succession of four juntas composed of three senior officers, one each from the army, navy, and air force. The first and most repressive junta consisted of President General Rafael Videla, Admiral Emilio Eduardo Massera, and Brigadier General Orlando R. Agosti (see Fig. 1). In 1981 Videla (whose term expired) was succeeded by General

FIGURE 1. The Commanders of the first junta, or "the gentlemen of the coup": (*left to right*) Admiral Emilio E. Massera (navy), President Jorge Rafael Videla (army general), Brigadier General Orlando R. Agosti (air force), June 9, 1977. (Photo credit: Guillermo Loiácono)

Roberto Viola, Army Chief of Staff. Though hardly conciliatory, Viola was a pragmatist who saw that the regime couldn't last forever and attempted to open talks with representatives of the political parties, though these were still illegal. Viola was unseated in late 1981 by the even more reactionary General Leopoldo Galtieri. In 1982, General Reynaldo Bignone was installed to preside over a "dignified" end to the Process and to orchestrate the transition to free elections. Even though the juntas were intended to provide the image of "impersonal" and "unified" military rule, each one was characterized by intense internal rivalry. The most brutal years were 1976–79 (with 1976–77 deserving special mention). The majority of the disappearances happened then, though the kidnappings did not stop until near the end of the dictatorship, and it is known that even after the election of Dr. Raúl Alfonsín a small number of individuals were still being held in military camps.

How DID ARGENTINA come to such a pass? There is, of course, no simple answer. Castro's coming to power in 1959 had worried Latin American conservatives and even some moderates. In March 1960, Argentina adopted the Plan CONINTES (Plan for Civil Insurrection Against the State). The offensive was not limited to "terrorists," but extended to their "sympathizers" and to "anyone helping to conceal insurgents." The country was divided into military zones, headed by commanders with wide-reaching powers. Certainly Washington offered no welcome to Fidel. He was seen as a potential weapon of the Soviet Union in the Cold War. The United States determined to keep Latin America on its side. In a speech to Congress in 1963, Defense Secretary Robert MacNamara declared:

> The best return on our investment in military aid probably comes from the training of selected Army officers and key specialists in our military academies and training centers in the U.S. and abroad. These students are carefully selected by their countries so that they in turn become instructors when they go home. They are the leaders of the future. . . . I don't need to dwell on the value of having people in positions of power who have a first-hand knowledge of how we think and act here in the United States. For us having these people as friends is invaluable. . . .[15]

MacNamara elaborated at the swearing-in of President Johnson:

> Our primary objective in Latin America is to aid, wherever necessary, *the continual growth of the military and paramilitary*

Forces, so that together with the police and other security forces, they may provide the necessary internal security.[16] [emphasis added]

The United States Doctrine of National Security struck a sympathetic chord with many in the Argentine armed forces. At the Fifth Conference of American Armies held at West Point on August 6, 1964, General Juan Carlos Onganía discoursed on the military as the country's "ultimate moral reserve":

It is clear that this duty to obey—referring to the authority of the government—will no longer be absolutely sovereign if, under the influence of exotic ideologies, the government exceeds its powers and presents a threat to the basic principles of a republican political system, or brings about a violent disturbance to the equilibrium of independence of our respective powers.

Since the people are powerless to exercise this right by themselves, it is the duty of the institutions which the people have armed and given the mission to sustain the effective validity of the Constitution, to act on their behalf.[17]

In power then in Argentina was Dr. Arturo Illia, a gentle physician. Less than two years after his West Point speech, Onganía unseated Illia, in what is generally considered the least justified coup of the century.

So to what extent was the last Argentine repression a "Yankee export"? It cannot be overlooked that many of the most promising Argentine officers were rewarded with special training at the U.S. Army School of the Americas. Founded in 1946, the soa specialized in counterinsurgency. It was located in the Panama Canal Zone until 1984 when it was relocated to Fort Benning, Georgia. Financed by U.S. taxpayers, the soa has trained 57,000 Latin American military men, including Nicaraguan dictator Anastasio Somoza, Panamanian drug lord Manuel Noriega, and Salvadoran death-squad leader Roberto D'Aubuisson. Ex-commander of the Dirty War Leopoldo Galtieri, who led Argentina to its grotesquely humiliating defeat in the Falklands, was another graduate of the soa. In September 1996, the Pentagon itself finally admitted that its students were taught torture, murder, sabotage, bribery, blackmail, and extortion for the achievement of political aims; that hypnosis and truth serum were recommended for use in interrogations; and that the parents of captives be arrested as an inducement for the prisoner to talk. The army could hardly do otherwise, in view of the training manuals that have surfaced recently. These course materials were used by Mobile Training Teams in Latin America from 1987 to 1989 and by the SOA from 1989 to 1991. The instructions clearly violate U.S. current policies.[18] The manuals—written in Spanish—drew on earlier models, presumably from the '60s and '70s.[19] Owing to its awkwardness, I would say that the English translation was done by a non-native English speaker. In the section called "Handling of Sources" special attention is given to planning:

> On planning operations, it is highly important to point out that, *even when there is not any activity felt on the part of the guerrillas*, an insurrection movement could be in gestation. Every countermeasure that concentrates only on the activities of guerrillas, without taking into consideration the secret organization and the great preparation before the violence explodes, is destined to fail. *The mere elimination of the guerrillas does not alter in any way the basic organization of the insurgents.*[20] [emphasis added]

In other words, communities living peacefully might well deserve violent attack; the behavior could actually be a form of "passive sabotage." Surveillance was crucial, particularly of political groups, diplomats, clergy, and the intelligentsia. "The terrorist groups usually come from middle and high classes," says the manual on counterintelligence.[21] "The universities play a prominent role in the recruitment of terrorists. They introduce anarchist and marxist doctrines and many of the student federations are controlled by radicals. The jail adds another element, although it does not play such an important role as the university's [sic]."[22]

The Dirty War regime eviscerated the best-educated generation in the history of Argentina. As I have noted, intellectual professions became "categories of guilt."

The manuals emphasize specialization: "The purpose of training consists in assuring that the employee has the necessary knowledge and training to perform his functions successfully. For greater security, the employee must be trained only in those specific aspects of the tasks that will be assigned to him."[23] In other words, if you were training to be a torturer, you shouldn't be concerned with anything else.

These September 1996 disclosures about the SOA were not exactly news in Argentina. Numerous survivors have told me of being tortured by SOA graduates. It was considered so prestigious to be sent to the SOA that certain goons lied about getting training there. One of the men who did *not* lie about his SOA background was Sergeant Elpidio Rosario Tejeda, known as *El Tejano* ("Texas"). (He also studied in Houston.) Tejeda was, as the manual recommends, a specialist. He was a mythic figure at the concentration camp of La Perla, a ferocious torturer who delivered his blows with an appalling micro-exactitude. Texas wore dark glasses and was rarely seen without his stick. "He knew the limits of human resistance," testified Graciela Geuna. "Once after he had beaten me, I managed to steal a razor blade from the desk. All I wanted was to kill myself, it was the only way to escape the horror. Texas confiscated it, saying 'You're not going to be able to die, little girl, until we want you to. We are God here.'"[24] In the words of survivors Patricia Astelarra and Gustavo Contemponi:

> He turned torture into an act of theater. He knew a great deal about anatomy, and so was able to direct both the placement and intensity of his blows for maximum pain. He was extremely focused and absorbed; the information he obtained he reserved for himself. He concentrated on "his" cases. . . . The efficacy he had as a torturer did not extend to psychological action; his function was simply to terrorize. Even the other officers resented him. When he was murdered [while out on a kidnapping] it marked the end of an era at La Perla.[25]

As these survivors have testified, Texas and other repressors periodically left the camps to act as instructors at training seminars in Buenos Aires. Their students were military men from other Latin American countries, including Bolivia, Paraguay, Brazil, and El Salvador.

The United States was not the only source of expertise for the Argentines. They looked as well to the French, who had fought "subversives" in Algeria and Indochina. In fact, *la guerra sucia* is a direct translation of DeGaulle's *la sale de guerre*, or Dirty War in Algeria. Like the Argentines, the French military insisted in Algiers that "we're defending the West here . . . a certain notion of what man is." The *CONINTES* plan had also been adapted from the French efforts to control this colony. In 1957, the Superior War College engaged two French Lieutenant Colonels, Patrice J. L. de Naurois and François Pierre Badié, both of whom had served in Indochina, to give instruction in the development of Marxism around the world and how best to lay it waste. The Argentines received advising from the French until 1975. "Torture is the particular bane of the terrorist," the French military insisted, "reports of results are magnificent."[26] Against allegations of atrocities in 1955, the French government commissioned the Wuillaume Report, which bears striking similarities to the junta's Final Report. No fewer than twenty-eight types of "services" were described—all clearly forms of torture—yet the word "torture" appears only twice in the document: of those instances one is a mitigating phrase ("physical maltreatment of the nature"). Euphemisms abound: "excesses," "methods," "long established police procedures," and "violence," which implied provocation.[27] As they prepared to leave office, the Argentine junta also spoke of "excesses" and "abuses." But it never mentioned torture, and denied the reality of concentration camps. Both documents expressly rule out any kind of investigation. The Wuillaume Report was buried; the Argentines must have figured the same would happen to them.

Giving credit where credit was due, General Ramón J. Camps, who bragged that he was responsible for 5000 disappearances, put things in perspective:

> France and the United States were the great disseminators of antisubversive doctrine. They both, but particularly the United States, organized centers to instruct in the fight against subversion. They sent advisors, teachers. They distributed a huge amount of bibliography. Unfortunately, all of that ended in failure, although it was possible to analyze why they hadn't triumphed. . . . There was a basic difference: they were fighting outside their own territory, in countries of different race, a different language, different customs. That situation is totally distinct from the situation in our [Latin American] countries.
>
> It is important to clarify that the French optic was more correct than the North American; the former had a global concept; the latter were all but exclusively military.
>
> All that was fine until we "reached adulthood," and applied our *own* doctrine, which enabled us to triumph against subversion. . . .[28]

According to Camps, the Terror was a rite of passage, a glorious coming of age.

THE "GENTLEMEN OF THE COUP" were ardent (though highly selective) students of history. They also had Argentina's own repressive traditions to draw on. The *picana*, the favored Dirty War instrument for electric torture, was invented for police use in 1934; since then it has been standard issue at precincts all over the country. Many of the Nazis sheltered by Perón found jobs modernizing the Argentine intelligence services. Some of these men would participate in the Dirty War, in a group known as Sol Argentino ("Argentine Sun"), based in Córdoba. The issue of torture has periodically caused scandal in the Argentine Congress. During the decade of the 1930s, a number of torture devices were invented by the infamous Leopoldo Lugones.[29] Tempestuous hearings in the Senate took place in 1946, 1949, 1953, and 1956, causing Ernesto Sábato to publicly rail against "this interminable history of torture."[30] The victims tended to be workers, labor leaders, dissident military, and intellectuals perceived to stray from "Western, Christian traditions," particularly homosexuals. Reading the testimonies from the 1940s and '50s is a shocking experience: They are all but identical to those of the Dirty War.

It cannot be said that the last repression was imposed on Argentina by outside forces. Foreign interests came together with a long history of entrenched conservatism, a tradition of the strong exploiting the weak, and quick recourse to violence.

IT IS TWENTY YEARS since the Dirty War coup. To what extent, and in what ways, has the country regained its bearings?

The regime was eventually brought down, but not because of its record on human rights. Rather, it crumbled under the weight of its own corruption, economic mismanagement, and military incompetence. In April 28, 1983, in a desperate attempt to distract the population and rescue its image, the junta went to war against the British for the tiny Falkland Islands (Las Malvinas) in the South Atlantic. The invasion was in every way a fiasco, and the defeat in every way humiliating. For the dictatorship, it spelled the end. On April 28,1983, as it prepared to exit from power, the regime issued a Final Report, proclaiming victory in its Dirty War against subversion, pardoning itself for any possible "excesses," and registering "genuine Christian pain over any errors that might have been committed in the fulfillment of its assigned mission." The long, dense report was read over national television against a kinetic filmed background of military actions against so-called terrorists. "This historical synthesis of a dolorous past . . . is intended as a message of faith and an acknowledgement of the fight for freedom, for justice . . . the right to life [and] . . . the safeguarding of human rights." In Section II, "The Facts," the regime charged "the enemy" with "the disappearance of the Republic as a democratic State." As for "disappeared" individuals, they were either "living in exile," "residing in Argentina with false identities," or "should be considered dead, even in cases when it is not possible to determine the date, place, or cause of death, nor the burial site of the remains." Certain people would be "absent forever," in the famous words of General Viola. As for secret detention centers, there were none; as for further information or explanations, there would be none.[31]

The country was outraged by this insult.

On December 10, 1983, Argentina held elections. Though there were candidates from smaller parties, the only real contenders were Dr. Raúl Alfonsín, from the Radical Civic Union, a basically centrist party despite its name, and Italo Luder, who had served in the cabinet of Isabel Perón. Alfonsín won overwhelmingly on his slogan "Democracy or Anti-Democracy" and his pledge to fully investigate and legally address the abuses of the prior regime. One of his first acts as president was to appoint the Argentine National Commission on the Disappeared, or CONADEP, to take testimony from victims of abduction and torture, from the families and friends of *desaparecidos*, and from other witnesses willing to come forward. Originally mandated to function for six months, the CONADEP's term was extended to a year because the committee insisted that the magnitude of its assignment outstripped the time it had been given. After twelve months of work, the CONADEP documented 8,960 *desaparecidos*. (Committee members have told me that had they been granted more time, they would have amassed more information.) The CONADEP's massive report, *Nunca Más!* (Never Again!) was published in Argentina in 1984, with numerous editions almost immediately selling out. Armed with the CONADEP's extensive corroborated evidence, Alfonsín announced that the nine ex-commanders of the first three juntas would be charged and tried. Over significant political opposition, he asked the Supreme Tribunal of the military to try its own, thinking that this would make a powerful statement about the institution's willingness to take responsibility and to enact a new moral code. But the military refused. And so, beginning on April 22, 1985, the ex-commanders were publicly tried in civilian court. For five months, day after day of testimony held the country rapt. There were hundreds of incriminating accounts from the witness stand, all of them Dantesque. Videla seemed not to be listening; he was elegant in a British suit, serenely reading his missal, betraying no sign of his bleeding ulcer. Massera strained, grimaced, and bared his teeth; he shook his fist and barked in his own defense, "I am responsible but not guilty." On December 9, 1985, the two of them were sentenced to *prisión perpetua*, their country's harshest legal punishment. In addition to being convicted for having directed systematized state terrorism, General Videla was found legally responsible for the following crimes committed by the army: 83 homicides, 504 illegal deprivations of freedom, 254 applications of torture, 94 aggravated robberies, 180 counts of ideologically falsifying public documents, four usurpations (of property), 23 counts of forced labor, one count of extortion, two extortive kidnappings, seven counts of child stealing, and seven counts of torture resulting in death. In addition to his leadership role in the terrorist state, Admiral Massera was held legally responsible for the following acts committed by the navy: 83 homicides, 523 illegal deprivations of freedom, 267 counts of torture, 102 aggravated robberies, 201 counts of ideologically falsifying public documents, four usurpations (of property), 23 counts of forced labor, two extortive kidnappings, 11 counts of child stealing, and seven counts of torture resulting in death. The remaining seven ex-commanders received sentences ranging from four and a half to 17 years; four other of the highest-ranking officers were cited for further investigation.

The prosecution of the ex-commanders was one of the most brilliantly plotted, eloquently argued, and closely watched trials of the century. Other members of the military and police were convicted in federal courts in both the capital and the interior. To cite but one prominent example, in August 1986, Colonel Camps, who had commanded the Buenos Aires Provincial Police and Central Detective Squad, was convicted in civilian court of 600 counts of homicide, and sentenced to twenty-five years in prison. Yet the overall effect was vitiated, according to many, by the limits that Alfonsín placed on the scope and time limit of prosecutions. Alfonsín wanted, above all, to reestablish democracy, gird its fragility, and guard its future. With the military restive and unrepentant, the balance was delicate. Even as the trials were going on, the military was promoting men who had committed abuses during the regime. Alfonsín greatly feared the destabilizing effects of widespread prosecutions and court cases going on for years. In fact on February 14, 1984, Alfonsín promulgated the controversial law 23.049, usually referred to as the Due Obedience law, which allowed lower-ranking personnel to claim that they had merely been "following orders." Excepted were "atrocious" or "aberrant" actions; although torture, rape, murder, and robbery were covered under these headings, kidnapping—which facilitated the other abuses—was not. Human rights organizations strenuously objected to the law, which goes against the precedent established at the Nuremberg trials of former Nazis.[32] In December 1986, Alfonsín set February 23, 1987, as the Punto Final ("final point"), or cut-off date for all trials related to the Dirty War. According to a 1988 study by the important human rights group CELS (Centro de Estudios Legales y Sociales), some 400 repressors benefited from Due Obedience; whereas 450 torturers or enforcers were tried prior to the Punto Final deadline, hundreds of other cases had to be dropped.[33]

What moral good comes of such measures? "Vengeance is understand-able, but it has no place in a rational society," I was told by the late Carlos Nino, Alfonsín's key legal advisor and the man who mainly drafted the Due Obedience and Punto Final laws. "I don't think that justice need be retributive. I don't have the Kantian view that a crime unpunished equals an absolute injustice. Symbolic prosecutions have great resonance, partic-ularly in a country that is not essentially violent and needs to heal."[34] Alfonsín's military advisor, Jaime Malamud, had a different view: "Look, this is a fascist society. We have to change its authoritarian structure. . . . And in the process we have to let a lot of people get away with [crimes]."[35]

The Dirty War happened because, in some measure, every part of Argentine society allowed it to.[36] How does a country confront—let alone punish—*that*? Even as the trial progressed, even as they watched and lis-tened, some Argentines wondered whether "it could really be true." *Será cierto?* they asked one another, with varying degrees of credulity and resist-ance. "A nation creates itself not just with what it remembers, but with what it forgets." So I was told by Oscar Camilión, a diplomat under Videla, and until recently the Minister of Defense.[37]

WHEN I FORMALLY BEGAN this work in 1989, the idea of a pardon for the convicted ex-commanders was inconceivable. Although it is hard to imag-ine that a convulsion like the Dirty War could be repeated, we know that sectors of its secret world still operate. And so, in certain places, do the attitudes and beliefs that allowed it to happen. In July 1993, a massive cam-paign of "ideological spying" was unleashed by the Ministry of the Interior and the Federal Police. Journalists, intellectuals, theater artists, human rights workers, and other predictable targets received death threats, and some were physically attacked. But they are not the only ones: The peaceful demonstrations of senior citizens unable to live on their pensions have been filmed by the Federal Police; some high school student councils are placed under military surveillance.

In a column called "Secret Argentina," James Neilson likened the country to Dr. Jekyll and Mr. Hyde:

From time to time, that "other" country—of the missing, of complicit silence, of demented militarism—becomes agitated. We know that it feels imprisoned in this democratic Argentina that believes itself to be mediocre, without ideals, a traitor to its own sacred mission. Remember well those years during which that "other" Argentina acted with absolute freedom, torturing and killing anyone whose presence it found irritating. *That* Argentina dreams of coming back.

No one knows how many are active in this obscene army of the night. Perhaps it's only a few thousand fanatics whose sporadic appearances don't mean anything. But even if their numbers are small, they will have collaboration from the many, who always adapt to the orthodoxy of the day. . . .[38]

In response to this, and other, protests in the media, Menem threatened a state of siege and announced the formation of a special commission to investigate "journalistic delinquency."

On November 17, 1994, in a landmark court decision, a Buenos Aires district judge fined the state and two former naval chiefs of staff, Emilio Massera and Armando Lambruschini, one million dollars each and awarded the monies to the sole survivor of the family of Hugo and Blanca Tarnopolsky, who in 1976 were kidnapped from their home with their daughter, one son, and daughter-in-law. The plaintiff, Daniel Tarnopolsky, was age eighteen in 1976 and not at home when the kidnap occurred. "Democracy must compensate for the crimes of these individuals," wrote the judge, "and it is fitting that the state itself pay some of the reparations." Within hours, Menem announced that the government would appeal directly to the Supreme Court (five of whose members were his personal friends). Commenting on the case, Argentine novelist Marcos Aguinis said, "Remember, this is a country where even the non-Jews know they have no rights. Ask anybody on the street, and he will tell you, there is one law for us, and one law for them. Nobody even expects justice here, and it is easier to forget."[39]

Such eruptions of the past into the present add another layer to this study. Testimony about those years reveals a lot about the moment in which it is given. Depending on circumstance, memory may be clear or dim, fluid or clotted. There may be guilt, resistance, fear, fury. Suspicion, distrust, despair. When the boundaries between past and present are seen to weaken, belief in the importance of giving testimony may diminish—or intensify. Over time, the purposes for giving testimony change. Practical, concrete objectives—like the amassing of evidence for trial—generate detailed accounts of specific actions and events. In these early testimonies incidents are tightly framed, reflecting, also, the physical isolation of the prisoners. Distance tends to allow for more reflection, analysis, the surfacing of connections—particularly since survivors listen to, and read each other, carefully. To better understand the Terror, and to trace its contours against the present, I have interviewed many of the same survivors repeatedly over the years.

Testimony is where the public and the secret Argentina intersect. To be immersed in testimony means to reside in both places at once— navigating by two sets of landmarks, trying to fathom two sets of codes, and two different, but interconnected, cultures. This is, of course, what the prisoners had to do, but *in extremis*. Often a matter of random chance, survival itself could be rendered unfathomable. The testimony of a man who had spent years in solitary confinement seemed, in some numinous way, to arise from a community. The account of a former organizer was so alienated it was hard to believe that he had ever worked among people. Certain prisoners are mentioned repeatedly in various testimonies. I came to "know" them, to anticipate their presence in other stories from that camp. Listening or reading, I would find myself "waiting" for them, but often they would simply disappear. I knew that in reality they were dead. But in testimony they were alive. And sometimes, I felt that I had "been there" when they died.

Alicia G.[40] is a name I heard often. She was sixteen years old, the youngest child of a close-knit Jewish family. "She had this radiance," survivors told me, and she was given little privileges, like social contact. She read books to prisoners who were blindfolded, several of whom I know. In the photos in her parents' apartment, she is slight, with long, unruly hair, and the open gaze of someone who knew she was cherished. On the day of my first visit, they said they were still tormented by not knowing how or when, exactly, she was killed. I suddenly felt sick, realizing that I knew. Alicia had also distributed shavers to men like Federico T.; "Bics or Gillette, whatever; she carried them in this little basket, and went from one to the other. I always took one and embraced her, but Jesus, it was sinister. They knew damn well how tempting it was to break those fucking things open and slit our wrists. But they also knew we'd never do that to Alicia. She was our darling. She was our angel. The last time I saw her was two hours before they took her to be shot. It was her 'last round,' and I think she knew it."[41] Some months later, the G. family let me know that Federico had written to them with other details about their daughter. "It helps to know that she was loved," they said. "Among the prisoners, at least, there was love in that hell of hells."

Among the most powerful connections forged by testimony are those that reunite the living. Parents have found their children, husbands have found their wives, and friends and lovers found each other. Though not with an intimate, I had this experience myself. Survivors of the death camp located in the Navy Mechanics School had mentioned a man they called Anteojitos ("Little Eyeglasses"). A small, round, nearsighted man who taught school and loved books. He was always mentioned together with others, some of whom are still missing. I gathered no stories that were specifically about this man; rather, he floated on the edges of other narratives. All I had were his nickname and kindly image, and to these I grew terribly attached. Try as I might, I could learn nothing more about him. Until the evening I met Susana Barros and in walked her husband, whom I immediately knew as Anteojitos. That he was alive seemed a miracle, and, in fact, it was.

Among my guides on this journey was Dr. Juan Carlos Adrover, a prominent lawyer who headed the Santa Fe branch of the CONADEP. One day he offered me this story within a story:

In 1984, we [the CONADEP] were taking testimony in San Rafaela, a small city nearby. The mayor kept saying, "Why have you come? We had no disappearances here."

"Then why have all these people formed a line?" And I went back to work. Toward the end of the day, I was approached by a middle-aged *campesino* who worked for a man who contracted a plot of land from the army. And he told me this: That during the dictatorship, he and his family were evacuated from this land six or seven times, and brought to stay for several days on the army base. When they returned, he noticed that the earth had been turned over. And once, he found a woman's sneaker and a gold chain, a choker. He buried these things and marked the tree, but said nothing to anyone. Until the CONADEP, until that very moment.

Later I went with a friend, a doctor, and we met this *campesino* who took us to "his" tree. Very gently we dug around, and found some little remains which I assumed were those of a dog. But I was wrong, it was a human finger with the fingernail still attached. By this time, the Punto Final had elapsed, and we couldn't investigate.

In his rational, lawyerly way, Adrover continued, "I put that little finger with its fingernail in a plastic bag and I keep that bag in my desk. Because to tell you the truth, I have the feeling that this whole country is a graveyard, and that we are all constantly walking on the bones."

1

A Lexicon of Terror

The aim of the Process is the profound transformation of consciousness.
                                    —General Jorge Rafael Videla, 1976[1]

We know that in order to repair so much damage we must recover the meanings of many embezzled words. . . .
                                    —Admiral Emilio Massera, 1976[2]

THE GRAND ORATOR OF THE PROCESS WAS ADMIRAL EMILIO MASSERA, master of the majestic rhythm, learned tone, and utterly confound-ing—but captivating—message. As a young man he had studied philology, and language would remain a lifelong obsession. Here is but one of his darkly shining verbal jewels: "Unfaithful to their meanings, words perturb our powers of reason." The quote is taken from "The Quiet and Subtle Cyclone," one of his most widely disseminated speeches. In his opening he makes clear that he speaks not only for himself, but on behalf of the entire navy, whose union with the army and air force is "brotherly" and "inde-structible." (They were in fact bitter rivals.) Grandly solemn, he says that his themes derive from a "meditation" on "objective reality," which he italicizes in the published text. That reality is "a veritable world war whose battlefield is the human spirit," a war in which "even the Word of God is used by murderers to invent a theology that justifies violence." Here, as elsewhere, Massera is tormented by the state of the language, which he compares to "an abject Tower of Babel," and warns his audience to beware of words. They are "unfaithful," will betray the unsuspecting, destroy the innocent. "The only safe words are our words." The warning is surreal, for it captures exactly what Massera himself is doing: spinning an intricate verbal web to ensnare his audience and "perturb [their] powers of reason."

Brutal, sadistic, and rapacious, the whole regime was intensely verbal. From the moment of the coup, there was a constant torrent of speeches, proclamations, and interviews; even certain military memos were made public. Newspapers and magazines, radio and television all were flooded with messages from the junta. The barrage was constant and there was no escape: Argentinians lived in an echo chamber. With diabolical skill, the regime used language to: (1) shroud in mystery its true actions and intentions, (2) say the opposite of what it meant, (3) inspire trust, both at home and abroad, (4) instill guilt, especially in mothers, to seal their complicity, and (5) sow paralyzing terror and confusion. Official rhetoric displays all of the traits we associate with authoritarian discourse: obsession with the enemy, triumphal oratory, exaggerated abstraction, and messianic slogans, all based on "absolute truth" and "objective reality."

The Dirty War, though unprecedented in its extent and cruelty, did not erupt from a vacuum. Rather, it drew on a reservoir of beliefs, phobias, obsessions, and rhetoric that have filtered down through a variety of ultra-conservative movements, tendencies, and regimes. Resonating through the speeches, articles, and proclamations are echoes ranging from the Inquisition to the Opus Dei, from the Praetorian Guard to the Nazis, from the *ancien régime* to the French war for Algeria. For all their shadings and variations, these elements had long coexisted in Argentine politics. In one guise or another, extreme archaic conservatives have always been a force—now in shadow, now casting the light. In the nineteenth century, the pioneering educator, writer, and eventual president Domingo Sarmiento called them "barbarians"; for the eminent contemporary historian Tulio Halperin Donghi, they constitute "the dark underside of Argentine politics." Virtually every institution and political party has been colored by, or has negotiated with, these extremist factions. For Argentines, the discourse is so familiar that even if one doesn't agree, the language—to some extent—gets internalized. The official rhetoric of the Dirty War drew much of its power from being at once "comprehensible," incongruous, and disorienting. "It made you *psychotic*," said Mother of the Plaza Renée Epelbaum. "We could barely 'read,' let alone 'translate' the world around us. And that was exactly what they wanted."[3]

The terrorist state created two worlds—one public and one clandestine, each with its own encoded discourse. I will examine each, and eventually

draw a straight line from the public pronouncements to clandestine practice, where language became a form of torture. But before we enter the
"night and fog" of Argentina, let us consider some of the texts and speeches
that were delivered in the (so–called) light.

Once again we need to emphasize that the coup of March 24, 1976—
coming after two and a half years of political chaos under Isabel Perón—was
generally met with great relief. Both within and without the country, the
takeover had long been expected. The junta's first proclamation opens with
an extended litany of the ills that have corroded the nation's institutions.[4]
The sentences are extremely long, solemn, and dirge-like, full of adjectives
like "exhausted," "impossible," and "defeated"; hinging on nouns like
"dissolution," "anarchy," and "frustration"; "corruption," "contradiction,"
and "loss." In the reader or listener, the preamble induces fatigue, discour-
agement, and a keen desire for a change of direction. Politics aside, on the
level of rhetoric, the coup is a welcome resolution.

The takeover is described as the result of "serene meditation," suggesting that the new leaders are clear both in mind and conscience. Further
on, the junta pledges to "fully observe the ethical and moral principles of
justice . . . [and to act in] respect of human rights and dignity." The new
government will be "devoted to the most sacred interests of the Nation and
its inhabitants."

The commanders have begun not by imposing themselves, but by
apparently acceding to the needs (the "tacit and/or explicit request") of the
citizens for order and decency. Where earlier the tone was funereal, now it
consoles, uplifts, offers a covenant. "Each citizen must join in the fight.
The task is urgent and arduous. There will be sacrifices, the strict exercise
of authority in order to definitively eradicate the vices that afflict the country." But only those who are "corrupt" or "subversive" need to worry. Only
those who have committed "abuses of power." The country was now
embarked, "with the help of God," on "a quest for the common good, for
the full recovery of el ser nacional." This expression recurs in these initial
documents and was throughout the regime a dominant note. El ser nacional
translates as "the collective national essence, soul, or consciousness." It
harks back to the Inquisition, helped justify the Conquest, and its variants
have figured in a host of reactionary movements ever since. It arises from
and speaks to "the delirium for unanimity," in the apt phrase of Argentine
historian Juan José Sebreli. El ser nacional was first used in Argentina by
Peronist nationalists in 1943, in Cabildo, a notoriously fascist, anti-Semitic
magazine, in an article entitled "We Are One Nation." One of the many
ironies of Argentine society is that el ser nacional has been used by Peronists,

anti-Peronists, military dictatorships, and some far left-wing groups as well. To the Gentlemen of the Coup, *el ser nacional* resonated with divine purpose, with the country's grand destiny. It reinforced the message that the coup was tantamount to normalization, integration. The expression also served to locate the Process within each Argentine; to resist the Process was to deny one's self.

Stalwart were these Gentlemen of the Coup, invulnerable to the pettiness of doubt. For a small minority, this precisely was a problem. The night before the takeover, Videla received a worried letter from Retired Colonel Bernardo Alberte, who in the 1970s had been General Perón's personal delegate. Born in 1918, Alberte was brilliant and eloquent; in officers school, he had graduated first in his class. He wrote Videla to inform him that three days earlier, security forces had attempted to kidnap him; and that a young colleague of his had been murdered, then "left to rot in an unmarked grave, his stomach slit and his entrails exposed." Alberte expressed concern for "the funereal discourse of certain comrades who insist on classifying the dead as 'desirables' or 'undesirables' and on concealing the assassinations as 'excesses committed in the line of defense.'" He lamented "the lack of questioning, reflection, or criticism." Then he asked the man who would soon be leading the nation: "What does it portend for us Argentines if we allow a General to deprive us of democracy with the argument that it could lead to *an atheist, materialistic, totalitarian government?*" (emphasis in original). Within hours Alberte was dead: In the middle of the night, a "security squad" threw him out the window of his sixth-floor apartment located, ironically enough, on the Avenida Libertador.[5]

Alberte would not have been fooled by the coming double-talk about democracy. The Process of National Reorganization would entail the immediate "dissolution" of all republican institutions—the Congress, provincial legislatures, and municipal councils; political parties, trade unions, and professional as well as student associations. Sitting members of the Supreme Court would be "removed" and new judges appointed. These actions were being taken "to ensure the eventual restoration of democracy . . . and the revitalization of [its] institutions.[6] The three commanders—Videla, Massera, and Agosti—carefully explained that they themselves would make decisions according to "a simple majority"—the very model of democratic rule. A model the rest of the country could follow "when it was ready."

The domestic press not only swallowed, but amplified, the double discourse on democracy. A March 25 editorial in the *La Prensa* is typical. Built into the message is the underlying premise that Peronists must be routed and the party forever prohibited:

> The truth is that a republic does not consist only in the observance of certain electoral and parliamentary rites. It rests—as the most enduring philosopher has taught us—on the principle of virtue.... Unless he were as penetrating as Tocqueville ... an observer of our contemporary reality might commit the crass error of thinking that our democratic institutions have fallen. . . . We repeat that even though a government has fallen, the institutions fell in 1973 [with the return of Perón]. . . . On the ruins of the economic and moral crisis, we must create the conditions that will allow an authentic democracy to function. Without ire or hate, but without forgetting the immediate past whose sorry lesson must be incorporated into our history so that the coming generations can keep themselves alert.[7]

Lest anyone misunderstand, the junta stressed that the country was *not* entering a period of "revolution." Since 1930, that epithet had been assumed by a host of governments—both military and civilian, nationalist and progressive, paternalist and tailored to the free capitalist market. "Revolution" was, in fact, one of the junta's forbidden words. The days of spontaneity and froth were over. The country was being rescued by a *plan*, the Process for National Reorganization, whose basic objectives— "to eradicate subversion and to promote economic development based on the equilibrium and responsible participation of the various sectors of society"—would be realized with "rationality," "resolve," "structure," and "sobriety." By realizing these goals—its "sacred responsibilities"—Argentina "would join the Western, Christian concert of nations."

What was the initial response from this "concert of nations"? They immediately recognized the new government. Editorials in the major foreign press were overwhelmingly positive; many expressed wonder that the incompetent Mrs. Perón had been allowed to stay in office for so long.

Two days after the coup, the junta announced that General Videla had been designated President of the Nation. He, as well as the other two members of the ruling junta—Admiral Massera and Brigadier General Orlando Ramón Agosti—had assumed office "as acts of service" and would receive no salary. Newspaper and magazine articles introducing Videla all emphasized his deep religious beliefs, devotion to his family, and austere personal habits (manifest in his spare physique). Videla looked every inch the gentleman; when out of uniform, he favored English tailoring and Scottish tweeds. (His wife's maiden name was Hartridge.) In a special, lavishly illustrated supplement, the women's weekly *Para Tí* described his public-school background as "similar to that of any other child." This they accompanied with a photo of a typical public elementary school. "From his father, also a military man, he learned early the meaning of the words discipline, valor, and sacrifice." This phrase was glossed with a picture of Videla gracefully drawing his saber at a military parade.[8] According to the press, Videla was at once elite and Everyman; modest and successful; a man of the missal and the sword.

In his first address to the nation, Videla stressed the theme of "subordination," which, he said, "is not submission, nor blind obedience to capricious orders. To be subordinate means to consciously obey in order to achieve a higher objective. . . . One historical cycle has ended," Videla proclaimed, "another one begins."[9] In this new epoch, all citizens were being called to battle. "Your weapons are your eyes, your ears, and your intuition. Use them, exercise your right to familial and social defense," said a communiqué issued to the public by the Fifth Army Corps. "Defense is not only military, but [a matter for] all who want a prosperous country with a future. . . . Citizens, assume your obligations as Reserve Soldiers. Your information is always useful. Bring it to us."[10] One was expected to denounce individuals whose appearance, actions, or presence seemed "inappropriate." The junta emphasized, "The enemy has no flag nor uniform . . . nor even a face. Only he knows that he is the enemy."[11] In a front-page article in *La Prensa*, the regime warned: "The people must learn to recognize the 'civilized' man who does not know how to live in society and who in spite of his appearance and behavior harbors atheist attitudes that leave no space for God."[12] Using Mao's famous phrase, the Argentine generals held that "the guerrilla must not be allowed to circulate like fish in water."

As Colonel C. A. Castagno had declared even before the coup, "the delinquents (subversives) cannot live with us."[13] As articulated by General Cristino Nicolaides, "an individual involved with subversion was *irrecuperable*"[14] Yet Massera would still insist: "A government is an essentially moral entity. . . [and] must never abdicate the metaphysical principles from which the grandeur of its power derives . . . every citizen is unique and irreplaceable before God." To gain support for the nefarious Process, the admiral appealed to the goodness of Argentines, to the collective need to rally for a lofty cause.[15]

The key word in the admiral's statement is "citizen," an echo of the Nazis' Nuremberg Laws, which stripped Jews of their citizenship, officially designating them as aliens. In Argentina nationality became a function of attitude. "The repression is directed against a minority we do not consider Argentine," said Videla, ". . . a terrorist is not only someone who plants bombs, but a person whose *ideas* are contrary to our Western, Christian civilization."[16] In a ceremony marking the 123rd anniversary of the Rosario Police, Chief Augustín Feced took Videla's reasoning on citizenship a step further. Not only was the "subversive" not Argentine, "[he] should not even be considered our brother . . . this conflict between us cannot be likened to that between Cain and Abel."[17] This quote, and other highlights of the speech, were published the following day in the newspapers. Feced, himself a sadistic torturer, was known in the camps as El Cura, "The Priest." According to "The Priest," not only was the "subversive" excluded from the Argentine family but from the whole Judeo-Christian "family of man." For the director of the Military Academy, General Reynaldo Bignone, subversives were not merely "anti-fatherland," they were agents of the "antichrist."[18] The missing and the dead were not victims, nor merely enemies; they were demons. And so was anyone who even *thought* otherwise.

Every day there were headlines like this: "Shootout With 21 Subversives," "Extremists Die in Córdoba," "Five Guerrillas Fall." The victims of these "shootouts"—the vast majority of whom were in fact unarmed and murdered as *desaparecidos*—were invariably referred to as "seditious individuals," "subversive elements," "delinquents," and "criminals." Occasionally a supposed alias was provided; almost never were the individuals named. Sometimes the articles said, "Efforts to identify these delinquents have proven fruitless," implying that the whole issue of the missing was an invention of the "subversives" themselves who, after abandoning their loved ones, had wiped away all of their own traces ("the enemy has no face"). Some articles justified the shootings by saying the dead had tried to escape from prison *(intenta de fuga)*. The victims were vilified as both "aggressive" and "cowardly." A not uncommon story in this vein (appearing as early as three days after the coup in *La Prensa*) involved a military ambush on the secret hiding place of a band of "terrorists": Immediately seeing the superiority of the "legal forces," the male subversive ignominiously attempts to flee, *using his children as a human shield*. So according to the official reading, the "subversive" is worse than merely "aggressive" and "cowardly": In trying to save his own objectionable life, he shows himself as essentially alien by violating the defining human pact, that of parents protecting their children. On a single page of *La Prensa* (April 2,1976), there were three related articles (stories of this type were commonly clustered). Two formed a symmetrical pair: "A Policeman Dies After Trying to

Question an Unidentified Person," which warned readers about strangers, and "A Terrorist Dies After Aggressing a Policeman," in the largest, boldest print on the page, which reassured the public that in spite of the attacks, the police would prevail. The message was reinforced by a third news brief on this page about the army's discovery of an arms cache at a farm in the province of Tucumán: No individuals were found at the site, but their (supposed) reading material—"magazines and books of Marxist ideology"—rounded out the incriminating picture. In but the first sixteen days of the new de facto government, 152 individuals died in political violence: 19 policemen, two members of the military, 68 "presumed guerrillas," nine civilians whose corpses were later identified, and 54 civilians whose identities remained unknown.[19] According to a judicial source who spoke to the underground press on condition of anonymity, by September 1976, the Process was conducting an average of 30 kidnappings a day; the whereabouts of only one percent of these victims had been verified: "The other 99 percent," he said, "had to be given up for dead."[20]

As evidence of atrocities accumulated—bodies, tortured and dismembered, were washing up along the Plate River—official denial became harder to maintain, and explanations grew increasingly bizarre. "We will not allow death to roam unconstrained in Argentina," intoned Massera in his famous "Dead for the Fatherland" speech of November 2, 1976. "We who believe in a pluralistic democracy are fighting a war against the idolators of totalitarianism . . . a war for freedom and against tyranny . . . here and now, a war against those who favor death and by those of us who favor life." Following Massera's logic, exclusion equals pluralism; repression equals freedom; carnage leads to life.

Massera delivered this speech to his subordinates in the Navy Mechanics School, where the year before he had created the regime's largest and perhaps most brutal concentration camp. Known as the ESMA, its Spanish acronym, it has come to be called the Argentine Auschwitz. Even as he spoke, prisoners in the complex were being tortured. Until about 1978, almost no *desaparecido* survived the ESMA.

The speech is a Dirty War classic, a dramatic weaving of myth, magic, lyricism, and lies, delivered like a sermon. It offers a history lesson in the form of a fairy tale:

Slowly, almost without our noticing, a machine of horror was unleashed on the unsuspecting and on the innocent, before the incredulity of some, the complicity of others, and the stupor of many more.

A war had begun, an oblique and different kind of war, primitive in its ways but sophisticated in its cruelty, a war to which we gradually became accustomed, because it was not easy to admit that the entire country was being forced into a monstrous intimacy with blood.

Then the battle began. . . .

Surmounting all obstacles . . . the Armed Forces went on the offensive. And there, in the northwest [referring to Tucumán, the 1975 defeat of ERP], our valiant comrades of the Army began a risky and patient war . . . the most moving in our memory.

Then, the Armed Forces began the Republic's process of reorganization and now with political [as well as military] responsibility, the offensive became more integral, efficacious—the Air Force and the Army have also suffered the wounds of this shameless war, they have contributed with their heroism to the enemy's defeat. . . .

[T]his is a war between dialectic materialism and idealistic humanism. . . . We are fighting against nihilists, against agents of destruction whose only objective is destruction itself, although they disguise this with social crusades. That is why we see their inexplicable alliance, their inexplicable victims. . . .

Just as centuries before the world was attacked by plagues, we today are seeing a new and hallucinatory epidemic: the desire to kill. . . .

We are not going to fight unto death, we are going to fight beyond death, unto victory.

For love of life, for respect of those who have fallen and will fall . . . for those who are being born, for those who are afraid and even for those who are confused after such torment and wish to be reborn as free men, for all of them I say: death will not triumph here. . . .

Because all of our dead . . . each and every one died for the triumph of life.[21]

Massera was speaking directly to the officers tapped to throw living individuals out of navy aircraft into the sea. As these men were being told by their chaplains, this was "a Christian form of death." Massera never mentions this. Rather he plays on the desire of these young officers to do something (exactly what, he never specifies) grand, heroic, in the face of "shameless" attack; on their esprit de corps ("for respect of those who have fallen"); on their belief that the armed forces are the country's "ultimate moral reserve" and that the civilian population is depending on them for their salvation. The subtext was this: They were not murdering human beings; their mission was to vanquish death.

The subtext of the death flights was at that point unknown to the general public, so for civilians the speech functioned somewhat differently. Its dissemination beyond the navy was intended to make civilians feel included, an integral part of the Process. Yet again Massera presents to the divided country an image of the armed forces as a model of unity, harmony, and mutual respect. He provides an "explanation" for the chaos of recent years, making clear that Argentines were victims, that the horror had been visited upon them. Moreover, he attributes to the "enemy" the very horror that the regime itself has created. Interestingly enough, even as he rallies the public, he does so by depersonalizing the enemy, which he describes as a "machine." Who after all could possibly feel any sympathy for a machine? As he often does, Massera calls for obedience indirectly. In a tone that oozes reassurance, he nonetheless suggests that the audience must assume some responsibility for the country's plight, by virtue of being unaware ("unsuspecting"), unprepared ("innocent"), or secretly guilty ("complicit"). He is careful not to scold or cast aspersions; after all, the armed forces have already stepped into the breach ("We will not allow death to roam unconstrained"). Secure in their "coherence" and power, the armed forces can afford to both forgive and reward: All those who have been "afraid" and "confused" yet wish to be "reborn as free men" shall be liberated, aggrandized, by adhering to the Process. He reinforces this call for unquestioning dependence with his plague analogy—epidemics, after all, can be solved only by experts, who must act urgently and without impediment. The messianism of the speech ("we will fight beyond death, unto victory") goes beyond proselytizing: It was intended to dwarf rational questioning and critique of the disappearances, to make logic seem not just petty, but fettered, unfree.

Massera compulsively plays mirror games with the "enemy," now from one side of the glass, now from the other. In "The Quiet and Subtle Cyclone" (Navy Day, 1977), he rails that "we live in a world where enemies are so mutually mimetic that their identities get confused; where people's minds are pervaded by the law of the jungle; where the sole fact of a person's existence is a provocation."[22] It is he who imitates his enemy; his mind that is savage; provocation arises from the existence of certain others. In "Dead for the Fatherland," he projects the state's terrorizing features onto the opposition. In "The Quiet and Subtle Cyclone," he accuses the "enemy" of "destroying clarity, of covering the vital centers of our universe with a heavy fog." As though the missing had *created* the Argentine *Nacht und Nebel*. Elsewhere, in the name of the regime, he assumes the discourse, attitudes, and images of the so-called "subversives." In a speech addressed to a gathering of businessmen, he declared: "We believe in a society that knows that he who is loved the least has most need of love; that he who has received the most will be called on to give the most."[23] The only things the Process truly freed were prices and interest rates. Yet against the euphoria of "sweet money," Massera repeatedly attacks materialism: "A civilization cannot take refuge in its caves of crystal and steel, in the shelter of its computers, as though it really had nothing else to offer. . . . We want a country where there is room for beauty, for creative heroism. We want a country where the economy is not its [sole] objective, nor money its idol . . ."[24] Given that Argentina's sudden wealth had been created through currency and credit sleight-of-hand, Massera was being shrewd in another way as well. Suspecting that the financial effervescence would not last forever, he wanted to ingather on "higher moral ground." On July 9, 1977, Massera declared:

> We believe in a country where the love of liberty and personal initiative will be so great that no one will feel that he is a child of the government, but rather its legal brother.
>
> We believe in a culture that is spontaneous and free, that will be no one's political tool, and in which the natural nonconformity of artists and intellectuals will be the most vibrant element of its construction, and not [a cause for] its dissolution. . . .
>
> We believe that the best proof that a country is civilized resides in its scrupulous protection of the right of its minorities to peacefully dissent.[25]

This speech, given in honor of Independence Day, began twenty-four consecutive paragraphs with the words "We believe" *(Creemos)*, followed by the various principles that define pluralistic democracy. It is pure theater: The script is incantatory; the theme is freedom; the *mise en scène* is marshal pageantry. "Offstage" people are disappearing, but that is a different show, with a cast whose days are numbered.

In its acoustical effect, we could say that the rhetoric of the repression was stereophonic. Argentines were surrounded, alternately chafed and soothed by its textures, described by its line. The highest-ranking participants all contributed their own notes and tones, flats and sharps, and

counterpoint. Videla's theme—especially when playing to foreign governments and reporters—was outright denial. Responding in late 1977 to a
question by visiting British journalists, he said, "I emphatically deny that
there are concentration camps in Argentina, or military establishments in
which people are held longer than is absolutely necessary in this . . . fight
against subversion. . . . I live with my family in a military zone and am
certain that I don't live in a concentration camp."[26] A year later (1978),
he maintained: "In Argentina, political prisoners don't exist. No one is
persecuted or constrained on account of his political ideas."[27] In July 1979,
he affirmed, "The basic principles established in the Constitution are
permanently in force."[28] Six months later he laced his denial with myth:
"Argentina has no Nazi vocation. It was born free, with a vocation for freedom, and will fight to maintain that."[29] One of Videla's most extraordinary
performances took place on U.S. television:

> We must accept as a reality that there are missing persons in
> Argentina. The problem is not in ratifying or denying this reality,
> but in knowing the reasons why these persons have disappeared.
> There are several reasons: they have disappeared in order to live
> clandestinely and to dedicate themselves to subversion; they have
> disappeared because the subversive organizations have eliminated
> them as traitors to the cause; they have disappeared because in a
> shootout with fire and explosions, the corpse was mutilated
> beyond identification; and I accept that some persons might have
> disappeared owing to excesses committed by the repression. That
> is our responsibility and we have taken steps to ensure that it not
> be repeated; the other factors are beyond our control. On more
> than one occasion, persons who were thought to be missing later
> appeared before the microphones on television in some European
> country, speaking ill of Argentina.[30]

To the frightened, anguished, disoriented loved ones of *desapareci-*
dos, these words were unbelievably cruel. Immediately broadcast back to
Argentina, they were repeated often by the various sectors of the regime.
At the Ministry of the Interior, it was the standard reply to parents who
came desperately seeking help. Fanny and José Bendersky lost their only
child, Daniel, a researcher at the Atomic Energy Commision who had
just received a scholarship to the Massachusetts Institute of Technology.
Daniel was kidnapped on September 16,1978. In spite of letters from MIT,
Senator Edward Kennedy, and various human rights groups, the young
man never reappeared. "Daniel would never just leave us," said Fanny,

her eyes welling up at the thought. "He was devoted, we were all very close. Daniel was committed to family, that's why they took him. His so-called crime was collecting money for the Mothers of the Plaza de Mayo." People who knew him all say that Daniel Bendersky was gentle, serious, and extremely protective of his parents. "They had so many ways," said his father, "of erasing people, of trying to make you doubt the truth of your own life."[31]

The individuals Videla described as "thought to be missing" had been so *in fact*. Even early in the regime, international pressure resulted in the release of a small number of *desaparecidos*. Ana María Careaga was one. The sixteen-year-old daughter of refugees from Stroessner's Paraguay, she was kidnapped by the Federal Police in May 1977 and held until September 30 of that year. The United Nations (which years before had certified her parents' refugee status in Argentina), the Organization of American States (OAS), and Amnesty International had all worked on her case. Three months pregnant at the time of her capture (seven months at the time of her release) Careaga and her husband were granted asylum in Sweden, where doctors who examined her testified that her body bore the marks of torture. She—and others in similar circumstances—declared before human rights organizations, the European Parliament, and certain media. Her two brothers-in-law were missing, and on December 8, 1977, Ana María's mother, Esther B. de Careaga, was also kidnapped. Such accounts as Ana María's were dismissed by the regime as part of an "international anti-Argentine campaign." In fact, on the very day of her release— September 30, 1977—the Argentine Foreign Relations Minister, General Oscar A. Montes, protested at the United Nations that "terrorist groups, hiding behind a campaign supposedly on behalf of human rights, are destroying [our] country's social and economic structure."[32]

Yet again the devouring regime was presenting itself as a victim. A *noble* victim. As Videla piously insisted from the first month of his tenure, "[establishing] the Process cost the armed services many sacrifices."[33] On May 14, 1976, Viola offered this *envoi* to the army's retiring colonels:

> The institution whose service you are leaving today is facing one of the most difficult hours of its history. It has assumed the responsibilities of government and the fight against treacherous subversion. It does so in full consciousness of its obligations and responsibilities, fully aware of the risks we face today and tomorrow, and for this reason we require of everyone, active or retired, a personal quota of sacrifice. . . .[34]

On the first Christmas Eve of the Process, Videla offered this summing-up to the country at large:

> Without a doubt, the year ends under the sign of sacrifice. A shared, indispensable sacrifice which marks the beginning of our way to the true reuniting of Argentines; through sacrifice will we be able to face the future, ourselves, and the world, with a new identity. [Sacrifice] will permit us to assume the essential task of the great Argentine family: that of national reunification.[35]

The theme of "sacrifice" was a classically Roman Catholic reference. Even more to the point, it played upon civilian shame. After all, the armed forces had stepped in because of popular failings. The last elected government had produced nothing but calamity. For Massera this was an irresistible subject. True to form in this Navy Day address, he emphasized the grandeur of surrender, and encoded the dangers of non-compliance:

> We have put an end to small-time objectives and gray propositions. Decadence has seen its day. For this conquest the Armed Forces call on everyone, but *most especially* on the young, on those who comprise this young Argentina, on those who are waiting for a challenge. We want to know what they have to offer the country. We want to know if they are capable of constructively channeling all that dynamism. We want to know if they are prepared for daily heroism, for anonymous heroism, for heroism in favor of life.
>
> I must tell you that in these moments all the country has to offer you is a creative adventure full of risk, discomfort, and sacrifice.
>
> But that is the challenge.[36] [emphasis in original]

It is interesting to note that in describing "the young Argentina," Massera uses the homey, affectionate, *esa Argentina cachorra, cachorra* meaning puppy. Massera often mixed his levels of diction in this way, to defuse tension, encode threats, and generally to offer the semblance of warmth. "Anonymous heroism," we know, refers to silent service in kidnap, torture, and death flights.

In extending this message to the civilians, the admiral plays, in his way, on a collective history of political frustration, incompetence, and defeat:

> We must be careful. We must all be careful. Even those in power must be measured; we must not forget that the majority of citizens

are offering the sacrifice of their patience and their silence, even though there is no lack of voices clamoring for immediate solutions through premature elections. . . .

Are we going to make do with mediocrity?

Are we going to make do with [a political order] devoid of intelligent life?[37]

Elsewhere Massera vowed, "We are going to end this loser's mentality; we are going to end this fatal conformity and resignation; and we are going to stop telling ourselves lies to hide this long absence of success."[38] Here again the admiral goes in for the rousing repetition of pledges, and for items arranged in a series to make them seem reasoned, logical, inevitable. "A government must above all be rational," he insisted. "Justice and ethics are rational."[39]

"This time we will win" was a leitmotif of the regime. But only if civilians were smart enough to stay out of the way until their reëducation was complete. Where Videla and Massera endeavored to persuade through "uplift," other spokesmen favored insults and bullying.

The notoriously anti-Semitic Interior Minister, General Albano Jorge Harguindeguy, was one. Two of his closest advisers were Nazi ideologues, expert in the writings of Hitler and other fascist authors. Harguindeguy, who ran his own kidnapping ring out of the Ministry, was responsible for handling writs of habeas corpus. He also set up a special department to receive the relatives of *desaparecidos*.[40] As countless families have testified, the basic posture at Interior was that the missing were all "fat and happy in Nicaragua." Harguindeguy's public pronouncements were similarly hard and scolding. His favorite theme was that Argentines were too immature to govern themselves. At a press conference in August 1976, he said that "there would [again] be political parties when the citizenry [learns to] vote rationally and not emotionally."[41] Two months later he allowed that:

[Whereas] subversive activities are practically nil, political activities are still suspended because many things need to be reorganized. Political parties need to be reordered so that they will have national—not sectorial—objectives, and so their leaders will be elected on the basis of their suitability. Civic reeducation is indispensable because politically the population has always acted according to its feelings instead of its mind.[42]

As time passed his message became if anything more closed and impatient: "The country should forget about political parties for the time being.

I want it to be clear that no member of the Armed Forces has had any dialogue with political parties. There has not been, nor will there be dialogue, for a long time."[43]

In November 1977, Secretary of State Cyrus Vance visited Buenos Aires where he personally handed Videla a U.S. State Department report according to which Argentina was harboring between 12,000 and 17,000 political prisoners, and had "presumably assassinated" 6000 other individuals.[44] By this time, there was intense protest in the foreign press. Harguindeguy was not one to back down. In fact, criticism only inflamed him. On April 25, 1978, he hosted a large gathering of reporters in the Casa de Gobierno, for whom he interpreted the past, present, and future:

> Those who in one form or another have been responsible for the blood that flowed in our country should, in the course of their own self-criticism, consider themselves marginalized from the national future. I will repeat once more what I am so tired of saying: political parties . . . as we knew them between 1973 and 1976, have no place in the Argentina of the future. Those whose electoral calculations and pacts brought us to crashing failure cannot today raise their voices to advise, nor even debate, the government. Consequently, before any activity related to parties [can be resumed], it is necessary that those who were incapable then of rising to the level of their responsibility . . . step aside and let themselves be replaced by new men who have better ideas and more strength.[45]

In other words, opponents of the Process should make themselves invisible, or they would be made to vanish. Such was the definition of "rational" rule for "thinking" citizens.

Compared with some of his peers, Harguindeguy's rhetoric could be considered high-flown. Others in the regime specialized in blatant terrorizing. Augustín Feced (Police Chief of Rosario) was one: "The enemy started this war with gunfire. With them we will dialogue, but only with lead. . . . No more words, only defeat and annihilation."[46] For those who needed literal translations, there was the unsurpassingly explicit Ibérico Saint Jean, governor of the Province of Buenos Aires: *"First we will kill all the subversives, then we will kill their collaborators, then . . . their sympathizers, then . . . those who remain indifferent; and, finally, we will kill the timid"* (emphasis in original).[47] It was the very baldness of this statement that made it so hard to believe. Yet this was indeed the monstrous plan.

Feced was wrong about only one thing. Words were still a precious weapon in the arsenal of the regime. The junta seriously undertook to "recover the meanings of many 'embezzled' words." High on their list for idiomatic repair were, as we have seen, "reality," "rationality," "truth," "sacrifice," "patriotism," "duty," "democracy," and "honor." They also redefined war and peace. For all its emphasis on "lucid" government, the junta's definitions of war tended to the mystical: "Unlike a classical [war], neither its beginning nor its final victorious battle are materialized in time. Nor are there great concentrations of men, weapons and materials; nor is the front clearly defined."[48] When pressed as to when the de facto government would come to an end, Videla always insisted: "The Process is not subject to a time frame, but rather to the realization of its objectives."[49] So the war could not be located—temporally, spatially, or materially. Its crowning triumph could not be measured. This was indeed a very new form of battle. People were disappearing, but aside from that, life was normal. Adults went to work, children went to school, families took vacations.

Yet "tranquility did not equal peace," and peace was not "the mere absence of explosives." As early as 1963, General Osiris G. Villegas (a pivotal tactician) was reinterpreting Karl von Clausewitz: "Peace," said the Argentine, "is the continuation of war by other means."[50] In May 1978, General Luciano B. Menéndez emphasized that "tranquility [had] returned to the people because subversive criminality has been annihilated in armed battle, but tranquility—if it is to be peace—must be won and guarded through constant vigilance."[51] Menéndez made this statement in Córdoba, near La Perla, the concentration camp he oversaw. For Harguindeguy, "Winning peace means nothing more and nothing less than getting Argentines [united] behind one idea of the country's objectives, instead of thinking about totally alien ideas."[52] Peace, then, was destroyed by independent thought; an individual quietly thinking was likely committing an act of war.

The junta abhorred both individualists and the masses. Their statements on the former echo almost verbatim their arch-enemy Perón (whose rallying powers the junta nonetheless admired). Here is Perón in 1943: "I am fighting to transform our country's individualist spirit because I think it arises from an inferiority complex." In 1949, he reiterated: "Individualism is amoral. It leads to subversion, to egoism, to the evolution of the lower forms of the species."[53] For Perón, as for the Dirty War juntas, "individualism" was far removed from any sort of heroism, particularly that of the "anonymous" kind, so highly touted by Massera. The Dirty War admiral—like his peers—excoriated the "impulse toward fragmentation . . . the abandonment of the search for Truth which has led to every man looking for 'his own' truth."[54]

Yet the junta continually warned against any identification with "the masses," which they held were "totalitarian." As glossed by Ibérico Saint Jean:

> Decades ago Argentina entered on the prickly path of a society [run by] massed which, grouped together in parties exercised an authoritarian, despotic power, endangering the very essence of democracy. . . . If the world were inclined toward quantity, we would be lost; but thanks be to God, we are an empty country, inclined to quality, which gives us enormous possibilities.[55]

The equation is simple and by now familiar: The Process was creating a nation for the immaculate few.

In the junta's analogies to cleanliness and health, we hear echoes of the Nazis. "These are difficult days," said Massera, "days of cleansing, preparation . . . this country has been ill for too long for a sudden recovery. That's why we must understand that we have only begun our period of convalescence . . . our recuperation of the nation's health . . . [and to do so] we must cleanse the country of subversion."[56] By the time the junta seized power, it had its whole Neo-Nazi "germ theory" in place. It articulated by Rear Admiral César A. Guzzetti for *La Opinión* on October 3, 1976:

> The social body of the country is contaminated by an illness that in corroding its entrails produces antibodies. These antibodies must not be considered in the same way as [the original] microbe. As the government controls and destroys the guerrilla, the action of the antibody will disappear. . . . This is just the natural reaction of a sick body.

It is worthwhile to note that under Perón (who gave asylum to hundreds of Nazis), dissidents were taken to a centrally located Buenos Aires hospital where they were tortured by the Federal Police. This was a daily occurrence, and known to the doctors and nurses who worked there.[57] The tropes of "sickness," "treatment" and "cure" had long been inscribed in the repressive practices of Argentina. The Mothers of the Plaza were immediately branded by the regime as "madwomen"—*las locas de la Plaza de Mayo* (see Fig. 2). The attributes we normally associate with health—clarity, vigor, independence—no longer applied. Health came to mean "proper social adaptation," that is, conformity, passivity, compliance,

FIGURE 2. The Mothers of the Plaza de Mayo are harassed by police during the March for Life, October 5, 1982. (Photo credit: Eduardo Longoni)

which were masked with grander words like "faith," "cooperation," "personal responsibility," and "maturity."

"Silence is health"—*el silencio es salud*—is an expression that numerous Argentines recalled for me as a slogan of that time. They are both wrong and right: The phrase was coined in 1975 by the Municipality of Buenos Aires in a campaign to reduce the din of traffic by prohibiting the use of horns except in emergencies. "Silence is health" originally had an ecological, communitarian ring, and gratified *porteños* (inhabitants of the port city of Buenos Aires) enjoyed the stylish posters, engaging ads, and aural relief. After the coup, "silence is health" took on a different meaning, and it was that which lodged in peoples memory. Interestingly enough, the generals did not use this expression. They didn't have to: The translation they wanted was made for them—reflexively by the people whose minds they had set out to conquer.

In the lexicon of the juntas, "silence" was loftier than "health." Its value approached the sacramental. It was referred to as a "sacrifice" offered by the "faithful," and as the penance required of the ungodly. As Massera explained to the National Academy of Law and Social Science: "Some must speak and some must be still, so we can listen to the voices of the just and to the silence of the sinners."[58]

Another reflexive translation that has lingered in the minds of many Argentines I know is *zona de detención*. During the Process, these signs were erected at bus stops in an effort to get people to stop clustering and tidily queue. In Spanish, *detención* means "wait" as well as "arrest." "Waiting at a bus stop," said a colleague, "always gave me the feeling I was lining up, oh-so-politely, to be taken away. Particularly when the police showed up and demanded everyone's documents." When an exiled academic who had surreptitiously slipped back to Buenos Aires saw the signs, it so frightened him that he immediately made plans to leave. "It sounds ridiculous." he said nearly twenty years later, "But it's true. I saw a sign meaning 'Bus Stop,' and all I could think of was being killed."

The censors of the junta were always on the lookout for suspicious terms, like "conditions," "contradiction," "criticism," "relative," and "reactionary." Journalists had to try to do without these words if they wanted to get their articles published without difficulty. Freudian discourse was so strictly forbidden that classical psycho-analysis essentially stopped during the Dirty War. Argentina then had (still has) more psychologists per capita than any other industrialized nation. "There's one in every family," goes the old joke. In Buenos Aires, analysts were so associated with one neighborhood that it was (and still is) called "Villa Freud." As I was told by one analyst, "The tools we needed for the 'talking cure' were off-limits. We had no safe way to communicate. And don't forget: Knowledge was dangerous. What we were told could be as perilous as what we might say." Practitioners who remained in the country devoted themselves to research. Argentina rapidly became the most important center outside of France for Lacanian psychology, which depends on a rarefied, highly encoded vocabulary. It is no exaggeration to say that the junta's linguistic proscriptions influenced the development of an entire discipline. (Of course by their lights Lacan would be no less "subversive" than Freud, but he was less famous then, and they could not begin to penetrate the language.)

No expression so infuriated the junta as "human rights." One could fill an entire volume with their bellicose statements on the subject. "We are jealous defenders of [a country's] right to self-determination. That is why we will not allow [groups] waving banners for 'human rights' to determine . . . our future," affirmed a spokesman for the air force.[59] Responding to journalists' questions in Brazil, Videla explained, "When we say that we want to respect human rights, we mean this to benefit all men of good will, Argentines and foreigners, who live in our country, who respect our laws, and who are collaborating in the development of our nation."[60] For certain members of the Church, "human rights" was the devil's own word play, a lofty-sounding label for mortal sin. As phrased by the Archbishop of San Juan, Idelfonso Maria Sansierra, "those who resort to 'human rights' have an atheist mentality, have committed criminal acts, and have political ambitions."[61]

This war of words culminated in a dramatic display in 1978, when the World Soccer Championships were held in Argentina. Taking advantage of their access, foreign journalists pressed the regime for information on reported disappearances, torture, and secret concentration camps. "What do you mean, 'human rights' [*derechos humanos*]?" the commanders fumed. "We Argentines are human, we Argentines are right"—*Los argentinos somos derechos y humanos*. The message was writ large on a huge banner in the reception area of Ezeiza, the international airport. Shiny decals with this slogan appeared in shop windows and offices, on private cars and taxi cabs. Employees at the Ministry of the Interior—who routinely shredded writs of habeas corpus—wore the decals and demonstrated in Plaza de Mayo. This group came face to face with another demonstration—parents, spouses, and children of *desaparecidos* who marched silently, wearing pictures of their loved ones and signs that asked; *Dónde están?* "Where are they?" The official reply? "We Argentines are human, we Argentines are right."

The decals seemed to propagate. In the windows of houses and apartments, on briefcases and handbags (see Fig. 3). Like charms, like defensive shields.

It turned out that Argentina won the World Cup. At the news of its victory, the demonstrations were so huge, so intense, that one foreign correspondent likened them to V-E day in Europe. For days and nights in every city and town, Argentines took to the streets, their cars and trucks and motorcycles bedecked with the flag. Those on foot came wrapped in sky-blue and white, the national colors. The athletic win was taken as vindication on every level. Three days after the victory, Videla proclaimed:

> The [games] are over, but they have left us with a teaching, the lesson that civic maturity is born of the deep sentiment of responsibility. It is the lesson of a diverse people who want to live in unity. . . . This unanimous cry of "Argentina!" that rose up from our hearts, this singular flag of sky-blue and white that fluttered in our hands, are signs of a deep reality that exceed the limits of a sporting event. They are the voice and insignia of a Nation that is reunited in the plenitude of its dignity. . . . All the Nation has

FIGURE 3. The signs these women are wearing ("We Argentines Are Human, We
Argentines Are Right") are part of the junta's campaign against human rights groups.
These women are in the heart of downtown, at Avenida de Mayo and 9 de Julio, on 7, 1979.
(Photo credit: Guillermo Loiácono)

triumphed. We are one people who today assume the challenge we
put to ourselves: that of creativity, of fruitful work, and shared
effort.[62]

More than one observer has noted the similiarities between the 1978 World
Soccer Cup and Hitler's 1936 Olympic Games. At no other time during the
Process was Argentina ever so massively, orgiastically fascist.

With the aid of the media, the Ministry of Education directed a special
linguistic campaign at parents: "How to Recognize Marxist Infiltration in
the Schools." According to this ubiquitous manual the "first sign" of peril
was "a certain vocabulary." Predictably, the following words were singled
out: "dialogue," "bourgeoisie," "Latin America" (for its Third World
connotations), "exploitation," "structural change," and, of course, "capitalism" and "socialism." Also, "popular," "leader," "uprising," "rebellion,"
and "revolution" (even in science). The word "cell" was strictly limited to
biology. Parents who sent their children to parochial schools or catechism
classes were warned about "pre-conciliar" and "post-conciliar," "ecumen-
icalism," "liberation," and "compromise." Parents were instructed to be

especially alert for more subtle dangers, like "group projects," which were used to evade "personal responsibility," and which functioned to "depersonalize" the individual child, making him or her vulnerable to "indoctrination." Such "work tables" could be infiltrated by subversive groups through particular students. According to the government, the following subjects particularly lent themselves to indoctrination: history, civics, economics, geography, and catechism. Parents were also to surveil Spanish and literature assignments lest they feature "engaged writers" in general and "Latin American novelists" in particular. Also proscribed were modern math and any science that derived from Einstein's theory of relativity. Just as the Process "watched over" parents, they in turn should "do their part" by regularly examining their children's homework and lesson books. There were also warnings about "parents' committees" formed to present "concerns" to school authorities. Individuals attracted to such initiatives were likely to be dangerous.[63]

Another special media campaign was targeted to women. "How have you raised your children?" "Do you know what your children are doing, *right now?*" Such messages were broadcast daily on television and radio, and featured in women's magazines. Maybe the "subversive threat to Western, Christian civilization" was the fault of Argentine mothers. "Young people have become indifferent to our world and are beginning to construct a private universe. . . . It is as though they are patiently waiting for the biological extinction of a strange and incomprehensible species . . . they are becoming a caste apart, a visible but secret society," said Massera upon being named Honorary Professor at the University of the Savior in Buenos Aires.[64] In other words, if your children are not part of the Process, they are not Argentine; if they are not Argentine, then they are demons. "Your weapons are your eyes, your ears, and your intuition."

Of the Gentlemen of the Coup it was Massera who dilated on the theme of women:

> For too long humanity has deprived itself of half of its available creative energy. By relegating women to a practically decorative role, [we have] wasted treasures of intelligence, imagination, courage, and sensibility. . . . This unsatisfied, unruly, fickle, insecure society whose materialism and supposedly revolutionary changes offer nothing but anguish . . .in a society created by men. . . . All of us Argentines want to modernize the country . . . want to bury the memory of failure, discouragement, and apathy, and we will succeed if women participate actively with

their ideas and valor. How can women be absent, when we speak
of a new birth.

We are calling [women] to be mothers of the Republic; to
teach it to walk, to teach it think, to teach it to smile.

Never as in these moments has Argentina so needed its
women, because never as in these moments has Argentina so
needed to be on the side of life.[65]

Here is a striking departure from the usual strains of fascist crypto-
feminism, in which women are called upon to produce sons for the Fatherland (Mussolini) or "Aryan children" (as in the case of the Nazis). Rather
the country itself is a baby, unable to walk, think, or express happiness—
the only approved emotion here. These basics, according to Massera, can
be taught only by women. *Argentine* women—with all the traits and equipment that nationality here implies.

Playing a major role in the junta's "feminist" campaign was *Para Tí*, the
largest-circulation women's magazine in Argentina. Similar to *Woman's
Day*, *Redbook*, or *Good Housekeeping* in the United States, *Para Tí* ("For
You") ran the gamut of fashion, domestic crafts, celebrity interviews, and
current events. The fashion pages often showed a military look, replete with
epaulettes, brass buttons, berets, and sailor hats. The cover photo of May 7,
1970, shows a vibrant woman in "uniform," saluting under the banner:
"For Women Without Barracks." *Para Tí* reproduced verbatim the junta's
discourse on "the enemy's unconventional war," on the need for "every
Argentine of good will to mobilize." Under the juntas, the tone of this magazine for ladies became suddenly defiant, "wised up," and aggressive:

We Argentine women will not be taken for idiots. *We have learned
a new language*, have new demands, and have chosen a different
road. . . . We are not the same as we were before. [emphasis added][66]

What accounts for the change? The writers—and readers—of *Para Tí* have
learned their lesson: "We were defrauded by democracy, which was not
what we had expected."[67] Recurrent themes in 1978 and 1979 include "the
benefits of limits" and "authority is not dictatorship," as they apply not
only in politics, but also in childrearing and education. The "Argentine
family" was a microcosm of the Process. At the same time *Para Tí* was
careful to include nonhomemakers in its target audience, and specifically
addressed "businesswomen," "doctors," and other "professionals." (It
seems that the Process was good for business. The magazine certainly
seized the moment to expand its readership.)

In general, the language of this magazine mirrored that of the regime, but it also developed a special idiom tailored to its audience (i.e., "Peace has settled in the living room, now it must take over the house.") When addressing its readers, it used the rallying, coercive "we," or the polite, respectful "you" (*Usted*, despite the familiar *ti* of the title), as in: "We are sure that you, like the majority of Argentines, gave your support to the Process that began on March 24, 1976. . . . On that day we took a decisive step toward political maturity."[68] It urged women to be active in every sphere of the nation's business, emphasizing that Argentine women were "advanced," "educated," "European." In May 1978, the magazine ran a feature on the recent detailed, quite technical, address by the Minister of the Economy, José Martínez de Hoz (who routinely gave the junta's longest, densest speeches). "It Might Not Have Seemed So But This Speech Was Also for Us," ran the headline in *Para Ti*. The article, which did nothing to gloss the minister's message, nonetheless said: "You cannot take refuge in the simple 'All I care about is when they raise the prices at market.' You have the obligation to know why that happens. You too are responsible. The future does not depend on the minister. It depends on all of us. It depends on you."[69]

It is the old story: "participation" is not really the issue, nor any sort of initiative or agency. (If it were, the magazine would have discussed the substance of the minister's speech.) What counts is the image of capable refinement. In fact in another issue (September 4, 1978) the editor asserted: "Caring for [our country's] image is also a way of forging the nation." The magazine became especially intense during peaks of the so-called "Anti-Argentine campaign." (Then, the discourse was "us vs. them.") In this regard, the two "hottest" times were the 1978 World Soccer Championship and the September 1979 fact-finding visit by the oas Inter-American Commission on Human Rights. (This commission came specifically to investigate reports of disappearances and concentration camps.) After Argentina won the soccer title in June 1978 the legions of foreign reporters left (or were expelled), but for months afterward *Para Ti* kept responding to the "hostility" of the foreign journalists and the "lies" about "so-called disappearances" and "human rights":

> We are prepared to demand a great deal of ourselves, but we are going to demand a lot of others as well. Of those who govern us, that they keep their word, fulfill their promises to the ultimate consequences. To those who *disappeared themselves* [we say] return, show your face if your conscience permits. If not, then

sincerely and with our hands on our hearts, we ask you to be quiet. Please, *enough*. . . . Enough demagogy, politicking, easy solutions, sentimentality, and false patriotism. In a word: we must once and for all put an end to populism. [emphasis in original][70]

Self-righteous aggression combined with a humble gesture of "sincerity" is another hallmark of the magazine's tone during these years. The accusation against the "so-called missing," is uncharacteristically slangy: *"A los que 'se borraron'que vuelvan, que den la cara si es que sus conciencias se lo permiten."* The literal meaning of *borrar* is "to erase." The reflexive verb *borrarse* means "to leave," "to split," "to beat it"—or, to erase oneself. The expression—doubly fenced off with italics and quotation marks—is yet another sign of contempt for the missing, who do not quite speak "our" proper language.

In 1978, appealing to its readers' savvy resolve, *Para Tí* launched a special international operation called "Defend Your Argentina." In a series of consecutive issues the editors replaced the usual recipes with scenic patriotic postcards (children with Argentine flags, national monuments, etc.) emblazoned with "Argentina: The Whole Truth." Readers were instructed to tear out these cards and send them to "those responsible for the Anti-Argentine Campaign" (all of whose addresses were provided): President and Mrs. Jimmy Carter, Senator Ted Kennedy, President Valéry Giscard D'Estaing, Her Majesty Queen Juliana of the Netherlands, and other world leaders; Amnesty International (Holland, U.K., France, Spain, and U.S. branches); Association Pro Human Rights; and *Le Monde, Paris Match, Der Spiegel, L'Unitá, Cambio 16*, and other publications of record. The campaign generated such a big response that the magazine repeated it over another series of issues. On October 23, 1978, *Para Tí* ran what the editors said was a survey of 200 women in Paris, "without a doubt the center of the defamation campaign." According to their findings, the majority of these Parisians did not know where Argentina was located, were unsure of the country's language, and believed that the typical Argentine woman was "submissive," "traditional," "poor, doesn't go to the cinema, doesn't read," "is short, dark, and has dark eyes." Some quotable dissenters found Argentine women "like other Westerners, but even more elegant than Parisians." The article ran with photos of the French capital, including one of a large demonstration urging the international boycott of the Soccer Championships. It is dubious that any such survey ever took place. The point of this article for the readers of Para *Para Tí* is the supposed ignorance behind the "Anti-Argentine campaign."

The writers of the editorials of September 1979—coinciding with the visit by the OAS Commission on Human Rights—were blatantly fed up:

> Yes, we suffered too much to again tolerate this insolence, to again hear those same voices that made terror and chaos our daily [reality]. . . . That is why today, with the excuse of the arrival of the Human Rights Commission, to hear them talking about these subjects, citing Pope John Paul II and the Gospels, makes us indignant. But that is their "style." They never miss an opportunity to talk about "the people," "mothers' pain," and "social equality." That is to say, they use a facile idiom, typical of those who . . . choose the road to demagogy. They speak for only one reason: to get votes. . . . So quickly do they forget their wrongdoings? So quickly do they wish to be relieved of their terrible responsibility? . . . If we err again it will be the end, we will have lost . . . our children's future.[71]

This editorial was preceded by a feature called "Today They Say," which assembled quotes and headlines "proving" that life was better, safer, more promising under the juntas. As the texts are intended to show, the source of the country's problems was Perón and everything that came in his wake. In another issue (September 10) the magazine published a survey of Argentine women, the great majority of whom believed that the country "was not ready" for a return to democracy, and that some political parties (particularly, but not only, the Peronists) should always be proscribed. All of the survey questions presume that democracy requires limits. Even more striking is the interview with Eduardo Roca, former Argentine Ambassador in Washington, D.C., and to the OAS, on the subject of "U.S. aggression." The elegantly attired Roca ridiculed Carter's informality, impugned the personal morals of Patricia Derian (Under Secretary for Human Rights), and attacked the credentials of State Department spokesman Thomas Reston. He also stated, "The New York Times is a paper that hates us," and that the OAS commission is "unlikely to be fair."[72] It is typical of *Para Tí* to name second-tier government appointees: The information helps readers to construct their knowing persona, their image of mastery.

In July 1993, I spent a couple of days in the Biblioteca Nacional reading nothing but *Para Tí*. The issues are collected in long, heavy, cloth binders, and are released from the stacks only one at a time. Every couple of hours, I had to stand on line and ask the librarian for another series. I was conscious that the young trainee was watching me, looking closely at the pages I asked to have xeroxed. It so happened that the government was then waging one of its "ideological spying campaigns," and I started to wonder whether the young man at the desk was really a librarian. The dates of my readings certainly betrayed the nature of my research. The next time the young man, who seemed about twenty-two, brought me my binder, he leaned down close and whispered, "You know the worst thing about this? I believed every word, my mother was a faithful reader."

HITLER ONCE SAID, "Without loudspeakers we never could have conquered Germany." In the Fuhrer's time, radio was the key advance. For the Process, it was public relations. Less than a month after taking power, Videla himself opened the 25th World Public Relations Congress, which had been scheduled that year in Buenos Aires. He then hosted a group of delegates in the Casa de Gobierno.[73] Five months later the de facto leader awarded a one-million-dollar contract to Burson Marsteller, the Madison Avenue PR giant, to "improve [his country's] international image." The agency began as it would on any other project, with a detailed diagnosis and strategy report. "The challenge was economic," I was told in 1996 by Victor Emmanuel who, as a thirty-year-old account executive, had been in charge of the job. "It was fascinating, enormous, we could say awesome. The aims were twofold: to introduce foreign investment and to promote foreign trade. In short, to bring Argentina into the twentieth century. Argentina had had years of protective, statist economics. And it was involved in a civil war. No one, but no one, invests in a country involved in a civil war. I'll be open," he offered, "I'm right wing. It was a real sloppy mess. You had the Montoneros blowing up kindergartens, school buses, making everything unsafe." He had just repeated two of the central distortions of the regime: By late 1976, even the junta conceded that the guerrillas had been militarily decimated, so any mention of "civil war" was by then poetic license; and the leftist Montoneros *never once* attacked a school, a school bus, or any facility for children. What did he make of the allegations of kidnap, disappearance, and concentration camps? "Their call was to get the mess over as soon as possible. A lot of innocent people were probably killed. But I wouldn't point the finger at any one party. There are always two sides to any story. And those who were writing about the repression were really only seeing it from one point of view. There *were* three troublesome issues: There was the Jewish issue, the terrorist issue, and the dictatorship issue. But it's the nature of people to find fault and criticize. Those who took opposing positions refused to look at the other side of the story." I pointed out that the regime had legalized the death penalty and so did not have to resort to kidnap and secret camps. "It was arguably almost necessary," Emmanuel replied. "The situation required full military force. Up until 1978, while they stitched the economy together. It's tough," he conceded, "the argument could probably be made for the other side, too. The ferocity could have been controlled. Should have been. But given the situation, immense force was required." With the hindsight of two decades, Emmanuel said that given the opportunity he would do the job again.[74]

The thirty-three-page initial report completed under his supervision often echoes the language of the regime, referring, for instance, to "the well-financed subversion campaigns of international origin."[75] Emmanuel and his team put the challenge in succinct, can-do language in the section entitled "The Communications Implications of Terrorism": "It can be categorically stated that terrorism and the manner in which Argentina eliminates it—particularly the accusation that terrorism by the right is not suppressed—are the only problems standing between the Videla government and free-world approval." BM, as the agency was known on Madison Avenue, warned Videla that this was a tall order, and suggested that its offices in eight countries all participate (the U.S., Canada, Japan, the U.K., Belgium, the Netherlands, Mexico, and Colombia). The targets of the campaign were threefold: "those who influence thinking," "those who influence investments," and "those who influence travel." Journalists, they knew, would be the toughest customers: "[Many] consider the Argentine government oppressive and repressive, a dictatorial military institution which deserves little more than condemnation." So prominent reporters got special attention, in the hopes that they would "help build a system of conduits in the leading newspapers and magazines [in the West]." Linked to this was a negative campaign aimed at the same individuals and groups singled out by Para Tí. Of the 53 U.S. reporters invited to Argentina, between 30 and 40 accepted. They were hosted by carefully selected Argentine editors who had been briefed on their guests' backgrounds, interests, and "the best approach for creating a positive and lasting impression." When the U.S. reporter returned home, the nearest Argentine embassy would follow up to keep the contact warm. Positive thinking was the key: "Terrorism is not the only news from Argentina, nor is it the major news." In addition, specially rehearsed Argentine editors traveled here to explain their country's dilemma, caught "between what was reported versus what really happened." A similar exchange was developed for government officials and business figures. Account executives at BM admitted, "We can never be certain that important business and financial publications will print news about Argentina along agreed-to lines." In order to fill this breach they used advertising. Videla was so pleased with the agency's performance that he renewed its contract—twice.

In October 1979, BM placed a long and lavish advertising supplement in the *New York Times Magazine*.[76] It is worth noting that the supplement appeared only a few weeks after the departure from Buenos Aires of the OAS Commission on Human Rights. I was told by Victor Emmanuel that the text and visuals were supplied by Argentina, "probably from the Finance Minister, Martínez de Hoz." "Argentina: Actual Reality" ran a full twelve pages dense with text and embellished with four-color illustrations. The front cover is a product map of Argentina done in primary colors and child-like forms: smiling cows, lollipop trees, and a giant beach umbrella. The red barns and green fields call up friendly reading primers; the airplane, boat, and ships along the "coast" look like toys in a bathtub. The Argentine airline Aerolíneas Argentinas is described, in naive verse, as "People Who Love People." By the time the reader gets to the back cover he or she has certainly "grown up." Against a velvety black background is an artful arrangement of diamond jewelry: a necklace, a bracelet, pendant earrings, and a ring, all by Ricciardi of Buenos Aires: "One of the few, finest, and the most exclusive jewelers in the world." The word "exclusive" is repeated toward the bottom of the page in relation to the store's address. Together the covers suggest a kind of life cycle: from child-like innocence to the utmost in adult snob appeal. (In other words, if you are good you will get the rewards.) Within, most of the ads are for banks, although insurance companies, hotels, steel works, and mills are also represented (and all offer special incentives). The first page of text, "Argentina: After the Decline," is topped with two adjacent photos. The first (reading left to right) shows Videla in an impeccable civilian suit: white shirt, white pocket hankie, dark tie with small white dots. The general is dressed entirely in black and white; there are no shades of gray. The photo on the right shows soldiers marching past the Casa Rosada. Visually the page is sober and perfectly symmetrical. The text, however, is a fairy tale about a country of "untold natural riches [and] a vivacious, adaptable people among whom racial, ethnic or religious conflicts were unknown." This land, we are given to know, was celebrated by the leading lights of Europe: Clemenceau, Count Keyserling, and Ortega y Gasset. But then "an unfortunate succession" of "governments with a partisan spirit inflam[ed] some social elements against others, initiated a stage of indisputable decline." The "collapse of republican institutions, of public security, and of the production machine was practically total" and completely the fault of "Marxist—Leninist guerrilla bands." Just in time, the Process, whose "legitimacy has been unequivocally accepted" rescued the country from "the Leninist militia." After just three years, the country can boast "a number of important achievements":

> Argentines . . . are again living with security. The nightmare of the subversive war is now behind them and now Buenos Aires at night is once again one of the most lively and best protected cities of the western world. This physical security is, in reality, a simple translation of an invisible security, provided by the authority of a Law recovered.

The opening lie is so bald it needs no comment. The language of the third sentence—at once magical and abstract—contains both truth and falsehood. The so-called "security" was essentially covert, but its workings (its "translation") were anything but "simple." The sentence is an evil tease: the meaning behind the words was beyond the comprehension of readers who really did not know what was going on in Argentina. For those who believed that the Argentine situation had indeed "improved," the word play was an in-joke. Investors were assured that they would derive "benefits" from the Process, which was oriented toward building "a stable and invulnerable democracy." Keen to the North American distaste for charismatic tyrants, the text asserts that "the military government presently in force is largely impersonal in nature." The word "impersonal" subtly suggests that claims of intimate loss (i.e., those of the Mothers of the Plaza) have no basis in fact.

The nerviest part of this supplement are the two pages devoted to "Human Rights in Argentina: 1959–1979." Why is the starting point 1959? Because it coincides with the first year of Castro's reign in Cuba. "This," say the authors solemnly, "is a historical account which centers on the human rights to life, to liberty, to property, and to the necessary conditions under which a civilized society may exercise those rights. . . . It is a truism that it is impossible to speak of 'Argentine terrorism' . . . we must understand that terrorism entered the country from the outside." Once again, poor Argentina is under siege from "those who decided on death as opposed to life." Directly or indirectly, Massera clearly had a hand in this text. The history of "institutionalized terrorism" (as the subhead puts it) is outrageously inaccurate and stylistically over the top. The rise of the guerrilla groups and the return of a revolutionary constitutional government (in 1973) led to:

> Hordes of youths with guerrilla banners occup[ying] the highest
> seats of the public administrations and universities. Faced with
> this the common man found himself disoriented. . . . Little by
> little, some understood that they were involved in a "war." . . .
> Then there followed violent student uprisings, in which fanaticism
> glorified crime. Everyday . . . there was tragedy. . . . People began to
> doubt the 'democracy of the vote' . . . as terrorists were being
> promoted to high public positions, with great publicity in the
> newspapers. Meanwhile misery was settling in their homes.

The authors explain by analogy: "It was as though the Symbionese Army
had occupied California and was planting its murderous cells throughout
all of the large cities of the United States." The comparison is ridiculous,
and the statistics are pure fabrication: Instead of the legitimate figure of
400 armed guerrillas out of about 2000 organized leftists, the text posits
40,000 in armed bands plus 30,000 sympathizers ready to replace them.
"In all, 70,000 persons who, at any given moment, were at the point of
destroying every vestige of civilization in a naturally peaceful country."
The "legitimate forces," it is said, destroyed approximately 9 percent of
these "terrorists." (A tacit confession whose real import is to impugn the
victims.) The rest "deserted," "disappeared," or are living abroad "enjoying the money they took with them . . . and occasionally find[ing] protec-
tors." References are made to "malicious broadcasts" that pushed some
countries to adopt sanctions. (One such leader was President Carter, who,
it was understood, was up for reelection.) Long-victimized Argentina
emerges as an example "of how a people can respond to . . . inhuman
challenge with courage, with faith in God and in their mode of life."
Argentina has assumed its duty. *('Have you?')* As the analogy to the Symbionese Army "makes clear," terrorism can happen anywhere. The essay
closes with a warning: "The task of the West is to take precautions." The
intention is to leave the reader uneasy, even guilty: If the West had been
more alert, maybe Argentina (and Nicaragua, El Salvador, etc.) would not
have been so "vulnerable." Reports of the regime's atrocities—the issue
that inspired the BM campaign—have been verbally airbrushed out of the
picture.

A more extensive supplement (31 pages) ran in *Business Week* on July
14, 1980. The hero of this story is none other than Ibérico Saint Jean ("First
we will kill all the subversives, then . . . their collaborators, then . . . their
sympathizers, then . . . those who remain indifferent; and, finally, we will
kill the timid"). Needless to say, his most famous statement—made four

years earlier—goes unquoted. Rather this is how he is introduced: "Few governments in history have been as encouraging to private investment as that headed by Governor Ibérico Saint Jean and his Minister of Economy, Dr. Raúl Salaberren." These are men like us: As the governor says, "We send our teachers to you so they can learn modern methods of instructing our pupils; it is evidence of our confidence in, and friendly feeling for, the United States." Saint Jean and Salaberren are pictured chatting comfortably with one Stanley Ross, identified as a "journalist and the writer of this special advertising section." It is the deeply tanned Saint Jean who anchors the photo: He sits across from his smiling companions, but leans toward them, his feet planted wide, his elbows on his knees, one fist closed over the other. "We have magnificent human resources," says this agent of the disappearances, later described as "an army officer with a reputation for independence, an attorney and a man of notable culture."[77]

MEANWHILE A SMALL GROUP of prisoners was being made to produce a newspaper for the Navy Mechanics School, commonly known as the ESMA. By 1979, the ESMA brass had decided that their New Argentina would need superior brainpower, and so designated certain captives as worthy for a "recuperation process." Their day was divided: The morning and afternoon were spent cuffed, shackled, and hooded, or at the very least "walled up" (blindfolded); at night they did their assignments in the glassed-in offices known as "the fish tank," an allusion to Mao ("The guerrilla must not be allowed to circulate like fish in water"). Susana and Osvaldo Barros spent their last days of captivity in the ESMA's fish tank and stressed that it was no guarantee of survival. Some of their fellow "reporters" were killed.

"Even the guards, the torturers, called us 'the journalists,'" said Susana, "and, I might add, with a measure of respect. The whole situation was insane, but it worked with a kind of logic."[78] The paper had everything but ads and editorials. Prisoners were assigned specialties: Susana, a biochemist, covered "international"; Osvaldo, a teacher, handled Latin America; a lawyer in the group was in charge of domestic news; an architect wrote on economics; a physicist covered science, technology, and education; and culture was handled by a girl named Mónica who loved to read the classics. There was also a section on human rights, written by a man who had "broken" and become a collaborator. "That was hair-raising," said Osvaldo, "he had completely internalized their language."

The morning papers in Buenos Aires are out by 2 or 3 a.m. "We got them all," said Susana, "*Clarín, La Nación, Diario Popular, Crónica Económica, La Prensa.* And there was a girl who translated political articles from the *Buenos Aires Herald*. Between two and about five, we read and synthesized everything we needed for our section, our 'beat,' I think you say. Between six and seven, the syntheses were photocopied and sent out. And don't think they didn't read every piece with close attention to style. If they saw something they didn't like, they'd let you know that you'd better take care.

"We didn't realize that our work was distributed outside the camp. We thought it was a way of evaluating our level of lucidity, our cultural 'value' for the 'new Argentina.' No one on the outside knew this paper was done by prisoners; they thought it was written by the staff of the Navy Mechanics School. It was sent to the news directors of radio and TV stations, magazines and dailies. If they used it, I can't say, but every morning it was on the desk of the Director of Channel 13. That," she said, "I learned later."

The paper—written by highly educated individuals—enhanced the school's image. It was incisive, sophisticated, and made the navy seem a little less reactionary. The "journalists" chose their stories independently, so to that extent they influenced the focus, and although they were subject to critique, they were never censored. At the same time the work was torment, a way of saying, "You may know 'everything,' but we control it all."

The human "conducting wire" between the junta's public and clandestine worlds was fifty-two-year-old Thelma Jara de Cabezas, who, while a prisoner in the ESMA, was forced to "give interviews" to the aforementioned *Para Ti*.[79] The piece appeared on August 10, 1979, shortly before the arrival of the OAS Commission on Human Rights. The headline stretched across two pages: "The Mother of a Dead Subversive Speaks Out." The facts behind the story are these: Thelma's seventeen-year-old son, Gustavo, had been kidnapped on May 10, 1976, while on his way to school. After addressing herself to the United Nations and the League for the Rights of Man, Thelma helped found and became secretary of the Commission of Families of Those Disappeared and Imprisoned for Political Reasons. She traveled to Mexico to meet with the World Council of Churches and then to Rome to solicit an audience with the Pope. She returned to Argentina because her husband was gravely ill with lung cancer. As she left the hospital on the evening of April 30, 1979, she was kidnapped and taken to the Navy Mechanics School where she was beaten and electrically tortured. As soon as they realized she was missing, Thelma's family and friends started pressuring the government to produce her alive. Thelma was forced to write misleading letters to her relatives, to Videla, to Pope Paul VI, and to the highest-ranking Argentine cardinals. If Thelma refused, not only she but her loved ones would be killed. Lest she have any doubts, her niece and her niece's husband were brought before her; both had been tortured, and their lives depended on her "cooperation." Her letters, all posted from Uruguay, insisted that she was living abroad, and that the Montoneros were threatening to kill her.

Over the course of several months, Thelma is taken to Montevideo several times by the navy, where she was photographed and interviewed by two reporters from Sun Myung Moon's *News World*, which is published in the United States. (Moon's sect was an ardent supporter of Latin American dictatorships.) Thelma was provided with travel documents and tickets on Aerolíneas Argentinas and lodged at the Victoria Plaza hotel. She was accompanied by several officers from the ESMA and was met by an intelligence man from Uruguay. In preparation for her interview with *Para Tí*, Thelma was brought to a hairdresser in the Belgrano section of the capital and then to buy clothes in Once—traditionally the Jewish part of town and, like Manhattan's Orchard Street, famous for its wholesale apparel. She was forced to try on different outfits until the enforcers approved of one. Her interview with the women's magazine took place in a café that had been cleared out by the navy. There was no one besides the reporter, the photographer, and a group of enforcers from the ESMA. As Thelma testified at the trial of the ex-commanders, "The journalist's questions were very aggressive, and all centered on 'why did I go to the human rights organizations?'" The story published in the magazine is a fiction invented by the navy.

For *Para Tí*, Thelma was dressed in a crisp white blouse and a Burberry plaid scarf. Her haircut is tidily stylish; her eyes are very sad. Her plight, she says for the magazine, is "all my own fault," for having trusted "in the sinister ways of subversive organizations posing as champions of human rights." For the "benefit of Argentine mothers," she confesses that after her son disappeared—"I had no idea he was connected to Montoneros"—she sought help in Europe. Clerics in Madrid took her to Italy, where she was personally introduced to the leaders of the Montoneros. She was then taken to the Catholic Bishops conference in Puebla, Mexico, where she was instructed to "pose as a Mother" (a slur on the Madres de la Plaza de Mayo). She was, she says, "a perfect instrument for the Montoneros." When she returned to Argentina, she learned that her son had been killed in a "shoot-out." Thelma is made to speak, not of grief, but of her "guilty conscience," "blindness," and "stupidity." She is "indignant" that Amnesty International has listed her as missing. She is made to say that she left Argentina because of threats by the Montoneros and is speaking out because "maybe they are doing the same to other mothers." She has learned her lesson, late but well: "I place all my faith in God." And what does she pray for? "That there will be no more mothers driven to despair and no more children who go wrong."

As if this were not enough, on the second page of this piece there is a boxed interview with visiting Nobel Peace Laureate Mairead Corrigan. The language of this smiling Irish pacifist is made to sound just like that of the Argentine regime: "I have been talking with many [Argentine] mothers, embittered and desperate that their families have been mutilated and their children killed by those who sow hatred and destruction." Her words on Ireland are transposed to South America: It is a conflict "between two cultures," she says, "but sooner or later we will win. It's just a shame that so many lives have been lost." In fact the Nobel Laureate was concerned about the human rights abuses of the junta. But that was hidden from the readers of *Para Ti*.

"WHAT WORDS CAN YOU no longer tolerate? What words do you no longer say?" In this way, I gathered entries for "A Lexicon of Terror," a record of the changes wrought in the Argentine language by the perpetrators of the Dirty War. Perversions of the language contribute to the sinister, indeed surreal, quality of life in Buenos Aires. In concentration camp slang, the metal table on which prisoners were laid out to be tortured was called *la parrilla*. Traditionally, *la parrilla* has referred to the classic horizontal grill—the centerpiece of the beloved social barbecue—and to the ubiquitous restaurants that serve grilled meat. Stand on any street corner in Buenos Aires and it comes at you from all directions: *Parrilla, parrilla, parrilla*—sustenance, pleasure and annihilation, all present in a single quotidian word. No wonder the present government, which pardoned the ex-commanders—has so often advised the public to "turn the page."

Mathilde Mellibovsky sits pondering my question about words. "There are so many," she says, not to me, but to a large photo of her daughter, Graciela, who in September 1976 was disappeared, tortured, and murdered. "Parsley," she says, *perejil*. That's what they called our children. Parsley is so abundant here, so cheap, greengrocers traditionally give it away. *No*, I always tell them, *no*. I wont say it, I won't have it. That's how they thought of our children—cheap little leaves made for throwing away."[80]

The slang that developed among torturers in Argentine concentration camps was an amalgam of borrowings and home-grown inventions. As a name for torturees, *perejil* would seem to have been translated from the French *persil* used against agitators for Algerian independence. Other expressions have their roots in Nazi rhetoric. Corpses—often hundreds of mutilated corpses, with limbs and parts deliberately confused—were buried in graves labeled "NN," denoting "no name" (from the Latin *non nominatus*). NN graves in Argentina go back at least to the 1920s; they were used for paupers and victims of the police. But today, in the minds of many, NN refers to *noche y niebla*, Spanish for *Nacht und Nebel*, or night and fog. Torture was often performed beneath portraits of Hitler whose recorded speeches were blasted through the halls. More than one concentration camp doctor was known as "Mengele."

In Argentina the infernal mist of *Nacht und Nebel* was ushered in by the unprecedented, obscurant usage of a single word: *desaparecido*. It was coined by the Argentine military as a way of denying the kidnap, torture, and murder of thousands of citizens. Then-commander of the army Roberto Viola put it this way: A *desaparecido* was someone who was "absent forever," whose "destiny" it was to "vanish."[81] Officially, a *desaparecido* was neither living nor dead, neither here nor there. The explanation was at once totally vague and resoundingly final. Night and fog drawn like a curtain in the collective mind.

Let us now draw that straight line from public pronouncements to clandestine practice. In the secret camps, torturers talked compulsively to their victims, ceremoniously repeating codified phrases: "You don't exist. . . . You're no one. . . . We are God." How can one torture a person who doesn't exist? Be God in a realm of no ones? How can a living being not exist? Be no one in a realm of gods? Through language. Through the reality created by and reflected in words. In the clandestine camps there developed an extensive argot in which benign domestic nouns, medical terms, saints, and fairy-tale characters were appropriated as terms pertaining to physical torture. Comforting past associations were translated into pain, degradation, and sometimes death. Although acts of torment are by their nature hellish for anyone, the names given to these practices carried an extra psychological twist for those raised in the River Plate culture.

Language helps to ritualize torture; it lends structure, provides a "reason," an "explanation," an "objective." ("Persuasion" was one of the euphemisms for torture.) Moreover, the special idiom provided categories for practices otherwise out of bounds. It was enabling. Constant talk of omnipotence led mortals to believe they could torment others with a godlike impunity. Euphemisms created psychological distance between the doer and his act. On December 12, 1976, Army Chief Roberto Viola devoted part of a 380-page secret manual to a series of orders on terminology. For clarity, the terms were arranged in columns:

Terms Not to Be Used	*Terms to Use*
❖ Subversive Forces	a. Subversive elements
❖ Guerrillas	b. Armed bands of subversive criminals
❖ Wearing uniform	c. Usurping the use of insignias, emblems, uniforms
❖ Army personnel taken prisoner	d. Kidnapped army personnel
❖ Guerrilla taken prisoner	e. Captured delinquent
❖ Guerrilla base	f. Criminal camp
❖ Guerrilla operations	g. Criminal actions

This abstract language obviously serves to objectify the army's targets. It makes a dramatic contrast to the rest of the manual, whose orders for kidnap (including of children), murder (including of popular leaders no matter the cause), the refusal to accept surrender, and the handling of corpses, are nothing if not explicit.[82] As a sign of the "maturity" touted by General Camps, the Argentines were commanded to drop "counterinsurgency"—a U.S. import—and to employ the home-grown "countersubversion."

Language as it was used in the camps was a form of torture. What follows are entries for a lexicon of terror, based on interviews I conducted or from testimony given at the trial of the ex-commanders or to human rights organizations. This lexicon gives a detailed picture of daily life in the camps and the thinking that went into their creation. It is no accident that official "germ theories" concerning "subversion" yielded a host of tortures bearing medical names. The accounts are harrowing. But testimony fulfills the sacred obligation to bear witness, and however discomfiting it may be for us, our pain, though great, is minor compared with that of the victims. We lack the right to turn away. After years of taking testimony, I am convinced that we will not begin to grasp what happened in Argentina unless we gain a sense of how these words were *lived*. We begin with *desaparecido* and *trasladar*, words whose deformations came to define an age, and whose pre-Dirty War meanings have fallen away almost entirely. The rest of the words are listed alphabetically.

A Lexicon of Terror

Desaparecido/a (n. Something that or someone who disappeared). The concept of individuals made to vanish originated with the Nazis, as part of the doctrine of Night and Fog. "The prisoners will *disappear* without a trace. It will be impossible to glean any information as to where they are or what will be their fate." (Marshall Keitel, explaining Hitler's decree to his subordinates.) In Argentina the model sequence was disappearance, torture, death. "The first thing they told me was to forget who I was, that as of that moment I would be known only by a number, and that for me the outside world stopped there." (Javier Alvarez, CONADEP file no. 7332)[83] Most *desaparecidos* spent day and night hooded, handcuffed, shackled, and blindfolded in a cell so cramped it was called a "tube." Some were given jobs. When their shifts were over, they were returned to their tubes where again they were hooded, cuffed, shackled, and blindfolded. Or they were sent to be tortured. Or they were murdered.

Ana María Careaga was sixteen at the time of her disappearance. She was recently married and three months' pregnant. "As soon as we arrived at the camp, they stripped, and began torturing me. The worst torture was with the electric prod—it went on for many hours, with the prod in my vagina, anus, belly, eyes, nose, ears, all over my body. They also put a plastic bag over my head and wouldn't take it off until I was suffocating. When I was on the verge of cardiac arrest, they called in a doctor who gave me pills. Then I had convulsions, lost consciousness. So he gave me something else and that brought me round. I wanted to die, but they wouldn't let me. They 'saved' me only so they could go on torturing me.

"They were always saying, 'We have all the time in the world.' 'You don't exist. You're no one. If someone came looking for you (and no one has) do you think they'd ever find you *here?*' 'No one remembers you anymore.' The impunity they had. One would go eat, another would take his place, then he would take a break, and another would replace him."

"The worst," she told me, "—so often I find myself saying 'the worst'; it was all 'the worst'—was after they moved me to the infirmary. The camp I was in was in the basement of the Sub-Prefecture of the Federal Police in the neighborhood of La Boca, Buenos Aires. A big police station in a busy neighborhood. There were small air holes between the ceiling and the walls, from which I could hear people walking by, cars and buses passing, life going on as usual—with us disappeared in a torture center. In the afternoon, when the sun was at a certain angle, I could see on the floor the shadows of the people passing by, getting in and out of their cars. Yes, that I think was the worst. To be so close to them, for them to be so dose to us, and yet so far away."

Trasladar (v. to transfer, to move). To take prisoners away to be killed. *Traslado/a* (n. transfer). *Trasladado/a* (n. one who had been transferred, one who was a transfer, one who had "got his ticket"). "You quickly learned that you were in the pit for only a limited period of time, difficult to predict. Then, transfer.

"The most terrible thing was that this period was indeterminate. It was impossible to conquer the fatalism and to understand that the visible end of the road was a dark point, a leap into the void, transfer. . . .

"There were various indications that a transfer would be happening soon. A week before, there would be a lot more intelligence officers coming and going, filling out forms. At first we didn't know what these forms were about.

"Another sign had to do with women. They'd check out all of them to see if they were pregnant; pregnant women were [usually] not transferred.

"The transfers didn't happen on schedule, but they happened in the same way. Movement began around two or three in the afternoon. And there was a special crew (all of whom were called Peter—*Pedro*—after the saint who has the keys to heaven).

"The 'lock' called out the code names of those compañeros who had been selected. They had to [exit their cells] and form a single-file line in the passage-way, still shackled and 'walled up' [*tabicados*, see below]. They had to leave behind any clothes: 'Where you're going everyone gets the same uniform,' or 'You're going North, you don't need all those clothes.' [The northern zones of South America are warmer.] Many compañeros were transferred in the dead of winter in only their underwear.

"A doctor . . . always accompanied the transfer. . . . All of the transfers were injected with Pen-Naval, a strong sedative. Then they were loaded onto trucks, from there into an airplane from which they were thrown alive, though unconscious, into the sea." (From testimony given to Amnesty International by Oscar Alfredo González and Horacio Guillermo Cid de la Paz)[84]

Lisandro Cubas, a survivor of the Navy Mechanics School, testified that, "In general, where the fate of transfers was concerned, the officers forbade it being mentioned. . . . [The crew] said previously [before the use of airplanes] the method had been to shoot people and burn the corpses in the Navy Mechanics School ovens or bury them in common graves in cemeteries in the province of Buenos Aires." (CONADEP file no. 6974)[85]

For survivors of the clandestine camps, *trasladar* carries more terror, more grief, than any other single word. "Tension reached untold heights for most of the prisoners. It produced a strange mixture of fear and relief, given that one both dreaded and longed for the transfer that on the one hand spelt certain death, and on the other meant the end of torture and agony. One [also] felt. . . fear of death, though not the fear of any death—which most of them could have faced with dignity—but of that particular death which is dying without disappearing, or disappearing without dying. A death in which the person dying had no part whatsoever . . . as though dying being already dead, or like never dying at all." (CONADEP file no. 2819)[86] At the trial of the ex-commanders a survivor on the stand told the judge, "Sir, it is very hard for me to use the word 'transfer,' because it was employed when they took someone we would never see again. So I will use the word only to refer to those persons, and in all other cases, must use the word 'move.'"

Asado (n. barbecue). Traditionally closely associated with *parrilla*. From the testimony of Jorge Carlos Torres, a seaman stationed at the Navy Mechanics School: "I knew that the bodies of the dead prisoners were taken away from the school in green trucks to the sports field at the far end, the other side of the Avenida Lugones, on the river bank. Two people were in charge of each truck and I once heard them say to the NCO on guard duty that they had come 'to have a barbecue,' which was a way of describing the job. . . . At night the bonfires of burning bodies could be seen. During the day this area was filled in with earth to extend the sports ground; I imagine this was how the remains of the bonfires were covered over. This is the field where I found a blue plastic bag. When I opened it I saw there was a fetus and some liquid inside."[87]

Avenida de la Felicidad (n. Avenue of Happiness). The corridor that led from the tubes to the operating theater.

Bodega (n. hold of ship; store). Navy's store room for *botín de guerra*.

Boleta (n. . . . ticket). "You've got your ticket," prisoners were told when they were about to be transferred.

Botín de Guerra (n. war booty). Belongings, including cars, houses, and land, taken from *desaparecidos* and detainees.

La Cacha (n. . . .) nickname for La Cachavacha, a television witch who made people disappear. The name of a camp in Buenos Aires Province.

Camión (n. truck). Syn. for *Traslado*. In the camp known as La Perla, prisoners slated for execution were taken away in trucks, driven out into the country, and then shot. In the words of La Perla survivor Patricia Astelarra, "In the concentration camp . . . time and space were used to maintain us—'the walking dead'—while we awaited the arrival of the truck. To this day, the revving of a truck motor gives me the shakes."

Capucha (n. hood). Section of camp where shackled, handcuffed *desaparecidos* were made always to wear hoods that covered their heads, faces, and necks. "The psychological torture of the *capucha* was as bad or worse than the physical. . . . With the 'hood' on, I became fully aware of my complete lack of contact with the outside world. There was nothing to protect you, you were completely alone. . . . The mere inability to see gradually undermines your morale, diminishing your resistance. . . . The 'hood' became unbearable, so much so that one Wednesday, transfer day, I shouted for them to have me transferred: 'Me . . . me . . . 571.' The 'hood' had achieved its aim, I was no longer Lisandro Raúl Cubas, I was a number." (CONADEP file no. 6974)[88] "It was raining, and I was in a hurry to get the kids off to school. '*Capirotes! Capirotes!*' I urged them, in a sudden panic. They had no idea what I was talking about. But I couldn't bring myself to say, '*Pónganse las capuchas,*' or 'Put up your hoods.' *Capirote* is totally archaic, rarefied. It means 'hood' but no child would know that. For me, *capucha* is a place, and that place meant torture and ultimately death for people I loved very, very much. And someday, I'm going to have to explain that to my kids." (Laura S., human rights lawyer and surviving sister of *desaparecidos.*)

Chupadero (n. . . . center.) Place where people were sucked up, i.e., a clandestine torture center. See *Chupar*. Syn. *gullet; drain.*

Chupado (past part. of *chupar);* n. *chupado/a,* someone who has been sucked up, i.e., disappeared). "'You're lucky that we were the ones to suck you up *(que te chupamos nosotros)*. You'll get bashed around, but you'll live. We're the only branch of the military that doesn't kill its *chupados* anymore. [A lie.] The country can no longer afford the luxury of losing strong arms.' This was systematically repeated by all the interrogators." (Oscar Alfredo González and Horacio Guillermo Cid de la Paz)[89]

Chupar (v. to suck; to suck on; to suck up; to swallow). To kidnap, disappear, assassinate someone.

Cinturón Ecológico (n. ecology belt). "Recycled" leftovers from officers' table occasionally served to prisoners as a treat. Ironic reference to the lands outside of Buenos Aires planned as a greensward; the project was so badly executed that after 150 years of no flooding, every time it rains the south side of Buenos Aires is inundated.

Comida de Pescado (n. fish food). Prisoners thrown from planes into the sea either drugged or dead, with their stomachs slit open. "I. . . . discovered a book in the documentation section [of the ESMA] which—significantly—explained the process by which a body decomposes in the sea." (Carlos Muñoz CONADEP file no. 704)[90]

Crucero (n. cruise). A cruise for *mercadería*.

Cuchas (n. kennels). Syn. in El Vesubio for the *tubos*.

Enfermería (n. infirmary). In El Vesubio, a central hall with three or four small torture chambers, all decorated with swastikas. In Campo de Mayo, the infirmary was near the operating theater. Although medical attention was given to the bodies of *desaparecidos*, they were psychically tortured: "There one would have to witness the torture and even death of others, as they tried to force prisoners to talk. The length of torture depended on how far the interrogator wished to go." (Juan Carlos Scarpati, CONADEP file no. 2819)[91]

Escuela de los mudos (n. school for the dumb). Enforcers' nickname for their concentration camp in the northeastern province of Misiones. Officially called La Casita ("The Little House").

La Favela (n. Portuguese for "shantytown"). Camp in the upper story of the Provincial Police headquarters in Santa Fe. At the time, Brazil had more shantytowns than Argentina. Moreover, many of the inhabitants of the *favelas* were black or of mixed race, which further incited prejudice among Argentines.

Grupo de Tareas (n. task force). Group that carried out kidnappings, torture, and other terror operations. Syn. *la patota* (the gang).

Huevera (n. egg carton). Torture chamber in the ESMA whose walls were lined with egg cartons to blunt the sounds.

Inmobilaría (n. real estate agency). Agency in the ESMA that falsified property deeds and defrauded prisoners of land, houses, and apartments whose ownership was then transferred to navy personnel.

Interrogación (n. interrogation). Torture.

Irse Arriba (v. to go up). To "fly" (see *El Vuelo*), be transferred. Syn. *Irse al norte* (to go north).

Los Jorge (n. pl. the Georges). Named for Saint George, who slew the dragon, they helped with transfers.

Leonera (n. lion's cage). "So called because it was the place where new arrivals were 'softened up.' It was like a collective cell where five to ten compañeros would be lying on the floor in very bad shape after torture. The first hour they used the electric prod without asking us anything. To quote them: 'This is to soften you up so we understand each other.'" (Oscar Alfredo González and Horacio Guillermo Cid de la Paz)[92]

Marcadores (n. markers). Prisoners who had "broken" under torture and who then agreed to cruise (see *crucero)* with their enforcers, and mark (identify) individuals (acquaintances, friends, intimates) for kidnap.

Los Marconi (n. pl. the Marconis). Camp personnel in charge of communications, named for the inventor of the telegraph.

Menéndez Benz n. Pun on Mercedes Benz, the manufacturer of the trucks used for transfer in La Perla. The director of the camp was named Menéndez, hence the gallows humor of the prisoners.

Mercadería (n. merchandise). Enforcers' slang for kidnap victim. Syn. *Paquete*.

Mojarrita (n. little wet thing; tiny river fish that children like to catch). Syn. for *submarino*.

Números (n. pl. numbers). La Perla slang for lower-ranking personnel who assisted in operations and other types of work. They generally came from other provinces, notably La Rioja and Catamarca. Patricia Astelarra remembered certain *números* staying on to watch torture sessions "out of morbid pleasure."

El Olimpo (n. Olympus). Camp in Buenos Aires named by Lieut. Col. Guillermo Minicucci. In the main "operating theater" there was a sign that said: "Welcome to the Olympus of the Gods. Signed: The Centurions."

Operación (n. operation). Kidnapping.

Pacto de Sangre (n. blood pact). Pact among officers, all of whom had participated in acts of kidnap, torture, and/or murder.

Pañol (n. store room). Camp store room for *botín de guerra*.

Paquete (n. package). Enforcers' slang for kidnap victim. Syn. *Mercadería*.

Parrilla (n. traditional Argentine grill for cooking meat). The metal table on which *chupados* were laid out to be tortured. "Your body jumps around a lot on the *parrilla*, at least as much as the straps permit. It gets twisted around, shakes, tries to escape contact with the . . . electric prod, which was handled like a knife by a 'specialist.' [He was] guided by a doctor who would say when more would kill you." (Antonio Horacio Miño Retamozo, CONADEP file no. 3721)[93]

Pecera (n. fish tank). Glassed-in offices in the ESMA where prisoners in recuperation did their jobs. Graciela Daleo was a typist: "One of the jobs I typed—I don't know who wrote it—was a long report about how to make investments in the Bahamas, Luxembourg, Panama, Switzerland, and Lichtenstein. There was also a section—quite technical—on the tax situation in these places. Another job was a survey developed in the camp and then sent to our embassies all over the world on Argentina's image abroad. What I typed were the replies to the questions, country by country. I was told that this survey, which was done in the camp, was sent to our embassies with a false title page, saying it had been done for the Foreign Ministry by *Burson Masteler* [sic] [emphasis added]."[94]

Los Pedro (n. pl. the Peters). Named for Saint Peter, who had the keys to heaven, they unlocked the prisoners' *tubos*.

La Perla (n. the pearl). Large camp in Córdoba. "La Perla, did it exist? Yes. It was a meeting place for prisoners, not a secret prison . . . the subversives were put there in the protection of each other's company. . . ." As told to *Gente* magazine (March 15, 1984), by the notoriously brutal camp director Luciano Benjamín Menéndez.

Picana (n. electric (cattle) prod). Main instrument for torture. Invented in Argentina in 1930 and routinely used in police stations ever since. Syn. *la máquina* (the machine); Carolina; Susana; Margarita (Spanish for "Daisy"; the third model featured a daisy wheel). "Be good," prisoners were told, "or you'll go dancing with Susana."

Pozo (n. pit). Camp, e.g., *Pozo* de Banfield, *Pozo* de Quilmes.

Quirófano (n. operating theater). Torture chamber. "The only furniture in the operating theater was a metal table on which the torturers strapped us down. This was a very sinister place, the walls were so covered with blood and stains that you could barely make out that it had once been painted yellow. The smell of burned flesh, blood, sweat and excrement, especially since there was no ventilation, made the air heavy, suffocating. The torturers took turns and kept a written copy of their 'work.' The doors were gray and just inside, on one side, were the forms the torturers filled out. . . . Children, women, pregnant women, the wounded, the sick—as far as the Argentine military was concerned, everyone was suspect. They only believed in 'the truth of the operating theater.'" (González and Cid de la Paz.)[95] In the camp called Vesuvius, there was a rhyming sign in the operating theater that said, "If You Know the Answer, Sing; If Not, Just Take the Sting." (*Si lo sabe, cante, si no, aguante*)

Rectóscopo (n. rectoscope). Anal torture device invented by Julio Simón, the extremely sadistic anti-Semite known as Julián the Turk (see Chapter 6).

Recuperación (n. recuperation). White collar/clerical/custodial job program inside the Navy Mechanics School, designed to "recycle" selected *desaparecidos* for use in the New Argentina. "The "recuperation" process came about as a result of a feud between [Admiral] Massera and [Captain] Acosta, known as Tiger. Under Massera, the ESMA was one of the bloodiest, most horrendous torture centers. It was purely an extermination camp. But as they brought in more and more *desaparecidos*, it became overcrowded, chaotic. There was more and more work. So they started having prisoners do some jobs. Now Acosta, even though he was a sadistic torturer, wanted to be known as an intellectual, as a refined kind of guy. So he devised the so-called recuperation process, and won the feud with Massera. Mainly we were pawns in the fights between officers. We still had no value in and of ourselves, in their eyes." (From my October 6, 1990, interview with Mario Villani, who spent four years in five concentration camps). "Acosta believed that if he gained the good will of those [of us] being 'recuperated,' that would help him win a political victory [after the dictatorship]. In our conversations with him, we were constantly having to simulate a change in our personal scale of values. . . . This duality demanded a great deal of psychic and nervous energy, and added to the constant tension of our situation." (Martín Tomás Gras)[96]

Sheraton (n. . . . Aires.) Camp located in a police station in La Matanza district of Buenos Aires. Also called the Funnel. A distinctive feature of the Sheraton was that some prisoners were allowed to write or phone their families. "As time passes and things get easier, it will be more difficult for them to kill us," wrote Ana María Caruso de Carri in a letter home. She was wrong; neither she nor any of the other prisoners in her group were heard from after December 1977.[97]

Staff (English) n. Group of prisoners who worked for the enforcers. Some were faking collaboration and survived to give crucial testimony; others really were collaborating. The authentic collaborators were called *quebrados* (broken ones).

Submarino (n. submarine; traditional Argentine children's treat consisting of a chocolate bar slowly melting in a cup of warm milk). Form of torture in which the prisoner's head was held under water befouled with urine and feces. When the victim was on the verge of suffocation, his head would be raised and then dunked again. After hours of being tortured by five men, Teresa Celia Meschiati "tried to kill [herself] by drinking the foul water in the tub . . . but [she] did not succeed."[98] *Submarino seco* (dry submarine). Form of torture in which the prisoner's head was covered with a plastic bag until he was about to expire. He would be unwrapped and allowed to get his breath, so torture could continue. This torment was used by the French in Indochina in the 1950s and in Algeria in the 1960s, and by the U.S. in Vietnam. In Argentina, kids are served *submarinos* most every day after school; it is still on the menu of any café. See *Mojarrita*.

Tabique (n. partition wall). Blindfold. *Tabicado/a* (adj. walled up). Blindfolded. Prisoners were blindfolded during their kidnapping and kept so during their captivity, causing eye infections, temporary and long-term blindness, and in some cases, infestations of maggots.

Terapia Intensiva (n. intensive therapy). Torture. On the door to the torture chamber in the camp called La Perla, there was a sign: "Intensive Therapy Room — Patients/Invalids Not Allowed." "The navy insisted that modern warfare had demonstrated that torture was the only instrument that could get the desired results, and they cited Algeria and Guatemala as examples." (Martín Tomás Gras)[99]

Trabajo (n. work). Torture. In some camps, "work cards" were filled out after every session. Arranged horizontally were the following headings: Interrogator, Group, Case (prisoner's number), Hour Began, Hour Finished, State (i.e., "Normal" or "Dead"). (Oscar Alfredo González and Horacio Gillermo Cid de la Paz)[100]

Tratamiento (n. treatment). Torture.

Tubo (n. tube). Tiny, narrow, prisoners' cell. Too low to stand, too low for some to sit up straight, too short for some prisoners to stretch out.

Los Verde (n. the green ones). Young NCOs assigned to guard the prisoners; usually 16–20 years old.

El Vesubio (n. Vesuvius). Camp in Buenos Aires, named for the famous volcano.

Vuelo (n. flight). Death flight. Death-flight duty was rotated to virtually all naval officers, who were ordered to load *desaparecidos* onto planes, undress them, and throw them into the sea. Some, like Adolfo Scilingo, were tapped twice. "I had no idea who they were. But there was a sixteen-year-old boy, a man in his sixties, and two young women who were pregnant" (see Chapter 6).

Zona Libre (n. free zone). Area cleared and secured by police and military in preparation for an *operación*. Syn. *luz verde* (green light); *zona liberada* (liberated area).

NICKNAMES AND NOMS DE GUERRE
OF CONCENTRATION CAMP PERSONNEL

Animals: Ant, Cat, Cobra, Crazy Bird, Crazy Horse, Giraffe, Hawk, Hyena, Jackal, Pacqui (short for Pachyderm; his speciality was breaking down doors), Penguin, Pirana, Puma, Rat, Rattlesnake, Shark, Tiger, Turtle.

Religious Figures: The Priest (numerous), John XXXIII, Monsignor. "Come, my child, give me your confession," said one of the Priests prior to beginning torture.

Medical Figures: The Doctor (several), Mengele (several).

Other Figures: Roland, Abdala, Quasimodo, Ataturk (or the Turk, of which there were several), Kung Fu, Serpico, Son of Sam (the son of General Suárez Mason, who was extradited from California to stand trial in Argentina).

Forces of Nature: Thunderclap, 220 (as in 220 volts); the Female Voice (a.k.a. Death With a Female Voice): "At night the *female voice* would arrive, a well-known officer of the *Gendarmería* who spoke in falsetto. The first thing he would do was to stroke one's testicles in anticipation of the pleasure of his task." (Miño Retamozo)[101]

Kin: The Uncle, The Aunt's Son, Baby (who left the "operating theater" every day at noon to go home and make lunch for his mother).

∗ ∗ ∗

As THE WISE NOVELIST Julio Cortázar said, "Under authoritarian regimes language is the first system that suffers, that gets degraded." I have come to believe that, even after the regime has ended, language may be the last system to recover. "Whoever was tortured, stayed tortured," wrote Holocaust survivor and eventual suicide Jean Améry. "Torture is ineradicably burned into him. . . . He loses something we will call 'trust in the world'. . . the certainty that by reason of written or unwritten social contracts, the other person will spare me . . . that he will respect my physical, and with it also my metaphysical, being. The boundaries of my body are the boundaries of my self."[102]

The body's knowledge cannot be contradicted, the body's knowledge is forever. As Foucault tells us, it is the knowledge of the body—of the punished body—that gives rise to the soul.[103] *Vos no existís, Vos no sos nadie* ("You don't exist," "You're nobody")—these expressions of ultimate scorn, these signs of ultimate vulnerability were indeed burned into the victims, and survive as marks on the body politic. All of society's institutions—political, military, and legal, religious, social, and domestic— were mobilized or appropriated for the purposes of clandestine torture and public complicity. To those who were subjected to such things as *el submarino* and *la parrilla*, it must have seemed that one's whole life had been "leading to" this; that torture was *always* already inscribed, and in the most "normal" communal pleasures.

It is difficult to know whether the continued usage of words like *parrilla* is a deliberate effort to salvage earlier untainted meanings, whether it is a sign of denial, or whether it is a sign that, come what may, life goes on. The 1985 trial of the ex-commanders, which held the country rapt for five months—ushered in a flood of terminology, and had some extraordinary effects on common usage. Adolescents started saying, "You don't exist!" meaning one of two things: "You're the greatest!" or "You're nothing, you're zero." Before the trial, the expression was not in general use. A locution one came to hear often was *darse máquina*, meaning "to give someone (or oneself) 'the machine,'" a reference to the *picana*, or electric prod. Today if someone says. *Basta con la máquina*, ("Stop already with the machine"), it means "Don't bother me," or "You're getting on my nerves." *Me cortás el rostro*, ("You're cutting up my face"), means exactly the same thing. Torture talk expresses mere irritation. In the same vein *Me mandó a los canas* ("he sent me to the cops"): "He really annoyed me." And *Pero me das una gomiada*, a reference to the rubber bludgeons used in the camps, was coined to mean, "Lighten up, get off my case." A particularly striking, newly invented tease or taunt was *Te doy una chicana*, a rhyme with and reference to *picana*, in a phrase that means, "I'm bothering you on purpose." At the 1988 Festival de Cine Español critic Juan Carlos Mareco drew attention with the following tribute to Spanish filmmakers: *Debemos rendirle* la obediencia debida *al talento de los artistas de ese país.* ("We must render Due Obedience to the talent of these Spanish filmmakers.") Mareco's statement was indeed very strange—"due obedience" is a strictly military term, and entered general usage only in 1984 when Alfonsín's controversial law was passed. It seems to me that such changes, such ravages of the language are manifestations that what happened in the camps did not just happen to those imprisoned there. In some sense it happened to everyone. Or at least, many people—on the evidence of the way they speak—have internalized that part of Argentine history.

The repression lives on in such aberrations of the language, in the scars it left on the language. When a people's very words have been wounded, the society cannot fully recover until the language has been healed. Words mark the paths of our experience, separate what we can name from ineffable terror and chaos. At once public and intimate, language is a boundary between our vulnerable inner selves and the outside world. When, like skin, the language is bruised, punctured, or mutilated, that boundary breaks down. We have then no defense, no way to protect ourselves. What we knew, we no longer know; names born of the truth of shared experience ring false. *On a mal dans sa peau*—we are uneasy in our own skin.

We must pay attention to this dis-ease, we must document its signs. We must make an artifact of this Lexicon of Terror, so that it will no longer be a living language.

2

Night and Fog

"TO BE OR NOT TO BE," RECITED THE ENFORCER KNOWN AS THE PRIEST, addressing the skull he held in one hand. "You shouldn't have got mixed up in politics!"

"Why didn't you tell me?" the skull "replied" in anguish.

"Ah," said the torturer, "that's how it is, 'To be or not to be.'"

"I," "groaned" the skull, "am Carlos Mujica, Third World Cleric, that's why I'm in hell. I'm a perverted sinner and suffer the eternal fires that I deserve."

The Priest—a civilian agent by the name of Magaldi—was enacting this scene in the cell block of La Perla. As everyone there knew, Carlos Mujica had been gunned down in front of his church in 1974; he was the first religious victim of the gathering repression, and his murder foretold the coming genocide. Born to wealth and highly educated, Mujica was despised by the authorities as much for being a traitor to his class as for his devotion to the poor.[1]

But the plot thickens. Before the literally captive audience of *desaparecidos* in handcuffs and leg irons, the Priest acted the Prince of Darkness wearing the bloodstained jacket of Carlos Cazzorla, who had been murdered as he tried to escape being kidnapped. He even complained to the skull that he had had to have the sleeves cut off because they were *just too bloody*. While the Priest did his show, Cazzorla's wife, Graciela Geuna, was in another part of the camp being tortured.[2]

It is unlikely that the Priest knew the whole of Hamlet's soliloquy. But many in his audience surely did—the enforcers called this camp the

University. As they sat unable to move, their wrists and ankles rubbed raw by the chains that held them, how could they not wish "To die, to sleep—/ . . . [to] end/The heart-ache and the thousand natural shocks/That flesh is heir to." In his demented way, the Priest was "hold[ing] a mirror up to nature." With their blindfolds raised, the prisoners finally *saw* each other—bruised and wounded, swollen, dirty, and discolored.

"Life in La Perla was nothing if not surreal," I was told by Patricia Astelarra, one of the few survivors of that camp. From its opening in March 1976 until the end of 1978, some 2000 individuals were disappeared there. Of these, 17 were liberated after one or two years; 20 were freed after two or three days; and about 100, having been "legalized" (officially charged and registered) were sent to the nearby prison of La Ribera. So out of these approximately .km to tke nearby prison of La Ribera. bo out of these approximately 2000 individuals, only about 137 survived. "Every layer of our reality was death," recalled Astelarra, "there was virtually no way to improve your chances of surviving. Your conduct had no effect on what happened to you. And their conduct was irrational. Why am I alive? My parents paid a ransom, and we have relatives in the army. But others had the same situation and were still massacred. Nothing you were or did mattered. They'd use it all—or not—and then annihilate you, if that's what they felt like."[3] In the book she later wrote with her ex-husband, Astelarra tells of a prisoner who went out of his way to be useful even in the "operating theater." When one day his name was called for transfer, he protested the error, and insisted that his case be checked. A little while later, the gendarme returned to inform him that there was no mistake, that everything was in order. After that group of transfers was gone, the director of the camp, Major Ernesto Barreiro, declared to the prisoners left in the cell block, "This is no place for mercenaries."[4] As everyone there knew, robbery was a hallmark of the hypocritical regime.

Barreiro himself was not merely a kidnapper, torturer, and assassin; he was also skilled in extortion. And like the Priest, he too went in for acts of theater. One of his memorable productions, a truly diabolical farce, was conceived for the Red Cross, which had come to investigate reports of human rights abuse. He had three prisoners—all kidnapped in 1976, brutally tortured, and then, after two years of capitivity, released under tight surveillance—testify before the delegation. On pain of death to themselves and their families, they all reported that they had been arrested but three days ago and were being very well treated.[5] A similar spectacle was mounted "for the benefit" of a recently captured left-wing journalist with media connections in Europe. After brutal torture and ongoing humiliation, he was told that foreigners were making "a lot of noise" about his case. Not long afterward he was brought to an office to meet with "a North American— Argentine human rights commission." Ingenuously taken in by the panel of "visitors" pretending to speak bad Spanish, he gave them his full testimony. The enforcers later told him that owing to an article that had recently appeared in Le Monde, they had no choice but to let him go. A few days later, they said they were sending him to France, but he was really getting the truck, or being transferred.[6]

Astelarra was also subjected to sinister theatrics. Pregnant at the time of her kidnap, she eventually gave birth in captivity. Malnourished and deprived of medicine, her health had quickly deteriorated. One day she was led blindfolded to an office where two officers told her she would get a surprise, and indeed they were right: a steak garnished with salad and served on her very own china—"So you feel at home."[7]

Traditional values and verities were twisted inside out. Codes of decency, domestic comforts, and high culture were translated into instruments of physical and psychic torment. In La Perla, torture was always referred to (by the enforcers) as "work." "Where's so-and-so?" someone would ask. "He's working. Mustn't be disturbed." "Work" was performed in five "operating theaters" that functioned simultaneously. As Astelarra and Gustavo Contemponi recalled, in the camp's lexicon a proper prisoner was one who was "useful"—that is, corrupt, treacherous, and/or violent with his peers. The path to "usefulness" was often paved with hope—to live, to escape, to testify. Freedom meant not doing anything that violated one's own beliefs and sentiments; in that context, freedom could be a synonym for self-destruction. But the same risk was inscribed in being proper. And in having hope. Benevolence on the part of the enforcers was always a show, a demonstration of their power and control. As Astelarra and Contemponi recount, the enforcers sought to manipulate the lowest human instincts—envy and competition, bullying and scapegoating—through torture, starvation, illness, and the constant threat of death. "The image you had to give was that no one cared about anyone."[8] From any angle, that was a dangerous game. "Normalization" was defined as a return to bourgeois values. "It is no accident," wrote Astelarra and Contemponi, "that the few survivors of La Perla are practically all middle- or upper-middle class, and have university connections. . . . 'Normal' values," as they used to say, "were work, studying hard in order to succeed, staying out of politics, and material well-being." Prisoners from the laboring classes were killed because they could not be "brought back," or "ideologically *normalized*."[9] For there to arise a New Argentina, any trace of class struggle had to be erased. As the torturer known as the Priest often said, "Religion is not supposed to modify the natural order, which by God's will means that those born rich stay rich, and those born poor stay poor."[10]

This theatricality—of which language was an integral part—served several purposes: as a torment for the prisoners, a sadistic pleasure for some enforcers, and as a distancing, enabling device for others in the chain of command. Survivors of La Perla, including Astelarra and Geuna, frequently mention Alberto Vega, a balding forty-eight-year-old major, junior grade, known as "The Uncle." Though obsessed with procedure, he was, as Geuna testified, "absolutely incompetent, [and his] presence in La Perla fomented lack of discipline and disorder."[11] A regular torturer at the camp, Vega, who had studied law, was a proponent of what he called "the modern concentration camp." He told Astelarra that he "dreamed of a having a real operating theater with tiled walls, surgical gowns, and rubber gloves." Incapable of confronting the blood, vomit, and excrement that were the physical evidence of his work, he compulsively cleaned the operating room, used a deodorizer, and ordered his subordinates to repaint the walls. The Uncle even hung art prints and posters, placed flowers and aromatic herbs around the rooms in which he tortured. Although his "modern concentration camp" was coherent with his view of political transformation and social order, he still resorted to denial both within and without the camp. In May 1977 when an elderly popular activist died in his bed and his aged wife—afraid of arousing the authorities—buried him quietly at home, Vega seized on the occasion to hold a press conference: "What's happening is obvious. There are no *desaparecidos*. As we see, their own organizations bury them in their houses." The main regional daily, *La Voz del Interior*, gave prominent coverage to the story, which they ran with pictures of Vega and the widow.[12] By then, Vega had personally directed or taken part in the kidnapping and disappearance of hundreds of individuals. Was the Uncle ashamed? Frustrated in the way of those who feel ahead of their time? With all his apparent contradictions, Vega did his job and, even after the dictatorship ended, stayed on active duty.

The Process needed to destroy all forms of intimacy that it did not control. Family ties, friendship, collegiality all had to be subordinate to the Process. This drive to dehumanize found its ultimate expression in the camps. Walled up in tubes, with their arms and legs in abrasive chains, the prisoners lived in an isolation so total that any social points of reference virtually disappeared. The battle, as I have been told by more than one survivor, was to remember that you were *human*. As one man put it to me, "The physical evidence goes against you, you're so weak, so sick and so tormented, you think, if you *can* think: I *am* my shit; I *am* these stinking wounds; I *am* this festering sore. That is what you have to fight. And it's goddamn difficult; because whenever they feel like it, they replenish the physical evidence that goes against you." The wedge they tried to drive between the victim and human sentience was the horror, the alienation, provoked by his own tortured body.

For Geuna, the blindfold was worse than electrical torture. "Gradually you became a little animal, with an animal's sense of death. They called us the 'walking dead,'" she testified, "and that's what you were. You were alone, suspended between life—though you did not feel *alive*—and death. That is what it means to be disappeared."[13]

The isolation served as well to keep prisoners from sustaining contact with one another. "The irony," said Astelarra, an intense sociologist in her early fifties, "is that we were supposed to distrust our fellow prisoners as much as we feared the enforcers." The kidnap of Astelarra and her husband is a case in point. "They were not looking for us, but for people we knew," Patricia explained. "When the prisoner they had as a marker in the car saw us come out of our house, she said, 'No, that's not them.' But they took us anyway and destroyed everything they didn't steal. The point, though, is this: While it's true she marked the house, she did so knowing that the people they wanted didn't live there. She took a chance that no one would be home, that maybe they would just turn back. When we appeared, they discovered her ruse, for which later she was brutally tortured. Collaborator or not, she got no protection or immunity; her terror, who's to say, might even have been worse. They loved it when someone 'broke,'" Patricia emphasized. "They used it to frighten, taunt, and divide us even more. The husband of the woman in the car had been a prominent labor leader. Under incredibly hideous torture, he 'cracked' and gave them some information. Then they wanted more, they wanted him to go to Buenos Aires and 'mark' some individuals. He refused. They said, 'We'll shoot you.' 'So shoot me,' he answered. The night they were going to take him away, they let him visit with his mother who in her youth had been in the Communist Party. They started in on the old lady, saying, 'Maybe we'll take you away with your son.' And she said, 'Fine, take my son, take me.' And they did. Shot them both. So here's the question," Patricia challenged, "Under torture he cracked, but given a free choice, he gave up his life. Is he a hero? A traitor?

"In every case," she continued, "you are the living symbol of everything society rejects. Dead or alive you can't win. In our Constitution, torture is a crime; but in the minds of many, surviving torture is also a crime, or implies a crime. I didn't give them any information, but they didn't torture me for as long as they tortured some others. The dynamic is finally mysterious. They found subtle ways to break people. Some who held up on the grill were suddenly collaborating three months later. How do you explain that? Please. No one could *determine* to live. They stripped us of that power. We who did survive are the emissaries of the horror. The horror. That too society rejects. So the isolation of the messenger never really ends."

Nor, for many, do the guilt and confusion over having survived. Victoria Benítez, a schoolteacher from the rural northeast, was arrested on the day of the coup.[14] Though she was always a legally registered prisoner (charged with "subversion"), she was subjected to a brutal regime. "They were always trying to get one of us to betray the others," she told me. "They would get you alone, without witnesses, with total impunity." Victoria has pulmonary problems, and believes that this got her released. But nineteen years after her ordeal, she was still tormented by the asthmatic woman with whom she shared a cell. "She was much sicker than I," Victoria railed, "everyone knows that an asthmatic can die of arrest at any moment. But they treated me, and ignored her." Weeping, she let out a long string of verbal indignities, all directed at herself. "They treated me, *me*," Victoria repeated several times, before sputtering, "My cellmate died." At this, Victoria's voice was subsumed by that of a man: Gruffly and in a low, growling register, she berated herself in the filthy language they had used when they searched her vagina for contraband.

For the Process, kinship was defined by citizenship, and only "authentic Argentines" could be part of the national family. The regime's depravity reached its outer limit with pregnant detainees. "Our bodies were a source of special fascination," Astelarra recounted, shuddering at the memory. "They said my swollen nipples 'invited' the prod, eased the passage of current. They presented a truly sickening combination—the curiosity of little boys, the intense arousal of twisted men." It was rare for a pregnant detainee to survive; most were killed soon after giving birth, and their babies sold to "proper" couples, usually from the military or police. Couples could sometimes choose their detainee, based on a description of her looks and level of education. The baby's biological ties and family identity had to be erased, lest it fulfill its "genetic destiny" and become a guerrilla. Since 1977, the Grandmothers of the Plaza de Mayo have searched for 220 missing children; of these, they have located 56 who were kidnapped with their parents who remain missing; 30 have been reunited with their biological families; 13 remain with their adoptive parents (in all cases civilians uninvolved with the repression who adopted in good faith); six cases are still pending in the courts; and seven are believed to have been assassinated together with their parents. The Grandmothers—who organized in October 1977—believe that there were many more children and babies born in captivity, but no one thus far has come forward to investigate their cases.

"They went out of their way to slander 'guerrilla families,'" I was told by Susana Dillon, whose son-in-law died during torture and whose daughter was given a lethal injection soon after giving birth. Under cover of night, two officers from La Perla brought Susana her five-day-old granddaughter. They conceded that the infant's parents were being held, but denied that they were dead. "According to them," said Susana, "'subversives' by definition cared nothing for their children. Nothing could be further from the truth. They were young and idealistic, had children out of passion and hope. My daughter had a terribly hard time conceiving; in order for it to happen, they had moved to the country and were living quietly, 'holistically,' we could say. They were overjoyed when finally she got pregnant. There was nothing they wanted more than to be parents."[15]

Yamila Grandi was two years old when her father and pregnant mother were kidnapped. Just before he was dragged away, her father scrawled on her bedroom door: "I love you Yamila, and cherish your mother." Nearly two decades later, the writing remains. "Somewhere in the world I have a sister or brother," Yamila mused sadly, "unless, of course, my mother died during torture."[16]

"Seeds of the tree of evil," the enforcers called the sons and daughters of "subversives." In their testimonies Astelarra and Geuna both dwell on the adolescents in La Perla. Between June and September 1976, approximately sixty youths from the Manuel Belgrano high school were kidnapped for no more than having been members of the student council. "They were children," wrote Geuna, "they had no idea what was happening. They called for their mothers in their sleep, played games in the showers. . . . The military couldn't decide what to do with them, whether to release them or murder them. Finally they reached a consensus: 'Better to nip them in the bud. When already they have these "social concerns," they shouldn't be allowed to grow up.' That settled it; they all got the truck."[17]

In spite of terror, torture, and depravity, prisoners did manage to resist the dehumanizing project of their captors. In La Perla, detainees memorized as many of each other's names as they could, repeating them, one by one, in the solitary darkness of their tubes. In the enormous Devoto prison in Buenos Aires where prisoners were "legal" (as opposed to those who had been illegally disappeared), the women were forced to change cells every few days so that no relationships could be formed. And every effort was made to pair detainees with "problematic" companions: hairdressers with anthropologists; Maoists with Trotskyites; Peronists with members of the Communist Party. "They wanted us to hate each other," recalled Norita, who spent a total of eight years in captivity, at first as a *desaparecida*, then as a political prisoner.[18] Norita volunteered to be interviewed, but insisted I not publish her last name. "Sometimes their strategies worked, but not always. One night as a punishment we were all forced to lie on the floor head to toe, head to toe. One woman caressed the foot of the woman beside her who then caressed the foot of the woman beside *her*, and so on down the line. We were very subtle, and they had no idea."

Victoria Benítez was also held in Devoto. "We were 800 women, and certain things we had no choice but to accept—like vaginal searches in front of thirty men all aiming their guns. But on other questions we could resist; we were always analyzing, making decisions about where to draw the line. For us, the boundary was group solidarity. Here's an example: We came from every background imaginable. The women from [the agricultural province of] Tucumán were not only far from home, but generally very poor. Those of us who did receive letters with a little money would buy cheese, chocolate, aspirin, whatever we could. The idea was to make a common store of provisions so no one would do without, and so when someone got sick, we could take care of her. As soon as they caught on, they forbade our buying 'in bulk,' as they put it. What they needed to prevent were our efforts to share. The jailers kept accusing us of being 'perverts,' or lesbians—to them any tenderness among us was twisted. One visiting day we had a horrific incident. One of the jailers—a woman—allowed a prisoner to embrace her child whom she hadn't seen in two years. The other women jailers rushed at this guard, beat her badly, and later bragged they got her fired for 'being lax.' Did they? Did they kill her? All we know is we never saw that guard again."

With it all, the women of Devoto wrote and circulated not one, but two magazines. "One on human rights," said Victoria, "the other on politics. We wrote on whatever scraps of paper we could find, rolled them into little balls, rolled the balls in plastic. We passed these packets to each other in the bathroom, often having carried them in our vaginas." She flushed with embarrassment, then added, "They were not going to crush our spirit. They were not going to keep us apart."

Devoto was not the only jail where prisoners risked their lives for the sake of writing. Abel Rovino, a poet and painter kidnapped in 1978, spent four years in captivity—going from a secret detention center to Devoto to the provincial jail in La Plata. "We copied books obsessively. . . . With 300 guards around it wasn't exactly easy; but [as I said] we were obsessed. We would roll the pages into *caramelos* [hard candies], wrap them in plastic, and swallow them. We copied each book three or four times, because the *caramelos* got damaged by the humidity in our mouths and at the other end. We had to save what books we could." Before they were moved to another jail or released, the prisoners swallowed the *caramelos* and later gathered them up in their feces. Rovino tells of Cacho Paoletti, a prisoner who wrote two books in jail, which were later published in Spain. As he wrote, his cellmates copied his verses for *caramelos*. When it came time for them to be released, each one carried out some verses and kept them safe. Years later when Paoletti was living in Spain, his friends sent him these "candies" in the mail.[19]

For Norita, the transition from secret camp to public prison was traumatic. "I'd been used to solitary confinement, starvation, the constant threat of death. When I was finally 'legalized' and got to the provincial jail I fell apart. Apparently it's not so unusual, when one goes from a hellish situation to one that is merely horrid. Your defenses relax, and you crumble. I was brought to this large cell, where the other women gave me perfume, shampoo, soap, talcum powder, cigarettes, water warm enough to bathe a baby. I was encouraged to use as much as I wanted, and for some reason didn't realize that I was the only one bathing this way. When a few days later the next just-legalized prisoner arrived, the women explained that now I could only smoke so much, use this much shampoo, and so on. 'All those things we gave to you, now we give to her.' It was a rare form of support. The gifts were not for you as an individual but were expressions of group solidarity. It was like giving a newborn everything she needs to stay warm, dry, clean, and comfortable."

Not long after Norita's arrival, the other women told her that the director would be coming by to see them. "Just do as we do," they explained, "and don't be afraid. That evening," said Norita, "the director shows up—a famous torturer from the previous dictatorship. So there he is, very imperious on his side of the grate. The cock surveying the henhouse. Extremely authoritarian, master of our lives, god of his universe. Grotesque, terrifying. 'What is it that you need?' he asks, whereupon everyone starts shouting: 'Packages!' 'Letters!' 'Chocolates!' 'Visits!' But all together in this incredible racket. But there he stood, cock of the walk, master of our lives, and pointed: 'You: package. You: letters. You: visits.' Then very grandly, he turned on his heel and left. 'What happened?' I asked my cellmates, who explained, 'Since any sort of organizing is strictly forbidden, we give them what they ask for, which is chaos.' We survived by creating chaos. By 'being a henhouse.' The director approved; it made him seem organized and effective in the face of screaming mimis."

Norita had been convicted by a war tribunal, and was released shortly before the election in 1983. She herself had had no political activities, but her husband—who was murdered by the regime—had been active in a leftist organization. The official charge against her was "illicit association." In preparation for her release, she had an exit interview with an official whose identity remained a secret. "He was dressed in civilian clothes, but his carriage was unmistakably military. Needless to say, I had rehearsed this interview in my mind for eight years. So I answered everything. But then he leaned forward, looked at me hard, and asked, 'Will you keep talking well of your husband?'

'Of course,' I answered.

'After all you've been through?'

'Absolutely,' I said, 'he was an excellent person. An outstanding husband, a devoted son, a wonderful father. I'm telling you what I honestly feel.'

'Right,' he said in that clipped military way. 'But didn't it ever occur to you that he was subversive? Think about all you've been through because of him. Maybe you made a mistake.'

'His life was his life. He died for what he loved, for principles he believed in. So I am not going to say that he was wrong. I will always say that he was an excellent person.'

"Whereupon this officer started to cry. At first I didn't know if this was theater, or the real thing, or what. We were in this enormous office with a huge crucifix on a sort of pedestal on the desk. I don't know if it was always there, or brought in especially for my appointment. He knew that before my arrest, I'd been involved in church groups. He took my hand, placed it on the figure of Christ, and said, 'You are not guilty, but I am.' And he wept, his face turning this deep shade of red.

"That's how I knew that democracy had already arrived. 'What's going to happen to me?' he asked, desperate, tormented. 'I don't know,' he wept, 'and I never will.'"

After years of serving the devouring regime, he was truly at a loss to comprehend her loyalty. And the realization undid him.

IN MY CONVERSATIONS with survivors and in my readings of testimony, I was continually struck by torture's web-like range of ambiguities. Mario Cesar Villani, who spent four years as a prisoner in a total of five clandestine camps, put it to me this way, "The situation of constant torture yielded an infinite palette of grays." According to Argentine human rights workers, Villani got to know more secret camps than anyone else.[20] He passed through all of the major camps located in the Argentine capital. A brilliant physicist who worked at the National Atomic Energy Commission, he is one of very few to have survived so long "inside." He achieved a rare understanding of his tormentors with whom he had complicated, but always adversarial, relations. Villani was more than a valiant enemy; he was intriguing and this, it seems, helped keep him alive. So did his keen attention to language, and his ability to decipher embedded codes.

Scion of a prominent, highly accomplished family, Villani grew up in the exclusive Barrio Norte section of Buenos Aires where he attended the finest academies, including an English-language high school. While a professor in the early 1970s in La Plata—a university city the junta considered a "hotbed of intellectuals"—and then as a researcher at the Commission, Villani was active in his professional guild. He frankly opposed the junta, but never belonged to an underground political organization and had never participated in violence of any kind. The National Atomic Energy Commission sustained a high rate of losses, with scientists being kidnapped in broad daylight from their labs. Villani resigned in protest the day his best friend there was disappeared.

A few days later—November 18, 1977—Villani was kidnapped by a heavily armed commando while driving in Buenos Aires. He was conditionally released in August 1981 under the terms of a special program called "supervised freedom."

Among survivors and human rights workers, Villani's memory, intelligence, and fortitude are spoken of with awe. He was a crucial witness at the trial of the ex-commanders, where he forced language to the center of the court's consideration. A walking dictionary of the slang that had developed in the camps, he initiated the court into the argot of physical and psychic torture. Villani's testimony was so authoritative that even attorneys defending the ex-commanders adopted his vocabulary.

Named "Witness of the Week" by *El Diario del juicio* (the newspaper devoted exclusively to the trial)[21] and quoted extensively in the general press, Villani testified for over three hours. He identified from personal experience 93 hands-on torturers, attending physicians, kidnappers, extortionists, and guards. He also identified scores of former prisoners and *desaparecidos*.

I had deliberately waited until I had gathered most of the words and expressions that would be included in my lexicon before calling Villani. His recorded testimonies were already the source of numerous entries. I knew that as a consequence of torture and prolonged maltreatment, Villani, now fifty, had lost the sight of one eye and sustained some neurological damage. Yet he'd gone back to work as a physicist and was employed at INTI, the National Institute of Industrial Technology. Although he had remained active in human rights, it had been several years since he'd given an interview. I need not have worried about Villani's stamina. He and his wife, Rosita Lerner, arrived at my Buenos Aires apartment at four o'clock on a Saturday afternoon and didn't leave until ten.[22] For nearly six hours they talked intensely, going far beyond the material in their previous accounts, casting new light on the night and fog of Argentina.

My sense was that life in the torture centers had been marked by an hallucinatory confusion induced, at least in part, by the double, even triple, discourse that went back and forth between the "no ones" and the "gods." Villani confirmed that impression: "It was a completely insane situation. The torturers and victims were all living together. Torturers were in constant contact with those they tortured. That is the basic difference between jails and concentration camps. In a jail, on one side of the bars you have the guards, the police, the administrators. On the other, you have the prisoners. In a camp, the two worlds intermix. The guards were there all day. When they wanted a break, they'd come play *trucco* with the prisoners."

I observed that *trucco* is the card game quintessence of bluff and bullying.

FIGURE 4.   Rosita Lerner and Mario Villani, September 1995. (Photo credit: Cristina Fraire)

"Exactly. Lots of talk, all of it lying and deceit. A national pastime. A good game, at least among friends. But it isn't as though we prisoners were playing *trucco* among ourselves, in a recreation period, for example, no not at all. The only time we played *trucco* was when one of the repressors felt like a game and came to our tube, to our cell, where we were shackled, cuffed, and blindfolded. We'd sit on the floor, with our ankles and wrists still chained and our *tabiques* [blindfolds] on our foreheads, playing cards."

A tall, extremely slender man, Mario shifted often as he spoke, stretching or contracting his long limbs, opening, clenching, rubbing his delicate hands. Each time he moved, he caressed his wife, who sat close to him, in some small and casual way. I hadn't realized that Rosita would be at our meeting, but as soon as they arrived it was clear that her presence was extremely important.[23] I sensed that I would first have to bond with Rosita before Mario would feel safe. Rosita made this easy, coming into my tiny kitchen so the two of us could chat and make coffee, I grinding the beans as she readied the pot. It wasn't only that her being there helped Mario to open up, to retrieve memories he'd suppressed. She seized the occasion to question him herself, using me as a witness as they crossed into zones they had previously skirted.

Rosita's probing tended to be psychoanalytical, reflecting her many years as a social worker. It is worth noting that Argentines often use clinical terms like "schizophrenic" and "psychotic" when discussing their country. Though a purist might argue with this use of specialized language, in itself it is important, as an expression of the general perception of political and social pathology. Two words with heavily Freudian associations—"sinister" and "uncanny"—are also commonly applied to current events. Whereas again a purist might quibble, the descriptions reveal the disorienting, even incapacitating, fear that has blighted so many Argentine lives.

Rosita conceded that torturers playing *trucco* with their victims was weird, but insisted there were far more sinister situations, where the lines between who was who and what side he was on *really* got blurred. Like the guard who brought his daughter in to meet some of his favorite prisoners.

Mario told the story. "That was Blood. His nom de guerre was Blood. It was always a relief to see Blood coming down the corridor. 'Good guy' was his role. I don't know anyone who said, 'Yes, this guy tortured me.' Blood went out on 'operations'—heavily armed groups who kidnapped people and brought them in. During interrogation, he'd say, 'Look, this one here is a son of a bitch. Talk to me, or I'll have to turn you over to *him*. And *he's* an animal.'

"Blood would sit on the floor of your tube and play chess, chat. And not about politics or information or people in the camp, but other things— what was going on in the world, soccer, whatever. Like someone who'd visit you at home. He'd talk about his kids, he talked a lot about his little girl. He worried if she shouldn't get good grades. He was preoccupied if a plant at home was dying.

"The overwhelming image I had of him—through his language, his way of recounting things—was that he felt more at home with the prisoners than with his fellows, his colleagues. Some prisoners even said to me, 'This one's *quebrado* [broken or twisted—a collaborator]. But *quebrado* from the other side. As though maybe he wanted to reassure himself, convince himself, that he was a human being, like us." Mario paused. "He said the girl was his daughter. I didn't believe anything I hadn't proved for myself. Ever." He toyed with the tidy, hard-covered notebook he'd brought with him. A light shade of khaki, the notebook blended in with the color of his trousers, with the color of the couch on which he and Rosita sat, their bodies always touching. He wasn't looking at either of us. I asked if he'd met the child.

"No. That was Guillermo, Guillermo Pagés Larraya, or Luis Guarini, maybe both. I don't remember. Both of them are still disappeared."

Rosita said that Blood brought the child, who was six or seven at the time, right to the tubes. Mario was leafing slowly through his notebook. From where I sat, I could see many blank pages. Finally he looked up.

"They came walking down the corridor together, holding hands. They stopped at Guillermo's cell, opened the door. And Blood said, 'This is Guillermo, about whom you've heard so much. And this—I can't remember the girl's name—he mentioned some detail about school or something. They all sat on the floor—Guillermo shackled and cuffed, his *tabique* on his forehead—and talked. Well, only Guillermo was in his cell—the tubes were only big enough for one—with the door open. Blood and the child sat on the floor of the corridor. And that's when he said, 'You've heard so much about each other, I wanted you to meet. And anyway I feel better with you all than with them.'

"One day Blood disappeared. I shouldn't say that. One day he didn't come anymore to the camp. Obviously he'd had work problems and had been moved to a different job. He wasn't good anymore for operations and the like."

Mario bent over his book, murmuring distractedly. His head was bowed over a neat column of small writing. "Don't think from what I'm telling you that I think he's salvageable, that he's a 'good guy.'"

"He's a monster," said Rosita.

"He was also a victim." Mario looked up from his book. "Horacio Martín Donati. Blood was named Horacio Martín Donati."

I asked how he'd learned this.

"With the advent of democracy, I began to testify, first at CELS [Center for Legal and Social Studies], then the [Permanent] Assembly [for Human Rights] and the CONADEP [Argentine National Commission on the Disappeared]. Others were doing the same. So the information stores grew and grew. The guy I knew as Blood, for example, someone else knew in other circumstances. Like when the kidnappers of Combal [a prominent banker] turned up in Switzerland the guy known as the Japanese, one of three captured then, had also participated in my kidnapping. Pieces of a puzzle.

"I'd been in so long, I'd gotten to know—at least to see—a lot of people. I left my 'C.V.'—the camps I'd been in and the dates—at CELS and the Assembly so relatives could contact me. We'd sit down with photos and I'd say, 'Yes, I know him. His number was X-86.' At that moment, his parents would tell me his name. Which I entered in my notebook.

"Here are the lists I brought to the trial. Repressors here on the left by their code name. In this column are their real names and ranks, and here, the camps in which they worked and the dates."

He shows me several pages of these columns, then flips back a few pages. "And here are the names of *desaparecidos* and *ex-desaparecidos*, with the camps they'd been spotted in and the dates. Some are the dates they were last seen. And here, if they survived or not."

In the far right-hand column, there is a "d" for *desaparecido*, or a "v" for *vivo*. Mario closes the book and leans back, stretching his legs, letting the notebook slide down between his hip and the corner of the couch.

"I started with little slips of paper. And eventually I had such a pile I was afraid some would be lost. So I began entering information in this notebook. In the camps, I could only make notes in my head. Which is a shame because I normally have a very bad memory. It's a long time since I testified. I'm sure a lot of this is more engraved in your mind, Margarita, than in mine. Memory loses its grip over time."

"I've always been struck," Rosita said slowly, "at the way memory seems to function in *ex-desaparecidos*. Once we were preparing testimony, for one of the human rights organizations. There was a group of *ex-desaparecidos* in the house all working together. With a good deal of difficulty, they were trying to reconstruct a certain event. Finally one of the women said, 'Oh right, it was the day they tortured——so badly she died that same night.' They were using this death, they kept using deaths, to locate themselves in time."

"A lot of things you'd like to forget," said Mario. "But there's the imperative to remember. A lot of things you *do* forget, and that's a torment too. Is forgetting a sin or salvation? Neither? Both?"

An infernal double bind. Damned-if-you-do, damned-if-you-don't situations were a constant feature, it seemed to me, of life in the camps. Either way there was the probability of death, your own or someone else's.

"That's absolutely true," replied Mario. "One time there was a guy dying after so much torture. He'd slipped into a coma, but they wanted to save him, of course only so they could go on interrogating him. So they brought him in and made us—other *desaparecidos*—give him artificial respiration, which is extremely exhausting, especially for people in the condition we were in. They laid him down on a mattress on the floor of the room where they did intelligence work. He was in such bad shape it was hard to tell if he was breathing. A doctor came and couldn't get a clear reading with the scope. So you know what he did?

"He inserted a needle into the guy's chest between two ribs, close to his heart. If the end of the needle moved, then his heart was beating. If it didn't move, then the man was dead. But I remember, with this type of artificial respiration, you're pressing down on the person's chest—and you have to do this hard, quite hard. I was terrified of disturbing the needle and wounding his heart, terrified I'd kill him. I remember how I tried to make him breathe, but in a way that wouldn't kill him.

"It was frightful. I didn't know if it would be better to bring him around or not. He'd only be tortured. But people survive torture. It wouldn't necessarily have been 'one last day. . . .' I'd survived torture. All of us in the room had. . . . I don't know. . . . The whole thing was. . . . It was. . . .

"He never came round. . . . There are so many incidents I just can't recover anymore. . . ."

Mario wraps his foot around Rosita's. For a moment none of us speak.

Then very softly, Rosita begins again. "Listening to Mario and other *ex-desaparecidos*, it has seemed to me that the worst was not physical torture, but these daily situations that were even more perverse, more tormenting than physical torture."

"Psychic torture was infinitely worse," said Mario, "because it was constant. I want to be very clear on this point. There were people in the camps who gave out no information whatsoever, collaborated not at all after hideous prolonged physical torment. There were others who collaborated, and there were various forms of collaboration, including participating in mechanical torture. But everyone, every single prisoner was subjected to psychic torture, which included the threat, and real possibility, of more mechanical torture. There were no exceptions, no breaks for 'good behavior.' Being given a job to do was no protection against torture, nor did it necessarily mean you'd been picked to survive. No, torture was constant and inescapable; and your death was always more likely than not."

My understanding was that everyone was physically tortured as soon as they were brought in. "Softening up" was another euphemism for torture, a way of establishing the "ground rules."

"That's correct," said Mario. "The only variation was time. I was interrogated under mechanical torture—with the electric prod and rubber truncheons—only for the first two days of my imprisonment. It became clear that they really didn't know why I was there—I didn't have the information they wanted—but there I was. . . . Subsequently, I was hit and beaten up many times but that, strictly speaking, is not mechanical torture. No, there were other things." Again he fell silent.

"Before being kidnapped," Mario began, "I had made a date with a close friend, the physicist Jorge Gorfinkel. We were to meet on what turned out to be my second day in the 'operating theater.' I was taken while driving to work and in the car was the agenda in which I wrote down my appointments. So they went to where Jorge had come to meet me—downtown, at the corner of Larrea and Córdoba—and kidnapped him. They told me this while I was being tortured on the 'grill.' They got Jorge because he'd kept his date with me. They knew that my knowing this would be a far worse torment than 220 volts. The remorse is almost more than you can take—'if it weren't for me, Jorge would be alive, he'd be *alive* if it weren't for *me.*' And from what they'd been doing to me, I had a pretty clear idea of what they must have done to him. . . ."

"Their very logic was a torment," I suggested. "Because you're being tortured, you have to be guilty. You even become guilty of *their* abominations."

"That," said Mario, "was one of their favorite tricks. An infernal 'sharing of responsibility.'"

This brought us to one of the most difficult issues, that of the so-called *quebrados*—the collaborators, or "broken ones."[24] It seemed to me that collaboration was yet another area where the lines got blurred.

"Absolutely. You had to walk a very fine line, making them believe you were useful, but without abetting them in a way that, morally, was going to do you in. You tried to communicate your own sense of what could make you useful. I knew electronics, which I'm certain saved my life. But other people communicated other messages, whether they realized it or not, and so they got selected for other jobs. Including mechanical torture."

But that too was a gray area. Was it not worse to be tormented by someone taking sadistic pleasure in it? Some survivors have testified that fellow prisoners managed to communicate solidarity even in the "operating theater," in the form of a caress or their own tears.

"Then the next question," said Rosita, "is whether it's better to die than torture another human being."

"That's how it was," said Mario. "Our choices were from a range of unthinkable options."

Mario was never asked to assist in physical torture, but he was asked to repair an electric prod.

"That was in El Banco. At first I refused. So they started using something called a *varivolt*, which basically was a transformer. When I saw the marks and burns on people's bodies, I told them, 'Bring me the prod.' I fixed it, but inserted a weak capacitor so that the voltage would be much lower."

It seemed he'd managed to subvert them.

"That's not to say it felt good. . . . But you're absolutely right," he said, "about this theme of collaboration. It could get very schizzy. Lucía, for instance, was a terrible collaborator, terrible. She'd go out on operations as a 'marker,' but even worse, she worked in Intelligence, figuring out whom they should kidnap, how it could best be done, who was connected with whom. She had her kid with her, a little boy. The kids spent the day in the washroom, since their mothers were often the ones doing the laundry. My electronic shop was across from the washroom and sometimes Lucía would come visit with her son. After a while she'd go back to Intelligence, but I'd let him sit on the table and draw pictures as I worked. Now apart from being a horrible collaborator, Lucía could show great solidarity with the other *desaparecidos*. For example, when one of the officers would give her sweets, she'd always share them with the rest of us."

"But it's not just sharing sweets," said Rosita, "it's also sharing her acts of collaboration, at least the rewards. I'm not saying that you all were collaborating, but here's another place where the lines are unclear."

I ask where Lucía is now, if they are still in touch.

"No," says Mario. "She took a different road. She went with the Cat."

"The Electronic Cat? The inventor of Carolina, an instrument of electric torture?"[25]

"That's the one. I don't know how they got together as a couple. He was a Professor of Electronics at the Navy Mechanics School, we were in the concentration camp there."

I ask if the Cat performed torture. If he'd tortured Lucía.

"I'm not sure," Mario replied. "But he came often to check in on Carolina. So certainly he was present during torture.

"Lucía and the Cat are the only such couple I knew personally. But of course there were others. [Admiral Rubén J.] Chamorro, for example, married a prisoner."

Lucía established an extreme type of relation with her captors, but all prisoners, I suggest, had to figure out some way of relating to their guards. They had to learn not just the argot, but the subtext. And a mistake could be fatal.

"Absolutely," said Mario. "Of course anything you did could end up being fatal. But the 'subtext,' as you put it, what they were *really* saying, could be extremely difficult to figure out. I'll tell you something that happened to me that was . . . I don't know how to describe it. But—— . . . Okay, now I've told you her name, but you mustn't print it. Or even repeat it. Because her family's still living. Her kids. Promise?

"We were both *desaparecidos* at Olympus. She was cleaning bathrooms, preparing meals, that sort of thing. It was a very difficult time, very rainy, there were floods, there was a lot of work, terrible food. Everyone was in a bad mood, which was extremely dangerous.

"A bond developed between——and me, a very subtle bond. We were able to get each other a little more food, pass each other a little toilet paper, or even say 'How are you?' (*How are you*? Talk about words from another language.) Even though this tie was extremely subtle, Covani, who was in charge of transfers, noticed that something was going on. He got the idea in his head that I had it for this woman, wanted to sleep with her. So he said, 'Skinny, you like the blond, don't you?' 'Who wouldn't?' I said. And he goes, 'Listen, I'll bring her to your tube, I'm on duty tonight. And in the morning, I'll take her back. No problem. A little present for you.' That night, he brought——to my cell. I told her what Covani had said and we spent the whole night talking, not just about that, but about all sorts of things. She told me about her kids, I told her about my wife, we told each other all about our lives. Of course nothing sexual happened. The next morning Covani came and took her back to her tube and I spent the day cleaning the bathrooms.

"Two days later there was a transfer, and the people who'd been picked were being herded together on the patio and loaded onto trucks. I see they're taking——. Covani comes over and says, 'You want to say goodbye?' So I went out to the patio, gave her a kiss, I don't know what I said to her, and came back. Then Covani puts his arm around my shoulders, sits me down with him on a little bench, very paternal, and goes, 'It's not getting to you too much, is it, Skinny?'[26] 'What do you mean?' I ask him. 'Because we're transferring her.' I had such a lump in my throat I thought I'd never breathe again. But I said, 'Come on, the world's full of women.' He patted me on the back and said, again very paternally, 'Very good, Skinny, very good.'

"He was testing me, to see if they should include me in the next transfer. He couldn't have cared less about my feelings for——, she'd already been programmed for transfer. As far as they were concerned, she was already dead. All he wanted to find out was if I was still useful. . . . That was when I pledged that, should I survive, I would dedicate the rest of my life to preventing any of those guys from enjoying the slightest impunity."

But Covani did get off—twice. The first time was under Alfonsín's Punto Final law, which decreed that accused officers who had not been tried by a certain date would not be tried at all. Then he was granted custody of a pair of twin boys he'd kidnapped from a *desaparecida* (killed soon after giving birth) in Olympus. When the woman's relatives started legal proceedings to gain custody of the children, Covani—whose real name is Samuel Miara—fled with them to Paraguay. Later he was extradited to Argentina for trial, but the judge ruled that to return the boys to their blood relatives would be psychologically damaging.[27]

"Right," said Mario. "Better for them to stay with Covani, who was a murderer, a torturer, a thief, a rapist. . . like all of them. . . ."

Even by those standards, some torturers stood out. Julián the Turk was one. Mario knew him well.

"Julián," he said, "was a Nazi, did unspeakable things to Jews, well to everyone, but Jews were his specialty. On the end of his watch chain was a big swastika. Julián was an animal, some kind of beast, also an opera fanatic, but a fanatic. I too love classical music and missed it terribly on the inside. Because I repaired electronics, I could listen to the radio—they couldn't control it, I had to listen or I couldn't fix the things. But then the guards would fight with me or between themselves over my music: 'Turn that shit off!' one would yell. 'It's boring!' One wanted news, another tango, someone else would be yelling for Bossa nova. . . . But Julián would bring me tapes, which he made himself at home. There'd be a selection of classical pieces, always one opera, for him—usually Verdi, anyway something Italian. We'd sit there together and listen, then he'd leave with the tape. A few days later he'd come with a new cassette."

Rosita broke in. "But he had to have his guard up all the time. Because as soon as the music was over he could start torturing again. One thing had nothing to do with the other."

Mario agreed. "Julián and I had a lot of run-ins. When he slapped me around, he sent me flying. He thought I was a very hard case, *un duro*. He even said, 'Nothing gets to you, does it, Skinny.' It was important for him to think of me that way. It meant I was useful, worth keeping alive."

It had to have been extremely difficult to develop these encoded behaviors. I asked if he was able to retrace that development, starting with his first two days of physical torture.

Mario thought for a moment. "In physical torture, there *was* a relationship, and it was complex, changeable even within the space of one session. One thing about mechanical torture is that it tends to happen along with interrogation. At least this was the case with me. Ostensibly at any rate, there was a reason for it. They wanted information, they wanted to punish me for past behavior and/or associations. So on one level there was clarity.

"I would say that they saw us, no matter our origins—guerrilla, student, labor activist, intellectual—as other beings. We were martians as far as they were concerned. For a guy to torment someone with 220 volts of electricity or with a rubber truncheon he first has to consider his victim a nonperson. And he has to believe that he is right to be doing what he's doing. Afterward, the *desaparecido* can go back to being a person, of sorts, a being not exactly of the human type. But someone the repressor could play cards with.

"I got to a point during torture where I'd think to myself, 'This torturer, this guy torturing me *now*, is a man like me.' I mean, I knew very well that I had never and would never use an electric prod on anyone. But it was important for me to realize that he was not a martian, not a cockroach, but a man like me. And this was borne out later, by Blood, for instance, who worried about his daughter doing well in school.

"This attitude was important on two levels. It helped me get along with them, to talk with them. And it was crucial in terms of my identity. Because if I looked at them like martians, I was doing the same thing they were. I was like them. So it helped me survive day to day, but even more importantly, I could inhabit my self.

"I had just one goal—to stay alive until the next day. A limited, concrete objective. If I got there, I'd have 'accomplished' something. Not that this was easy. There were explosions, with Julián, for example, over stupid things. There were so many days I wasn't at all sure I'd make it. But it wasn't just to survive, but to survive *as me.*"

Rather than some form, some mutation, of *them*?

"Yes. That terrified me."

This was but the second time Mario had spoken of fear. On both occasions, he had connected terror with moral, rather than physical, dangers. It dawned on me that he hadn't once mentioned hope.

"From the moment I was kidnapped," he said, "I believed I was condemned to die. I always thought, Here everyone is a dead man. Maybe there would be exceptions but basically we were there to be exterminated. I didn't know how or when it would happen—if they'd shoot us, strangle us, cut off our heads—none of that was clear. Today we know the mechanisms, but then we didn't. At one point, we found out that people were given pills that knocked them out. But we didn't know that then they were thrown out of airplanes. I know some people had hope, but I did not. Which made certain situations even spookier."

For example?

"Like the 1978 World Soccer Championship. I was in El Banco. The guys running the camp decided that as this was an historic event for Argentina they would arrange for everyone to enjoy it. In quotes. Or maybe not in quotes. See? The limits become blurred. Back and forth between the double message. They didn't have the means to put together an auditorium or viewing room. So they brought in a TV—stolen, of course, and repaired by me—and put it up on a high platform at the end of a long corridor. The tubes lined this corridor. They opened our cells, let us raise our *tabiques* to our foreheads and sit in the doorway on the floor. Still shackled, still cuffed, we watched the game. And shouted the goals." [It is customary in Argentina for soccer spectators to shout a prolonged "Go-o-o-a-a-a-l-l-l-l" each time their team scores.]

"This is the part that drives me crazy," said Rosita. "They made them shout the goals."

"The whole thing was very mixed-up," said Mario. "It's not that they said, 'Now, you're required to shout the goals.' But these were people who if they hadn't been *desaparecidos* would have been home, or at the stadium, watching and shouting the goals. Some—whether they knew it or not—had already been programmed to die. Were in fact scheduled for the next transfer. So the whole thing took on a different meaning—to be there, perhaps on a death list, shouting the goals."

"In fact, most of those people were transferred," said Rosita. "Hardly any survived."

"But not everyone was conscious that we were condemned," said Mario.

I asked if that perception made him feel like an outsider, even among his fellow *desaparecidos*. He said yes, that was part of what made it so spooky.

Rosita went on. "I don't think the prisoners were meant to enjoy it at all. With or without the quotes. It was a show of power. 'We will allow you to. . . .'"

Mario agreed. "It was extremely cruel. Because the sensation you have is that the outside world has disappeared. That you've left the world. And so these signals from the world are very. . . . I don't even know how to put it."

Messages concealed within messages, something we normally associate with theater and art, characterized daily life in the camps. Many survivors have testified that especially at the beginning it could be hard to understand even on a literal level. Right away, just through the strangeness of their captors' words, prisoners got the message they were aliens.

"It was extremely confusing," Mario began. "There were words I heard for the first time in the camps. Then there were others—like lion's cage, operating theater, and so on—familiar words, that took on totally different meanings there. Those shifts were also extremely disorienting."

"Sinister."

"Exactly, two realities colliding in one word. Other expressions—*picana, sos boleta*—I knew from detective novels. But now they were part of my everyday reality. 'You'll get your ticket,' for example wasn't a threat they used just in the 'operating theater.' They used it all the time, and for trifles, for bullshit. Like when they'd bring me a radio or TV (stolen, of course, from someone they'd kidnapped) to fix, and I'd tell them, 'I can't, I don't have the parts.' They'd say, 'You'll fix it or we'll give you your ticket.' The meaning of that bit of slang—'*We'll kill you. We'll kill you for nothing. We'll kill you because we feel like it*'—was our everyday reality.

"As I said before, right after they disappeared me, I didn't understand a lot of what was said to me. And then when I got out, people didn't understand a lot of what I said to them. I realized I was still thinking—and talking—in camp terms.

"'You don't exist' was a favorite of theirs on the inside," said Mario. "It's interesting," he went on, "the slang in the camps was a mix. Some of it was definitely born there. But some came from the jails. Because many of the guards and torturers came from the penal system and police. Much of the *lunfardo* [slang] in this country comes from the marginal sectors, people who tended to land in jail. Originally *lunfardo* provided a way that prisoners could talk among themselves and not be understood by their jailers. A code. So those running the jails learned it in order to break the code. And then the situation became reversed—the prisoners had to learn the codes of their captors. The amazing thing—maybe it's not so amazing—is that there did develop a common code, and that this united us."

Rosita is aghast.

"Let me explain," says Mario. "In Olympus, there was a patio out back. Sometimes they would let the pregnant prisoners go out and take a little sun there. One day they decided that the pregnant women could do with a little outing and so they got together a group of five or six. They included me too, for a reason I've never been able to figure out. With a couple of guards, we were taken to Chacabuco Park. We must have been a very strange-looking group, given where we'd come from. And then they made us ride the kiddie train. We must have looked very strange indeed. Afterward they took us to one of the cafés that bordered the park and we all had a beer. We sat around this table, drinking and talking about things going on at Olympus. For a moment I thought, 'What if someone overhears us?' Then I realized that no one could have understood what we were talking about—we were speaking in code, as it were. Not deliberately, it was just how we spoke then. And it hit me: Here I am, sitting at a café—out in the world, but not a part of it. Not a member." In the night and fog of Argentina, language itself became a prison.

"One of the first things I came to learn about Mario and other *ex-desaparecidos*," said Rosita, "was that they relate to words differently. How can I explain it? Have you ever been with deaf-mutes? They have a particular code—if they move a finger, for instance, that means a certain thing. Well, that was the image I had. Let me give you an example. Once a group of us were preparing a [testimonial] document. At one point Isabel, who was disappeared as an adolescent, said, 'I was trying to see her, but I couldn't, I didn't have her in the center.' What can this mean, I wondered. After a few minutes it came to me: She'd been trying to see out a little corner of her *tabique*. She'd devised some way of seeing, slightly anyway, even though she was blindfolded.

"At the beginning, being with these people could be very difficult," said Rosita. "They communicated differently, minimally. They'd had to develop a minimal way of making contact. Gestures, looks, signals that in normal life would go unnoticed. Inside, they had to go unremarked. What is extraordinary is that with such restricted means of communication they were able to discern in whom they could trust and in whom they could not. And deep, abiding ties developed among those who were together in those camps. Nearly all of the *ex-desaparecidos* we know are basically introverted, close-mouthed. I think," she reflected, "that these are the ones who best withstood the camp. They could more easily focus within, they needed less contact with others, were accustomed to less contact. For this type of person, a small gesture has more weight than for an extrovert who needs a great deal of togetherness."

"Certain neurotic aspects of my personality saved me," said Mario. "In normal life my neuroses are a problem, but on the inside they were immensely useful."

Rosita offered an example. "Our apartment is quite small. The living/dining area is right up against the kitchen. Mario often sits down at the table, which is three feet from the kitchen, to study or go over calculations. One night I have dinner on the stove and go out to do a last-minute errand. Mario is at the table, his head in his numbers. When I come home, there's smoke in the lobby. I go upstairs, there's smoke flooding out from under our door. I go in and there he is, intent on his calculations, totally oblivious to everything else. The smoke is so thick we all—not to mention dinner—could have burned to a crisp.

"Mario," she continued, "has an extraordinary ability to disconnect himself from what's going on around him. He can take himself out of time. He could spend hours and hours blindfolded in his cell doing the most sophisticated, complicated physics problems. Others had to count sheep, which must have been much less effective."

"Now," said Mario, "I have to rid myself of these neurotic strategies."

"If something bad has happened to Mario, it doesn't show," said Rosita. "I can tell, but the signs are so small. He has to relearn how to express what's going on with him."

"These traits weren't born in the camps," said Mario. "I had them before. It's just that on the inside they were useful. Maybe I have this personality structure because I'd lived through similar situations before being disappeared and they developed in response to that. Yet even on the inside I was aware that anywhere else my behavior would be considered extremely neurotic. This became a problem for me toward the end when I was in the Navy Mechanics School and selected for its 'recuperation process.' And with that," said Mario, "I encountered the dangers inherent in hope. As I said, before I hadn't expected to survive. But then suddenly the implication was that they'd decided I would live. With hope came fear, a host of fears. At least for me. Uncertainty provokes anxiety, dread: What if . . . ? What if they killed me anyway? Hoping to live fills one with feelings and desires that had long been dormant. It became very much harder to take it one day at a time. That structure had been crucial in holding me together. And what if they released me? What shape was I really in? Would I be fit to live 'normally' among people, among people I loved? What could be left of my previous life? I had no idea.

"The dynamics of the double discourse changed," said Mario. "We spent half the day chained and walled-up in our tubes. The other half we circulated comparatively 'freely,' in the fish tank."

So everyday prisoners experienced something of both fates.

"Exactly. And some people were transferred from the fish tank. Mainly we were pawns in the fights between officers. We still had no value in and of ourselves. In their eyes."

Family visits were part of "recuperation." They were introduced gradually, with prisoners being allowed an hour or so at home in the company of an armed guard. Eventually the prisoner would be allowed overnight, even weekend visits, without a guard.

"There was no point even thinking about trying to escape," Mario insisted. "They let me know they'd done impeccable research on all the members of my family—the buses my nieces and nephews took to school, the bus my brother-in-law rode to work. No, there was no way. They'd have killed everyone. And after I was released—they called it 'supervised freedom'—I had to call in once a week, then once a month. I'd have to meet them at a cafe. 'We just want to make sure you're doing okay, Tito.' They called me Tito."

Even after the election of Alfonsín, Villani got calls. The voice on the wire was always friendly, solicitous. He was given "emergency numbers," in case he should ever "need" them. Villani recited those phone numbers at the trial of the ex-commanders.

"What I didn't say was that the day before my father [who had filed habeas corpus] and I were to testify, my father, an architect, got a call at his studio. When I go to meet my father in the witness room, he's already waiting for me, very shaken and upset. 'They said I should tell you to keep your mouth shut or they'll kill everybody, the whole family.' He says this over and over, trying to convince me we shouldn't testify.

"'Excuse me,' I say—this is a very traditional family in which one doesn't lightly contradict one's father—'Excuse me, but I think we'll be safer if we say here and now you were threatened.'

"My father finally testified, but said nothing about the incident. Then I gave my testimony, and as you know I didn't exactly hold back. After I finished I went up to Strassera [the prosecutor] and told him privately about the threat. 'Oh, I get them everyday,' he said and slapped me on the back. It was the last threat I or any member of my family ever received."

"Their presence," said Rosita, "is threatening enough. I'm going to tell you something now you wouldn't believe if you read it in a book. The night we went to see *The Official Story* [the first Argentine commercial film to deal explicitly with the Dirty War] we took my daughter, Mariela, who at the time was ten. Afterward she was full of questions, and so as we walked along we tried to explain certain things. Then we got into a bus to go home. She and I immediately went to the back, as the bus was quite crowded. I sat down with her on my lap and waited for Mario to join us. But he didn't. He bought our tickets and then kept standing near the driver. How odd, I thought, he never does this. It was very strange. And then it was time to get off. Mariela and I exited from the rear, Mario from the front. This is really weird, I kept thinking. And then he told us: The man sitting across the aisle from us with his wife was one of the repressors from the Navy Mechanics School. Now there was a lesson for Mariela: They're out, unpunished, literally right next to us." The enforcer they met was known as Jackal. A naval employee at the ESMA, his real name is Rubén Omar Vitale, and he specialized in kidnappings.

"Another one that got off on the Due Obedience law," said Mario.

By the time of this interview in October 1990, Mario had also crossed paths with Julián the Turk. "Always by chance," he tried to joke. "The first time was in 1982 or 1983. I don't remember precisely. It was well before the trials. On my way to work I always traversed the Plaza Pizzurno, in front of the Ministry of Education. I'm walking along, as usual enjoying the lovely spot, when all of a sudden I hear, 'Tito! How're you doin'?'"

"Talk about surrealism," said Rosita.

"So I go, 'Julián, what's up, what're you doin?'"

"'C'mere,' he goes, patting his bench, 'sit down, how are things?'"

"'Fine, fine, working. You?' He tells me he's doing surveillance. 'On me?' I can't help but ask. 'Nah,' he goes, and gestures, self-importantly, to the Syrian Embassy across the square. Who knows," said Mario, "maybe he *was* spying on the Syrians. At least it was clear he wasn't spying on me. If he were, he never would have let me see him. Still, for all the banter, the encounter left me feeling bad. Very bad. Sour."

I am amazed at their strange camaraderie.

Mario takes this in, then leans toward me to explain, "Julián, as I said before, was truly an animal. But he could also show real solidarity. Bear in mind the context," he says. "For instance, one of my jobs was to clean the bathrooms. Of course we never had toilet paper. What we had were newspapers and magazines stolen from the homes of *desaparecidos*. These we tore into little bits and hung in a plastic bag. But this was terrible—unhealthy, scratchy—remember, our bodies were extremely tender—and carried bad associations. Occasionally, Julián brought in real toilet paper. Bought it himself, with his own money."

Rosita says not a word but looks stricken.

"I realize," said Mario, "that maybe this shows more about *us* than it does about Julián. But the truth is, we were extremely grateful for the paper, and it was he who supplied it."

The next time Mario met Julián was in 1985, in the heart of downtown, at the corner of Paraná and Corrientes. Mario was coming up out of the subway and there, half-sitting, half-leaning on the window of the pharmacy, was Julián. "We looked at each other, both of us pretty surprised," said Mario, wearily. "'Tito, what're you doin'?' The whole thing starts all over again. 'It's been so long!' he actually said.

"'Look, Julián, I don't have time to hold up this wall, I have to go to work,' I said, and tried to walk past him.

"He grabs my arm, and says, 'C'*mon*, a cup of coffee.' I get back my arm, and he says, all injured, 'At least tell me how you're doin'.' I tell him I'm doing fine. But it's clear that he's in a bad way."

"Not exactly a high-level spy," says Rosita.

"Right," says Mario. "'But you've got a lot of contacts,' I tell him, 'you always said you wanted to go to Paraguay. Why don't you?'"

"'They're bastards,' he goes."

"'Just what I always told you.'"

"'Shithead!' he says. 'You should be doing better, Tito. A genius like you. Let me help. Go see Sivak.'" Osvaldo Sivak, the owner of Buenos Aires Building, was kidnapped twice in the 1970s for ransom. The second time his captors—and presumed assassins—were agents of the Federal Police. At some point before the industrialist was killed, Julián was Sivak's custodian.

"So it's the end of 1985," Mario continues, "we've been through the trials of the ex-commanders, and there's Julián sending me to Sivak's company for a job.

"'Tell them I sent you,' he says.

"'And whom shall I say? Julián the Turk, or Julio Simón?'"

"'Shithead!'" he goes, '*flaco de mierda!*' He didn't know I knew his name.

"'Thank you very much,' I said, 'but I'm doing just line.' Except that was only partially true. Because then I did something I hadn't done in a very long time. I went to my office by the most roundabout way possible in the event I was being watched. Seeing him was like a time warp. Instincts came alive from a time I thought was over." Mario shook his head and attempted a smile. Hanging over this interview of October 1990 was the bitter certainty that the convicted ex-commanders of the Dirty War would soon be set free in an executive pardon. President Menem was vaunting this unprecedented gesture as "necessary for the healing of Argentina."

"They're no longer content with double discourse," railed Mario. "They're rewriting the whole text. They're rewriting history."

Was this not another way in which language could become a prison? Words thrown up like walls to block the collective memory?

"They can't totally erase us from the history," said Mario. "We're *there*. They can fence us off, but we're *there*. And we have to insist on our *thereness* because it may be a form of safety. Let me explain. When I first began to testify at CELS, for example, I'd insist they black out any details that could reveal my identity. I would go over the transcripts and listen back to the tapes. It took a while before I fully trusted those taking my testimony, even though I knew they were sterling people and even though I wanted very much to trust them.

"Then with the CONADEP, a group of *ex-desaparecidos* went to Olympus. I'd known the place very well, after having done all sorts of repairs there. At one point, we got to a door that wouldn't open. I said, 'Behind this door is a water pump.' They all looked at me a little strangely. But I knew because once when it was flooded, I'd fixed it. I gave a minute description of what we'd find when we got the door open. And that's exactly what we found. Afterwards there was a televised press conference, and they asked us if we wished to participate. To my astonishment, I heard myself say, 'Yes.'

"It was the first time I spoke out publicly. Suddenly I'd realized there were no torturers at my side threatening to blow me up. Rather the torturers were in my head. Inside I was still a prisoner. And realizing that set me free.

"There was nothing they could do to me anymore. The whole country had seen my face. Finally," said Mario, "I was safe. At least as safe as anyone in Argentina can expect to be."

One of the men due to be pardoned and freed "in time for Christmas" was the totally unrepentant ex-commander of the navy, Emilio Eduardo Massera. He was given Argentina's harshest legal punishment: life in prison.

Prisión perpetua—the very sound of it is ringingly final. The plosives beat down like a gavel; liquid double vowels at the end are open, flow on as though for all of time. In Spanish, this punishment is phrased to extend beyond the measure of a human life, beyond the measure of time. The language leaps over the venal realm of politics, dwarfs the realm of history. Linguistically, *prisión perpetua* is absolute. As it applies to the men who

were ultimately responsible for the torment of those like Mario Villani—
and the silenced tens of thousands— *prisión perpetua* has all the clout of a
dead letter.

"I am responsible, but not guilty," said Massera when in 1985 he took
the stand in his own defense. "My judges may have the chronicle, but history belongs to me and that is where the final verdict will be decided."[28]

History as a means to afflict the collective memory, history as night
and fog. Cynical and facile, this view of history is itself a crime against
humanity. The chronicles of survivors like Mario Villani are infinitely
harder to construct. I am haunted by the many blank pages in Mario's
notebook. Several days after our meeting, I was alone with Rosita. I asked
her why in his notebook he's written so little that is personal.

"The notebook," Rosita's voice grew weak. "He told me, 'When I open
it, I hear the screaming.'"

3

"Life Here Is Normal"

JULY 1990: MIDWINTER IN ARGENTINA. "LIFE HERE IS SURREAL," PEOPLE tell me over and over. And it is true. I am walking through downtown Buenos Aires—the very heart of Buenos Aires—on my way to an appointment. A small crowd—mostly women, quite well-dressed—has gathered before a construction site at the corner of Florida and Viamonte. The younger ones push close to the large sign, call out the designers whose creations will soon fill the renovated mall. Galerías Pacífico—famous for its splendid frescoes—has been closed for several years. In the early 1970s, it was full of costly imports from Paris and Milan, London, New York, San Francisco. Shopping there epitomized leisure and luxury. By the time of the dictatorship, the store was less glamorous but still pleasant. And one couldn't hear the screams of those being tortured in the basement. One was oblivious to the fifteen tiny cells, whose walls were marked with the desperate graffiti of those who were murdered there. But everyone knows it now; we've known since 1987 when the secret camp was discovered. If we'd forgotten, we'd been reminded last month when newspapers ran photographs of the renovations, showing the cells, the shooting gallery, and the phrases, initials, and dates—all between 1977 and 1981—scratched into the walls. But on this bright, midwinter morning Dior, Chanel, Issey Miyake— *these* are the names that people want to read.[1]

I am walking to the home of Matilde Mellibovsky, one of the founding Mothers of the Plaza de Mayo.[2] Matilde is a tall, fair, elegant woman in her sixties with long red hair, high cheekbones and green, Eastern European eyes. She lives in a small, curving street, whose ornate French and Italianate buildings seem to embrace you. It is mild enough for us to go out on the terrace.

"I saw a violent kidnapping there," she tells me, pointing to the house across the way. "In '75.[3] I was wandering around, unable to sleep, must have been three in the morning. I stood looking out the window, toward Nueve de Julio [a major boulevard], everything was so quiet. All of a sudden, there was an eruption of men in the son's bedroom." She points to the tall windows on the top floor. "Things were flying around—sheets, clothes, books. With a great deal of violence, they were taking the boy away. I turned off the light, and peeked through a tiny opening in the curtain. 'I'll be safer in the dark,' I remember thinking. 'Safer in the dark,'" she repeats with an edge, and looks away.

Next door is the Israeli Embassy. In this country where anti-Semitism is endemic, the Jewish State is represented in a great historical palace. It is more than a government outpost, it is a place for the community to gather. Parents like the Mellibovskys went there for help, after their children had disappeared. The appearance of anti-Semitism was something the "gentlemen of the junta" tried hard to avoid. It would have worsened its relations with the United States, endangered its weapons trade with Israel. Yet though Jews comprise only about two percent of the general population, they account for 10 percent of the missing. Tapes of Hitler's speeches were blared through certain camps; some enforcers wore swastikas and performed their "work" under a portrait of the Fuhrer. As we have seen, the Dirty War dictatorship was intensely verbal, and had a diabolical genius for appropriating language to which it had no moral right. The regime *was* shot through with a hatred for Jews, but that did not stop it from pilfering the Warsaw Ghetto cry, "Never Again!" *Nunca Más*! they wrote in their Final Report, claiming eternal victory over subversion.[4] Within the Jewish community, the dynamics of the Terror were extremely complicated and divisive. I am a Jew, and this is one of the most vexing chapters in a book that is full of vexation. It is but a facet of the prism, albeit a crucial one, for certain themes—identity, memory, collective trauma, contamination of history—come into startling focus.

This is our first meeting, and Matilde is watching me closely. I've been referred by a mutual friend; still, she is guarded, formal, vaguely defiant. She says her daughter was kidnapped not far from where I currently live. When I tell her I knew that, she seems to soften, ushers me back inside. All over the living room are pictures of Graciela Mellibovsky, who disappeared on September 25, 1976, at the age of twenty-nine.

"I'll introduce you," she says and leads me to a poster of Graciela wearing the uniform of the prestigious Colegio Nacional de Buenos Aires. She touches the picture, as though brushing a lock of hair from the young woman's eyes. Large, dramatic, almond-shaped eyes like Mathilde's. "What a beautiful girl," I say.

"Graciela *is* a beautiful girl," says Matilde, stressing the verb. "Also nervous, obsessive, agitated, doing everything at once. I don't want to 'improve,' or 'recreate' her," she tells me, "I want her with all of her faults."

The two were alike—headstrong and quick, sometimes too quick, to speak. For years, they had terrible arguments, but that improved as they both grew older, and as the times got dangerous. Everyday, it seemed, someone else they knew was taken. "They came of age during '68," she says, proudly. "They wanted to change the world, and why not. Graciela was a Peronist—since high school, she'd worked in the *villas miserias* [shantytowns]. She'd leave with clothes from her own closet, come home with her shoes full of mud. I begged her to leave, at least for a while. But she was adamant. 'If we go, who will be left? It would just be giving them the country.'

"Not long after, I dreamt she was being kidnapped. She was being rushed by a band of men, and they were stuffing her into a tiny car."

And that, essentially, is what happened. The last time Mati saw her daughter was the day Graciela disappeared. A political economist who also taught and did translations, Graciela lived on her own. Still, Mati—a compulsive cook in those days—used to keep the kitchen filled with her daughter's favorite treats. She was delighted when, early one Saturday morning, Graciela called, suggesting they meet for a sunbath. They spent a few hours in the plaza at Charcas and Cerrito, surprised the weather was cool. It was a normal visit. The mother scolded her daughter for talking too fast; the daughter made fun of her mother's home remedies. They parted happy, relaxed, and slightly pink.

Graciela went home carrying the tart her mother had baked her. She planned to shower, dress—carefully, her mother surmised, knowing her daughter was a little vain—and see a movie with friends. Matilde and her husband, Santiago, had their meal and lay down for siesta. At four o'clock they were awakened by the telephone. A male voice wanted to know if Graciela was there. "Who's calling?" Mati asked. "Who is it?" But the voice would say only that he was a friend, and hung up.

Graciela had met her friends at around three. Within half an hour, the group was kidnapped, from the corner of Córdoba and Francisco Acuña de Figueroa. By now the day was exceedingly hot and humid. Mati had gone back to bed but couldn't sleep. She and her husband went out; he to an exhibit, she to a concert in San Telmo.

"I had a horrible feeling walking the streets," Matilde recounted. "The afternoon papers had banner headlines: 'Shoot-Out With Five Subversives.' You saw those stories most everyday. Only the cops ever had guns."

She met Santiago at his mother's, then the two walked home along Santa Fe, a main avenue full of shops and cinemas, restaurants and cafés. They were both tense and distracted, and neither dared to mention the phone call. They entered a café but left without ordering, bought tickets for a film they didn't see. Unable to eat, drink or talk, they finally just went to bed.

At 3:30 in the morning, there was a violent commotion at their door. Fifteen soldiers in civilian dress were breaking in. Apparently there'd been a mix-up; this was the second crew assigned to kidnap Graciela. They assaulted both Matilde and Santiago, hitting and kicking them, twisting their heads and limbs. They ransacked the house, took everything that belonged to Graciela—her schoolbooks, souvenirs, things she'd had as a child. They dragged Mati out of the apartment, shoved her into a car and sped to another apartment the family owned. If Matilde didn't open it they'd blow up the building, they said, producing a grenade. But Graciela wasn't there either, so they shoved Matilde back into the car, sped to her sister-in-law's, and tore apart that place, too. An hour later, they dragged her home again. "So now what are you gonna do?" one of the soldiers asked her. "I suppose I'm going to cry," she told him. But she didn't. By now it was dawn, and all they could do was collapse.[5]

As soon as possible, they sent their son to Spain. Santiago's sister and her family went to Mexico. Other relatives made a point of never mentioning Graciela's disappearance. "So there we were," said Mati, "the two of us—alone and out of our minds."

She stared for a moment at a photo of her daughter (pictured in Fig. 5). "One day I was walking down the street, just walking, going I don't know where. I suddenly realized there was a man keeping step a little behind me. He was laughing one of those soft, cultured laughs. I whirled around and demanded to know what was funny. 'But, *señora*,' he said condescendingly, 'don't you realize you're talking to yourself?' 'Yes!' I *screamed* at him. 'Yes, I am talking to myself because my daughter has been disappeared my daughter has been kidnapped my daughter is missing!' Well that shut him up. But he looked at me with loathing, and walked away.

"I am a very ordinary, common, vulgar woman," says Matilde. "Of course I read, my father taught me early. But I was always in the kitchen, I

FIGURE 5. Buenos Aires, 1989: Matilde Mellibovsky holds a photo of her daughter, Graciela, during a march preotesting President Menem's executive pardon of military officers awaiting trail for crimes committed during the Dirty War. In 1990 Menem also pardoned the ex-commanders who had been convicted in 1985 of crimes against humanity. (Photo credit: Eduardo Longoni).

liked movies, I daydreamed. I had an idea of 'doing something' (as we used to say) once the kids were older. But they took my daughter and the next day I was a Mother of the Plaza de Mayo. There was no other choice. Now come into my kitchen."

The kitchen is enormous, tiled in royal blue. There is a large, round welcoming wooden table. On the wall are black-and-white crayon drawings, vaguely figurative, which I assume have been done by the grandchildren. Matilde stands behind me as I look more closely at the drawings. Then very softly she says, "Every time I dream of her, I get up and make a drawing. She comes to me, and I make a drawing. . . .

"I think often of how she must have died," she continues, eerily calm. "The worst must have been for her to feel so alone, in a concentration camp one is so utterly alone. And so I think of how she must have died, to be with her there, to be with her then."

How she must have died. . . . The images conjured by the phrase are too much to bear in this homey kitchen, smelling now of coffee and warm milk. For me, at least. Matilde has learned to inhabit a zone where past, present, life, death, lucidity, madness have changed, intermarried. At once present and absent, sustaining and sustained, Graciela is *there.*

"It's such an *intimate* thing to lose a child," I blurt involuntarily.

"Now you've said something profound," says Matilde. "You'll come often, and we'll talk."

OUR VISITS GO ON for hours. Matilde is full of stories she tells in bits and pieces, fits and starts. Certain fragments recur so often they come to seem like legends unto themselves. Some days her memory floods, and the details of several narrations are swept along together, like the furnishings of a many-roomed house being washed away.

Today when I arrive Matilde is calm, absorbed in a book lavishly illustrated with old photographs. *One Hundred Years of Moísesville* celebrates the best-known Jewish colony in Argentina, founded in 1890 as a refuge from the czar's pogroms. Graciela's great-grandparents are buried there; it's where Matilde was raised. We page through photos of dazed arrivals in the Argentine port; weathered farmers in their wheat fields; children in schools, Hebrew and secular.

Until the mid-nineteenth century, there was but a handful of Jews in Argentina, virtually all New Christians who had converted, but hadn't convinced the Spanish Inquisition. In the New World, they observed no Jewish rites, and practically all of them married Catholics. In the eighteenth and nineteenth centuries, there were occasional French and German arrivals who came to expand their already immense fortunes. They as well tended to assimilate, so there was no specifically "Jewish presence" in Argentina.

Yet even before the arrival of the Jews from Eastern Europe, there was significant anti-Semitism in the Argentine press. In 1881, Jews were referred to as "noxious insects, powerful parasites." An influx of their numbers was likened to "an injection of leeches."[6]

"Argentina was supposed to be a Promised Land," Santiago would tell me, "a land of milk and honey. I have here the Czar's original decree ordering my grandfather, Leon Mellibovsky, to leave the royal territory within forty-eight hours. Neither he, his family, or their descendants could ever return. He got the news on a Friday morning and, as you know, Jewish law forbids sadness on the Sabbath. But it seemed to him the *last* Sabbath, and he broke out crying during dinner on Kabbalat Shabbat. Sinning, he told his family they were banished, and then they all sinned together, I suppose. My mother's family also fled in terror. With us, foreboding is bred in the bone."

Santiago still insists he has no memory for history. "Dates and names are like things that float away from me; before I know it, they're over the horizon. Images are different," he says. "Once I've seen it, a face or an image is with me forever."

There is a wall of faces in the House of the Mothers of the Plaza de Mayo (located near the Congress). Photos of their missing children. It was Santiago who conceived the idea, developed and copied the negatives, cropped and arranged the prints. Above the panel are Santiago's words: "All Mothers One Mother All Children One Child." "The unification of all the mothers," he tells me, "the unification of all the pain." For the last fifteen years, Santiago has marched every Thursday with the Mothers in the Plaza de Mayo.

"Well, go ahead," he challenged me one day, "aren't you going to ask?"

"Ask what?"

"Why the Mothers were so brave and the fathers so cowardly? It's a favorite question among journalists."

I remind him that I am not a journalist.

"I'll tell you, anyway," he says. "We made an agreement. Since the father was the family's provider, he would be more of a 'watchdog.' At the beginning, the Mothers met secretly in church basements, each one arriving and going home by circuitous routes. Some fathers went too, but remained outside in order to witness, and testify, if anything should happen. We knew that if *we* were to occupy the Plaza, they'd mow us down. They had gunners on all the roofs. So you know this.

"But I tell you, we haven't held up. Many fathers have died, committed suicide. Fathers are pathetic, you see. The violence we feel toward the guilty ones we turn on ourselves. In Argentina, the guilty remain faceless. So when we look in the mirror, we want to draw blood.

"If it weren't for Matilde, I would be dead. Of this I am certain."

The two seem a study in contrast. She appears nervous and jittery, blindly fiddles with small objects. His demeanor is reserved, fastidious, and rather stern. He focuses on details his wife ignores, meditates before he speaks, is given to long periods of silence. He rarely pronounces his daughter's name, and cannot speak of her in any personal detail. When I ask if the two of us might talk alone, he says, "Bring batteries and lots of tape."

Our appointment is for the following Saturday.[7] When I arrive, he is more subdued, more self-contained, than ever. Once seated, he barely moves. His whole body emanates tension.

He tells me he spent the morning making salad—washing four kinds of lettuce, chopping tomatoes, peppers, beans, mushrooms, sprouts. "Each ingredient must be done separately," he explains, "they each require different *knives*."

"We don't have to do this," I tell him.

"Oh, yes we do," he says. "I'm prepared."

I take out the tape recorder and say—lightly, I hope—"Now, don't be afraid."

"I'm always afraid"—right away he's talking—"I live in a permanent state of fear. I have known repression in the Republic of Argentina since I was six years old. My first image of terror goes back to September 6, 1930, when the fascist revolution broke out against the government of Yrigoyen.[8] We had a house then right in the center of the city, we were hiding in the basement, hiding from 'The Cossacks,' that's what we called the Argentine cavalry. From the little windows that gave onto the street, we saw the Cossacks with their sabers unsheathed, hitting people with the broad, flat side of the blade. I was twelve, peering out at the young aristocrats who supported this revolution, the young nobles in their fancy cars, with soldiers on the running boards shooting their pistols *tac, tac, tac!*"

He takes a breath.

"What I hadn't seen from my little window was how they'd killed my best friend. He had just gotten his first pair of long pants and couldn't wait to show his parents. During a lull, he'd gone out, tried to cross the Plaza de Mayo. They blew him to pieces with a *dum-dum*, a bullet that explodes on entering the body." He sighs, slumps down. "The most advanced bullet is no longer the *dum-dum*, but the Ithaca which can penetrate iron. They killed my daughter with such a bullet, in the back.

"How do I know? I have the signed confession of my daughter's torturer. Oh yes, the document exists. But I won't show it to you. And I won't tell you his name. You heard what I said about fear.

"What I'll tell you is this: He went to work like an executive, wearing a suit and tie. He tortured all morning, went out for lunch, then tortured in the afternoon. In the evening, he went home to his family.

"Is this recording? In 1983, Graciela reappeared. By then she was dead, but as Matilde says, Graciela is always present, always. What I mean is this: There was an international meeting here of statisticians. And the human rights group of the American Statistical Association began investigating the cases of two of their fellows—one of whom was our daughter. Graciela's torturer sent them a letter, saying he had information. And so they returned to Argentina, and met with that bastard who, for an unrelated offense, was in military prison. He said he knew where our daughter was buried; for five thousand dollars he would tell. He wanted half the money up front. No deal, we told him, no fucking deal.

"We later found out where our daughter is buried. Not from the one who actually killed her, but from someone who hauled the bodies. It's a common grave, in a corner of a cemetery near Quilmes.[9] Easy access in and out, a consideration for the trucks.

"We are legally entitled to an exhumation, but there are five hundred people in this grave. We'd need the permission of every other family, and somehow that doesn't feel right. I've seen photos of other mass graves in Argentina—pits full of broken bones, all mixed together.

"You know, the funeral was invented by Neanderthal Man. He couldn't bear the carnivores tearing at his dead, feeding on their flesh. So he covered his dead with piles of rocks. And don't we still leave stones when we visit a loved one's grave?[10] The gesture is born of an ancient connection—the primal need for a tomb. The oppressors well know: *Consume the dead, and you consume the living*.

"What else can I tell you. After fourteen years, every day I feel more desperate. There's no anesthesia for this pain, no scarring over. They say time heals—but no, *el tiempo no lo cura, locura*. Time doesn't heal, it makes you crazy.

"I see my daughter being tortured. I see her alone, about to die.

"I am holding the paper signed by the man who tormented her."

He is holding nothing. He stares down at his empty hands, and is silent.

ANDRÉS FRANCISCO VALDEZ tortured many people, but Graciela Melli-bovsky stood out in his memory: "... a political economist ... yes ..." and then he described her ordeal under torture.[11] He further declared that sometime during September 1976, Graciela was taken out and shot, as her father had told me.

He stated this, as the document says, "In the city of Buenos Aires, on the seventeenth day of May, in the year 1984, in the headquarters of the Argentine National Commission on the Disappeared." Taking his testimony were Raúl Aragon, Susana Aguad, and Dr. Raúl Rayes. All together Valdez deposed on six occasions: April 2 and 11; May 17 and 31; June 6 and 27, 1984. Sessions were relatively short, as he was a prisoner then in Penitentiary No. 17, having tried for more than his "fair share" of the spoils stolen from detainees.

Valdez gave information on scores of former colleagues and *desaparecidos*. In the early '70s, he was a low-ranking army officer; in 1975, his career took an upward turn. According to his deposition, he attended the School of the Americas, at Fort Gulick, in Panama, which specialized in counterinsurgency, intelligence, and interrogation. Valdez said he studied primarily with Green Berets who had served in Vietnam and French Black Berets who had fought in Cambodia. Upon returning to Argentina, he was promoted to a job in "intelligence," which was, of course, a euphemism.

Valdez's deposition was more an attempt at commerce than an act of confession. He inserted errors to render his testimony inadmissible in the upcoming trial of the ex-commanders. For example, he asserted that in 1976 Graciela Mellibovsky was held in a camp called Olympus; but El Olimpo did not exist until 1978. And he tormented her parents with an image they can neither trust nor forget. An image—perhaps invented, perhaps not—of their daughter in extremis.

Valdez made no pretense of remorse. Susana Aguad put it to me this way: "He'd come forward to make a deal. He thought if he testified for us, he wouldn't be court-martialed by them. Anyway, he eventually found himself a deal. Some embassy got him out. He's got a new country, a new name, a 'normal' life with his family."[12]

UNTIL 1983, WHEN Valdez came forward, the Mellibovskys had hope that their daughter was alive. Within hours of the violent break-in at their apartment, they began a desperate round of visits to the police, the military, embassies, human rights and Jewish organizations. There was no official trace of Graciela. Yet there was a sign that she was alive. Five days after being kidnapped, Graciela called. Matilde gives me her notes of their conversation, which is too painful for her to recount.

Just before the line was cut, Matilde asked, "When will I see you, will I see you again?"

Graciela answered, "No, mamá, never. . . ."

Others permitted themselves a different view. "According to what we're seeing, the tendency is not to kill them. So it's best to do nothing. Anyway, there's nothing to do." Such was the advice given to Santiago, the very week of Graciela's call, by a senior functionary of the DAIA (Delegation of Argentine Jewish Associations). Representing congregations, schools, and cultural organizations, the DAIA is the official link between its members and the Argentine government.

Soon after, Matilde got an appointment with the same official, Marcos Barbarosch. "He was pathetic," she told me, "totally useless. He tried to ignore the reason I'd come, he even cut me off to take a phone call from a friend. I kept telling him my daughter had disappeared, but he talked over me—*his son*, the financial genius, *his son*, the soccer star of San Lorenzo. . . ."

Barbarosch came to have nicknames among relatives of the Jewish disappeared. One was "guard dog," another was "barbed wire." And that is mild compared with the enmity these families reserve for the highest officers of the DAIA, the organization founded to protect them. It was formed in 1936 to combat a wave of Nazi inspired violence in Argentina. From its inception, it is worth noting, communists and anarchists were excluded. DAIA leaders have been mostly lawyers and businessmen, skilled in their professions but amateurs in terms of organizational leadership. The most common charges against the DAIA were that it was "mediocre," "middle-brow," "presumptuous." The DAIA has always believed that Jews should speak with one voice, and refers to itself as "the community." A prominent philosopher put it to me this way, "These were people who fought to death over the subcommittee on refreshments. What can you expect?"[13] Still, the DAIA has always protested clear cases of anti-Semitism, and even organized a highly effective general strike.

How could such a conflict have arisen? The answer is found, though only partly, in the schizoid history of Jews in Argentina. The largest Jewry in Latin America, the community has by and large done well. Yet anti-Semitism is entrenched in every major institution, particularly the Church, the military, the government and public schools. Every setback in the economy has engendered scapegoating of the country's Jews. And every attack on democracy has featured Jew-hating rhetoric. Labor unrest unleashed a full-scale pogrom in 1919.[14] In the '30s, inspiration came from the Nazis. After the war, Argentina accepted refugees from Hitler's Holocaust even as it welcomed Martin Bormann, Josef Mengele, and Adolph Eichmann. Ex-Nazis modernized the Argentine secret service.

There has never been serious hope among Jews here of eradicating anti-Semitism; rather, the task has been to set "acceptable" limits. But in the chaos of the early '70s, the very concept of "limits" had no currency. And then the Gentlemen arrived, to save "Western, Christian civilization." To a Jewish ear, that clarion call was nerve wracking to say the least. But on the part of some it engendered a paradoxical reaction: to insist that as Argentine citizens Jews could *not* be considered foreigners, that subtextually the junta was including them in "Western, [Judeo-]Christian civilization." They reassured themselves with their history of obeying the laws, of enriching Argentine culture and institutions. And wasn't Israel a highly valued partner in trade? At this time of national reorganization, Argentina *needed* its well-educated, industrious Jews. Certainly the Process would work. How could it not?

As if in answer to a prayer (and *not* just a Jewish one), the dark skies of Argentina were suddenly pierced with the golden rays of prosperity. The new finance minister—José A. Martínez de Hoz—made speculation the order of the day; at a time when the dollar was weak, he printed money, artificially inflating the ranks of the Argentine rich. There were long after-noons spent shopping at Galerías Pacífico, Harrods, and designer bou-tiques. Trips to Europe, Miami, New York—life was better, was it not?

True, people were disappearing. *"Por algo será"* ("There must be a reason"), they said.

Three Jews *had* been singled out: Freud, for undermining the Chris-tian family; Marx, for opposing Christian capitalism; and Einstein, for challenging Christian notions of time and space. Jews *as such* were not being threatened, only "subversives." Synagogues, schools, and other Jew-ish institutions were functioning unmolested (in contrast to the situation in Uruguay, for example). Face to face with people like the Mellibovskys, what could the DAIA say?

To find out, I returned to Buenos Aires in July 1992. Marcos Barbarosch was "unavailable" every time I called, but two men who led the DAIA during the Terror agreed to meet.

"The safety of the whole community was in my hands," insisted a very agitated Nehemias Resnizky, president from 1976 until 1980.[15] He did not want me to record our conversation, and tried physically to eject me when he saw my machine. "These are sensitive subjects," he screamed, but even-tually gave in.

"We had to watch, wait, maintain access," he repeated.

"No," say the Mellibovskys, "to them, our children were a threat. And we were a nuisance. Thank God for Marshall Meyer."

An American Conservative rabbi, Meyer, who died in 1993, had arrived in Argentina in 1959 and stayed until 1985. He was the only foreigner named to the Argentine National Commission on the Disappeared (CONADEP). By nature outspoken and political, he was regarded by the Jewish "estab-lishment" with a mix of hostility, envy, and amazement. At the time of Meyer's arrival, Jews who wanted to affiliate had few options. Almost all temples were Orthodox, with rabbis who had superb Talmudic training, but who lacked secular higher education. As a result, most Jews avoided synagogues. But underneath was spiritual yearning. Meyer, they say, was like a gift from God. His services galvanized the community, particularly the young. A protégé of Abraham Joshua Heschel, Meyer founded the first

Conservative rabbinical seminary in Latin America (renamed in his honor) and the unprecedented Bet El, a synagogue rooted in the Prophetic Tradition and Liberation Theology. From his pulpit, Meyer openly denounced the generals and their Dirty War. Services overflowed, and not only with Jews: Catholics, Protestants, atheists, and of course members of the Secret Service came to hear Meyer's news. He received death threats every week, but still met with relatives of the disappeared, visited jails, and marched with the Mothers of the Plaza de Mayo. Yet he agonized that he was endangering the community. He meditated on his mentor, Heschel, who had angered some Jews by marching on Shabbat with Martin Luther King. "I'm praying with my feet," Heschel had replied to those who charged that he should have been in *shul*. "So how could I stop?" Meyer asked, rhetorically. "I knew that my teacher, a *tzaddik*, would have told me, 'You'll endanger their souls if you are silent.'[16]

"My political position," stated Meyer, "was very clear, and I said it to Resnizky: 'You don't have cordial relations with Hitler.'

"It's not that I think the DAIA was evil," Meyer glossed, "but they were silent, acquiescent. They are guilty of sins of omission, which in Jewish law are as bad as sins of commission." The specter of acts omitted—and committed—by the DAIA still haunts the Jewish community.

By September 1976, when the Mellibovskys made their first desperate visit to the DAIA, reports of Nazi activity in Argentine jails were circulating internationally. Graciela had disappeared on the 25th, and called home on the 30th. On the 28th and 29th, the U.S. House of Representatives had a special session on human rights in Argentina. Burton Levinson, president of the Latin American Affairs department of the Anti-Defamation League (ADL) of B'Nai Brith, testified that anti-Semitism appeared to be a factor in abductions. Also testifying was Father James Weeks, an American priest who had been kidnapped, jailed, and then expelled from Argentina. "In their talk and behavior," Weeks declared, "the kidnappers were like Nazis."[17] The DAIA certainly knew of this session, as they were constantly in touch with the ADL.

Soon after the coup, Morton Rosenthal, a New York rabbi, started getting visits from Argentines whose loved ones had disappeared. By the end of 1976, Rabbi Rosenthal, director of the Latin American Affairs Department of the B'Nai Brith ADL, had a list of over 600 *desaparecidos*. Most, but not all, were Jews. Rosenthal, like Meyer, received anyone who needed help. Of the Jews who went to him, many complained about the DAIA.

"So I sent them these six hundred names," Rosenthal told me in the summer of 1992,[18] "and got no response. Then, about two months later, I had a visit from one Alfredo Baumetz—vice president of B'Nai Brith and a member of the DAIA. 'Where did you get those names?' he kept asking. He brought no information, and requested no cooperation. All he wanted to know was where I'd gotten the names."

Soon after, Rosenthal got a letter from the late Helmut Heinemann, German-born and a top leader of B'Nai Brith in Buenos Aires. "He was extremely irate," said Rosenthal, "I was endangering the community—according to him—and should *stop*."

Rosenthal would not stop. As he saw it, he had a moral obligation to act. Against the better wishes of his immediate superior, and over the opposition of B'Nai Brith, he forged on with the Argentine Prisoners Project, a series of booklets with photos and brief bios of detainees and *desaparecidos*. Rosenthal raised the monies himself, and eventually had 25,000 such pamphlets in circulation.

"Officially," said Rosenthal, "the DAIA didn't obstruct me. They just didn't help, though we promised them anonymity." Nor would they publicly discuss the disappearances.

In 1977, however, they had no choice. On April 15, Jacobo Timerman—the country's most famous journalist, and perhaps its best-known Zionist—was kidnapped from his home by a military commando because the generals suspected that one of Timerman's business partners, David Graiver, was bankrolling the Montoneros.[19] (Timerman, who survived torture, deprivation, and two years of captivity, rendered the ordeal in the indispensable *Prisoner Without a Name, Cell Without a Number*.[20]) There was immediate international protest to Timerman's abduction. A few days after Timerman disappeared, Meyer requested a special meeting at the DAIA, located in the heart of Once, a neighborhood full of Kosher stores and Yiddish signs.

"I said I was going to raise money for a full-page ad," Meyer recounted in one of our last conversations. "It would call for the immediate release of Timerman, and all the other disappeared. Well, all they heard was 'Timerman,' and their immediate reaction was, 'What if he's done something wrong?' As though *anything* could justify disappearance. What about habeas corpus, for God's sake? It was a terrible meeting, in fact the last."

Careful to stay uninvolved with Timerman, the DAIA nonetheless spoke out against several concrete instances of anti-Semitism. But then, on July 27, 1977, the DAIA itself was threatened when Nehemias Resnizky's twenty-two-year-old son, Marcos, was abducted, ostensibly for being "politically suspect" and the son of a Zionist leader. No one can fault the father for doing everything possible to save his son. Given his position,

Resnizky had extraordinary accesss. He went directly to the highest eche-
lons, including Cyrus Vance and the Argentine Minister of the Interior,
the notoriously anti-Semitic Albano Harguindeguy. Ninety-six hours after
he'd been taken, Marcos—who had been hideously tortured—was driven
home by government agents. Recovering him had proved a bloody ordeal.
He'd been taken by the First Army Corps, who did not want to give him
back. So the armed forces of the Interior Department went in and murdered two of his captors. Marcos was then flown to Tel Aviv, where he'd
been granted asylum. The father, too, could have left the country. But he
did not. He continued as president of the DAIA and, at least for a time,
bereaved parents sought his help.

"They couldn't refuse to receive us," said Matilde, "that would have
been too obvious. But they wouldn't see individuals, or couples, only
groups. They'd herd us around, make us wait in the hall. There would be
more than a hundred of us, we'd fill an auditorium. All the officers were
nervous, but Resnizky was a wreck. He kept leaping from his seat, the man
next to him literally had to hold him down. To one of these meetings came
a Polish couple by the name of Russ. Both had survived Nazi concentration camps, in fact that was where they'd met. After the war, they'd 'started
life over' in Argentina. Now both of their children had disappeared. Señor
Russ came with a letter of protest in which he compared the DAIA's conduct to that of the Polish bourgeoisie in the thirties. A number of us were
taken aback, but his charges were so well formulated. And he'd been there,
we had not. In any case, Resnizky should have resigned. After recovering
his son, it was clear he couldn't agitate for anyone else."

From 1977 on, DAIA statements and publications indicate ever closer
relations with General Albano Jorge Harguindeguy, Minister of the Interior. This ministry was integrally involved in the disappearances, and had
its own budget for arms. By now, there was a large number of exiles—
forced and voluntary, Jewish and gentile—and they were testifying to the
press and human rights groups. On March 4, 1978, the Polish novelist and
painter Marek Halter wrote in Le Monde that "Jews in Argentina were
more frightened than those in Hungary." Harguindeguy was furious, and
told Resnizky to write a rebuttal. After some temporizing, Resnizky
declared that "[Halter's] article was prejudicial, and harmful to our country . . . [and] contained information that was absolutely inexact [sic]. Jewish religious, educational and cultural life was normal. That," he stressed,
"has been and continues to be our objective. Jewish life and Zionist activity are free in Argentina." That statement was circulated internationally by
the World Jewish Congress. In late April, the Congress met in Herzlia,

Israel. In his address to that body, Resnizky focused on neo-Nazism in the United States and Europe. Yes, he said, there were anti-Jewish incidents in Argentina as well, but they should not be exaggerated "lest they benefit interests outside the Jewish community." In other words, the leadership should not appear alarmist or "pushy." The DAIA, Resnizky said, had made good use of its access to the government in order to have several anti-Semitic magazines banned. About detainees or *desaparecidos*, he didn't say a word. But he reminded his fellow delegates that chapters could not get involved in foreign domestic matters without the express prior permission of the local Congress authorities. In the case of Argentina, that meant the DAIA.[21]

Resnizky was proving to be a good ambassador. And so in 1978 the junta had him make a video of his recent statements. That film was seen by Esteban Takacs, Argentine Ambassador in Ottawa and a delegate to the Canadian Jewish Congress.[22] The film seemed to prove that official Jewry in Argentina was constrained by persecution, or "captive," the one exception in the Congress's nonintervention policy. That perception was strengthened by the visit of Renée Epelbaum, a prominent Mother of the Plaza whose three children were missing. When the Canadians made overtures, the DAIA threatened to bolt firom the World Jewish Congress.

"So," said Rosenthal, "because the DAIA was dishonest about the situation in Argentina, organized world Jewry was essentially passive." Resnizky had also paved the way for General Videla's 1978 visit to the States.

Rosenthal was fighting an uphill battle within his own organization. But that changed in 1979, when Ben Epstein, National Director of the ADL, traveled to Buenos Aires. What follows is from an internal memo, dated February 16, 1979:

> As an American student in Berlin in the 1930s I saw Hitler rise to power and the almost immediate consequences. I have seen Spain under fascism and Russia under communism. . . . But [none] of this prepared me for the [time] I spent in Buenos Aires. . . .
>
> I found the Jewish community . . . well informed, sophisticated, rich and frightened. . . .
>
> My meeting with the DAIA was in many ways a frightening experience. The fear of being overheard, the care with which they choose their words, and their request that I take no notes was the

climate of our luncheon. . . . The most shocking thing to me was to hear intelligent Jews condone the disappearance or arrest of people if they were communist. They failed to understand my distress, [accepted] the designation of communist without evidence, trial, or public examination of the allegation.

The clean streets, the orderly activity, the quiet kind of atmosphere is [like what] I remember [from] the first year of Adolph Hitler. Like Germany, this is repression without accountability. . . .[23]

Even after the OAS visited Argentina in September 1979, and issued its devastating 1980 report on human rights abuses there, the DAIA held its line. "We are not going to publicize our concern unless it is absolutely necessary," Mario Gorenstein, now president of the DAIA, told the *Los Angeles Times* in September of 1980. In December of that year, Gorenstein publicly battled Jacobo Timerman, who had accused Argentina of "being fascist."

The DAIA had most everyone stymied, even Cyrus Vance. In a confidential ADL memo, dated May 11, 1981, Vance was quoted as having expected the DAIA to set forth their problems during his recent visit to the Argentine capital. On May 12, Gorenstein was in Washington meeting with members of the House. He downplayed concerns about the disappeared, and said that only a hundred Jews were missing. In fact, Rosenthal had sent the DAIA his most recent list, with over 700 missing Jews.

IT IS HARD to say which of the DAIA's omissions and commissions most embitters parents like the Mellibovskys. Perhaps it is the *Special Report on Detainees and Desaparecidos* issued by the organization in January 1984, after the democratic election of Alfonsín. They did the report as soon as the president announced the formation of the CONADEP, or Argentine National Commission on the Disappeared. With great ceremony, they brought their report to the CONADEP as though to say, "Here, you're just getting started, we've been at it for years." In the Introduction, the DAIA not only states, but underscores that "[We] assumed, with neither evasion nor vacillation, the defense of Jews whose disappearance was reported to our institution. . . . [This, from] our unconditional commitment to the integrity of Jewish life, the defense of Jewish interests, which are inseparable from human rights."

"Such lies stop the heart," says Matilde.

And then there is "Appendix 11," or the infamous "195." This consists of a list—195 detainees and *desaparecidos*. Why 195? No one seems to know.

(By then, Rosenthal had sent the DAIA 1200 names.) The list is remarkable in other ways, as well. For one thing, it's full of mistakes. Known survivors are listed as dead, or missing. Eusebio Fingerhut had the dubious pleasure of presenting himself at the DAIA and asking, "So, do I look dead?" Fingerhut had testified in exile, but apparently the DAIA wasn't paying attention. According to this report, Santiago Mellibovsky waited nearly a year before reporting the disappearance of his daughter. And only one of Renée Epelbaum's missing children is included; it is well known in Argentina that she lost all three. Certain names have clarifying tags: "Presumed guerrilla," "presumed Montonero," "worked in shantytowns," "active since youth in politics."

"It's a police report," Matilde fumed. In protest, a group of families (including the Mellibovskys) wrote, and published, an extensive rebuttal.[24]

I asked Gorenstein why the report was so controversial.[25]

"Look," he said, "anything was insufficient if it didn't bring back their relatives. No matter what you did, if it didn't work, they were suspicious. Blah, blah, blah, I've heard it all. The DAIA *did* try."

Gorenstein is a fair, portly man who flushes easily. He is an exquisitely dressed attorney given to emphatic gestures and imposing postures. Even when he is calm, he speaks loudly.

I tell him I'm puzzled by the ideological tags. That was not the kind of information supplied by parents. Could the list have come from the Ministry of the Interior?

"Very possible," he says, sitting up straight, "we were always in close contact."

I ask why the list is so small.

"Every case reported to the DAIA is on the list," he says, without blinking. "Not everyone came to us for help." He leans toward me, across his desk. "Do you know who, more than anyone, came running to the DAIA when they were in danger? The ones who most clamored for the DAIA to respond? The marginal ones, people who for ideological reasons—or whatever reasons—weren't interested in the Jewish community."

"Seems strange," I say.

"Well, I've been able to prove it. And I don't see that those who were saved, those who managed to survive, realize what it means to be a Jew in a situation of discrimination. They haven't become active in the community, on the contrary. Perhaps for this reason, the work that you are doing is beside the point. People who could testify, who could give an experienced Jewish perspective aren't around."

"What," I ask, "is 'an experienced Jewish perspective?'"

"To work for the continuity of the Jewish community in Argentina. To be concerned."

What about his conflicts with Marshall Meyer, I ask.

He says he has none.

"You threw Meyer out of a World Jewish Congress Meeting in São Paulo in 1980."

"Oh, that, right. Well, he was out of order. Like any organization, the Congress has its structure. The DAIA is the official Argentine delegate. We were *letting* Marshall be there. In fact I, as president of the DAIA, let him come. Others didn't want him. And he, in his usual spectacular fashion, introduced subjects out of context."

"What was the context?"

"Other subjects."

"Marshall brought up the disappeared," I say.

"Politically, the DAIA is the head of the community. That's just how it is," he says tightly. "And it's been that way for decades."

"But why not discuss the missing? People were being taken even as the meeting happened. And by then it was known that outside pressure was important."

"That goes beyond the community, as such. It seems to me," he says, shaking with rage, "that a few pages from this book are missing. A few pages have been torn out. If we're going to tell things—Marshall Meyer, São Paulo—let's tell it all. I'll add the material.

"Did you know that as president of the DAIA, I got *Holocaust* on Argentine TV? The generals were worried that the scenes of the Warsaw Ghetto Uprising would incite the guerrillas. 'You're not thinking of Argentina's image,' I told them, and that did it. I'm not saying there weren't mistakes, there were, and some out of fear. I admit there was fear. And that's why I can't tell you everything, and I may change a few names. . . .

"Did you know they called me to have Jewish school children lead a parade through the streets of Buenos Aires in favor of the Malvinas war? Why me, I said. What about the Catholic schools? They're far more numerous. Well, that stopped them dead. I was opposed to any sort of acquiescence."

What he recounted about *Holocaust* is true. But there's more to the other story. On April 2, 1982, the country declared war on England over two small islands in the South Atlantic, the Malvinas if you are Argentine; the Falklands, if you are British. As anyone could predict, Argentina hadn't a chance. Five days after the Argentine invasion, such as it was, the DAIA issued a long, flowery statement, from which I excerpt:

. . . The Jewish community . . . celebrates this historic moment together with other sons of the land. . . . The Jewish people, pilgrims through the ages in search of their ancestors' land finally recovered, have had enough experience to understand and support the act of recovery of the Malvinas for the national patrimony. . . .[26]

According to Morton Rosenthal's confidential memo of May 4, 1982, the statement was written by the Argentine government, and brought to the DAIA by government agents who asked the organization to issue the declaration as its own. Rosenthal got this information from an anonymous caller who said his father was active in the DAIA.

My interview with Gorenstein, which lasted nearly two hours, was full of such partial truths, untruths, and calumny. Gorenstein closed our interview with a blustering anecdote intended to prove his power and assimilation.

"I'd got this call from [General Ramón J.] Camps [Buenos Aires chief of police]. He wanted to meet. I didn't want to, but people said I'd better. All right, but I set conditions. He meets my conditions. You see, I knew Camps was a real anti-Semite, but a real one, and I had an instinctive strategy. He would think I, as leader of the Jewish community, would be less than Argentine. Well, I wanted him to know that I am Argentine. So I said, General, you're from the Cavalry, aren't you? In such-and-such year, you were in such-and-such regiment? *I'm* interviewing *him*, see. But how do you know? he asks. And I tell him, I did my military service in that regiment. I'm giving him the message he's talking to an *Argentine*. Well, I have the advantage of rank over you, he says. Very well, I reply, I accept the rules of the game. . . ."

But "the game" would have him only as a pawn.

"EVEN JEWS PICK ON the Jews," Resnizky railed at me in Buenos Aires. "I am *not* a Prophet, I am a human being. And these were inhuman times."

Unlike Gorenstein, he is a deeply troubled and, I think, remorseful, man. In responding to protest by the Mellibovskys and other parents, he admitted that "more could have been done." After lung and brain cancer he's dying, he tells me, and he indeed looks ill. We need an *objective* history, he says imploringly, and gives me two bulging files of clippings and documents from the DAIA, nothing that adds anything new. He insistently taps his finger on the cover of the *Special Report*, whose very purpose was to obscure the truth.

Resnizky's behavior is fraught with the double discourse that makes Argentina so maddening, so surreal. The Terror depended, at least in part, on the skillful wielding of contradiction. On the one hand, there was no official anti-Jewish policy at the highest levels of the regime. The generals were too careful of their image vis-à-vis Washington for that. Israel was a leading buyer of Argentine wheat, and Argentina a major customer for Israeli weapons. That was an irony that cut both ways. Even as exiles poured into Israel, Uzis were being used in the Argentine camps.

As was noted earlier, Jews—less than 2 percent of the Argentine population—account for about 10 percent of the missing. The explanation, however, does not point to an out-and-out Jew hunt.[27] Rather, Argentine Jews are largely urban and well educated. They are well represented in journalism, the arts, psychology, and psychiatry—"categories of guilt," in the parlance of the regime. Having your name in the wrong address book was also a category of guilt, and so was getting caught by random chance. In common with the Nazis, the Argentine commanders directed their violent policies toward those they considered aliens. But where Hitler's definitions of Otherness were clear and specific, those of the Argentine tyrants were comparatively fluid and ambiguous. The Argentine junta, as we have seen, was obsessed with the "hidden enemy."

Since late 1976, it has been documented that once in the camps, Jews were subjected to special torments. Verbal abuse and other degradations came straight from the Nazis; pictures of Hitler embellished numerous blood-stained walls. (Marcos Resnizky was tortured in such a room.) And yet what the DAIA said was largely true—schools and synagogues, even the Zionist Youth, were active. So the Repression, they argued, wasn't a "Jewish problem." But "Jewish life" was no exception. By the "rules of the game," anyone could be "sucked off" the street and disappeared.

Says Rosenthal, "The Prophetic tradition of social justice is understandably alien to Latin American Jewry. Social *injustice* is the norm. That's what makes the work so difficult. They can hardly envision social justice. More primary is the violation of solidarity. In the Middle Ages, whole communities would raise ransom—even for strangers, for Jews captured by pirates. But the DAIA refused to rescue their own."

Nor, I would add, did they acknowledge their fallen. In its attitudes and behavior, the DAIA reflected not only the passivity of the general population, but the habits of the regime itself. "The repression is directed against a minority we do not consider Argentine," said then de facto President Jorge Videla in 1976. Likewise, with few exceptions, detainees and *desaparecidos* were not considered part of "the community." In discarding lists of the missing, the DAIA—symbolically, if not literally—threw away human lives.

"In my hands," said Resnizky, holding his hands out in front of me, "lay the safety of the whole community, the community *as such*." Jewish law forbids trading one life for another. And most any law—sacred or secular—may be broken in order to save a human life. Says the Talmud, "One who destroys a single life . . . destroys an entire world; and one who preserves a single life . . . preserves an entire world."[28] "A miracle, a universe," is a human life in the Jewish tradition.

Granted, the DAIA was a political, not religious, entity. And its mandate is entirely secular. Yet like the regime it, too, manipulated religion. The junta blamed parents, especially mothers, for having raised "subversive" children. The DAIA waged a similar campaign, saying to parents like the Mellibovskys, "This is what happens without Jewish education." As though religious Jews had not disappeared. As though secular individuals do not lead hallowed lives.

Politically, the DAIA's lack of acuity is astonishing. "Divide and conquer" is what tyrants always do. Insisting that it alone could speak for "the community," the DAIA fatally weakened its position.

But why were they so ill-prepared? I asked Gregorio Klimovsky.[29] A renowned mathematician and philosopher, he has always been highly visible as a Jewish intellectual, and served on the Argentine National Commission on the Disappeared. Mild and quietly jovial, he is known for his benevolence.

"I'm going to say something that is perhaps unjust," he said slowly, "but I believe it nonetheless. The leadership was not so uncomfortable with what was going on. People talk about the poor, frightened Jewish community. I don't see it that way. They simply didn't want to do anything. Some have even said so. What about the 'abuses'? 'A shame,' they said, 'but that is the price that must be paid.'"

Terror does ghastly things to the human mind and heart. And Argentines were terrorized, had been since before the coup. The country as a whole was largely silent during the Dirty War. Since torture and death were castigations for *thoughts*, people tried to stop thinking. "We knew but we didn't know," would later become a refrain.

But what about intellectuals who, in the comfort and safety of their offices in foreign universities and think tanks, also believed "that *that* was the price that had to be paid" for so-called order? They had a lot more power than the DAIA, and basically nothing to lose. In an essay on *Prisoner Without a Name, Cell Without a Number* for *Commentary* (the politically conservative Jewish monthly), Mark Falcoff took Timerman to task for writing that Argentina was "fascist" and "totalitarian":

As is necessarily the case in any urban setting where the forces of order must contend with the virtual invisibility of the enemy, a blanket repression is often the only means which offers any hope of success. In such situations—let us not mince words—the distinction between terrorist and suspect, between sympathizer and activist, indeed, between innocent and guilty, is often lost— but in the end the job can be done, if the will is there to do it.[30]

To my mind, when the distinction between innocent and guilty does not matter, civilization itself has been murdered. Of course, others have a different view, like Ronald Reagan, who reversed Carter's stand on human rights and ended the U.S. arms embargo to Argentina. Reagan and Gorenstein were both elected in 1980. Reagan was probably never briefed on Gorenstein, but the Argentine certainly got the message from the American. And from prominent neoconservative coreligionists.

The DAIA behaved reprehensibly, it is true. But it was absurdly out of its league. "We are a generation traumatized by the Holocaust," Resnizky wrote and said repeatedly, though he never elaborated. Rather, he is obsessed with "the dignity and decorum of the Jewish community," one of the signature phrases of the DAIA's *Special Report*. Again, shame attaches not to the violent, but to the victims. Why insist on "decorum"; why omit "safety"? Because the former has the ring of aristocracy; the latter speaks of need.

If the DAIA had been looking for lessons from the past, it did not have to go back fifty years, or even leave Argentina. All it had to do was recall a pivotal incident from its own recent history. When Eichmann was executed in Israel in 1962, hideous riots broke out in Argentina, culminating in the "Sirota affair," in which neo-Nazis kidnapped a college student named Graciela Sirota and carved a swastika into her left breast. The reaction was hysterical and schizophrenic—people wanted anarchy so they could get revenge, but also a military crackdown so there would be law and order. Then the president of the DAIA, Dr. Isaac Goldenberg, cut through the horror and confusion to proclaim: "We must defend democracy and its lapses. Even when Jews are the victims. We must insist on due process, on innocence until guilt is proven."[31] How could the DAIA have forgotten their own visionary? How could it squander such inherited wisdom?

"MY DEAR FRIEND," said Jacobo Timerman,[32] "I'm not *defending* anything. But you expect too much. History leaves no lessons. For the human race refuses to learn. Least of all about terror. There's not one example of a people that has learned from its past. Individuals maybe, but no communities, and certainly no nations.

"Yes, the DAIA was the Argentine *Judenrat*.[33] Yes, they gave names to the generals.[34] But we must judge them as criminals, not as Jews. Throughout history, *everyone* has been complicit."

Certain individuals have learned from history. Even as the DAIA prevaricated, Graciela Sirota—the woman with the swastika carved into her breast—was fighting for human rights. Marshall Meyer, Morton Rosenthal, Israeli Ambassador Ram Nirgad, Cyrus Vance, Jimmy Carter, to name just a few—actually saved lives. Such individuals do forge community consciousness. Meyer created Jewish Liberation Theology in Argentina, and risked his life to do so. His former congregants and students carry that with them and will pass it on. In joining with like-minded priests and ministers, and with secular human rights groups, Meyer demonstrated that Jews did not have to segregate themselves in order to be safe. Or to throw off their Judaism to accommodate the "rules of the game." Those lessons may seem elementary, but in Argentina, they marked a Jewish revolution.

MY LAST EVENING of that month in Buenos Aires I spent with Matilde. When in March 1992 the Israeli Embassy was bombed, Santiago was home taking a nap. The window by the bed exploded, and flying glass lacerated his head and face. Yet hours later, he was on television news, bearing witness to the death and wreckage in his neighborhood. Their apartment was nearly destroyed, but thanks to good friends, it was soon made livable.[35]

As always we go out on the terrace, though it is freezing cold. The Israeli Embassy has been reduced to a miniature desert. In truth, all that remains is coarse gray sand. People were killed across the street. The building itself looks mortally wounded. The walls are collapsed, pipes and wiring hang. Matilde tells me again about the kidnap she saw there in '75. How sudden, how violent it was, how the boy who was taken never came back.

4

The Land Mourneth

In Corrientes, practically nothing has been investigated. The whole subject is taboo.

—Sergio Tomasella

The *campesinos* are still so afraid that the elders have yet to tell the youths what happened, what happened *to them*. The one thing they have learned from history is that knowledge is a very dangerous thing.

—Father Jorge Torres

THIS IS THE STORY OF A REVOLUTION SO SMALL, SO MODEST, AND SO far away from Buenos Aires that the vast majority of Argentines have no idea that it actually happened. In the remote northeastern province of Corrientes the peasants have lived since the Conquest in medieval poverty—isolated, exploited, and silent on the ranches *(estancias)* of their *patrones*, or *trabajando a la golondrina*—poetic Spanish for itinerant labor, an expression in which desperately wandering workers are metaphorically transformed into the comforting image of swallows. Impelled by unlivable conditions, strengthened by the Living Gospel, and guided by the priests, nuns, and bishops associated with liberation theology, the peasants began—slowly, tentatively, and peacefully—to organize. They needed more efficiency in the backbreaking labor of growing tobacco, wanted the right to set their prices as guaranteed by the Constitution, were desperate for schools, clinics, and asphalt roads. So careful was this movement that land reform was excluded from its lexicon, in favor of the less incendiary statement *la tierra para quien la trabaja* ("who works the soil deserves the land"). In the feudal context of Corrientes, such acts of peasant analysis were in themselves revolutionary, and incited reprisals from the whole series of elected and de facto governments of the early 1970s. By the time of the 1976 coup, the movement's most important leaders were already in prison, and most of the others were too frightened to meet. The material aims of this movement were so reasonable and necessary that, when it implanted itself, the local infrastructure of the Dirty War coopted the major gains and distributed them as lordly gifts. At the same time, it decimated what was left of the Agrarian Leagues, occupied remote villages with tanks and trucks, and billeted soldiers in rural nurseries and schools. The dictatorship completed the campaign of destruction begun by its predecessors. Terror was shamelessly out in the open. Activist priests were run off the road, nuns were strip-searched in their homes, peasants were tortured in the fields. In the feudal province of Corrientes, the forces of repression were the same quartet as always—the landowners, the military, the police, and the traditional hierarchy of the Catholic Church. Impunity is their portion, their bounty from the deep and narrow straits of local history.

WERE IT NOT FOR the International League for Peoples' Rights and Freedom, I might never have learned of the obscure Agrarian Leagues. At its Third Congress, held in Paris in 1987, the league focused on the problem of impunity in the fragile new democracies of Latin America. It was resolved that each member country would hold a Tribunal Against Impunity with direct testimony from survivors and witnesses, expert counsel for the prosecution and defense, and distinguished international judges. The trials themselves would not be legally binding, but it was hoped that their moral power would have legal effect. At the very least, the countries would be shown to be in violation of international human rights conventions that they had previously signed.

The Argentine Tribunal Against Impunity took place in Buenos Aires on the crisp fall day of May 4, 1990, in the Centro Cultural General San Martín, a subsidized hub of theaters, libraries, galleries, and meeting rooms. The event was opened by the 1980 Nobel Peace Laureate Adolfo Pérez Esquivel, Argentine Coordinator of Servicio Paz y Justicia (SERPAJ), a lay ecumenical organization whose mission is to battle human rights violations by means that are exclusively nonviolent. As phrased by Pérez Esquivel, "We . . . [have] a commitment to the whole continent: to live the Gospel, with a preferential option for the poor, for the most needy."[1] Deemed a "maximum security risk" by the last military regime, Pérez

Esquivel was illegally arrested in 1977, savagely tortured, and kept hidden for fourteen months in the municipal prison of La Plata. The judges from abroad were Antonis Tritsis, from Greece, former Minister of Education and Religious Affairs under the presidency of Andreas Papandreu and past president of the European Community Ministers Council; and John Quigley, professor of International Law at Ohio University. The Argentine judges were likewise eminent: criminologist Eugenio Zaffaroni and prosecutor Ricardo Molinas, vice president of the American Association of Jurists.

There was real urgency here. Barely seven months before the Tribunal (on October 13, 1989), President Menem enacted an executive pardon to, as he said, "balance" the "two demons" of the Dirty War. A total of 280 individuals supposedly went free—76 accused of leftist subversion, 30 military officers accused of abusing civilians, 164 officers alleged to have participated in recent armed uprisings, and three officers previously convicted of negligent mismanagement of the 1982 Malvinas war. The pardon was unconstitutional and incredibly dishonest: Three of the supposed "subversives" were in fact dead, their bodies years ago claimed by their families; in spite of six years of democracy, nine of those pardoned were still languishing in the netherworld of *detenidos-desaparecidos;* the cases of six others had been dismissed by the courts; and four had already been released.[2]

What hung in the balance was this: Less than a month before the Tribunal, Menem announced that he would also pardon the convicted ex-commanders and have them home "in time for Christmas." Many still believed that Menem could be stopped. The presence of a judge from Greece had particular resonance, given that country's recent parallels to Argentina. In 1975 the Greek colonels responsible for the coup of 1967 and the repression that lasted until 1974 were tried publicly by a civilian government swept to office with more than 50 percent of the electorate. The colonels were originally sentenced to the firing squad. But then, on the principle that "death should be banished from governance," President Konstantinos Tstavos commuted their terms to life imprisonment. Accused of "showing weakness," Tsatvos replied: "When we say 'life imprisonment,' we mean 'life imprisonment.' Not one of the colonels ever released. As they prepared the trial of the ex-commanders, Alfonsín and his advisers had looked to Greece for inspiration and precedent. It was hoped that Menem now would do the same. At the Tribunal in Buenos Aires, the Honorable Antonis Tritsis was absolutely stunning. Elegant, urbane, and fluent in two ancient and four modern languages, he drew in his oral decree on 2000 years of legal precedent, moral philosophy, and literature. Far from an ivory-tower intellectual,

Tritsis invoked "the sacred will of a democratic people," and supplemented his scholarship with underground rock and poetry. All of us in the court-room hung on his every word.

The auditorium was filled to overflowing. Before the proceedings got under way, the room buzzed with an intensity that bordered (odd though it might seem) on exhilaration. Strangers introduced themselves without restraint, clasping hands or kissing on the cheek. Reunions were intense, though one I witnessed was silent—the embrace between two men who had lost track of each other in *capucha*. Shaking, they sat down, the bald man pulling lightly on the other's hair, who gently slapped the first man's bearded face. When they could speak they said exactly the same words at exactly the same moment—*estás vivo, no puedo creer*. I can't believe it, you're *alive*. They kept shaking their heads and kneading each other's hands and knees and shoulders.

Such grateful scenes would give way to testimonies of frightful horror, and still, after fourteen years, of convulsive grief. The point was not to prove the guilt of the junta and its minions—there was no room for doubt about that. Nor were there any cries for vengeance against the perpetrators (punishment, yes, within legal means). It was clear, and truly awesome, that the witnesses were fueled not just by abuse and loss and injury, but by an urge that was deeply creative. *Todo se ha dicho*, the generals had ruled, "it's all been said." And since then, both elected presidents had declared, "It is time to turn the page." With their stories the witnesses proved that the "book" was *theirs*, and still in the process of being "written."

As I studied the room, I was struck by a man sitting by himself who seemed to know no one. He was extremely thin, with a narrow, bony face, and nervous deep-set eyes. He wore work clothes and heavy boots. His hair was longish, golden red, his skin was ruddied, roughened, almost burned. He seemed intensely aware that he looked like no one else in this big-city auditorium. He listened to the proceedings in a state of apparent agitation, shifting in his seat, with his arms crossed and wrapped around his torso. But when he was called to testify, his demeanor abruptly changed. He strode with an assertive step to the front of the room, accepted the micro-phone with a practiced hand, and faced the audience with disarming directness. In a thick provincial accent, he spoke to "the historical, collec-tive, unending repression against peasants." The former Secretary General of the decimated Agrarian Leagues, Sergio Tomasella had traveled 1000 kilometers by overnight bus from Corrientes. His testimony (given entirely without notes) unfolded with the impeccable logic and flowing eloquence instilled—I learned later—by a Jesuit education.

"The line is continuous—those who took the land from the Indians continue to oppress us with their feudal structures. And the same Church that blessed the indigenous genocide of the seventeenth century has blessed the very system that keeps us poor, illiterate, isolated, and afraid. 'He hath anointed me to preach the gospel to the poor; he hath sent me to heal the brokenhearted, to preach deliverance to the captives.' This is the Gospel according to Luke. Yet in Corrientes 50 percent of the land is owned by thirty interrelated families. And the *peone* [peon] who wants to own the little patch he has farmed for twenty or thirty years is treated like an unrepentant sinner."

Tomasella himself was arrested in 1974 during the government of Isabel Perón and held prisoner for nearly five years. His wife, also a delegate, was kidnapped, beaten, dumped blindfolded from a truck, and left before dawn on an isolated road.

"The forces of the Dirty War simply began where the previous so-called democracy had left off," he said. "My wife was taken a second time on the very day of the coup. In the countryside, the repression was shameless. They took people in front of their families, tortured them right in the fields, charging the *picana* on the battery of the truck. This happened to my brother-in-law, Juan Antonio ('Tonito') Olivo, in front of his wife and children. They pursued my sister all the way from Corrientes to Buenos Aires, where she'd come to work as a domestic. They kidnapped her on a city street and *nada más* [nothing more]—another *desaparecida*."

Tomasella knew that much of his testimony was coming to us as news. This was primarily an urban audience. To forge a common link, he mentioned Sister Caty. "When I was in jail, our *compañera* Caty stayed with my wife and mother. When my wife fell again, Caty came to Buenos Aires to protest, to search for all of our prisoners and *desaparecidos*. You know Caty as Alice Domon," he says softly, and there are gasps of recognition. A French nun long resident in Corrientes, Domon was kidnapped, along with ten other individuals, including two Mothers of the Plaza, on December 8, 1977, from the Santa Cruz Church in Buenos Aires. The group was meeting to collect contributions with which to publish the names of their missing loved ones in *La Nación* on December 10, International Human Rights Day. The notorious "sting" was orchestrated by Naval Captain Alfredo Astiz, who had infiltrated the Mothers by convincing them that he was one of "theirs," the brother of a *desaparecido*. To the Mothers, he was *El Angel Rubio*, "The Blond Angel." The case of Domon and Sister Leonie Duquet, who perished together in the ESMA, caused a major international scandal and is still an irritant between Argentina and France, which condemned Astiz in absentia. If Astiz attempts to leave Argentina, he will be arrested by Interpol and escorted to Paris to serve a life prison term.[3]

"So what do I want to denounce?" Tomasella asks rhetorically. "That we live under a permanent state of oppression. The last military regime simply took advantage of that history. The governor we had just prior to the coup was a Peronist who owned 40,000 hectares. Peasants were the last group he wanted to hear from. In Corrientes practically nothing has been investigated. The whole subject is taboo.

"So what do I think about this fight against impunity? That it too has historical roots, going back to the seventeenth century, to Bartolomé de las Casas [1474–1566; Spanish missionary and chronicler who crusaded on behalf of the Indians]. We are here to confront both streams of our history. To confront and admit that our whole society is repressive. And why? Because our whole society is dependent. Foreign monopolies impose crops on us, they impose chemicals that pollute our earth, impose technology and ideology. All this through the oligarchy which owns the land and controls the politics. But we must remember—the oligarchy is also controlled, by the very same monopolies, the very same Ford Motors, Monsanto, Phillip Morris. It's the *structure* we have to change. This is what I have come to denounce. That's all." Tomasella held out the microphone, ready to leave, but was immobilized by the *vivas!* and prolonged, passionate applause.

"Please . . . keep the microphone," requested the intrigued and visibly moved Judge Tritsis. "What is your profession?"

"Campesino, of course," Tomasella replied, with some astonishment. "I plant tobacco to sell at market. In order to eat, with my wife and children we plant peanuts, manioc, yams, lettuce, squash, a few tomatoes. I have seven and a half hectares. So if you like I'm a landowner," he says. "But 80 percent of our campesinos are tenant farmers, and 50 percent of the population of Corrientes has had to leave because they can't survive. And why can't they survive—in a province whose soil is fertile, a province that is rich in water and sun? Because 90 percent of the land owned by the *latifundistas* [large landowners] is uncultivated, or badly farmed. This means that 40 percent of our total arable land lies fallow, untended. The owners can't be bothered—they live here, or in Paris, or in Punta del Este. They keep their money in foreign banks. They won't farm to capacity, or allow anyone else to plant, work, harvest. The very earth they hold captive, the God-given earth they abandon. Come to Corrientes and you will see: 'The land mourneth.'"[4]

Many in the audience are openly weeping. Tomasella takes this in, and goes on, quietly and evenly. "When you shudder at the *villas miserias*, try to imagine where these people come from, think about how they got here. We are trying again to organize, but it's hard, people are afraid, and so they leave. And what happens then? They starve anyway. And precisely because they are hungry, they are considered suspicious, 'subversive.' And we all know what that leads to."

"How do you see the future?" asks Tritsis. "Last question," he adds, as though embarrassed at his own unwillingness to let this witness go.

"I look forward," says Tomasella, "with a great deal of enthusiasm. . . ."

"Where does this enthusiasm come from?" the unsettled Tritsis wants to know.

"I believe that truth and justice will eventually triumph. It will take generations. If I am to die in this fight, then so be it. But one day we will triumph.

"In the meanwhile, I know who is the enemy, and the enemy knows who I am, too."

WHEN I LAND at the airport in Goya, Tomasella's home city in Corrientes, there is a line of military police awaiting the arrival of my plane. It is not I who am the object of their scrutiny but Sergio, who is always under surveillance. I learn that in spite of a "counterspy" in the post office, my letters and telegrams were all intercepted. As they stood around the airfield, the officer in charge stood behind Sergio, chatting him up in a jokey, menacing way.

"So you're going a lot to Buenos Aires these days, Tomasella. So many hours on the bus. If you want to fly, talk to us, we could make an arrangement."

Even at the punning reference to the death flights of the last repression, Sergio had kept his back to this crude loquacious spy. When we leave the airstrip, Sergio escorts me right through their line, allowing no sign of recognition that the military police are even there.

It is three years since I first met Sergio at the 1990 Tribunal Against Impunity. He had embraced me warmly then, mistaking me for Brazilian. "*Compatriota,*" he'd said, holding my arms and smiling into my face. When I told him that, no, actually I was from New York, he froze. "You could be CIA, for all I know," he had cried, springing back with genuine fear in his eyes.

Susana Dillon, a Mother of the Plaza de Mayo, had come to my defense, but Sergio was unmoved.

"Do you know Judge Quigley?" he'd challenged. "Why not?" he demanded. And then he stomped off.

A SERPAJ representative tried to soothe me. "They've lost so many, you have to understand that he's right to be afraid. Let him go, we'll help you, but this will take time, you must be patient."

It is now August 1993. Late winter here is balmy. The air is moist, redolent of citrus and the heavier scents of horses, dark earth, and the fumes from beaten down, corroded old trucks. *Otro mundo*—another world—is how *porteños* refer to this region. Just a few days before my arrival, an altar-boy had dreamed of a cask full of gold coins hidden in the basement of the colonial church built by the Jesuits in nearby Santa Lucía. Upon awakening, the boy had followed exactly the instructions of his dream, and to everyone's astonishment, found a trunkful of seventeenth-century Spanish gold. In the wake of the "miracle," I am told, there was scandal: the Vatican was insisting that the centuries-old agreement between a Renaissance Pope and the Catholic Kings be honored, which stipulates that half of the money belongs to Rome.

Sergio has come to meet me with his brother-in-law, Jorge Soler, a quietly warm and serious man. He is the son of a mechanic who emigrated from Spain. I learn a lot about the family from Jorge, particularly at the beginning, while Sergio still seemed to be sizing me up. Jorge is deeply bound to this clan, stayed close all through the Terror, as he calls those years when, in close succession, four members of the family fell. Jorge and his wife Marta live with their children in the small riverbank city of Goya; he is a sales representative, she an agronomist.

We drive in Jorge's car about ten minutes on a straight, flat, dusty road flanked by unworked, partly flooded fields overgrown with reeds and grasses. Occasionally rising up from shallow pools are solitary willows whose branches droop down into the dark gray water. Most everywhere I look there are horses—most of them tethered to trees, though a few are loose, and some are pulling *surkis*, simple two-wheeled wooden carriages. Just beyond what the eye can see are the Paraná River and the rice paddies along its banks. We pass through the military checkpoint and enter the town's low-key morning bustle: children in their white Catholic-school smocks; men lugging crates, machine parts, and plastic vats of gasoline; Indian women selling produce they've arranged on the ground. We proceed to the center of town, and stop at the home of Sergio's mother, Doña Elena.

Doña Elena is the clan's beloved matriarch, and her house is the natural—and frequent—meeting place for everyone in the family. It is to this address that I had sent letters to Sergio, who lives in the country, without mail or phone, about eight kilometers away. Built close to a hundred years ago, the house is old by the standards here. Cool, high-ceilinged, and colonial in design, it has a large patio in the back bordered by a small arcade of bedrooms and what used to be the family store. Growing on the patio are orange and lemon trees, squash, lettuce, tomatoes, bougainvillea, and geraniums. What shade there is is provided by the wash hanging on the line. Like Sergio, Doña Elena is very fair-skinned; her abundant red hair has by now faded to a sandy amber. Well into her seventies, she still has freckles on her arms. She has a broad, open face, light blue-green eyes, and a strong, high-pitched voice. Although her legs are badly swollen, she seems always on the move—cooking, washing, tending her plants and her grandchildren. She welcomes me with straightforward, unaffected warmth. Sergio goes off to do some errands—which unsettles me—but Jorge stays and the three of us go into the kitchen for steaming cups of *cafe con leche*.

Doña Elena talks fluidly in the light, slightly musical accent of Corrientes. She was born, she offers, in the "Italian colony" of Santa Lucía. Her parents emigrated from northern Italy and worked, she says, "like donkeys" in the tobacco and cotton fields with their children. "We all worked together, my parents, aunts, uncles, cousins. Without *peones* [peons], of course. Just ourselves. Gradually my father and uncles bought small parcels of land and even added animals. I had a brother-in-law who by the time he died had 30,000 hectares. The same day he made the purchase he dropped dead. It took everything out of him, the poor man."

Doña Elena married in the early 1940s, had seven children, and with her husband continued with *la chacra*—the local term for field work—until 1961 when they moved to Goya and opened a store, selling groceries, stationery, and household goods. "At that time, the *chacareros* [field workers] could still survive on tobacco, which has always been our mainstay. If not, we could never have opened our store. After the harvest, they could buy a mattress, a poncho, a chair, in good years even a bedframe. This isn't to say they weren't exploited—they were, and without mercy. Many were required to buy food and other staples from their bosses, who then charged high interest on the credit. We know *chacareros* who worked twenty, thirty years for the same *patrón*, raised their children, had grandchildren and then, when they were old—and *campesinos* are old by the time they're forty, destroyed before they're sixty—got thrown off the land with no place to go. After paying the owner 45 or 50 percent of the harvest every year. They even had to pay on their own soup gardens and fruit trees. After a generation and a half, the avocadoes and oranges they'd planted for themselves were lovely, mature, generous—ripe for stealing. The *patrones* simply destroyed these families, whose members were forced to scatter. I know one woman who hasn't seen her children for ten years. It's a sorrow," says Doña Elena, her voice rising, "a desolation."

"Even when you had the store, only the *campesinos* who were close in to town could come," interjects Sergio who has now, to my relief, rejoined us. "Because there were hardly any roads, and during the rains you couldn't go two kilometers. Every year there are these vast lakes, acres and acres totally under water. If you got sick, you simply died; the horses wouldn't move, there was no way to get the truck out—if you had a truck—it was impossible to go on foot to your neighbor. Until the early 1960s, the department of Goya was the 'tobacco king' of Argentina. Visualize the contrast," Sergio commands, "for close to a century, most of the people sitting around Argentine city cafés smoked cigarettes made from tobacco grown here, *here*."

Sergio may be off by a few percentage points—statistics for earlier years are hard to come by—but his argument is valid and important. In 1959–60, 47 percent of the tobacco consumed in Argentina came from the province of Corrientes; by 1968–69, that figure had dropped, stunningly, to 13 percent.[5] The story of this collapse not only helps explain the formation of the Ligas Agrarias but also illuminates how the age-old feudalism here was quickly put to the service of multinational capitalism. At the turn of the century, Corrientes was indeed *el rey del tabaco*, supplying a thriving domestic market. In 1896, in just the city of Buenos Aires, there were no fewer than 681 tobacco manufacturers, and most of these were small, artesanal. By 1942, the number of manufacturers had shrunk to 165. By 1971, there remained only five domestic cigarette companies: Nobleza, Particulares, Massalín y Celasco, Piccardo, and Imparciales.[6] Until 1961, unfiltered cigarettes made from dark tobacco predominated in the Argentine market. By 1962, U.S. tobacco companies, specializing mostly in filtered blond cigarettes, were directing a massive ad campaign at middle-and upper-class women, appealing to their yen for status, glamour, and refinement. At the same time, they saturated the market with product smuggled in. A mere six years later, in 1968, the consumption of blond tobacco was twice that of the traditional dark blend: 881 million packs of blond cigarettes compared with 428 million packs of black. Overall consumption had also increased substantially.[7] The five remaining Argentine producers decided to join, rather than fight, the foreign invaders: Piccardo made a licensing agreement with Liggett and Myers (L&M); Massalín y Celasco with Philip Morris; and Nobleza with American Tobacco ("Lucky Strike"). The two remaining manufacturers made contracts with German companies: Imparciales with Reemtsma Cigaretten Fabriken; Particulates with Brinkman A.G.

The "king of tobacco" was now rather more like a pawn. With their diversified foreign investments, the large landowners could easily weather the change. To further protect themselves, they under-reported the local harvest. This did two things at once: drove up the prices they were paid by the big tobacco companies, and drove down what they owed to the peasants working their land. The means by which they achieved this, the notoriously crooked *clasificaciones*, were a major impetus behind the establishment of the Agrarian Leagues.

The growing season for tobacco is longer than a year; one by one the tiny plants are cradled in, and must be tended individually against bugs and disease. If the planting survives to maturity, the crop is picked leaf by leaf, and it is backbreaking work, particularly in a place like Corrientes where it is done mostly by hand. Classifications of the leaves by "type," that is to say, according to whether the leaves were large or small, smooth or wrinkled, had always been used by the landowners to gain an edge on the market. The concept itself is suspect, since tobacco leaves are shredded in the manufacture of cigarettes. Still, *clasificaciones* here are as old as tobacco itself. In years when demand was high and landowners could sell a great deal of tobacco, they reduced the number of categories; when demand fell—as it did from the mid-1960s—the owners, under contract with the multinationals, decreed as many as five classes of leaves, and would sell from only the two "highest." The lower categories, if they were purchased at all from the *campesinos*, fetched extremely low prices. The *campesinos* were required to divide the leaves themselves, an added burden to their already exhausting harvest labors. Often, however, when they delivered the crop, these classifications were revised, to the advantage of the *patrón*. There was no oversight or official control of this process; it was purely an owners' maneuver, against which the peasants had no ally or representation.

However, two events—both of which occurred outside of Corrientes— provided hope and inspiration for these peasants. The first was the Cordobazo, the tumultuous strike that took place in Córdoba, Argentina's second largest city, in late May of 1969. In power at the time was General Onganía, who three years before had seized the presidency from the democratically elected Arturo Illia, and whose economic program stressed containing wages and limiting workers' rights.[8] On May 29, the city exploded in an uprising led by automotive workers and university students; within hours there was massive participation, and for two days there was intense combat between military and police, and rioters who occupied the city center, burning cars and buses. The Cordobazo ignited a chain reaction in a number of cities around the country; it also proved that workers could fatally destabilize a military dictatorship they rightly despised: Within months Onganía was toppled by the somewhat more conciliatory General Levingston.

The second development—a more direct model for the tobacco growers of Corrientes—took place in the adjacent rural province of the Chaco. It was there, on November 14, 1970, that the first Agrarian Leagues in the history of Argentina were founded. The *chaqueños* (residents of the Chaco) had been energized by the peasants in Paraguay who, in conditions of great danger, had organized in 1969 the Organizaciones Campesinas against the harsh dictatorship of Stroessner. The *chaqueños*—whose main crop was cotton—rose up not only against generally unacceptable conditions, but against a specific foe, a company called Agrex. The Agrex Plan entailed the direct transfer of one million hectares of government-owned land in the Chaco and in the province of Formosa to a consortium of North American companies backed in Argentina by PAL, a business owned by the Lanusse brothers, Pedro and Alejandro, a general, who would seize the presidency (from General Levingston) within a matter of months. The peasants who had farmed those lands for the last half-century were to be summarily evacuated. Coming on the heels of the Cordobazo and solidified with support from the International Movement for Rural Catholic Youth—a non-governmental agency (NGO) recognized by UNESCO—the newborn Agrarian Leagues must have looked formidable. And in fact they were, for they put a halt to the plan and sent Agrex packing.[9]

"As our own problems worsened," Sergio explained, "these models were terribly important. Having left here in the early 1960s to work for a couple of years at the Peugeot factory in Buenos Aires, I'd personally had experience with the auto workers union. It was a revelation, let me tell you. The idea of organizing was totally foreign here, unheard of. Perhaps even more moving to me than the solidarity within the union was the support that came from without—from students, for example, other unions, progressive artists, and intellectuals. That one sector of society would try to understand, and support, another sector—well, that was completely new. I understood right away that you need support *across* the lines. And, naively, I have to say now, we thought maybe, just maybe, it could happen here."

On January 29, 1972, some 3000 peasants gathered in the colonial plaza in front of the white Jesuit church in Santa Lucía to declare the founding of the Agrarian Leagues of Corrientes. The Leagues were totally democratic in structure, and had no affiliation to any political party. No decision was ever made by the central committee without its having been ratified by the local chapters. The individuals at this founding meeting were elected delegates, sent from local councils in every corner of the province, and nearly half were women. Many had traveled for over a day to get there, going miles by foot or *surki* from their settlements to a road where the bus would pass, then waiting there for hours in the subtropical summer heat and humidity. The Leagues' initial goals were clear and specific: (1) the division of harvested tobacco leaves into two, rather than five, classifications; (2) the right to set minimum prices based on the cost of living (in 1966, the earnings from ten kilos of tobacco enabled a peasant to buy twenty kilos of meat; by 1971, with the same amount of tobacco he could buy only six); (3) the assurance of being paid upon delivering the harvest, instead of months later at an always unpredictable rate; (4) League representation in the Provincial Institute of Tobacco; and (5) tractor loans by the provincial government to the many regions that lacked such basic equipment. Then Governor Navajas Artaza, owner of Las Marías, one of the province's most important agro-industrial corporations, responded by offering an eight-year plan that would benefit 500 small tobacco growers.

"At that rate," exploded Sergio, "it was going to take *112 years* to help the 7000 peasants who owned a piece of land and so qualified as small producers." These 7000 represented less than a third of the province's tobacco producers: 70 to 80 percent were sharecroppers, tenants, and migrants— all wretched, unprotected by labor laws, and omitted from the government's offer of a "solution."[10] It was precisely in order to protect this, most unfortunate sector of the *campesinato* that the Agrarian Leagues were formed. The government was simply refusing to recognize the situation that furnished Leagues' raison d'être.

The Leagues of course rejected the governor's overture, and sent its own representatives to Buenos Aires. As Secretary General, Sergio led the delegation, which included several priests who were advisors to the leagues. They were received by the minister himself, who turned out to be Antonio Di Rocco, who had been dismissed from a provincial ministry in the northeast through the combined efforts of the Agrarian Leagues of the Chaco, Formosa, and Missiones. Di Rocco had a long history of betraying peasants to the military and police. For this, he had been rewarded with a minister's portfolio and luxurious offices in the Argentine capital. Di Rocco greeted the delegation with seigneurial Old World charm, and then made clear that if the peasants continued to agitate, they would be crushed.

A dangerous pattern was emerging here: As the Leagues gained access to higher levels of government, they were at the same time exposed to reprisals from higher-powered forces. On February 25, 1972, soon after the meeting in Buenos Aires, General Alejandro Lanusse sent his Minister of

Social Welfare to Corrientes (the provincial capital) to announce that help was on the way, in the form of an official team of technical experts. On the day that this minister arrived, the commander of the Second Army Corps let fly with a public attack on the "ideological aggression" of the peasants, their clergy, and lay supporters. According to the general, "It was the responsibility of every true republican to reject the whole lot of them."[11] Five days later, when the official team of experts arrived in Goya, no League representatives were even invited to the meeting until a protest outside the building gained some of them entry. Even as plans for help were being announced within, the 3000 peasants waiting in the square outside were roughed up by soldiers and police.

"'*Double discourse*,' they call it in Buenos Aires," said Sergio, making a bitter joke. The Agriculture and Cattle Ministry of the Nation did later provide the temporary services of an economic "swat team"—for which Governor Navajas Artaza claimed full credit.

"Nothing at all would have happened without the pressure of the Agrarian Leagues," said Sergio, hotly. But the help was counterbalanced by heightened surveillance and outright harassment by the military and police. Merchants weighed in with their own form of pressure by threatening to withhold credit from *campesinos* who, having yet to be paid for the harvest, had no cash. "The blatant hypocrisy of all those ministers and officials began to harden a number of us. Not that we were considering anything violent—we were not—but neither were we walking away. Nothing had come of our demands, nothing at all. 'Put all of us in jail,' we published in one of our circulars, and we meant it. 'The government has to choose between the truth and lies, justice and injustice, hitting on the weakest, or making changes so that no one is left defenseless. For ourselves, we have chosen: Take all of us, if you must, like you did to Norma Morello.'"

Norma Morello—whose name I would often hear invoked with reverence—was a teacher whose pupils, for as long as they lasted, were mostly the children of sharecroppers. Morello, a practicing Catholic, believed that peasants should organize, and even before the founding of the Leagues, lent her house for meetings. On November 31, 1971, she was kidnapped by a terrorizing daylight commando that used an airplane to take her away—over the tobacco fields, into the clouds, and, finally, beyond the sight of the children and grownups who, rigid with fear, watched from the ground. Her capture had been ordered by SIDE, the national intelligence service, and coordinated from Buenos Aires. As soon as the plane leveled off, the soldiers onboard started torturing Morello with their fists, truncheons, and *picana*. Physical torment would become an almost daily ordeal over the next five months, first in the prison in Rosario, and then in a post of the Second Army Corps. Morello was held at the disposition of the national executive (Poder Nacional Ejecutivo, or PEN), further proof that the Leagues were considered a threat to the nation.

Morello's release, nearly five months later, was a spectacular victory for the Agrarian Leagues, particularly since it was won in a face-to-face confrontation with then dictator General Lanusse. It was a cooperative effort by the Leagues of Corrientes and the Chaco—where on April 14, 1972, Lanusse had come to visit. Within days, the beloved "Coca" (as she was called) arrived in Goya, where she was met by some 5000 peasants overflowing the main square. "I come to you fresh from my apprenticeship," began the teacher, "an apprenticeship in the world of terror. It taught me—teaches us—that violence is not born of the people, but of those who wield power in this system that day by day has become harder to change. *Compañeros*, we need to really *see* the kind of world we want to create and be aware of the risk that this entails. But we must conquer being afraid, for our fear is their favorite instrument, the tool with which they seal our mouths and tie our hands. A united people can achieve anything. If that weren't true, I wouldn't be here."[12]

Coca's presence invigorated and inspired the *campesinos*. But there were further insults and danger ahead. The famous economic "SWAT team" came and went and accomplished nothing, in terms of the needs outlined by the Leagues. A demonstration scheduled by the Leagues in the main plaza of Goya was first prohibited, then violently put down by special antiterrorist police squads. For the Leagues this was a double blow: The brutality from without was creating division within. "Most of our people had never been able to think about much more than bare survival, and all this so-called 'dialogue' we were attempting was clearly posing a threat. It was very hard," Sergio recounted, looking past us out the window to his mother's patio. "A lot of them simply went back into the hills, where they did what they were used to—'hiding,' you could say, behind a system which held no surprises, but which was working them literally to death. They felt safer with their *patrones*—who were behind all the violence we'd suffered—than with us. We should have foreseen this, prepared for it, but we didn't."

"But you learned from it," said Doña Elena firmly, "and you went on. The delegates and leaders went back to the hills," she tells me, "*ranchito por ranchito*, and most of those peasants came back."

Nearly 15,000 families were officially registered with the Leagues, which was indeed impressive participation. (In the four impoverished provinces of the Northeast, League membership totaled 45,000 families.) As the local councils redoubled their grass-roots efforts, it appeared that the Leagues were about to realize a gain: Langusse announced that he himself would visit Goya on July 15, 1972. His meeting with the League central committee, charged but nonviolent, was carried live by radio. *Campesinos* all over the province gathered to listen in squares (where the Leagues had mounted speakers in the trees), rectories, garages, stables, certain stores, and in the far-off, desolate hills. Before he departed, Lanusse was handed a letter that articulated their boldest proposition yet: the expropriation of uncultivated lands and their sale to working peasants. Sergio was a drafter of the letter, which comes out against any form of charity or patronage; rather, it argues for the rights to services that promote self-sufficiency: health care, sanitation, education (86 percent of students were dropping out of elementary school to work in the fields), roads, equipment, and land. The land was to be sold, not given, at fair prices; and state credit extended for its purchase and for tractors and other equipment to be used by local cooperatives. *La tierra para quien la trabaja*: Even Lanusse conceded (or appeared to concede) that those who work the land have a right to own it. He ordered the governor to begin a program of expropriation; but the only parcels put up for sale were floodlands, totally unfit for farming. And they came not from the largest landowners but were exacted from those with mid-sized and smallish extensions. The aims of this so-called solution were three: to insult, confuse, and divide all those who should have been natural allies.

"The subject of land is an ancient taboo," says Doña Elena, putting a finger to her lips.

"What you have to understand," says Sergio, "is that this was not a 'radical' project in the sense that they understood it. We were trying to right a radical wrong. Going back to the colonial era and the first years of independence, many of the large landowners simply stole their thousands of hectares, evacuated or peonized the inhabitants, while their lawyers wrote false deeds 'showing' family ownership going back several generations. They hadn't even been here that long, in fact, most of them had recently arrived. Every province," he explained, "has what we call *tierras fiscales*, or land that is owned by no one. By law, those lands come to belong to the person who cultivates them."

Sergio is right. This legally ratified concept was dealt a fatal blow in Corrientes in 1825 when one Pedro Ferre simply appropriated vast parcels of *tierras fiscales*. The trend was started, and soon the province was stripped of virtually all its *tierras* fiscales.[13] "The essence," insists Sergio, "of our redistribution effort was a return to legality. But *real* legality, not fake."

Embedded in this history is the major difference between the Leagues in Corrientes and those in the Chaco. The latter were able to beat back the Agrex Plan because it was to involve *tierras fiscales*, which are abundant in the Chaco. But the Correntinos, having little in the way of unowned land, have no such leverage.

After the humiliation of the floodlands incident, the Leagues intensified their actions, seeking support from labor unions, and artisan and student groups. In preparation for the return of Perón, the first democratic national elections since 1966 were to be held in March 1973. True to their charter, the Leagues endorsed no candidate, but pressed their demands to the entire slate in a massive demonstration. By a small margin, Corrientes elected a Peronist governor, Julio Romero. But here the Peronist Party differed little from the two entrenched landowning parties, the Liberales and Autonomistas, which merged for these elections. As Sergio had told us at the Tribunal, Romero himself owned 40,000 hectares and his relatives many thousands more. His siblings, cousins, and friends were given high-level posts in the government. The elections in Corrientes represented not change, but continuity.

Two weeks after the election, the Leagues staged their biggest and bravest action: a strike in which they held back the entire tobacco harvest. No crops would be yielded until two conditions were met: that the *clasificaciones* be limited to two categories, and their prices for each type be met. The Leagues had the unprecedented active support of some eighteen labor unions, including the regional delegation of the CGT (General Confederation of Labor), university groups, and, of course, the progressive wing of the Catholic Church. On the day the strike began, March 25, 1973, the Leagues blocked all the major roads in the tobacco region. Cars were allowed to pass only if they paid a small toll, which was used to maintain soup kitchens for the striking peasants. Even more than the demands themselves, this was the action that ignited official wrath. "The idea of peasants out in the open, being fed on public support and generosity, was more than they could handle," recalled a priest who was there. "They simply boiled over." On Route 27, just a few kilometers from Goya, the police released a variety of noxious gases, then attacked the unarmed peasants with heavy clubs. But the strike, the roadblocks, and the soup kitchens were kept going through the efforts of some 40,000 peasants.[14] To protest the violence, Sister Caty, together with ten *campesinos*, maintained a hunger strike in the Cathedral of Goya.

After thirty-three days, the Leagues claimed victory. The price for tobacco was raised; payment would be made within thirty days of delivery of the harvest; and the *classificaciones* were reduced from five categories to three. Small though they were, in context these gains were revolutionary. Yet the importance of the strike went far beyond the material rewards. The *campainato* had risen up to express itself.

And that would never be forgiven.

SERGIO WAS THE FIRST of the Leagues' political prisoners.[15] At the time he was secretary general, and a sharecropper in Perugorría where Anita, his future wife, was born and raised. He "fell" on November 28, 1974, during the national state of seige declared by President Isabel Perón. Sergio was arrested without charge and transported to Resistencia, capital of the Chaco, and held there in the federal prison. Later he was informed that he was a "political," meaning that under the terms of the state of siege he was considered "a menace to the security of the Nation." Beyond that, there were never any specific charges against him. "None of us ever carried guns," Sergio has declared, "there wasn't a single bomb here, not one. We didn't kill anyone, we didn't even attack a truck or any kind of vehicle." Under the Argentine constitution, political prisoners had the option to leave the country provided they were granted asylum by a nation that did not border Argentina. (Even before the coup, however, this right was capriciously withheld.) Sergio refused the option. "My duty was to stay here by my *compañeros*, even though they were agitating for my freedom. As long as there was the dimmest hope for democracy, I couldn't leave."

Sergio watched the coming of the Dirty War coup from the vantage of prison. "At the beginning we received newspapers and magazines, had access to radio and sometimes TV. We could write to our families and to foreign embassies and to organizations like the International Red Cross. We could receive packages of food, clothes, and money, which was very important. Medical care was terrible; in the whole prison there wasn't a single eye doctor or dentist. There were, however, all sorts of books, including Marx, Lenin, and Mao. But we were not allowed to work, except if we wanted to paint seashells or something like that. The enforced tedium, together with the menacing information that steadily came in, was a torment. Particularly as every day there were more and more political prisoners. And then in mid-September 1975, I learned from the newspaper that Anita had been kidnapped on the Day of the Farmer [September 8], which the Leagues had declared a day of mourning. I cannot describe the anguish that caused me, even now," said Sergio. "What I can say is that as a group we were terrified. We knew that in Chile, for example, virtually all the political prisoners were shot as soon as Allende was down. Why would it be different here? Considering our history. We took to making dark jokes, like 'reserving' the wall where we 'wanted' to be shot, 'cultivating the crows' so as not to be eaten by 'strangers.' . . ."

Sergio learned of the coup the day it happened from a radio broadcast that was blared through the prison. Life "inside" quickly changed. Political prisoners were pulled from their legal limbo and officially labeled as "subversives." The food, always inadequate, was now usually rotten and crawling with bugs. "We were literally starving. Every now and then they would throw us a bone with a little meat on it—we'd pounce on it like dogs, all of us in a pile, and then of course they'd send us right back to solitary 'for fighting.'" The general behavior of the jailers became more violent; torture became routine. Guards uncomfortable with the new regimen were shot. "New prisoners arrived in very bad shape," recalled Sergio, "wherever they'd been before, they had really been worked over." By mid-April 1976, prisoners were forbidden to write to their families; by early May visits were also proscribed. There were no more pens, papers, or reading material of any kind. Radio and television were allowed (except to those in solitary) but in a situation of unrelieved passivity, these too were a kind of torment. The only human connection to the outside world was Bishop Bisoboa of Resistencia, who came to visit and hear confessions. The bishop was so compelling that even the police posted outside the confessionals obeyed his order to leave. A few days after he delivered a public sermon on behalf of the prisoners who he declared were being tortured, it was reported in the local press that Bisoboa had been the victim of an accident "caused by an inexperienced driver." What really happened was that a large truck had borne down on the cleric's jeep and forced it off the road. Then soldiers pulled the bishop from his vehicle and broke his arm and several ribs. He was, of course, forbidden to return to the jail. The prisoners had lost their last human link to the outside world.

But they could still be tormented with "outside" accoutrements, like the radio news. On Sunday, December 12, 1976[16] seven prisoners were removed, with great violence, from the jail. "Whenever there was a transfer, it was terrifying," Sergio recounted. "We never knew where they were being taken or why. The prisoners were always abused and beat up. And of course they never came back. This time it felt even worse, it had never happened on a Sunday before. The names were called out one by one, and we all had a terrible feeling. The next day we heard the official explanation on the radio news: that while a group of prisoners was being transferred from

Resistencia to another prison, the truck was attacked by 'their terrorist *compañeros,* trying to free them.' In the shoot-out with these 'Montoneros,' all of the prisoners, themselves 'subversives,' were killed. A close call for the forces of order, et cetera, et cetera. Of course we knew it was a lie. The specifics I learned later: The prisoners were driven to the remote settlement of Margarita Belén where, staggering and disoriented from electrical torture, they were finished off with machine guns. Seeing them being taken was torment enough; hearing the propaganda was unbearable. In their hands, even the radio was an instrument of torture."

DURING THE YEARS of her son's captivity, Doña Elena was pursued and hounded by the military and police. The catalogue of her losses is extraordinary: Two of her children and one nephew were missing; Anita was taken away before her eyes; Anita's brother was tortured in front of her; *compañeros* from the Leagues were in jail or unaccounted for. Because she went back and forth between Goya and the country, she has a rare perspective on the repression here—on its brutality, to be sure, but also its ambiguities, nuances, contradictions. She was mostly in Perugorría, working in the tobacco fields with Anita's family and cooking at a rural school. "They came looking for me in the hills! Tramping around *la chacra.* I can't tell you how many times they took my picture!" They also broke into her house in Goya, beat up her teenage daughter as she slept in her bed, and stole all of Sergio's farm tools on a false tip they were weapons. "Once," she recounted, her voice going shrill at the memory, "after they'd broken in and once again found nothing, they needed someone to sign this special document. They pulled a man off the street, a man who was just passing by, and at gunpoint told him to sign. The man couldn't read, and was too frightened to make his mark, or even speak, so they hit, punched, kicked him—you can't imagine the *sound* of those blows on his body—then pushed him into a truck and that was that, he was never again seen by anyone!"

That was the work of the Federal Police. Although certainly there were oppressors in the local police, many on the force had relatives in the Agrarian Leagues. "They themselves were the sons of *campesinos,*" explained Jorge, "starving *campesinos,* that's the reason they became cops. Or soldiers."

"Before the coup," recalled Doña Elena, "the army itself helped women whose men were in prison. On visiting days, they'd come around, giving us pasta, sugar, and other food. Every week they did this. And when the feds were looking for my daughter Norma [whom they eventually found in Buenos Aires], two policemen 'stood guard' outside our door."

Everything changed from the moment of the coup. Most of the local police force was replaced with special squads from the provincial capital. Tanks patrolled the quiet streets of Goya, the provincial two-lane highway, the rice paddies, the floodlands, the desolate hills. Perugorría was "enemy territory," but "captured" without the slightest resistance. Doña Elena was living in the hills outside the village with Anita, who was arrested within hours of the takeover. "Suspicious" *campesinos* were rounded up, tied together, and carted away, like cattle, in roofless wooden trucks. At the same time the local community of nuns was placed under house arrest, depriving the village of its only nurse and medical practitioner. The soldiers painted every house and building, including the church and its altars, with the colors of their regiment, white with a yellow stripe. Charged with a particular sting were the soldiers' parties, which all the *señoritas* were expected to attend. The day after several young women declined to dance with the soldiers, a group of officers and subordinates strode into the Provincial School and raped them, and some others, in revenge. Villagers stayed as much as possible in their houses, and women never went out alone. Soldiers and spies were everywhere—"like the Holy Ghost," I was told by one battle-worn, chain-smoking nun.

Yet Doña Elena felt safer in Perugorría than in Goya. "Well, what was safe? We didn't know anymore. In the city, the terror got to me more. At night they shone lights in your windows. There was no respite. All those lying officers who denied that they had my son. 'No, *señora*, we know nothing, *señora*, please, perhaps tomorrow. . . .'" She mimics perfectly their syrupy loathing.

"But in *la chacra*" she says in her own energetic voice, "many of the soldiers were boys, they literally ate and slept in my kitchen, the kitchen of our school. 'You're underfoot,' I'd tell them, 'can't you see I'm making lunch for 150 children?' I could tell when they were homesick, knew when they got drunk, heard them at night singing and playing their guitars.

"I saw others drag Tonito [Anita's brother] into the field, torture him right there with that thing of theirs wired to the battery of their truck. I saw them hold a gun to his daughter's little head—if she screamed or made a sound, they told her, they would shoot the whole family. The child stood there rigid, facing the field, her eyes wide open, too afraid to blink. And when they were done with their *picana*, I saw them tie Tonito up with chains, and drag him away like an animal.

"Like an animal," she repeats, brokenly, but looking me straight and level in the eye.

As WE PREPARE to leave, Doña Elena gives Sergio two kilos of bread. Although Anita has a mound-shaped clay oven in the yard, her mother-in-law wants to save her the labor. We set off in Sergio's ancient truck, shouting over the noise of the gears and motor. We keep the windows all the way open against the exhaust smoke that darkens the cabin. I try not to cough or let the absence of shocks pitch me around.

"Anita is convinced she had a miscarriage last year because of this truck," Sergio shouts mournfully, looking away from me, out the window. "All the bouncing, she thinks, made a hemorrhage. And once it started," he says bitterly, "all we had was this truck to get her to the hospital." He is quiet for a while, then insists, "With it all, we are among the more fortunate."

After about twenty-five minutes, we turn off onto a dirt road. Further on, we come to a wooden fence; Sergio jumps down, lifts the log that is the latch, and drives in. We are now on land that belongs to him. Where we enter it is at once scrubby and subtropical. There are bare spots and puddles in the forest, but also oranges and lemons, sugar cane, a skeletal tree I don't recognize trailing bright red flowers. Three children come running to meet us: nine-year-old Emiliano, the elder son; seven-year-old Alicia, coltish, long-limbed, her blond hair flying; and Serguito, the trailing five-year-old, at once jubilant and out of breath. They're jumping, it seems, over everything at once—the truck, their father, even me. Anahí, their first-born, has stayed behind with her mother. She is a tall, slender, shy-looking twelve-year-old, with Sergio's fair skin and Anita's long, heavy, dark hair. Anita has the round face and short, solid body characteristic of the Guaraní, the region's predominant indigenous group. She is a woman who radiates quiet strength, whose embrace is both warm and calm.

Sergio goes to the field to help Matías, the young man who works for them several months a year. After the harvest here is finished, Matías thumbs his way across the country to the province of Mendoza (which borders Chile) to pick fruit. Matías is hitched to a plow drawn slowly by a single horse. Sergio goes out to relieve Matías, helps him to unharness the leather straps, which he then steps into himself. While Sergio plows, Matías goes to feed the other two horses, which are tethered to a couple of trees. It is late afternoon; the sky, where it meets the field, glows apricot and violet. Sergio is bathed in this ravishing light, his body looks larger, fuller, more substantial. Here, I think, is one of nature's cruel and mocking tricks. This is the light which in Renaissance paintings depicts the aura of heaven; it is painful to see it now, showered on a thin man harnessed to a thin horse, farming as they did before the Bible was even written.

Anita shows me to the *galpón*, a long, three-walled rectangular drying shed, constructed of mud and straw. It is divided in half: one part is for the chickens, the other is for cooking over a fire laid on the ground. There is a long wooden table where the family eats, and a storage loft full of tools, sacks of feed, and tied-up sheaves of tobacco. Suspended from the walls and ceiling are bunches of maize, dried meat, and more shedding, dusty sheaves of tobacco.

As Alicia dances around the chickens, Anita relights the fire. Emiliano brings water from the pump, which gets boiled for tea and Matías s *mate*, the traditional herb tea steeped in a gourd and sipped through a metal straw (see Fig. 6). Anahí quietly gathers an assortment of cups and goes to wash them in a plastic basin in the yard. While the tea is steeping in the

FIGURE 6. Sergio Tomasella pouring *mate* in his galpón, the shed used for drying and cooking.

kettle, Serguito is sent to fetch Matías and his fether. Anahí has arranged the cups on a large plate, and offers me my choice. All but one of the cups are ceramic, some white, some painted, all of them chipped. There are six of these, one for every member of the family. So I choose the small tin cup with the curling lip. Anahí looks disconcerted, but says nothing. Anita comes over and, handing me a different cup, explains, "That one is for Sergio. His lips are so sensitive to the heat that he can't use ceramic. And we fill it just part way," she says, "up to here." She'll tell me later that Sergio had skin cancer brought on by exposure to the sun. Before he comes in, his cup is poured and set aside to cool. The children rip into the bags of bread, gulp down hungrily the torn-off chunks they soften in their tea. Sergio and Anita look at each other but say nothing, and neither of them eats. Sergio doesn't linger, since he wants to finish plowing before the sun is completely down. In the time before dinner, the older children are required to study. They sit together at the wooden table, leaning in, as they read and write, toward the lantern. Serguito plays outside with the cat, and chases chickens.

For dinner we'll have polenta, cooked slowly over the fire. "It's something Sergio can digest," Anita explains, "the years in jail damaged his stomach and intestines." As we cook and clean up, she tells me that she hadn't intended to marry. Her calling, she felt, was with the Leagues. At sixteen, she was the youngest League delegate in the province. "Women were very important in the Leagues," she tells me, "nearly half the delegates were women. And the men listened to us, respected us, we usually had a few more years' education. Sergio was the most educated of everyone, the most prepared. He was our leader. But there was a part of him that always seemed lonely. I think that's what made me soften. It was I," she allows, almost shyly, "who introduced myself to him."

Anita credits her parents as the "gestators" of her activism. "For themselves they couldn't militate," she said, suddenly blinking back tears. "They had suffered too much, were too beaten down. But somehow they taught us lessons they themselves had been denied: that if you speak, others will listen; if you are deserving, you will be respected. They were the creators of our spirit, and we understood that we were the ones who would act" Don Emilio and Doña Isabel (see Fig. 7) were sharecroppers when they wed. To this marriage each of them brought three children from previous unions; together they had six more. Like all of their twelve sons and daughters, Anita was obliged to leave school for la chacra, but having studied until age twelve, she was comparatively advanced. From an early age Anita stood out, so much so that a local patrón wanted to "adopt" her and sponsor her

FIGURE 7. Don Emilio and Doña Isabel with their children. Anita Oliva de Tomasella
stands in the back holding a baby (*third from left*).

education. "I begged them to let me go," said Anita, "and was devastated
when they refused. They had fought and struggled to raise us all together
under one roof. If one of us left, they felt, it would be like a tear in the family they had woven together. I didn't understand it then, but they were
right, and I thank them for it. The 'yours, mine, ours' household they created was extremely rare. When a parent dies, or a couple separates, in a
family that has no land, the children get parceled out and never live with
each other again. Sometimes they never see each other again. What my
parents were trying to do, what they did, was to go against the forces of
history. That's not how they put it," said Anita, now weeping unashamedly,
"but that's what it was."

In the late 1960s and early 1970s, it was all but unheard of for a man like
Don Emilio to allow his fourteen-year-old daughter to travel. But having
safeguarded the structure of the family, Don Emilio could afford to be

permissive. The first time Anita rode a bus, she was almost fifteen, and did so accompanied by Tonito, who was older by about a year. At this point, their periodic trips to Goya were for meetings of a Catholic youth group. "We all lived in such isolation, just meeting each other was a revelation," Anita recalled, "just knowing the others existed." The Grupos Rurales, as these groups was called, were the precursors for the Agrarian Leagues. At first Anita went to meetings under her brother's wing. "And sometimes," she recounted, "papa still said no." But soon enough she was traveling alone, not just to Goya, but to settlements all over the geographic department of Perugorría. Tonito was the first in the Olivo family to join the Agrarian Leagues; Anita followed quickly and was soon elected a regional delegate.

Sister Anne Marie, the chain-smoking nun in Perugorría, would later recall for me the first time she witnessed Anita in action. "Sister Marta and I had just arrived in this area and it was our first introduction to the Leagues. It was already dark when we set off on horseback with Father Simi, who navigated through the hills by reading the stars. The meeting was way off on the other side of the stream, which was fnghtening for us, who knew nothing of the landscape, to cross. We finally got to this grange which was totally filled with men. The only exceptions were Doña Elena and this *waïná*, 'a little slip of a thing,' to say it in Guarani. She was barely twenty years old, and she was running this whole meeting of *campesinos*. With a composure that was extraordinary. *Correntinos* like to talk, as no doubt you've noticed, but Anita kept everything on track. No one could do this with her skill. Scores of extremely *macho* peasants listening quietly, asking her questions, thinking things over. To me," said the nun, "this was clearly a sign of grace. And we came to see that the grace of this *waïná* was partly inherited."[17]

For a time the French-born Sister Marta and Anne Marie (originally from *Córdoba)* lived on the Olivos' land, in a *rancbito* built for them by Don Emilio and his older sons. It was a time of crisis over a school that was desperately needed but continually denied to the families living on this side of the stream. During the rains, flooding made getting to class on the other side impossible, for months at a time. The affected families waited for good weather, then staged a strike, keeping their numerous children out of school. When the province held firm with the insulting excuse that the region was "underpopulated," Goya's progressive bishop, Alberto Devoto, secured backing from a German foundation and, practically before he asked, a patch of land from Don Emilio. While the mud-and-straw school building was under construction, classes rotated all day long from the Olivos' shed to the table where they ate to shady spots in the yard. Sometimes children slept there. In no time the school had 150 pupils coming to study every day. The curriculum was organized by two lay educators and the pioneering nuns from the French order in Perugorría. Sergio's mother'. Doña Elena, lived here, too, as the official cook. Until construction was complete, she fed scores of children from the Olivo family hearth.

The school soon became the hub for all the settlements on the near side of the stream. In addition to classes, there were concerts, cultural activities, and meetings of all sorts organized by parents, musicians, youth groups, and—though Don Emilio himself never joined—the Agrarian Leagues. "Everything was out in the open," said Anita, "when the police asked what we were doing, we invited them. We had nothing to hide. And some of them even came."

Things changed abruptly in 1973 when the Peronists were elected to power. In order now to hold a meeting of any kind one needed advance police permission. Although the province had no choice but to accredit the clearly needed and thriving school, on the same day it did this, it fired all of the nuns and secular teachers and prohibited them from entering the premises. The school continued to function, though with different teachers. Doña Elena stayed on to cook, and also worked in the fields with the Olivos.

Soldiers arrived by tank, Don Emilio would later tell me.[18] "We were all out in *labacra*, and there they were, coming over the ridge, a battalion ready for war, against a schoolhut full of children." It was 1974, and they had also come to claim their spoils—the tractors lent by the previous military goverment by agreement with the Agrarian Leagues. "They came during the harvest," Don Emilio would recount, "when we really needed those machines." The peasants using them were forced down at gunpoint, and the vehicles were tied up and dragged away through the high tobacco, like prisoners of war. And soon the *clasificaciones* were raised from three to seven, higher than they'd been for over a decade.

The tractors were later returned to the peasants by none other than the occupying forces of the Dirty War. The *clasificaciones* were eventually lowered to five. The province (now being run by a general) provided elite SWAT teams, as well. From other parts of Argentina came doctors, agronomists, and engineers lured by contracts for high salaries and large houses; their wives came, too, for the uplift and adventure of teaching French to "promising peasants." Of course these efforts toward "progress" were intended not to educate, but to confuse; not to enable, but to paralyze. The campaign of terror coexisted with the programs for assistance and soon enough overtook them. The French teachers and their husbands left. The school became a billet for soldiers, who played among the children when they weren't in their tanks trawling the fields for "subversives."

On my next trip Anita took me to her family. The Olivos' land, higher up than Anita and Sergio's, is also more wooded, more rugged. Over the years and with the efforts of the entire family, they now own about twenty hectares, not all of it fit for farming. Mostly they grow tobacco, but some onions as well, and keep a kitchen garden for their own sustenance. In the years the children were growing up there was no road that went anywhere near their homestead; the only precarious access was by horse. During the rains, there was no access at all; even now with the road, the rains can make travel impossible. We enter past a couple of grazing horses, tied loosely to a pair of trees; an old, but functional, *surki* is set out on the patchy yard, its harness and straps pointing away, toward the road that leads to the village. There are two *galpones* full of tobacco sheaves, corn husks, jerked meat, and enormous, balloon-like squash suspended upside-down. Nearer the house there are palm trees and poinsettias; on the rose bushes, handkerchiefs are spread strategically to dry, their corners supported by thorns. Parading among the oranges that have fallen into the dust are a clutch of white chickens and a single mahogany-feathered, scarlet-combed cock.

Though he is slightly bent and stooped, Don Emilio is still an impressive-looking man. He is long-limbed and very lean beneath several layers of clothing, of which the outermost consists of pleated black pants tied with a rope, a white shirt, woven vest, and a black beret, worn at an angle over his waving, collar-length silver hair. Don Emilio is famous for being taciturn, and for a sense of humor "so dry," I was told, "it makes you thirsty." Doña Isabel has dark hair drawn tightly into a bun; she is small and always, it seems, busy. Most of what the family eats is grown right here; bread is baked outdoors in the turtle-backed clay oven. The mud-walled, straw-roofed house—originally one interior space—is now a warren of rooms gradually added on. The cookroom—with two hearths, of which one is reserved for big cauldrons—was built a few steps away from the living quarters as a precaution against fire, a constant source of worry here. Part of an earlier house had in fact burned down; Anita, Sergio, and the other siblings recently rebuilt the parental home.

The tenor of this quiet family is a contrast to that of the voluble, high-energy Tomasellas. Anita has told me that her mother, who is vulnerable to restlessness and depression, dreads the rains, which she says keep her "all locked up in walls of water." Yet the Olivos are beloved and highly respected here; Don Emilio is the wise local elder, revered for his ability to settle disputes. Don Emilio is not a man of politics but a man of faith. And he has always trusted his children. But the reaction provoked by the Agrarian Leagues was like nothing he had ever seen. "I hear in the village they're going to kill you," he had warned Anita in 1974. But she promised that nothing would happen, "because we're not doing anything wrong." The innocence of her reply is, of course, astounding; more amazing yet, I have heard it echoed many times. "We had no idea that they *hated* us," Anita will try to explain, and again I am staggered. To an outsider it is clear that the social system is based on the contempt that comes of exploitation. But for the vast majority of peasants the only world they'd ever known was that of their *patrones*, whom they had often served for generations. Extreme isolation combined with total dependence, illiteracy, poor health, and exhaustion do not encourage self-respect, let alone analytic vision. As long as the peasants were blindered, effaced, a kind of harmony could reign. "As soon as we made them see that we were *human*, we were done for," wept Anita. "I see that now, I didn't understand it then. That was our crime, to be human, to want to *create*. To create ourselves, a community, ideas, projects. They wiped out this energy for creation. But what if they hadn't, I keep wondering, think of all the things we might have done."

There was a deeply personal, even familial quality to the repression here. And as in families certain behaviors are so ingrained as to become automatic. September 1975: Don Emilio had already gone to bed when there was a loud banging on the wooden door. Four men immediately stepped in: two elite policemen accompanied by two civilians (local markers) wearing, of all things, wigs. "They asked if they could speak with Anita," Don Emilio recounted slowly, as is his way. "They said they'd just come from the nuns' little house, so I thought, well, all right, 'she's in the back, washing up the dishes.'" Just months ago, he'd warned his daughter that he feared for her life, yet at this moment he reflexively accommodated the authorities. Only when Anita was marched past him with a gun held to her ear, did he perceive what was happening.

Doña Isabel is hearing this story for the first time, and keeps repeating, "They came here? *Here?*" At the time she was in the hospital in Curuzú Cuatiá, close to where Anita was released, that is, dumped out of the truck. (In the highly descriptive language of Guaraní, the literal meaning of Curuzú Cuatiá is "cross of papers." In colonial times, the settlement was important for the exchange of messages.) Though she knew that her daughter was kidnapped, her family had spared her the details. Neither of these elderly parents can specify the date of Tonito's disappearance; as they sift through a string of kidnaps and arrests—"after Sergio, after Anita, after Rogelio, before Don Curimá"—I get an image of beads being fingered on a rosary of disaster.

Anita spent a year and a half (1976–77) in prison. She insists that that is where she learned to program her day. "In the fields, everything you do is dictated—by the weather, the season, the position of the sun. In prison, you have to make decisions. And we did it collectively, the whole pavilion of women. We organized squads to do the washing, cleaning, and other tasks; we had study and discussion groups. We were efficient, orderly. We were also terrified; that's how we handled our fear. Norma Morello was like our patron saint. When they tortured me, I repeated her name, silently, over and over. If she withstood this, so would I." Anita got released through the efforts of Sister Caty, who arranged for asylum in Mexico. She left Argentina on June 17, 1977, and went to Mexico City. "Prison prepared me for exile," Anita insists, "I'd have never survived without that 'training.'" She lived in a communal apartment, and made do with a variety of jobs. She eventually formed a cooperative with a group of women, making stuffed animals they sold in local markets. After more than a year in exile—and over two years without hearing from him—she got her first letter from Sergio, who had been incommunicado since 1976. The process of his release was complicated and frightening, coming as it did after a military, not civilian, trial. There seemed to be no rational explanation for the convictions handed down. As Sergio recounts in his written testimony, men who were blind, crippled, old, ill, drew fifteen, twenty, twenty-five years. A twenty-year-old got thirty years for distributing leaflets at his university. Having been deemed (for whatever reason) "recuperable," Sergio was released. That label too was a deception, because some "nonrecuperables" were freed, while some "recuperables" were not. Sergio was let go on December 8,1978.

"We went to the prison to meet him," Jorge told me, "We had never been so terrified. We were convinced that as soon as he walked through the gates of that prison, supposedly 'free,' they would shoot him. In my dreams, I heard the machine guns, saw him crumble to the ground, all bloody and torn apart. It was still a shock to see him, he was in terrible shape." Sergio was clearly unsafe in Argentina. The Leagues had been crushed, many friends were dead or in jail, and he was anxious to be with Anita. Because of his family's origins, he was entitled to an Italian passport. During the months it took to get his papers from the Italian consulate in the city of Rosario, he lived clandestinely in Buenos Aires. Then, after more than five years' separation, the couple was reunited in Mexico.

"Exile was a torment for Sergio," Anita continued. "He was sick and very weak, worried about his *compañeros*. He couldn't get a grip on the city, couldn't deal with the noisy, crowded streets. For a while he did construction, but that was too much. So he stayed home and worked with us. He sewed and I went to market to sell."

At the time of my first visit in 1993, Anita was trying to start a sewing cooperative, but without success. "There are all these imports coming in from Brazil," she explains, "we could make clothes faster, better, and sell them even cheaper, right here. People know us, they would buy what we make. The problem," she says, "is the word 'co-op.' It makes them scared of being raided, even killed. These families are starving," she says, "but they're too afraid to organize, even just five women sewing! The *milicos* taught them well," she said, using derogatory slang to refer to the military: 'Fear us, fear each other, fear yourselves.' There are people here who blame Sergio for what happened, not the *milicos*, but Sergio. My sister-in-law Margot was one of them. She *saw them* torture Tonito, but in her mind, the guilty one was Sergio. Who was in prison, *incomunicado*."

By 1995, Margot was dead: a long, slow suicide of confused rage, depression, and self-neglect. "She refused to really *think about* what happened," Anita told me. "Sergio went to her on her deathbed, but she cursed him." Margot wouldn't admit it, but she, too, was a victim of the Dirty War, and so are her two orphaned children.

It is dark by the time we eat dinner, and all of us are tired. Afterward we sit, hardly talking, watching the fire die down. Then Alicia shows me how to work the pump so I can wash, and holding the flashlight, walks me to the latrine. The family sleep all in one room, in a small, partly open building about fifteen yards from the *galpón*. They create a bed for me on a table, softening the top with towels. Serguito jumps in bed with his parents, Alicia asks for a story. Out of the darkness comes Sergio's bemused, affectionate voice, saying it's time to go to sleep, in Latin. He repeats this, in French, and then again in German. Softly, slowly, rhythmically, he glides from Spanish to Latin to French to German. The children repeat the phrases after him. Gradually, their voices trail off to an intermittent murmur. From Alicia's corner there now comes silence, and from Serguito who was fussing. Patiently, peacefully Sergio continues, until all of us are translated from weariness to rest.

FOR HIS EXPOSURE to foreign languages, Sergio credits the seminary where he studied as an adolescent. The order was originally German and some of the priests were European. The dominant force, however, was the local bishop, Monsignor Alberto Devoto, a native Correntino and a visionary believed by many to have been a saint. At the Tribunal Against Impunity where I first met Sergio, SERPAJ had distributed a tribute to the late bishop on the fourth anniversary of his death, calling him *"el santo* who lived in Goya."[19] Devoto was decades ahead of the Second Vatican Council (convoked by Pope John XXIII, 1962–65), which emphasized rigorous social analysis, advocated the serious study of Marxism, and pastoral responsibility to the poor.[20] Devoto was a major figure in liberation theology and the Third World Priests' Movement (El Movimiento de Sacerdotes para el Tercer Mundo, founded in 1967).[21] It was he who, as far back as the 1950s, originally suggested to the *campesinos* that they form a sort of guild. And although the business of the Agrarian Leagues was handled by the peasants, Devoto was a constant inspiration, reference, and guide. He worked not from above the community, but from within. In accordance with his vows of poverty, the bishop lived in a precarious barrio on the outskirts of Goya. To the places he could not go on foot, he traveled by horse, bus, or by thumbing a ride on a passing jeep or *surki*. He knew every inch of his diocese—from the *villas miserias*, to the tobacco fields, rice paddies, and hidden *bañales* (hollows with a natural stream). Today his photograph is found on the altars in peasants' homes. "They ask for him when I celebrate Mass in certain places," recounted Father Jorge Torres, who was also active in the Third World Priests' Movement and an advisor to the Agrarian Leagues. "'But you know he's dead,' I have to tell them, but they reply, 'No, he's a saint. And they pray to him for help. Even today."[22]

By his own example, and by educating a whole generation of priests, nuns, and lay activists, Devoto prepared the ground in which the Agrarian Leagues of Corrientes would eventually take root. The process was "antlike," in the words of one priest, requiring decades. Acción Católica Argentina, founded in 1948, was the first Catholic youth group devoted to work in rural areas. Mostly, it sent urban adolescents and young adults deep into the provinces where there were few churches and clergy. The orientation was confessional rather than political, paternal rather than empowering, observing as it did the traditional divisions between the material and spiritual, history and the eternal. Those, precisely, were the divisions that Devoto (and later liberation theologists) rejected. Over the years Acción Católica would refine its mission and, in 1958, a more specialized offshoot, the Rural Movement (El Movimiento Rural de la Acción Católica)—which spawned the Grupos Rurales—was born. Here the ecclesiastical was combined with a (strictly nonpartisan) struggle for social justice and liberation of the oppressed.

"Yet it still had all the limitations of a traditional church-related organization," recalled Victor Arroyo, a sixty-year-old priest who was trained by Devoto and worked with him closely.[23] "It had a vertical structure, too much obedience to the clerics. But there were individuals, like Norma Morello, who had direct knowledge of the reality here and were extremely important. And don't think that way off in the hills you won't find individuals who are—" he gropes for a word, then asks if I know French. "—des personnes reveillées [people who are alert, astute, literally 'awake']. Slowly, slowly, we established links with these leaders, without whom the Agrarian Leagues never would have formed."

The polyglot Father Arroyo taught at the seminary while Sergio was a student there. Sergio had introduced us on the day of my first arrival. On my second visit to Goya, in July 1995, I talk for hours with "Cuki," as the priest is called, in the kitchen of the house where he grew up. Large and airy, it is now the parish house where congregants freely come and go. Arroyo is warm, voluble, and direct. His family was vigorous not just economically, but intellectually and culturally as well. One of his sisters is an educator trained as an anthropologist; another, who lives in Buenos Aires, does research in Paris, and wrote a book on human rights. Arroyo lived in this house with his parents until they died, his mother in 1990, his father in 1991. "Sister Caty was one of my mother's dearest friends," he recalled. "A very sweet woman. What I remember most of all were her hands. They were tough from all the work she did—picking tobacco, sinking fences, everything the peasants did she did. You know how when you take the hand of a campesino, the skin is dry, hard, leathery? That was Caty's hand."

Arroyo entered Devoto's seminary at the age of twelve, but wasn't ordained until he was twenty-four. In the meanwhile he studied philosophy and letters at the University of La Plata, a campus known for its political activism and called, before the generals "intervened" it, the South American Sorbonne. Arroyo returned to Goya to be ordained, and then in 1967 joined with Devoto in the formation of a conciliar diocese. "Devoto was a complicated character," reflected Arroyo. "He wasn't like [Miguel] Hesayne, [Jorge] Novak, or [the deceased Jaime] de Nevares, all bishops with an international profile.[24] He was introverted, so gentle as to appear timid. But his spoken language and pastoral letters were extremely forceful. Thousands of peasants would gather to hear him preach, which he usually did in a field, standing on top of a crate." The bishop was frankly a socialist, and wrote that capitalism, "even though it's touted as 'Western and Christian,' only fosters injustice."[25] His pastoral letters assailed the government for its reliance on torture, and inveighed against the "gross worldly comfort" of the Church, which he strongly suggested was failing its mission. "Each one of us," he wrote, "must address the need for deep spiritual renewal. We must abandon our position as 'settled' Christians removed from human agony; we shall encounter Christ only in the encounter with our neighbor."[26]

"Devoto only appeared timid," said Arroyo. "With total *sang~froid* he performed acts that were extremely provocative." In theological terms, one of the most extraordinary of his actions took place during the dictatorship of Onganía, a general who stressed religious pomp and display. "In penitence and protest," the bishop canceled the 1968 Midnight Mass of Christmas Eve. "In order to listen to the clamor of the poor crying out for justice," the bishop and about 350 of his followers observed a fast, in accordance with which he neither gave nor accepted Holy Communion, the wafers for which he had personally locked away.[27]

"In this conciliar diocese," Arroyo explained, "the bishop wanted the clergy to do manual labor, so I moved to a neighborhood that was very poor and spent two years baking bread. Of course everyone knew I was a priest, but I was also their baker. Then I worked as a mechanic for Citroën, which I preferred. I was even elected Secretary of SMATA, the autoworkers union. Afterward I founded a plumbers' cooperative here in Goya. That was wonderful, I went from house to house, installing gas, plumbing, fixing the pumps. But then the bishop sent me out to the country and basically that's where I've been ever since. I live here, but every day I go out to the hills. It's been years since I 'had,' as they say, a church."[28]

Devoto, he says, was brilliant at forming teams—a teacher, a doctor, a priest, a social worker—who would go and reside, temporarily, in some remote village. "You have to realize what it took for them to get there," Arroyo recalled, "without maps, without roads, travelling by *surki* to settlements virtually untouched by the 'outside.' It was slow, slow work. The difficulties were profound. There were peasants who barely spoke Spanish; resistance, for them, meant keeping Guaraní. Now I believe it's crucial to keep one's language," said the priest, himself fluent in Guaraní, "but you also need to understand what's going on around you. Otherwise, you're done for."

Underpinning these efforts were the writings of Paolo Freire, which were banned by the Dirty War regime. Of particular importance was Freire's concept of *concientiza*çao—conscientization, in its awkward English translation. As the pioneering Brazilian educator emphasized, the term goes beyond the French *prise de conscience*, often cited as the nearest linguistic equivalent. *Concientiza*çao is a rigorous process of confronting, analyzing, and committing to change the structural atrocities served up as normality, order. As one's own normality and order. It demands, precisely, the lucidity that oppression works to extinguish, the desiring passion that oppression works to kill. *Concientizoçao* means, then, to bear witness, with all the dread, horror, and resistance that that implies. "[It] involves an excruciating moment," wrote Freire, "a tremendously upsetting one, in those who begin to conscientize themselves. . . . Because conscientization demands an Easter . . . it demands we die to be reborn. . . ."[29] Rebirth, for Freire, means emerging from the darkness of fear, especially the fear of freedom.

The peasants of Corrientes literally wore the vestments of their own destruction. "Even today," recounted Father Arroyo, "you see them in the hills, wearing the neckerchiefs of their bosses' political parties—sky-blue for the Autonomistas, red for the Liberales. Each party has its so-called patron saint. So you see the depth of their confusion, everything was all mixed up: work and hunger; obedience and betrayal; holiness, sham, and degradation. An endless series of tightly tangled knots."

It was a battle to reclaim (among other things) the meaning of the sacred symbols and the meaning of the holy lexicon. Intrinsic to Catholic liberation theology is the unfettering of language. Until Vatican II, in official Church documents, "development" had to be used in place of "evolution"; "renewal" in place of "reform." Other once-forbidden terms were "structures," particularly "change of structures," "socialism," "temporal commitment," and, needless to say, "revolution." The Third World Priests were careful to emphasize: "We do not 'own' words. . . . We cannot decree the banishment of certain words, even if we sometimes wish that we could. We must pledge to read faithfully the signs of the times, to witness this unfolding of words, which is the very unfolding of history."[30]

For the peasants of Corrientes the Agrarian Leagues opened up a whole new era of words. "Meeting," "council," "representative," "rights" were at first alien terms, as were idioms pertaining to the commercial market. Many of the peasants could neither read nor write, so the language used in meetings and speeches had to be grounded, clear, and easy to remember. The Leagues' mimeographed bulletins featured drawings and scripted dialogues. "We had to be very careful," I had been told by Sergio. "Every document had to reflect reality as the *campesinos* understood it. It had to be *their* language." At the same time there were words that had to be taught— "taxes," for one, which for many was either new or wrapped in confusion.[31] Income was so regularly withheld from the peasants, and by so many different and threatening means, that specifics got blurred. The peasants were literally at a loss to name, to define, mechanisms that made their lives extremely hard. So a crucial part of this struggle for self-liberation entailed the learning, the acceptance, the integration of a foreign language—a process that, under any circumstances, takes time. And time, for the Agrarian Leagues, was yet another enemy. Yet today in the minds of many peasants this lexicon of social justice was nothing but a formula for disaster.

Arroyo himself was arrested by the military in mid-1977 and held for a week blindfolded, cuffed, and shackled. "They ran the *picana* over my hand," he said, "but that was just to scare me. They didn't torture me like they did the others. There was a group of boys from here—Abel Arce, the Coronel brothers, and Don Curimá— not one of them could read, not one of them had shoes, and now they were also bruised and disfigured. They killed Abel precisely because he was too marked up to be released. Curimá never reappeared. The others they kept for six, seven years." The names of these boys recur in my visits here, because of their youth, the wretchedness of their families, and because the memory of their desperate condition still haunts surviving prisoners.

Arroyo tells me that he was taken with a cell of ERP (People's Revolutionary Army). "Or so they said. I was never really sure. What I do know is that a leader from the Leagues in Formosa came here in September of 1976. He needed work, I gave him work, no questions asked. In December he left, saying he was being called to Buenos Aires. That's where they got him. They tortured him without mercy, really destroyed him, and he 'sang,' gave them all the names he knew and the places he'd been. He did apparently have a cell here. I find that very interesting, because it was highly unusual, especially after the coup, to have a group of politicized *campesinos*. This fellow's name was Morrell, he was tall, dark, like a typical *crillo* [Creole] and moved easily among the people here."

I asked if he was sympathetic to guerrilla groups like ERP. "Look," he said, "I was a worker priest. A lot of people came to me. Some were explicit, some were not. Anyone who comes to me needing work or food or a place to stay gets them. I didn't pay too much attention to the subtle ideological differences. They were all basically populist with a Peronist cast. In these parts, they weren't doing armed resistance. It was all conscientization. To tell you the truth, I'd forgotten about Morrell. I thought they got me for my time in the auto union."

Not unexpectedly, Bishop Devoto was followed and threatened by the local enforcers of the Dirty War. "They repeatedly broke into his house and went through all his papers," said Arroyo. "Then they started roughing him up. He was so vulnerable, always on foot or hitchhiking. We wanted him to leave his barrio, come live here, in this house, where he'd be safer, but he refused until 1978, when they made a serious attempt to kill him.

"With it all, he never stopped visiting the jails. Wherever 'his' prisoners were—Resistencia, Buenos Aires, all the way down to Rawson [in Patagonia]—that's where he went, and always by public transportation. Whether or not the prisoners were Christian. He withstood terrible humiliations—long waits, strip searches, internal body searches. But he wouldn't be deterred." After Anita's arrest on the day of the Dirty War coup, it was Devoto who managed to locate her place of captivity. And somehow he got her parents in to see her, with himself as the chaperone of the visit.

Devoto presented a dilemma for the highest authorities of the Catholic Church, whose own equivocations were highlighted in its handling of his situation. For the first time ever, the Papal Nuncio, Pio Laghi, paid a visit to Goya in what was clearly an effort to protect the bishop. "Pio Laghi celebrated a special Mass in the cathedral here with all the trappings and solemnity that went with it. But he also made clear that he wasn't very happy with *us*'" recalled Arroyo. "He said we were overly concerned with politics. On the subject of the general repression, political prisoners, and disappearances, he was ambiguous—at least privately with us. Publicly, he was silent."

At the time of this visit in 1995, church authorities were newly embroiled over the controversy surrounding Pio Laghi. A few months earlier, former Navy Captain Adolfo Scilingo exposed the official cover-up of the Dirty War death flights by admitting to his own participation. What to many was even worse, Scilingo was absolved when he made confession to a military chaplain.[32] "It created a chain reaction here," 1 was told by Arroyo. "It brought back into public discussion the whole subject of the ambiguity of the Church. The bishop we have now [Tockler] is from the north of Germany, and also, how shall I say, 'ambiguous.' (Like his recently appointed peers in the Chaco, Misiones, and Formosa.) About a month ago, he convened a meeting of priests in order to propose that we send a letter of solidarity to Pio Laghi. Now the majority of us were educated by Devoto, grew up with him in the largest sense of that term. 'Write a letter yourself,' we told the bishop, 'but we won't sign.' There was no way he was going to convince us. And he is not going to drag us back to a conservative church that stays out of politics and takes its orders from Rome. Even though he's been here for twenty years he doesn't understand that in Latin America you cannot be 'everybody's bishop.' This is a very conflicted society. You're on one side or the other. There is no middle way."

IF ELSEWHERE IN ARGENTINA "the Scilingo effect" was dominating the news, here it was hardly mentioned unless I brought it up. Father Arroyo was the only person with whom I spoke who introduced the subject. The issue has been buried by the local press, which is openly controlled by the arch-conservative police, political, and judicial establishment. It is common knowledge that more than one prominent reporter is a mole for the national intelligence service.

"It isn't only that people won't talk about these things, they are afraid even to *hear* about them," I was told by Victoria Benítez, who had gathered testimony for the local commission of the CONADEP. Known by everyone in Perugorría as "Vitoti," she was arrested with Anita on the day of the coup. She was born in the one-room house where we sit in the dusty dimness of a winter afternoon.[33] A curtain divides the space in two; placed discreetly in the farthest corner behind the drape is a white enamel bowl, a communal receptacle for urine. The daughter of a seamstress, Vitoti is not, strictly speaking, a *campesina*. An unabashed atheist, she taught in the Provincial School, located by the wooden gate where our bus entered the village.

Vitoti got involved with the Leagues through friendship, she tells me, with Anita, Sergio, with the families of her pupils, and the Sisters, who never scolded her for her lack of faith. "More than anything, I was a messenger for the leagues, encouraged people to attend the meetings, or if the rains had kept them away, went around to let them know what happened. After a year and a half in prison and six years in exile in Mexico, Vitoti came home when the dictatorship ended.

"You need to realize," she commands, "that one of the hardest, most frightening times was during the trials of the ex-commanders. The politics was double-edged: On the one hand, there were prosecutions, but these were for show. Soon enough, Due Obedience and Punto Final made the real message clear: *The genocide was legitimate.* Finally, we gathered very little information. Families were too afraid to testify. Accuse the government? To them it was a capital crime."

If in Buenos Aires Alfonsín's election ushered in the "days of euphoria," here the return to a formal democracy provoked a spasm of terror. Father Torres returned from exile in 1984. He had "fallen" soon after Sergio, in November 1975. Upon the death of Bishop Devoto (of natural causes) in 1984, Torres was appointed acting administrator of the diocese. In 1985, he was descended upon by the federal police, who had an order for his capture. Even as the CONADEP was gathering evidence against the junta, Torres was wanted for his activities while in exile. "Finally," he said, "they let the whole thing drop, precisely because I had the rank of bishop." But it is plausible that the Church engineered these efforts to arrest him. "There was a whole campaign that the diocese was being run by a 'subversive,'"he recalled.

Torres was born near Goya, in the town of Mercedes, to a family of humble origins. "Employees," he tells me, "of various types. I've been here since 1969, and started working with a group of young *campesinos* because they asked me to. I'm a rural peasant by adoption, if you like, not by origin." He has the simple, snow-white church in Itatí, a village contiguous to Goya. The main road is paved, but the dust obscures the asphalt. Horses and *surkis* mix with bicycles and cars. As I enter the village, I see that ahead of me a horse has got loose and is prancing down the middle of the street, with children and adults running after him. They eventually catch him and tie him to a tree; by the time I arrive he is stomping and snorting and raising clouds of ocher dust.

Torres is muscular, bespectacled, and wears his hair in a ponytail. He resisted going into exile. "But I was clearly a dead man. My comrades insisted it was better to be a living martyr." But coming home was also traumatic. When I ask about the sequelae of the repression, he says, "There are too many to count. Fear, deep fear is the first thing. What happened has not been passed down from the elders to the youths. Fathers haven't told their sons, uncles haven't told their nephews. So the facts and events aren't known in the rising generation. At every level. When I came to Itatí in 1986, I tried in catechism and confirmation classes to raise these issues because it was plain they knew *nothing*. But some parents came and asked me please not to recount 'those things.' In the schools it's even worse than in the families. In about 1989, a group of young priests ordained early in the presidency of Alfonsín requested a meeting with those of us who had been active in the '70s. At least they *wanted* to know, and were objecting to the official silence of the seminary. But they, I'm afraid, are the exception."

I ask if his congregation—which extends to the Paraná River and into the hills—is at all afraid of him because of his past. "When I first returned," he says slowly and visibly taken aback, "I didn't want to go back to some of the settlements. The losses had been so great. You see, we'd had so little time that when their leaders 'fell,' they couldn't carry on without us. Or not for very long. Although there were some secret meetings of the Leagues until August of 1976. Do you realize what that means? The passion? The *hope*? But they had no idea what they were up against, weren't equipped for such an enemy. We should have prepared them more fully, more deeply."

He sighs. When he begins again to speak, he is still looking away. "So I thought that maybe I should leave it alone. But they all asked me for masses and novenas, all insisted that I come. Not out of vanity, but I wanted to know why. It's not that they're drawn to the Church, especially with the hierarchy we have now. They're loyal to their country priests, and we all came to them through Devoto, whom they revere. What happened is there, all right, but deep in their hearts, like in a place that's secret, locked away."

WITHOUT THE WILLINGNESS of local guides, I could not have gathered any of this history. Without Elsa from SERPAJ in Corrientes, I could never have connected with Sergio. He, Anita, and Doña Elena passed me on to all the others with whom I spoke.[34] But those who wish to talk are the exception, and so perforce this narrative is skewed. So much, even privately among *correntinos*, has been erased, unexplored, or left unsaid. In this sense my three briefest visits, all made in July 1995, were searingly illuminating.

Soon after my arrival in Goya, Sergio took me to María Esther Gómez, the mother of *desaparecido* Abel Arce.[35] She lives with her nephew and niece on an isolated homestead toward the river. We went, perhaps unwisely, in Sergio's truck, in the evening in a driving rain. But Sergio once lived out here and knows the landscape like the back of his hand. He got us to Señora Gómez by incredibly subtle markers: the low vestigial stump of a vanished fence; a vine-obscured ditch; a particular fallen tree.

Abel Arce was twenty-one years old and a conscript in the 121st army regiment in Goya when he disappeared. In late May 1977, his mother was expecting him to come home for his weekend leave, but he never arrived. Before his capture, he was last seen at the base on the 19th of that month. According to the accounts of surviving witnesses, Abel passed through a number of prisons, including the Goya Racecourse, a secret detention center. Abel came from a family of tobacco workers, and was a member of the Agrarian Leagues.

The Gómez house consists of two whitewashed rooms, dimly lit by candles. There are numerous Virgins, altars, and images of saints. The place is immaculate, fastidiously maintained. Abel's father, now deceased, was blind. So his mother drove the *surki* when they made inquiries for their son. To spare her fragile husband, she sometimes went alone, as on the day the cart flipped over, leaving her totally paralyzed from the neck dovm. By the time we arrive, the señora has been bathed and her snowy hair combed for the night. She lies flat on her back in a fresh-smelling nightgown on sheets that are smooth and very white. Her nephew positions himself across from me, stares hard, and barely says a word. His wife is also silent, and sits so still in the shadows that she all but vanishes. The señora's voice is very soft, her words passive and resigned. She frequently asks Sergio for dates and other specifics, like the number of Abel's regiment.

"They said he'd gone AWOL, I didn't believe it. They'd taken a lot of *compañeros*, so I figured they had him too." She mentions the three Coronel brothers, who came to see her upon their release. "They said he was all beat up. But that's all we ever knew."

I want to know what opinion they had had of the army before what happened to their son. She tells me, very quietly, that they never had any opinion at all.

"Not at all?"

"No, no."

"They were just there?"

"Yes . . . we never . . . thought anything."

"When your son went into the service . . ."

"Normal."

Sergio says that most people liked army service for their sons. "It would 'wake him up,' as parents used to say, 'make a man of him.' There was an expression," he asks the family, "'for boys who didn't go, who didn't qualify, what was it?'" They all ponder for a moment, then the señora says something, chuckling, in Guaraní.

"Dog meat," Sergio translates, "*carne de perro*."

I mention the army's well-publicized fabrication that Abel had stolen a pistol.

She murmurs as though to agree, then says, "We don't know about that." But I know from Sergio that she does.

I talk for a moment about the importance of gathering these stories. "So that something should be left. So that people should know." Weakly, she murmurs approval.

"That the official stories ate mostly lies about 'subversives.'" As I pronounce this word, the nephew starts with indignation and exclaims in agreement. It is the first time he has uttered a sound.

Emboldened, I ask if they have tried to locate Abel's remains. But no one answers.

"I think that around here the subject's off-limits," says Sergio, in a delicate attempt to urge her on, "or it seems that way to me . . . at least I, personally, know of no one. . . ."

After a silence, I asked, "Is that right, señora?" and she answered with a barely audible "*Sí*."

IN PERUGORRÍA WORD got round fast that Anita was in the village, and
Carmen C. was expecting us.[36] A schoolteacher who once lent her house
for a meeting of the Agrarian Leagues, Carmen was arrested with Vitoti
and Anita. I was warned that she is fragile, but Anita insists that we draw
her out. It's been a while since she has seen Anita; she fairly flies out of her
house to greet us. Carmen is short, slightly plump, and still teaching well
into her fifties. In spite of Anita's description, she looks vigorous, buoyant,
and prosperous, to judge by her recently acquired television. She chatters,
at first about mutual friends, then more intensely, about trifles. When
Anita breaks in to explain why we have come, she leaves the table to get us
sweets, which she fussily passes around. As she listens to the jist of my
book, she undergoes a startling transformation. She seems to fold in on
herself, appears to grow physically smaller.

"I didn't do anything wrong," she stammers, in a voice alarmingly like
that of a girl.

"I know that," I tell her, but she has started to cry.

"The other teachers still look at me, say I'm a criminal. They whisper
when we have meetings, and I am so, so ashamed."

The shame, I suggest, isn't hers.

"But I was in jail!"

"But—"

"No *but*! I was in jail!"

She seems too shaky to do an interview, and I suggest that we stop and
just visit.

I am haunted still by her helpless send-off, "I never understood what
happened. I just never, ever understood."

BY LOCAL STANDARDS the Puntíns have done well for themselves. They
are mechanical jacks of all trades, fix jeeps and trucks and *surkis*, and
what can't be repaired they sell for scrap. They also have cows and pigs.
We are greeted by their strikingly beautiful, extremely suspicious daughter whose guard-dog demeanor immediately softens when she recog-
nizes her "idol," Anita. She is unwed, about thirty, and lives with her
mother and several brothers, only one of whom is home. The father is
deceased and his survivors are a tight little clan. They admit us to their
table, sit all together on one side, and wait for us to explain ourselves.
It's important that Anita speak first. While she breaks the ice, I get
accustomed to the room. The house has no wiring and, on this winter
afternoon, the interior is dim. It is full of decorations, some of which
I can barely make out. Sepia photos of serious, stiffly posed Spanish

ancestors abound. Propped in a corner is an enormous bass fiddle lacking strings.

"Anything with politics we hate," they tell us. "Anything like that turns out bad."

In late January of 1977, they received a letter posted from the province of Misiones. Brother and sister tell us the story, in a manner that is totally inscruuble, while the mother rocks slightly, but quickly, back and forth. "'I saw your son, Hector Rolando, being kidnapped by the army on January 21 in Sauce at the turn-off to the highway. You must do something for this boy, if you can.'

"Papa was so frightened. 'If you move from your house, they'll kill you all,' a lawyer told him. And so you know what he did with the letter?" They stare at us, unconvincingly defiant.

"He burned it. And that is how the matter ended."

DESPAIR, PARALYSIS, INCOMPREHENSION: For the peasants of Corrientes, these are the legacies of the Dirty War. Elsewhere in Argentina, charges of impunity are a clarion call to protest; while, here, that is a word I rarely heard pronounced. "They'll do what they always do," say *campesinos*, with resignation.

Peasants here today have no organization of any kind that exists solely to represent their interests. The Agrarian Leagues were the first, as well as the last, attempt by the peasants to create such a body for themselves. In 1993—the year of my first visit to Goya—the multi-sectorial Forum for Justice had just been established to address the extreme legal vulnerability of the poor in the context of a reactionary, highly politicized judiciary. "We concentrate on cases where human life is imperiled because of violations of human rights," I was told by Sister Martha Peloni, one of the Fonmi's founders.[37] She wears the brown-and-white Ursuline habit and lives in the colonial Convent of Saint Teresa, located in Goya's *plaza mayor*. "We've brought actions for peasants who were illegally forced off land they'd been farming for twenty years, tiny parcels of land that belong to no one. Baby trafficking is a big issue here, and neither the press nor police will even touch it. And of course police brutality, which is endemic here." The Forum for Justice was inaugurated in Goya on May 8, 1993, with a series of human rights panels and presentations. The day after the initial program, Peloni received a visit from a journalist who is also an undercover spy for the SIDE. "He was oh-so-*simpatico*," recounted Peloni. "He doesn't know that I know what his real job is. So he says, 'Martha, I'm bringing you a message from the Chief of Police, who is very concerned about you. Be careful, he says, watch out. Because they've started to see a resurgence of Third World idealogues. And to protect you, they're giving you a private guard from the police. He'll go everywhere with you, so nothing should happen.'" At this point, Peloni said, she was laughing out loud. "'What do I want with police protection? I'm going to court this week with a case of police brutality!' And he said, 'Martha, you'll end up dead of a heart attack from the psychological job they'll do on you. They'll drive you to an infarction.' 'Well,' I told him, 'I'll just have to report this, won't I?' And I did. And so the judge called in the Chief of Police and the 'journalist,' whose name is Juan Carlos Izquierdo, from the Autonomist—Liberal Pact. And the police chief says, under oath no less, 'I just want Martha to take care of her health.' And the judge bought it! So does that give you an idea of our courts?"

When I arrived for our meeting, at 7:30 A.M., there was a curious-looking chubby gentleman standing by the Convent's carved wooden door. "Right," said Martha, "*el gordito*, he's my 'spy.' He must have known you were coming." As I was leaving she asked me to check on his presence. He had gone. "He must be writing his report," she concluded, "he'll be back." Sister Martha's phone is tapped and her mail arrives unopened only if her "counterspy" in the post office gets to it first.

Just prior to my visit of July 1995 the public hospital serving the region of Goya received a government award for having provided the highest number of organs for transplant of any institution in Corrientes. "They had this whole ceremony," Peloni told me, "it was hair-raising. Because of course what this means is that the organs of the poor have some value, but the individuals themselves do not. We studied the numbers for donated organs, they are terribly high, way out of proportion. It's very clear that patients—some of whom weren't in danger of dying until they came in—are denied care so that the hospital can make some money off their kidney or liver. When the award was announced, I brought the clippings to class for the high-school girls to study. 'How should we read these articles? What is the meaning of this news?' Well, they had no idea. They thought we'd just been given an honor. It was, after all, an award with all the trappings, and with pictures to 'prove' it. So you see, we have work to do." Sister Martha smiled, but her eyes were weary.[38]

As I write this, in February 1996, the peasants near Goya had just been given a new *patrón*—the army, which is the largest landowner in Argentina. Having had its budget slashed by the federal government, the army has turned to farming to raise cash.[39] *Campesinos* who would otherwise be migrating "like the swallows" are now sharecropping for the same institution that decimated the Agrarian Leagues. That these peasants have work is of course a very good thing. If the conditions are benign, so much the better. But this form of relief carries a price: In workers in whom passivity was ingrained through terror, it will not encourage free inquiry or reflection on the past.

Wrote the wise Gustav Meyrink, "When knowledge comes, memory comes too, little by little. Knowledge and memory are one and the same thing." But here, for the sake of "safety," knowledge has been locked away like a substance that could explode, stamped out like cinders that could ignite. Fire is a hazard, that's certainly true; but its warmth, energy, and light are essential, and can be tempered. Guided by the late Bishop Devoto, Sergio, Anita, the Fathers Torres and Arroyo, and the chain-smoking, battle-worn nuns all carefully, very carefully, lit the spark and are among those who continue to cradle the embers. And they were not alone. In these feudally poor, oppressed tobacco fields, the Agrarian Leagues were kindled by 15,000 peasants who united for the first time in their collective history. This should be known, this should be remembered.

5

The House of the Blind

You got to a point where you didn't dare to direct your gaze, you were no longer *able* to focus.

—Soledad B., August 8, 1993

Us? We knew nothing. Nothing. Even now, you have to wonder. Did it happen? Can it be?

—Suki M., May 8, 1990

O N AUGUST 21, 1979, SUSANA BARROS, A DIMINUTIVE WOMAN WITH waist-length black hair, left her biochemical lab at her customary hour and walked to the Avenida Rivadavia. She stopped at her usual corner and stood waiting for the #128, the bus she always rode home. It was a balmy evening in early spring. The sun was down, but the sky was glowing, a deep violet blue. Susana remembers feeling dreamy and drinking in the breeze which, even in the onslaught of traffic, tasted of flowers.[1]

Her reverie ended with the grating arrival of the bus. She climbed on, greeted the driver, paid her fare, and, nodding to a couple of acquaintances, headed for a seat near the rear of the vehicle. Before she could sit, the bus stopped. A soldier in civilian clothes climbed on and, waving a pistol, grabbed Susana and pulled her violently backward.

"*Por el pelo, no,*" a woman pleaded softly as Susana was dragged past her, "not by the hair." Visual images are splintered and confused; what Susana remembers clearly is the silence: Except for the woman, no one said a word.

Not that the protest had registered. By her hair Susana was dragged to the sidewalk, where a second soldier was waiting. As the two men punched and kicked her, the bus pulled away, merging with the flow of traffic down the avenue. Susana was stuffed into a white Renault and soon deposited at the Navy Mechanics School.[2] As the #128 completed its route—as passengers sat there or stepped down the aisle and disembarked—Susana was being stripped, blindfolded, tied to a bedframe, and electrically tortured.

We know what happened to Susana. We do not know what happened on the bus. But from my interviews with others who saw abductions, I will hazard this: No one spoke. The driver's eyes avoided the rearview mirror. The passengers shrank away from one another, fearful and suspicious. Everyone rode to his usual stop, faithful to the stricture of routine.

By 1979, the passengers of the #128 had to know what they were seeing. The Mothers of the Plaza had been marching since 1977. In 1978, the World Soccer Championship erupted in scandal when foreign journalists and representatives aggressively pressed the generals on allegations of disappearance and torture.

But my interest in the #128 centers not on what the passengers knew or did not know but, rather, on how the regime—whose essential creation was a hidden world—manipulated public space. Buses and trains, streets and neighborhoods—and the ways in which we inhabit them—have much to do with our sense of reality. I am haunted by the woman who softly entreated, "Not by the hair." What was she pleading for? Did she know? If I could ask her today, would she remember?

We can but wonder. None of the witnesses has ever come forward.[3]

RELATIVELY EARLY IN my researches, in May 1990, I did an interview that struck me then as anomalous. This conversation, with a woman I'll call Suki M., took place at her home in Villa Devoto. An outlying district of the Argentine capital, Villa Devoto houses the country's largest prison. Under the generals, Devoto (as it is called) specialized in "subversives." Male prisoners included common criminals; all of the women were "politicals" (in the parlance of the guards). A high percentage of the inmates had spent months, or years, in clandestine camps. On the scale of things, getting sent to this prison helped, but did not guarantee survival. Particularly in the early years of the regime, inmates could be subjected to torture and secret executions. On March 14, 1978, Devoto was stormed by an army SWAT team that, on the pretext of "mutiny," murdered scores of prisoners (the exact figure is unknown). Witnesses from the neighborhood—blocked off and occupied that day by soldiers "armed to the teeth"—testified to seeing the army enter the jail and to hearing the repeated rounds of machine guns. The junta prohibited any coverage of the event, but could not prevent word of mouth, or the aggrieved protest outside the jail by inmates' relatives, who carried flags and mournfully intoned the national anthem.[4]

In Suki M.'s neighborhood you perceive no sign of a prison nearby. The houses are large, impeccably maintained, and of European architecture. Surrounded by palms, cacti, and jacaranda, there are numerous Swiss-style chalets.

"*Us?* We knew nothing. *Nothing.*" Suki waved my question away. A professional party planner, she rejected my query with outgoing charm. She offered me candy, fancy gumdrops elaborately sculpted into leaves. The house is bright and decorated to the hilt. The furniture is soft, comfortable, and upholstered in exuberant florals. On every table there are photos and family mementos (she and her husband have three sons).

"My work," said Suki, "is to plan for the joyous occasions in people's lives—weddings and anniversaries, birthdays and bar mitzvahs." She showed me a box full of samples—engraved invitations and placecards, monogrammed matchbooks, styrofoam scaffoldings for the artful arrangement of flowers.

Suki talked and talked, about this, about that, in a highly sociable stream of consciousness. All of a sudden she was telling me about a kidnap she witnessed in the street. She had just dropped off an order for invitations and was walking back to her car.

"Just a normal young woman," she said, as though thinking out loud, "really a girl. Two men shoving her, stuffing her—*oof!*—into a car."

When I asked when this happened, all she would say is, "Then."

"Terrible," she shuddered, but no other details emerged.

Silently, she gathered our cups and placed them on a tray. "Even now," she mused, "you have to wonder. Did it happen? Can it be?"

"But you saw," I said gently.

"No," she insisted, "we knew nothing. Even now."

The woman on the #128. Does she know nothing? Even now?

I WAS THERE; I SAW IT; I couldn't have known a thing. To my surprise, this paradox emerged as a significant pattern in my interviews. Because the majority of victims were taken from their homes,[5] lots of Argentines saw kidnappings and knew perfectly well what they were witnessing. Who intrigued me were those who simultaneously saw and didn't see; understood and didn't know. Who, years after the public trials of the ex-commanders, could not make sense of it all. Who, when asked if they ever saw a kidnap, first answered automatically in the negative. I am not referring to ardent supporters of the generals. But, rather, to individuals with no taste for politics, who simply wanted to raise their children and live their lives. More is at play here than denial. As official rhetoric worked to conquer the mental space of Argentine citizens, in shared physical space, a coercive discourse was also brought into play, one that could turn a "normal" setting into a bizarre, and disorienting, theatrical. The performance of normal daily actions, like riding a bus, could make one an impotent player in a deadly spectacle. At the same time everything was normal—the corner printshop, the #128, the bustling avenue that pointed toward home. The Terror needed a setting that was largely undisturbed. For if the setting radically changed, how could one assimilate what was happening there? If the missing were eerily present by virtue of their absence, in what sense were those present really *there*? Space was manipulated to make one thing clear: It was strictly forbidden to get one's bearings.

The regime made a clear distinction between those who could live "in society" and those who could not. Yet living "in society" was also a form of captivity. "The enemies of the Process," declared Massera, "are those who in their hearts hate the yearning for a dictatorship."[6] The theater of this war "without battlefields or boundaries" was the human spirit. Of all the forbidden kinds of knowledge, self-knowledge was the most transgressive. The woman on the #128, whose own hair prickled as Susana was dragged away, could not help but register visceral empathy, that tenderness of the flesh which is the signature of a sentient human being. Involuntary, small, and immediately stifled, the woman's voice ("Not by the hair") literally escaped her. To live "in society" was to be caught between one's own humanity and inhumanity—with sentience, empathy, and social intelligence in conflict with blind instinct to survive. Or with shrewd instinct to flourish.

Once again it is worth noting that the coup was seen as inevitable and had massive civilian support. The locus of democratic government was all but abandoned several days *before* the coup (which happened on March 24). The exodus was under way by March 22, when numerous legislators carrying bulging packages of documents were seen leaving through the small side doors of the enormous baroque Parliament.[7] Even before the Congress was officially dissolved, the people's representatives basically surrendered the territory. On March 23, the front page of *La Razón* was emblazoned with: "The End Is Imminent. It's All Been Said."[8]

It was clear that anything associated with "populism" (an aberration, according to the official lexicon) was doomed. As soon as the military took over, activities that entailed debate in free assembly were prohibited. Labor unions were banned, professional guilds controlled, and student councils made suspect. The free exchange of ideas—defined as "any activity taking the form of indoctrination, proselytizing, and agitation"—was forbidden in public space. The very notion of communal space ceased to exist. Under cover of business as usual, isolation was the rule. Within forty-eight hours of the coup, a front-page headline in *La Prensa* proclaimed: "Activity All Over the Country Is Normal":

> Yesterday was another day of absolute tranquility in the interior of the country, with general activities proceeding with their usual rhythm.
> Business and industry, as well urban and suburban transportation, were normal. By the afternoon, more people could be seen downtown, shopping and carrying out their usual activities in provincial administrative offices, which also functioned normally in accordance with the orders of the junta.[9]

It was understood that each province had a newly designated military superintendant and that key functionaries appointed or elected during the last government had not only been fired but of "any goods in their possession belonging to the national, provincial or municipal patrimony." Former officials were immediately forbidden to use any "offices, houses, vehicles, fuel, or service personnel" that had been part of their compensation or necessary to the performance of their duties. Any infractions would be handled by military courts. The message was clear: nonparticipants in the Process literally had no place in the new society, nowhere to go, and no way to get around.

In fact, everyone was given rules for navigating public space. On March 28, 1976, a directive by the Third Army Corps (which would soon establish La Perla concentration camp) was published in the national and local dailies. The directive was presented in the form of a parable. In Córdoba the day before, a woman was driving a green Renault, accompanied by her young daughter. Upon discovering that she wasn't carrying her documents, she tried to evade a military checkpoint by abruptly turning and heading in the opposite direction. She failed to stop when the army fired two shots into the air, leaving them no choice but to aim at her car and kill her. "In order to avoid the repetition of such unfortunate occurrences," the Army "was suggesting" that the entire population observe a six-point set of instructions to facilitate security and stem anxiety on the part of army personnel. On approaching a military checkpoint, Argentines were advised to refrain from "sudden movements," "getting out of the car without first being asked," and "maneuvering in a way that soldiers might misunderstand." Proper identification was to be carried at all times. As the regime repeatedly stressed, trouble tended to arrive with "unknown persons." On the same page as this directive published in *La Prensa* were further updates from around the country on the recuperation of "absolute normality": the streets were quiet; the banks were open; factories reported "very low absenteeism."[10]

To a panicked and deeply riven society, the junta immediately held out the promise of wholeness. The first editorials after the coup were uniformly graphic: According to *La Opinión*, the nation had been "mutilated," "dismembered."[11] Yet all could still be healed by the gentlemen of the coup: As expressed by *La Prensa*, after its time of "sickness" and "delirium," the nation would "convalesce"; it would never again be "disfigured," its "loveliness would be eternally restored."

Integral to the Process was beautification, which began immediately. Three weeks after the coup *La Prensa* ran the following editorial:

> All over the Republic a thorough cleansing is under way. From the walls and facades of public and private buildings, squads of peons, neighbors, and volunteers have taken up the task of washing away the inscriptions and graffiti that . . . constituted a veritable violence against the soul. . . . The walls are being cleansed of that filth, those signs of tribal frenzy. Soon enough the surfaces will shine through, released from that nightmare by the action of soap and water. . . .

Yet still *La Prensa* warned:

> The country is called to the practice of new customs. The walls and surfaces must be cleaned. But minds too must be cleansed, for that is where "the error was born."[12]

Running across the adjacent two columns on the same level as the paper's logo, is the large, sanguine headline: "After the Nightmare." Its author, whose mind required little in the way of "cleansing," shows an exemplary sensitivity to locale:

> Obviously, the elements of our environment are the same as before [the coup of] March 24. Yet still it seems that the clouds floating through the vast blue sky, the birds and trees, the pavements and

cobblestones, the buildings, the voices that reach our ears all seem new, endowed with a most agreeable timbre, as though we were witnessing for the first time their inherent grace....

This demonstrates that our surroundings ... have a decisive influence on our state of mind. (There's truth to the saying, "landscape embodies the soul.") It feels to all of us that this is a time of renascence, that a special vital energy has saved us from the consequences of an accident, gained us this sweet state of convalescence....

Sweet though it may be, thankfulness is to be seen as a tonic:

After the nightmare [of the last years] we have been granted unclouded happiness.... After the nightmare, and inspired by this historical moment, we must promise ourselves to forever eliminate even the possibility of nightmares.[13]

"Cleansing," a key word in the official lexicon, entailed first of all the erasure of recent history. Murals, posters, graffiti—any evidence of prior political life—was considered filth and washed away. Popular expression was a "nightmare," "tribal frenzy"—either way, a rampage on the bastion of thought. The environment had to be bright, beautiful, and *soigné*: a setting for, and mirror of, the exalted virtue ("inherent grace") of the Process.

And, indeed, the streets of Buenos Aires were clean, full of flowers, free of crime. In its showcase capital, the regime wanted little overt militarism. Membership in the First World, an Argentine obsession, was contingent on being considered "authoritarian not totalitarian," in Jeane Kirkpatrick's famous distinction with little difference.[14] Enormous loans from the International Monetary Fund, Chase Manhattan, Bank of America, Citibank, and a host of other institutions, ushered in an intoxicating couple of years of "sweet money" *(la plata dulce)*, which brought further embellishment and distraction: French and Italian clothes and cosmetics, German cars, electronics from the United States and Japan. Newsstands were full of *Vogue, Donna Bella, Uomo, Marie Claire*. As French journalist Marie Muller observed in 1979, Buenos Aires was hot with *Saturday Night Fever*: "Travolta calendars, Travolta ashtrays, Travolta posters, all the teenage girls eating their hearts out for John Travolta. Disco in all the clubs...." As for the adults: "Even at the height of summer, the sunny Argentine capital was on the go and on the make: a city of busyness and business ... no one waits for anything, everyone is occupied, preoccupied, serious, and very politely indifferent."[15]

Poverty had no place in this shining capitalist scheme. Along with the leaflets, graffiti, and other "filth," the shantytowns were eradicated. At the time of the coup, the shantytowns comprised 5 percent of the city's population. By the end of its first year in power, the regime reported that 76 percent of the slum dwellers in the capital had been "removed." Police, army, and security personnel made night-time raids on the *villas miserias*, using trucks, dogs, machine guns, and tear gas to flush out the families who lived there. Allowed only the belongings they could carry, the inhabitants were rounded up, shoved into trucks, and dumped in the wastelands beyond the city limits. By morning, the remains of the *villas* were gone, bulldozed into oblivion. "Our only intention," affirmed the head of the Housing Commission, "is that those who live in our city be culturally prepared for it. To live in Buenos Aires isn't for just everyone, but for those who deserve it. . . . We ought to have a better city for the best people."[16]

Growing up in the embassy district of Palermo Chico, María Claudia A. was, by her own description, among "the very best people." Of French extraction, the A. family came to Argentina in the mid-nineteenth century. The family includes captains of industry, breeders of cattle, power brokers in the Navy and the Catholic Church. Like everyone else in her circle, Claudia (as she is called) traveled exclusively by limousine and was always accompanied by bodyguards. "We'd come out of school and they'd all be waiting for us at the gates—suits, sunglasses, walkie-talkies, guns in their shirts. Protecting us from 'subversives.' What did we know. We skipped right over, glad to see them." Now in her late thirties, Claudia is an academic who lives abroad and specializes in literary representations of the Dirty War. "I study literature to get at the truth, at the horror that was hidden, but happening all around me. In my totally insulated, impenetrable world, the horror was *invisible*."[17]

By virtue of their wealth and long history in the country, the A. family (and the rest of the oligarchy) had always occupied a space apart. Their environment had always been regulated, but voluntarily and by themselves. Most Argentines lacked the resources to construct a world so enclosed, opaque, and self-referential. Still life went on "normally" in various classes and milieux.

"The Process simply passed me by," Clara G. recalled, in November 1995. "I know it sounds amazing, but it's true." In 1976, Clara in her twenties, newly separated, and raising small children on her own. "Every day was a drama. I was working two jobs, sometimes three. I'd been studying, but had to stop. The logistics of my life were all-consuming." An energetic, heavyset woman, Clara looks older than her age. After years of apprenticeship, work, and saving, she has her own business designing gardens. "At the same time," she reflected, "I *knew*. In about 1977, my sister-in-law came back from Mar del Plata all impressed at seeing Videla on the beach. 'What do you mean you took his picture? That murderer! That son of a bitch!' I don't know where it came from, I just exploded. Neither of us ever mentioned it again. Believe me, politics was the last thing on my mind. I was totally unconnected, paid no attention to the news. My life was work, diapers, shopping, diapers, cooking, diapers, work, diapers, and sometimes sleep. How did that knowledge [of the atrocities] seep in? I really don't know."

Raúl T., a computer specialist now in his forties, recalled, "A typical night out went like this: You'd meet for drinks, see a show, have dinner, go dancing, then have dessert as the sun came up. This was a way of life. This was Argentina." There were also the ominous Ford Falcons without license plates; searches by soldiers with machine guns. The bearded Raúl T. was stopped so many times, he developed a patter to keep the soldier calm. "I'd heard of people being shot because they'd moved a hand to their pocket when asked for their papers, so I'd say, very slowly and respectfully, 'My ID is in that bag. May I reach for it there on the seat? Thank you. Now I'll hold it upside down so that when everything falls out, you'll see I have no weapons, nothing to hide.' I'd talk him through every step, so that he wouldn't be startled by the jangle of my keys, and shoot. Needless to add," he said, ironically, "I always thanked him when he'd finished." The "civilized" Raúl T. had a very good act. He was in fact an "enemy of the Process." In addition to his professional work, he was a part-time rabbinical student and helped track prisoners in Devoto.[18]

Visitors to Buenos Aires often remarked on the "unreal" quality of life there. Unlike the vast majority of Argentines, foreigners had access to coherent information. The contradictions between what these visitors knew (or had experienced) and what they saw could be overwhelming. Shortly after the coup, Jerónimo José Podestá, the former bishop of Avellaneda (a city just outside Buenos Aires), was forced into exile, which he spent in a highly politicized Argentine "colony" in Mexico. On several occasions in 1976 and 1977, he returned clandestinely to Argentina. "I was dumbfounded and frightened by the easy, insensitive collusion of the greater part of our society, particularly the managerial classes, in the face of state terrorism and genocide."[19]

In February 1979, Ben Epstein, U.S. National Director of the Anti-Defamation League of B'nai Brith, went on a fact-finding mission to the Argentine capital:

> When you see the busy streets and the wonderful shops and the number of people who are out making purchases, it is a complete contradiction to what you were told [regarding the repression, inflation, and high cost of living]. They say they are spending money today because it will be worth less tomorrow. Incidentally, Buenos Aires is one of the most beautiful cities I have seen— physically. It reminds one of Paris with the broad boulevards, beautiful parks, lovely shops. You can walk in the streets at midnight without any disturbances, you see no policemen, you see no military. When I asked one of my Argentinian Friends how was this possible, he smiled and said, "In Buenos Aires you are safe in the streets at any time, but you are never safe in your home."

Epstein returned to New York tormented by what he had seen:

> You must look into the eyes of the parents when they sit across the coffee table from you and tell you all they want is to know whether their child is alive or dead. . . . You have to sit across the table from a father and mother where the father talks and the mother sobs. And yet, outside the traffic rushes by, the hustle and bustle and noises of a big city continue as if everything were perfectly normal.[20]

As Epstein was aware, the scene was abnormal only because these families had someone who was *listening*.

The activity that Epstein and many others remarked was, at least in part, a cover for anxiety. The apparent order and prosperity had come as paternal gifts to a civilian population that had shown itself incompetent to manage its own affairs. The gifts themselves were perplexing: No one really understood the phenomenon of "sweet money" and, judging by the unprecedented capital flight, virtually everyone mistrusted the economy that had spawned it.[21] "Sweet money" was spent on imports, travel, and foreign investments. Hardly anyone saved or invested money in Argentina. Underlying the polished urbanity was the suspicion that what had been given was likely to be taken away. That the population was yet too "imma-ture" and "emotional" to vote, let alone govern, was a constant of the junta's rhetoric. Official lies and censorship about the existence of concentra-tion camps made it truly difficult to comprehend the scope of what was happening. (Only after the regime was it discovered that there was a vast network of camps.) Oracular pronouncements were a constant, a kind of weather. Like cold fronts and pressure zones, reports of disappearances were the arcana of the atmosphere, unpredictably drifting in, elusively drifting over and out. These conditions made for a complicated mix of reactions: cunning and regressed obedience; complicity and shame; opportunism and terror. "What dictatorship?" Muller, the French journalist, was asked by a young worker whom she described as "sincerely surprised" by her questions. "I'm like Saint Thomas," claimed another man, "I only believe what I can see."[22]

Despite the many layers of denial, there was physical evidence of a world "offstage," a universe beyond the confines of "society." In out-of-the-way streets, on isolated highways, along the Atlantic Ocean and Plate River, corpses periodically were discovered by civilians. Riddled with bullets, missing digits and teeth, most of the bodies were too ravaged to be identified. The first body to wash up—just a few days after the coup—was described in the media as that of "a drunk Korean fisherman," and there the improbable story sank. Early on the morning of Sunday, July 3, however, passers-by saw a man wrested violently from a green Ford Falcon, tied to the Obelisk in the Plaza de la República, and machine-gunned by the men (wearing civilian dress) who had transported him there. The site, the exact geographical center of Buenos Aires, is the local equivalent of Boston Common, the Arc de Triomphe, or the Lincoln Memorial. It is a monument to democratic governance.

In his next column James Neilson, a well-known Anglo-Argentine journalist, published "Tolerating Horror" in the courageous English-language *Buenos Aires Herald*:

> In some fortunate nations the discovery of a single corpse would be enough to keep the press and police occupied for several days. The mystery of the corpse would become a public obsession. . . .
>
> Nothing of the kind happens here.
>
> Argentines have been so cauterized by violence that they will accept almost anything. A political crime has to be on a grand scale or be particularly horrendous in order to penetrate the public consciousness. . . .[23]

Barely eight weeks later, on September 6, the handcuffed, shackled, and mutilated corpses of three more young men washed up on the coast of Uruguay. One of these bodies was soon identified as that of Floreal

Avellaneda, a fourteen-year-old *desaparecido* from Buenos Aires.[24] When it was published, a lawyer told me, the age of the helpless victims caused "but a momentary collective shudder."

Unknown to the general public were the experiences of two agricultural workers who witnessed mass executions and discovered common graves on military land near La Perla. José Julián Solanille was forty-seven at the time, the father of ten children. From 1976 until 1978, he did day work at Loma del Torito, a ranch that bordered the concentration camp. On a Sunday morning in May 1976, Solanille later testified, "I was rounding up the animals when I met my neighbor Señor Giuntolo . . . who said he wanted to verify with me whether the rumors he had been hearing were true. Both of us on horseback, we climbed the hill to where we could see the mass grave [Giuntolo had heard about] 200 meters away. There were cars and trucks there, and among the other men in uniform was General Menéndez [who as head of the Third Army Corps ran La Perla]. Shooting started while we were on the hill and we saw a hooded man whose hands were tied behind him, who kept falling and getting up until he just fell. They kept shooting and other people kept falling, also with their hands tied, and wearing black blindfolds. The way the sun was shining, the black really stood out. They must have shot about fifty people." During the two years he worked at Loma del Torito, Solanille saw approximately 500 graves of all sizes, some of them immense.[25] "What struck me most was not seeing so many corpses—because there comes a moment when one gets used to it—but the two lovely girls who were thrown out of a helicopter and landed a few meters from my house. The girls were blonde, looked like twins; one had red boots, the other only one moccasin; they were wearing jeans and a sweater. They were sixteen or seventeen years old. After they had been there two days the gendarmes took them away and buried them in one of those graves. . . . There is one that I know is still intact. . . . Its mouth about six meters and it was very deep. Once some of my animals fell in and there was everything—whole corpses, bones, remains of every kind."[26]

Neilson was certainly correct that consciousness on a grand and public scale was closed to the horrendous violence. Yet scores of people have told me they felt *personally* wounded by the murderous desecration of Republic Plaza. Many were haunted by rumors they could neither prove, dispel, nor even comprehend. How could a person simply *vanish?* All over the country, there were accidental witnesses, like Solanille and Giuntolo, who were devastated by what they knew and who suffered alone, for years, in silent terror.

By December 1976 (just eight months after the coup), 1000 prisoners were known to have been shot; 20,000 individuals had been reported missing; 300,000 were officially exiled. According to a source in the Argentine Judiciary who in 1976 spoke on condition of anonymity, 400 writs of habeas corpus were being filed every week in Buenos Aires; the national weekly average was 800. The same judiciary source emphasized that these figures represented less than half the number of actual disappearances, since most families with *desaparecidos* were too frightened, ignorant, or isolated to connect with one of the rare lawyers willing to submit a writ of habeas corpus.[27]

"Normality" notwithstanding, the human landscape had definitely changed. By August 1976, approximately 100 of the country's most prominent reporters had been forced to leave.[28] Over the course of the regime another 92 journalists would be disappeared.[29] By October 1977, one in twenty-five Argentines was living abroad, for a total of one million out of a population of just under 25 million. Among scientists, researchers, and professionals the proportions were staggeringly high: between 40 and 50 percent had emigrated.[30] Enormous numbers of literary, theater, film, and visual artists were also forced to leave the country, as well as many publishers, producers, and gallery owners. Over seven years, Operation Clarity (run from the Human Resources Department of the Ministry of Culture and Education) removed 8000 "ideologically suspect" individuals from jobs in universities, secondary and elementary schools, libraries, and cultural institutions. Many of these educators and intellectuals also left, or were forced "underground."[31] Their jobs were eliminated, taken over by the military, or filled by civilian appointees. Others, knowing they were at risk, lived clandestinely or semi-clandestinely, publishing or producing work under pseudonyms. They were there, but they were invisible.

These changes in the human landscape were not reflected in the distorting mirror of the media. Especially cynical were the columns (in *La Prensa*, for example) on the activities of Argentines living abroad: The focus was on businessmen and entertainers; needless to say, forced exiles were excluded. All the dailies ran richly photographed supplements on the junta's beautification projects. Real estate and restaurants, fashion and travel (all linked with "sweet money") were prominent in the news. Clearly the function of these pages was to ground Argentines in a flatteringly seductive image of the place in which they lived. The very busyness of the cultural pages was a cover for the human void.

While omitting blacklists, death lists, book burnings, and the liquidation of libraries, the literary and cultural pages reported on a host of "First

World" arts activities. In just the first weeks and months of the regime, Buenos Aires hosted an international book fair, the Bolshoi Ballet, Django Reinhardt, an Australian art exhibit, a Bach festival, and a series of visiting orchestras at the renowned Teatro Colón. Throughout the days of the regime, imported opera, orchestras, jazz, chamber music, and dance (ballet, modern, folkloric) flourished. So did foreign films, particularly from Europe and the United States. Scanning the major dailies during the regime's most brutal years (1976–80), we see listings for movies by François Truffaut, Werner Herzog, Ettore Scola, Joseph Losey, Jean-Louis Trintignant, Luchino Visconti, Carlos Saura, Woody Allen, Martin Scorsese, John Cassavetes, Robert Wise, and Paul Mazursky. James Bond, Jean-Paul Belmondo, *Planet of the Apes*, and *Superman* were box-office sensations. Strangely enough, there are even ads for *Midnight Express*, a harrowing true story of torture in a Turkish jail, and a few erotic films, "strictly prohibited to those under eighteen." The movie pages give the impression of considerable cinematic excitement in Buenos Aires. But the message is misleading: Films were severely edited for Argentine consumption (10, which featured the bikini-clad Bo Derek, was subjected to over sixty cuts). The number of films being made *in* Argentina had plummeted; the production of Argentine art films was essentially dead.

The same sort of mirror game was being played in the book pages. Assiduously grooming Argentina's refined international image, literary coverage in the conservative *La Nación* emphasized foreign writers, regularly reprinting texts (by such authors as Octavio Paz, Eugéne Ionesco, Wassily Kandinsky, Umberto Saba, Severe Sarduy) that had originally appeared in *Le Figaro*, the most conservative major daily in Paris. Unrepresented in *La Nación* were the numerous Argentine writers who had been forced to flee, or whose work was considered "suspicious." In early 1977, in its "World of Books" section, *La Prensa* published an interview with Paula Speck, a visiting doctoral student from Yale who found "literary interest in this country much higher than that in the United States. It's something really exceptional. And I have had this substantiated all over Buenos Aires. I've walked many of its streets, taken buses at random to 'discover' the city, been to the Abasto [the central market]. So I make this statement sincerely and with pleasure."[32] Even if Speck was being less than sincere, her comments would have helped fill in the picture of a society whose literary refinement was admired by foreign scholars. And even as writers were being kidnapped, tortured, and disappeared, there *were* some authentic literary events. Between June and August 1977, Jorge Luis Borges—who disappointed many for refusing to speak out against the junta until the trials in 1985—gave an important (and intensely advertised) series of lectures at the splendid Teatro Colón: *Borgesian* lectures, of course— eloquent, learned, playful meditations on "The Divine Comedy," night-mares, "The Thousand and One Nights," poetry, Buddhism, blindness, and the Kabbalah.[33]

News from "without society" barely appeared; when it did, it was manipulated and tightly controlled. In the early days of the regime, several newspapers published filings of writs of habeas corpus (along with notices of foreclosure, and other legal proceedings). These lists alone meant nothing to the uninitiated. Soon enough even they were discontinued. Only the *Buenos Aires Herald* and *La Opinión* (until the kidnap of its editor, Jacobo Timerman) published clearly identified lists of the missing with any regularity. In May 1978, during the uproar that accompanied the World Soccer Championship, *La Prensa* published a list of 2000 *desaparecidos* with their National Identification Document numbers. It did so on more than one occasion, always for an exorbitant price, as I was told by various of the victims' relatives who had dealt with the paper. "It was totally cynical," said Renée Epelbaum, who lost all three of her children. "They knew we would have paid anything. They made huge profits on our misery."[34]

Like echoes from faraway trenches, there were periodic reports of "shootouts with subversives."[35] Some days, three or four such articles were clustered on a single page. On the rare occasion when a photo ran with a story of a "shootout," the image was invariably dark and grainy, to fit the *Nacht und Nebel* beyond the city limits. The stark contrast between the "battlefield" and the readers' beautified surroundings made it seem like news from another world, skirmishes with a different species. On April 6, 1976, *La Prensa* ran a three-column photo on page one to gloss the fatal defeat of twenty-one unidentified "terrorists" in the province of Buenos Aires. In the photo, a long, dim, all but deserted avenue stretches to a narrow point on the tight horizon. Telephone wires and a traffic light overhang the asphalt. According to the caption, this is where the "encounter" took place. The legend also tells us that the battle took place between "the beer hall on one side and a high school on the other," neither of which can be identified in the photo. The real message of the caption is: *Trust us. This is what you see. This is what you know.*

The late Guillermo Loiácono took more pictures of the repression than any other photographer. He also collected obsessively, and his archive of images from those years is the largest in Argentina, and quite likely the world. The grandson of Czechoslovakian immigrants, Loiácono was the extremely intense son of a doctor. Several years before his death, we did a series of interviews in his studio. He got his first staff experience on *El Des-camisado* and *Notícias*, two landmark Peronist newspapers, both of which were closed in 1975. Six months before the coup Loiácono founded the first photojournalism agency in Argentina and, during the regime, divided his time between industrial shoots, sports, and politics. Many of his political photos were published unsigned or pseudonymously in Europe and Brazil. "We did so much political photography for the simple reason that it never occurred to the military that we would use the medium to express opposition. They never deciphered our language. At official ceremonies I'd be the first to arrive and the last to leave. They seemed to be flattered, and so access was rarely a problem. But I was always waiting for the gestures they made when they thought no one was looking, for the social groupings that revealed dangerous political alliances. I was particularly interested in politicians from earlier governments—civilian as well as military—to show the continuity, the wide spectrum of interests that had combined to produce the repression. In the first months of 1978, when the junta saw our pictures in *Paris Match* or *Stern*, it assumed they were taken by foreigners as part of the so-called 'Anti-Argentine campaign.'"

Loiácono and his colleagues didn't realize until 1981 that they had in fact created a movement, a photography of resistance. By 1981 the repression was winding down a little, though it was by no means over. With about eight other photographers, Loiácono organized an exhibit in San Telmo, the historically working-class neighborhood associated with the birth of the tango. The photographers were free to hang what they wished, and every picture was signed. "Each one of us was taking responsibility for his own actions and career. I won't say we weren't nervous, even scared, because we were," recalled Loiácono, who hung several pictures of Videla. "We had predominantly two classes of visitors. The guys in the green Ford Falcons, they came in, grabbed a catalogue and left. They didn't even look at the images. Their issue was who, not what was in the show. Now the other group was interesting. Word had got round in the neighborhood and so, at around 10 or 11 in the morning, the old *señoras* would stop in, with their string baskets full of fruits and vegetables. These women were seventy if they were a day, and were incredibly supportive. They came day after day and sent their families. One kid asked his father, 'Why weren't these pictures published in the newspapers?' Well, they had been. That child's question led us to an extremely important discovery. Take a picture out of context and its meaning changes. And not just its meaning, but what you literally *see*."[36] That viewers returned to the show repeatedly testifies to the complicated process of peeling away these many layers of deceit, and regaining familiarity, and trust, in one's own powers of perception.

THE HIGHLY PHOTOGENIC Mothers of the Plaza de Mayo were an especially difficult problem for the junta. The Argentine press did its utmost to ignore the Mothers, otherwise it slandered them as "madwomen" (*locas*) or "communists linked to nihilist perversion." (Only the English-language *Buenos Aires Herald* gave them reliable coverage.) From the roofs of every building on the Plaza soldiers aimed at them with machine guns; they were set upon by mounted police; they were threatened with dogs. Yet "pedestrians ignore[d] them, and the din of traffic drown[ed] out their conversations, except to those close by," according to an early article in the *New York Times*.[37] During the World Soccer Championship in May–June 1978, the Mothers were a magnet for the massive gathering of foreign journalists. Images of the Madres—in their sensible shoes and support hose, wearing kerchiefs they had embroidered with their childrens' names—suddenly flooded the world.

Even in the context of this intense war of images, the June 16, 1978, issue of *La Prensa* was extraordinary. In the "Weekend With the Family" page, there are two pieces side by side: one on quick and easy recipes (soup and tuna tart), and "Plaza de Mayo: Yesterday and Today," illustrated by two nineteenth-century prints. "This weekend we'll explore a very special part of Buenos Aires which, since 1810, has fomented the ideas of freedom. Of this [history] its public buildings and monuments, houses, gates, and churches are a living testimony." There follows an embarrassment of detail about architects, arches, cupolas, gardens, walkways and lighting. This "exhaustive" article on the Plaza totally excludes the Mothers and the square's modern association with social protest. Also ignored are the Plaza's roots in the Inquisition, which did not officially end in Argentina until 1813, three years after the country won its independence from Spain.

Every city in the Empire had been established with the selfsame ritual: the erection and benediction of the *rollo* or *picota*, the stone pillar or wooden pole against which infidels were to be tortured. Being a city lacking in stone, Buenos Aires was invested with a massive wooden pillar, cut by the conquering Spaniards from local trees. The Plaza Mayor (later renamed the Plaza de Mayo, or May Square) was conceived in 1580 as a place for executions: to be strewn with flesh and hair and digits; foul with blood and the fluids of death. On days when all was calm, the site, and people's minds, were meant to be haunted. Even as the Inquisition wound down, the square remained the site for public punishment. The fight for

Argentine independence began in 1810. Three years later, the Inquisition was officially banned from the fledgling country and torture specifically outlawed. On May 25, 1813, a chill morning toward the end of a rainy autumn, the founding fathers organized a public burning. In the southern hemisphere, the coming of the Age of Reason would be marked by fire, to cleanse, reconsecrate, the very spot where the Inquisition had been blessed. While the crowds looked on and dignitaries gave speeches, the wooden racks and stocks and "horses" used in torture were consumed. From this date, the square would resonate with protest as well as power, be a magnet for marches, strikes, and popular celebrations. "Every time we march," says Matilde Mellibovsky, "I think back to the banning of torture *exactly here.*" Certainly the Mothers chose this spot for its high visibility and its proximity to the seat of power. But they also sought to anchor in communal space the most humane current in the Republic's history—the Enlightenment, another dirty word in the official lexicon.

Were any of these details included in *La Prensa's* "Weekend With the Family" page? Certainly not. No matter what the world was saying, the Mothers were *not* news. They had nothing to do with the Plaza.

RELATIVES OF THE MISSING were devoured by the sensation that *they themselves* were lost. As though still unable to believe it, many parents I interviewed dwelt obsessively on the disjunction that "everything was different everything was the same." People were disappearing and life went on. In the words of architect Enrique Fernández Meijide: "They took Pablo, our seventeen-year-old son, from the family apartment at 2 A.M. A few hours later, the neighborhood woke up as usual: Newsstands were open, buses were running, children were going to school. I stared through my window as though it were a telescope and the street below a faraway planet. It's a perception that stayed with me for years."[38] Pablo's mother, Graciela Fernández Meijide, is today a senator from the progressive Frepaso party. She recalled, "I'd be somewhere very familiar, like at the corner of my house, and not recognize it, literally not know where I was. I'd be on a bus, and suddenly race down into the street, convinced that a child I saw was Pablo. And then of course it wasn't. And then again I would have no idea where I was." Shortly after the election of Alfonsín, Graciela was put in charge of taking testimony for the National Commission on the Disappeared. "This story that I'm telling you now, about myself," she said, "I heard from others hundreds of times."[39]

The most extreme story of disoriented captivity "in society" was told to me by "Soledad B."[40] A quietly intense, somewhat formal woman in her early fifties, Soledad was anxious to talk, but insistent that I not publish her name. "We have been too much exposed," she said. "Print whatever is useful, but please understand, we need to guard a small private space." She had learned of my work through a prominent human rights lawyer, and invited me to her home in one of the central provinces. Soledad's younger sister disappeared in April 1976; I know from another source that her last act before being executed in La Perla was to embrace each man on her firing squad. "You are the last human beings I will ever see," she is reported to have said. "I do not want to leave this world embittered." Soledad learned through survivors that the day her sister died the whole camp went into mourning, even—perhaps especially—the men who shot her. "The letters I have received from survivors talk about her dignity," said Soledad, "and this helps, to know that she found such strength, such clarity, within herself."

Soledad's sister was kidnapped from her home by the army, which then occupied the apartment for a day and half, tearing into everything, leaving it a shambles. "This may be too stupid to recount," she said abashedly, "but it was a Monday evening, 9 P.M., I was sitting with my husband and suddenly my sister's name rose up out of my throat. All of a sudden, I was repeating my sister's name, unable to stop. This made my husband quite impatient, after all it was very strange. But I learned later that that was exactly when the army was breaking into her apartment." Soledad comes from a large, wealthy, rather conservative family. She attended rigorous Catholic schools in the progressive mold of Vatican II. In April 1976 (when her sister disappeared), she was nursing her four-month-old daughter and attributes a later diagnosis of breast cancer to the trauma she experienced then. "They called three days after my sister's kidnap, demanding an enormous ransom and making specific threats against my baby," Soledad recounted. "Our family sold houses, we sold cars, we sold land— we sold everything we could. Did we believe it would save my sister? That they would spare my baby? It was unthinkable to refuse. One way or the other, they were pulling the ground out from under us."

Soledad's parents were led on a wild-goose chase for their daughter. Ordered not to inform the police, the courts, or any other organization lest their daughter be immediately killed, they were instructed to go to a specific place with the ransom. The elderly couple went to a number of these exchange points; their money was always taken, their daughter was never there.

"There came a moment when those of us on the outside actually envied those inside, in prison. There was so much insecurity outside, so much terrible persecution. It was such anguish to have no one to talk to, no one you could trust. Even close friends stayed away. Suddenly we were 'dangerous.' You didn't trust anyone, you suspected everyone, you didn't want to connect. You got to a point where you didn't even look around. We had a friend who was taken because they wanted to know who it was she was looking at. You were no longer able to focus, didn't dare to direct your gaze. I was always behind the door, always waiting for when would they come. I would have given anything to be in jail. The waiting would be over. And I was sure that it was safer." Soledad had spoken in a rush and now was spent, on the verge of tears. "I do not know how to communicate the dimensions of this," she said weakly.

Soledad's yearning for a conventional jail—implying cause and effect, order and definition, transparency and due process—was an image that embraced far more than her personal grief. It was a moral fantasy, in a world from which the assurances of morality had all but disappeared.

ONE OF THE RUMORS allowed to circulate by the junta involved "reeducation camps" in the deserted expanses of southern Argentina. As late as 1984 (Alfonsín was elected in 1983), General Menédez kept up the charade with *Gente* ("People") magazine: "La Perla, did it exist? Yes. It was a meeting place for prisoners, not a secret prison . . . the subversives were there but in the protection of each other's company."[41] "Given our country's historical habit of keeping political prisoners, this seemed logical," recalled Susana Dillon, a Mother of the Plaza from Río Cuarto in Córdoba province. "That was the model a lot of us had in mind. I for one expected my daughter to be released. Eventually, not necessarily soon. It never occurred to me that Rita—or anyone—would be given a lethal injection after giving birth. Until 1982 (when I learned through survivors that my daughter and son-in-law were dead), I envisioned a general amnesty, a collective coming home. I did not—perhaps could not—imagine that there were death camps."[42]

But of course there were—341, according to the on-site investigations of the CONADEP. (It is possible that there were others.) More than half were controlled by the First Army Corps, whose jurisdiction included the capital, the province of Buenos Aires, and part of La Pampa. Some of the largest, busiest camps were hidden in the beautified capital (Olympus, the ESMA, Automotores Orletti, the Athletic Club). Most of the camps were in police stations and military establishments. Some, however, were located in civilian facilities, like appropriated school buildings (La Escuelita in Bahía Blanca, the College of Physical Education at the National University of Tucumán). In the city of La Plata, a camp was located in the former transmission station for Radio Provincia. One of the camps in Córdoba was housed in the headquarters of the provincial water authority. In the province of Tucumán, converted properties included an historic sugar mill on a large estate and a new motel. Private estates, like Mansión Seré in the province of Buenos Aires, were also used. So were factories, like Acindar, one of whose directors was Martínez de Hoz, named Minister of the Economy in 1976.[43]

Without realizing, civilians walked past some camps every day. "The camp where I was was located in the basement of the Sub-Prefecture of the Federal Police in the neighborhood of La Boca, Buenos Aires," recounted Ana María Careaga. "A big police station in a busy neighborhood. There were small air holes between the ceiling and the walls, from which I could hear people walking by, cars and buses passing, life going on as usual, with us disappeared in a concentration camp. In the afternoon, when the sun was at a certain angle, I could see on the floor the shadows of the people passing by, getting in and out of their cars. Yes, that I think was the worst. To be so close to them, for them to be so close to us, and yet so far away. It was surreal. We were in the world but not part of it, alive in the realm of death."[44] The realm that insistently called itself "life," "civilization," "society," required inhabitants whose faculties were essentially deadened.

The two worlds intersected on the level of personnel. The camps were staffed not only by police, security, and military, but by civilians as well. Survivors have testified that physicians, lawyers, technicians, and common criminals were also hired for torture. These men (and women) lived not where they worked, but at home. Recalled Careaga, "One day, as one of the torturers was getting ready to leave, he said to the others, 'See you tomorrow, gotta run, gotta pick up my son at school.' How, I thought, can this man have a child? Be married? Go play with his kid after torturing people all day?"[45] Yet he did. That was his job. Jorge Antonio Bergés, an obstetrician/gynecologist who specialized in the torture of pregnant *desaparecidas* and in the trafficking of their babies, also returned daily to his wife, his classes at La Plata medical school, the patients in his private practice.[46] So did numerous others.

Personnel was fluid in other ways as well. It has been proven that workers were "marked" for disappearance by their supervisors and employers. Particularly in small factory towns and villages, this wreaked havoc. Near the end of 1975 Acindar required its 500 workers to be photographed for new factory passes. These pictures were later passed on to security and military agents who used them to carry out kidnaps.[47] "Everyone

and no one [here] is a 'cop,'" observed Bernard-Henri Lévy, the French
scholar of the Gulags, who visited Argentina several times, until getting
kicked out during the World Cup in 1978. "The 'cop' is in the street, in
people's heads. The 'cop' is the lovely waitress, whom you find so deli-
ciously attentive and whom you at once also distrust, lowering your
voice when she approaches. It's the next-door neighbor, who if he ever
overheard us, wouldn't hesitate to save his skin by turning us over to the
hangmen. . . ."[48]

Even as internationally the junta flatly denied the camps, it exploited
several of them for maximum local terror. The colonial-style Mansión Seré
was one such place. Formerly the primary residence on the Seré family cattle ranch, the property was controlled by the Municipality of Buenos Aires
until November 22, 1976, when it was ceded to the air force. The Mansión
Seré was located in the Castelar suburban district just outside the capital.
The prisoners were kept in inhuman conditions, made harder to bear by
the haunting sound of breezes and birdsong. David Brid spent twenty-
seven days shackled, hooded, and forced to listen to his father being tortured. The elder Brid disappeared from the Mansión Seré; years later, his
son was still emotionally incapacitated. Neighbors heard soldiers call the
place "Attila"; they themselves called it "The House of Terror," and later
testified to hearing screams and shooting during the nights. Most everyday, they said, air force helicopters landed and took off from the surrounding grounds. One night four young men escaped, running handcuffed and
naked through the quiet streets. A series of fires eventually wrecked Mansión Seré: According to the air force, the arsonists were Montoneros;
according to those who lived nearby, the place was burned by the air force
itself, which wanted to destroy the evidence.[49]

COTI Martínez was also located in a suburb of Buenos Aires, the town
of Martínez. It "specialized" in well-known journalists (like Jacobo Timerman and Rafael Perotta) and former senators of the last democracy. The
goings-on at COTI Martínez were flaunted to the neighborhood. The terror
was so intense and unrelenting that even during the CONADEP investigations of 1984, witnesses were too frightened to give their names. Several
members of the commission told me that the neighbors who managed to
testify could not help but "shake and stutter." It was clear that without ever
setting foot in the camp, they too had been tortured. As one man recounted
to the CONADEP in January 1984:

I have lived here with my family since 1973. When we came this
adjacent building was empty. At the end of 1976 they began to

make modifications. They built an enormous dividing wall there, erected a barbed wire surround, and put gratings in the windows. There was the constant sound of people coming and going. At night the searchlights were beamed in all directions. Firing could be heard from morning to night, as though they were practicing shooting or trying out weapons. Heart-rending cries could also be heard, leading one to assume that the prisoners there were undergoing torture. Large boxes and coffins were often brought out of the building, as well as mutilated remains in polythene bags. We lived under constant stress, as though we ourselves were also prisoners; we couldn't invite anyone over, such was the extent of the terror gripping us, and for nights on end we found it impossible to sleep.[50]

In keeping with the medical terminology featured in the official lexicon and in the repressors' slang, the Alejandro Posadas Hospital was also used as a concentration camp. Located just outside Buenos Aires, it operated under the supervision of Federal Security and the Air Task Force in cooperation with the police from the nearby towns of Castelar and Morón. The majority of the repressors were supplied by the army, but—in a crowning piece of irony—others came from the Ministry of Social Welfare's Public Health Department. In yet another piece of perverted masquerade, victims were dressed in the uniforms of hospital staff. The workings of the camp were out in the open so that the doctors, nurses, and patients of Posadas would also be terrorized.[51]

THERE ARE THOSE who say that what went on still haunts these places. A police reporter told me that in the commissary of La Matanza (Buenos Aires Province), young officers insist "this building is full of ghosts" and sleep with all the lights on. The same reporter has interviewed a retired police chief who once hoped to be an artist, and who now spends his days in pajamas drawing "what is always there when I close my eyes." From a large, worn manila envelope, the journalist removed highly detailed renderings in India ink of fingers crooked in spasm, a lacerated nipple, a dead man's staring eye above his smashed-in nose. Page after page of isolated human features, their injuries obsessively worked. Not a single human body, nor even a face, is rendered whole.

Is it possible to exorcise the horror that clings to these places? Or should the horror be memorialized, and the places be preserved? Can atrocious violations of public and private space be truly healed? And should they be? How, and by whom, should the artifacts and memories of divisive history be framed in communal space? Coming to terms with these places, their past uses and continued presence, as artists have done in Figures 8 and 9, is yet a highly charged and complicated drama. And so are the legacies of living for years in an environment where, as the generals phrased it, "tranquility does not equal peace."

Extortion and robbery were part and parcel of the repression. Kidnaps were intended to net not just human "merchandise" but "war booty" as well. Victims lost their houses, cars, furniture, clothes, even personal items, like photographs and mementos. The objects that make a house a home often ended up in concentration camps for the enjoyment of the staff. The comfort, the sense of rootedness those things once brought, became a nasty joke. "In the ESMA," recalled Susana Barros, "they had all our books in the library. One day when I was cold, a guard offered to lend me my own

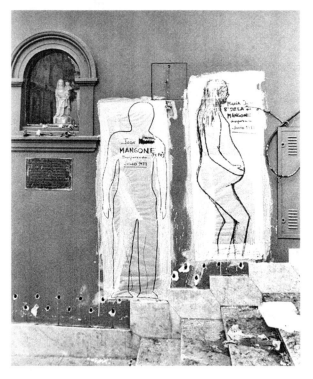

FIGURE 8. As the dictatorship crumbled, the walls of Buenos Aires began to speak. These figures appeared in 1983 on the bullet-pocked façade of the Metropolitan Cathedral on the Plaza de Mayo. María and José Mangone were friends of the photographer. (Photo credit: Guillermo Loiácono)

FIGURE 9. These figures appeared in October 1983 during the March of Resistance, which became an annual human rights event. (Photo credit: Guillermo Loiácono)

sweater. She was *wearing* my sweater. Needless to say, I refused." The prisoners who got released often had nothing, nowhere to go. Whatever place they had created for themselves was gone. "We didn't even have cigarette or bus money," recalled Barros, "let alone clothes or furniture. We were reduced to a state of total dependence. We lived with my in-laws who were very kind. But on top of everything else that has happened, you feel very regressed. And lost. Which is, of course, exactly what they wanted."[52]

In July 1993, I accompanied an *ex-desaparecido* to one of the towns just outside the capital. At the time of his kidnap, he had owned a house there. After months "inside," he was taken by two military officers to a public notary where, "on pain of death" ("as though we were making a deal, they killed you when they got the urge") he signed over ownership of his house. He had always been curious as to what they'd done with the property, as to who actually lived there. We'd arranged by letter that soon after I arrived in Argentina, we'd go and knock on the front door. We set out from Buenos Aires on a Saturday afternoon, taking the bus he'd once traveled most every day. The closer we approached, the more rattled he became and we got off, mistakenly, a couple of stops too soon. From that vantage, the neighborhood looked different to him. We passed a father and son working on their car, and asked directions to a school located close to his former house. "Please," said the older man, "it's cold, my boy will drive you." I felt my companion stiffen. "No, no," he insisted, already walking off, "we'll find it, don't go to any trouble." He was suddenly frightened that they were cops. (I don't think they were.) We wound through the streets, passing landmark stores and cafés. Then my companion stopped and quietly stared. The façade was different, and so were a number of other features. It had clearly changed hands a number of times. But that was the place. We shouldn't have come. "I see myself ringing the bell," he fretted, "and 'Colores' or 'Julián the Turk' answering the door. Crossing paths with them by chance is one thing, I'd handle it, but to go looking for them, no, this is insane. Of course," he insisted, "I know they're not here, but I keep seeing them behind the door." Among survivors, such feelings of menace, displacement, and dispossession never entirely go away. Certain places, even if one owned them, remain off-limits.

In contrast, the convicted ex-commanders had been moving about with surprising freedom. Even before their presidential pardon, they had a flexible routine, which included day-trips and excursions. When asked by reporters what life was like in Magdalena Prison, Viola (who got seventeen years), replied, "Well, I wouldn't call it a torture center."[53] Massera, sentenced to *prisión perpetua*, was often seen in Recoleta, one of the tonier neighborhoods of Buenos Aires, where he used to visit a certain tailor. As a novelist friend told me, "I went one day for the newspaper, and the vendor at the kiosk said, 'Guess who just passed by?' I thought he meant a friend of mine. But no, he meant Massera." Even as a supposed lifer, the admiral was spruce. We learned this from certain photos taken by Marcelo Ranea in June 1989 and published immediately thereafter in the newspaper *Nuevo Sur*.[54] He'd been out walking and saw Massera enter an apartment building. "I waited there for hours," Ranea recounted, "I knew that eventually he had to come out."[55] The pictures rocked even *porteños* who normally are proud of their cynicism. To the sudden uproar, the government offered no response. Within days, however, Ranea's apartment was broken into and torn apart. Amidst the wreckage was one small island of order: the passports of Ranea and his wife, opened to the pages with their photos, were neatly laid out on the pillows of their double bed. In classic Dirty War style, the photographer was being "invited" to leave the country. He did not. Ranea, a warm, burly, talkative man in his late forties, believes the photos had a tonic effect. "It isn't just confirming the rumors, though that was clearly important. For years they had us all in their sights, well, now, they have to know that *we're* watching *them*." Still, the information confirmed by the photo hurt. "The point of the sentences was to separate these men from the society they tried to ruin, to shield us from their presence," lamented Renée Epelbaum. "They're mocking us," she said bitterly, "they're insulting the memory of our children. It seems every time we get a little justice—as in the trials, the convictions—its gets undone."[56]

Osvaldo Barros, a survivor of the ESMA, joked sarcastically, "Massera is enjoying 'conditional freedom,' just like they gave to me." He was referring to the arrangement under which some detainees got released. Periodically they had to call in, or meet their repressors "for a chat," at some café. "Don't worry," one woman was told by her former torturer, "we won't lose you." In mid-1995, a reporter met one of her ex-guards, ironically enough, on the steps of the federal courthouse. "How are you?" he wanted to know. And then came the bloodcurdling threat, "How is the family?" Ana María Careaga doesn't know if she's ever crossed paths with the men who tortured her body with the electric prod. "I was blindfolded on the 'grill,'" she said. "It's terrible. They can see me, but I can't recognize them."[57] Many Argentines have told me they get an odd feeling sometimes on a bus or subway. "You never know who you're sitting next to," they say, "that normal-looking man, well, God only knows what he might have done."

At tense political moments, President Menem has from the beginning of his tenure exploited such anxieties about the environment. Upon assuming office in July 1989 (a time of economic crisis), he enacted sweeping, brutally sudden cutbacks in public spending; at the same time he launched a driving campaign to privatize major services and institutions (including telephones, transport, some research establishments) that had been traditionally subsidized. The first year of Menem's administration was characterized by months of hyperinflation: During the first two months of 1990 inflation rose 190 percent. When he took office, the exchange rate was 655 Argentine australes to the U.S. dollar; by March 1990, one dollar fetched 4500 australes; in February, the exchange had spiked to over 6000.[58] According to an official report, 35 percent of the total population was unemployed or underemployed.[59] The Secretary of Labor in Santa Fe reported in February that the city was seeing 100 firings a day and that March would be worse.[60] For Argentines who still had work, the average monthly salary was the equivalent of $70.[61] In February alone the general consumer price rise was 70 percent; it was higher for food. Menem pressed on with his program, letting it be known that public employees would be reduced by 20 percent; "disemployment" combined with social assistance programs was seen as a means to break the unions.[62] It was a scenario that could only produce social unrest. By February 1990, food riots broke out in various cities around the country and continued through the month of March. In the news day after day there were photos of housewives looting their neighborhood stores. In early March, it was announced that the government would raise money by auctioning off a group of old, but well-running, Ford Falcons. The public was invited, March 9, at 10 A.M.: 146 cars would be on the block in the parking lot of the Federal Police.[63]

If the Terror has one reigning symbol, it is the Ford Falcon. They were seen everywhere—always without license plates, cruising the streets or quietly parked and waiting. Thousands of individuals were "sucked up" off the streets, stuffed into the trunk of the car, or thrown onto the floor of the back seat, and transported to secret detention centers. The cars were also used to haul dead bodies. Even the cops sometimes complained about these cars, how they smelled of vomit and sweat, feces and urine—"the stink of fear," as one of them put it in his confession.

So who would buy one? What is the significance of selling not just symbols, but *instruments* of terror? Particularly in a moment of national anxiety? I was told that each car fetched about $10,000. One and a half million was not going to do much to heal the ravaged economy. So the measure was not, essentially, fiscal. The auction had all the trappings of a sinister two-step, or *paso doble*. First, the cars were put on display: a warning of what can happen to "suspect" individuals, mothers, say, who riot because their children don't have food. Then the cars were transferred to the general population. But who, according to Menem's corrupt, exclusionist government, is considered part of the "general population"? The precise meaning of the auction was hard to pin down. Its essence might just be that it was a show, a spectacle orchestrated to engender fear and disorientation, and to elicit—from those who could afford the sticker price—complicity.

Menem (whose term extends until late 1999) has repeatedly shown anxiety about the right to free assembly, and antipathy to public marches and demonstrations. In July 1992, on the eve of a rally for public education, he warned, "Such mobilizations are ripe territory for terrorists. It would be a shame to have another contingent of Mothers of the Plaza de Mayo, clamoring for their children."[64] Thousands of students, teachers, and parents still turned out for the peaceful march, on a frigid afternoon.

FUELING ANGUISH AND bitterness is the fact that numerous establishments that once housed concentration camps have continued to function as public institutions. If one building can be said to symbolize the genocide, it is the Navy Mechanics School (ESMA). It is here that the death flights originated. Columned, stately, immaculately white, the enormous central building is surrounded by acres of emerald-green lawns and manicured playing fields. The complex fronts on the Avenida Libertador, a busy and elegant boulevard. Its foyer is graced with one of the most extraordinary marble staircases in Argentina. Planning and preliminary interrogations were carried out in the Gold Room. Historically, and still today, the Navy Mechanics School is an elite training institution. As early as 1976, stories were circulating about the place, which the junta countered with the most cynical and sinister measures. During the 1978 World Cup, the basement of the ESMA was converted to dressing rooms and relaxation areas for the soccer players.[65] Soldiers supplied the athletes with towels and other amenities while upstairs, out of earshot, torture went on as usual. In 1979, in preparation for the investigative visit of the OAS Human Rights Commission, the ESMA did a massive "transfer." The prisoners not murdered then were moved to an island in the Tigre Delta. The torture room known as the *huevera*—where to blunt the noise the walls were covered with egg cartons—was repainted and labeled Audiovisual. "But," recalled Susana and Osvaldo Barros, "they left everything else exactly as it was. The bed, the picana, everything. Neatly arranged, impeccable. Another 'operating theater' was labeled Photography. In *capucha*, they brought in beds, arranged them in tidy little rows, and hung a sign that said, Junior Officers."[66] (The resourceful OAS commission still issued a blistering, richly documented report.)

Of the three military forces, it is the navy that has the highest number of implicated officers and proven murderers still on active duty. As a string of public scandals makes clear, the school remains a bastion of cynicism, bad faith, and defiance. In May 1993, the director of the Instituto Edward Shields, a private high school in Palermo, one of the more prosperous neighborhoods of Buenos Aires, announced that as Shields was growing too large for its space, gym classes would now be held on the playing fields of the Navy Mechanics School. As was publicly revealed at the trial of the ex-commanders, the playing fields were used for "barbecues," naval slang for the burning of corpses. A small group of parents, including a father whose sister is still missing, objected to Shields's arrangement, taking care to be tactful and moderate in their language. But the school held firm, arguing the fields were already being used by other prestigious schools, and by the employee soccer teams of the Banco Nación. "We must not raise our children with hatred and rancor," declared school director Cristina Leguizamón, "we cannot raise healthy youths by keeping old wounds open. . . . The relation of the [Navy Mechanics] School with painful episodes and circumstances of the past should not affect our decision. We regret the dissidence, but realize that it is impossible to satisfy the tastes, desires, and feelings of everyone." The father asked that his daughter, Natalia, be allowed to skip physical education when classes were held at the ESMA. Here the debate turned nasty, with a teacher exploding at the girl whose aunt was disappeared: "If a car kills someone," she shouted, "do the rest of us stop crossing the street?" That day, the school's principal sent a letter to every household, vowing that "a few would not spoil things for the many." In a sinister round-robin, initiated by the Navy, six prestigious schools later shared these playing fields, as though boys and girls playing soccer would erase the atrocities that went on there.[67]

In 1995, Scilingo's confession and the navy's attempts to promote several documented murderers of the Dirty War (including the notorious Alfredo Astiz), kept the ESMA much in the news. On the occasion of the 19th anniversary of the coup, the Mothers of the Plaza staged a march in front of the building, where they had a sign that read "Escuela de Torturadores y Asesinos" ("School for Torturers and Assassins"). When policemen began to take down the sign, Hebe de Bonafini, president of the Mothers, moved to intervene, and got hit several times on the back. The police also hit another Mother and broke the camera of the Mothers' photographer. Coverage of the march showed a number of participants bleeding from their injuries.[68] This was ugly, but minor, compared with what happened one month later.

On April 28, the mixed-up remains of at least six individuals were discovered in a garbage bin on property belonging to the ESMA. After examining the skulls, ribs, femurs, and pelvis, scientists concluded that the deaths occurred between five and twenty years ago and that the bones had been kept somewhere else until very recently being discarded. It was impossible to reconstruct a single jaw, indicating that the victims' teeth had been removed to frustrate subsequent attempts at identification. The presence of but a single pelvis suggests that an attempt was made to conceal the sex of the victims as well. When asked about "the important findings," the navy declined to comment.[69]

Five months later, in October 1995, the ESMA's pool was selected by the capital's Ministry of Education and Sports as the site for a citywide high school swim meet. In the context of recent news, the decision seemed particularly obnoxious. The prestigious Colegio Nacional de Buenos Aires—ninety of whose graduates were disappeared—immediately withdrew its team from competition. Opponents held that the ministry's choice of location "constitute[d] a violation of collective memory, a disaparagement of those who died or were murdered at the ESMA."[70] One commentary noted that the young Fernando Brodsky, kidnapped from his family's bathroom and last seen in the ESMA, had been a competitive swimmer.[71] Responding to charges by human rights groups that the ESMA was "a symbol of death," an official of the Ministry of Education indignantly enumerated activities of daily life: "We give classes twice a week for students of the Institute of Sports, and the River Water Polo Team practices here every Tuesday." The meet was indeed held at the ESMA, but only about twenty out of 120 invited swimmers attended. Journalists were barred from the pool. But one of the coaches spoke to reporters outside: "How long," he asked, "are we going to live anchored to the past?"[72]

Controversy continued in the days after the meet when it came to light that, until just recently, students from the School of Exact Sciences of the University of Buenos Aires had also been using the ESMA pool. There was as much surprise as outrage: Exact Sciences has a long history of political engagement and in its lobby is a plaque with the names of over a hundred missing professors and alumni. Faculty and student associations convoked a public ceremony of repudiation, attended by human rights groups, the Association of Ex-Detainees and Desaparecidos, and the University Federation of Argentina. Supporting the arrangement, a member of the sports program declared, "The ESMA is as much a state entity as the School of Exact Sciences. We do not believe in opening up the wounds of a sinister past; we should rather look forward, all Argentines united in peace and tolerance." As if that weren't cynical enough, he added, "Sound body, sound mind." For the student secretary of human rights, "This is not just any swimming pool, this is the Argentine Auschwitz."[73] Less than twenty-four hours after the event, the Secretary of Academic Affairs, who had quietly made the arrangement with the navy, resigned.

IN 1993, I VISITED a house in which the Dirty War unequivocally lived on.[74] It is in the city of Rosario, a tidy working-class neighborhood where in most buildings three generations live together. In the 2800 block of the calle Santiago, the houses are small, low, and pastel, painted pink or aqua or yellow or lavender. All except for the house in the middle of the block, which had always been yellow but was, when I saw it, gunmetal gray. The address is 2815, and the house was still legally owned by María Esther Ravelo, known as Pinina. She lived there in the early 1970s with her husband, Emilio Vega, and their eighteen-month-old son, Alejandro Iván. Emilio and Pinina had met and married while students at the provincial School for the Blind. Emilio had lost his sight in an accident; Pinina from an adolescent virus. Independent and industrious, the couple (both originally from the old-fashioned, rather sleepy provincial capital of Santa Fe) bought the house in Rosario because it came with a small soda factory. They named their company LODI SRL; Pinina and Emilio washed the bottles and filled them with seltzer, their sighted employee made deliveries with the truck. By all accounts, they were very well liked. Neighbors helped with Iván, and Pinina was known for her great *empanadas* (meat pies).

On the night of September 15, 1977, the entire neighborhood was sealed off and occupied by a large military commando outfitted for war. The improbable targets of this major operation were the quiet, home-oriented Emilio and Pinina. Soldiers shot their seeing-eye dog, bashed in the door, killed the couple's employee, and kidnapped the entire family. Another crew loaded all of the couple's belongings—furniture, utensils, even the chandelier—into an army truck, and drove away. Two days later, the National Gendarmes moved in and took over the house, which they soon began to use for parties. There was activity during the day as well: Retired policemen regularly stopped by, on official business about their pensions. The baby was returned to a relative, but his parents never reappeared. Seventeen years after the kidnap, and eleven years after the restoration of democracy, the house was still occupied by the police. Pinina's mother, Alejandra Leoncio de Ravelo, is now close to eighty. Together with Emilio's mother she raised Iván, worked tirelessly to find the boy's parents, and for the rightful return of their house. She is founding president of the local Mothers of the Plaza de Mayo.

In August 1993, I spent a day with "Negrita," as Pinina's mother prefers to be called. She never left her native city of Santa Fe, but lives alone now in a small, cold, extremely modest house. The terror here was unabashedly inquisitorial. Survivors identified two judges—both of whom were handily promoted *after* the regime—who stationed themselves just outside the torture rooms, at the ready to take "confessions." Hard though it is to believe, a young couple here was disappeared even as they were getting married. They had just repeated their nuptial vows and been blessed. Then the army strode down the aisle and took them away, before a church full of people.[75]

Negrita was anxious to tell her story, but got easily agitated and upset. She began by saying that on September 17, 1977, two days after the break-in, she got a phone call from Pinina. Emilio, she said, was sick, she had to take him to the doctor. The baby was with Negrita's cousin in another part of Rosario; would she come get him and keep him with her for a couple of days?

Negrita immediately got on a bus for the three-hour trip to Rosario. "As soon as I saw him, I thought something was strange. Iván was always very well cared for, but that day his clothes were a mess, didn't fit, they didn't even match, and he had nothing, not even his little bag. So how was he going to spend a few days with me? This wasn't Pinina, she was always organized. I couldn't bring him on the bus like that, I had to buy him a little outfit to take him home. My cousin said that the baby was brought to them late at night by two civilians, very well dressed, very fine hands. After a few days, I returned to Rosario and went to my children's house. As I turned into the block, Doña Laura—their closest neighbor—grabbed me, pulled me inside, and locked the door. Soldiers were still posted on their roof, they'd said they were waiting for me. What could they want with an old woman," Negrita shouted, "what could they want with a couple who was blind? Well, they figured if they got rid of me the whole thing would die down. There'd be no one to make a fuss."

Neither Emilio nor Pinina seems to have had any political activity. It appears they were looking for information on Emilio's brother, who was political, and who is also missing. "An army guy lived two doors down," said Negrita, "and I've always wondered. . . ." Whenever she referred to a military man, she used the derogatory *milico*.

Shortly before my visit, Negrita had learned from Doña Laura that five days after the break-in there was still a body in the house, decomposing. "For so many years, none of the neighbors could bring themselves to tell me. It was terrible for them. We think it must have been their driver, because Pinina called me. None of us knew his name," wept Negrita, "none of his relatives ever tried to find him."[76]

Because the kidnap took place at night, the neighbors did not specifically see Emilio or Pinina or Iván. What they saw were things being carted away, among them a rolled-up carpet, very long and fat. Some of the neighbors think that someone must have been rolled up inside. The only eyewitness account is Iván's. "He was in very bad shape, always jittery, nervous. By the time he was three, I had him in therapy," said Negrita, weeping. "As soon as he could draw, he did so compulsively, always the same thing, over and over: His father in a truck. So it seems he saw his father taken away." Iván has never drawn his mother, which suggests that Pinina was the one hidden in the rug. From the time he was four, Iván was obsessed with plastic soldiers. He would tear off their heads and hang them by their necks from the windowframes. Negrita would ask, "Sweetheart, what have you done?" "They're bad," he'd say. "I want more." It was a game he played over and over. To this day, Iván starts to shake in the presence of soldiers.

According to his grandmother, Iván has always been a loner. He is quiet, gifted with his hands, and left high school to study electro-mechanics in San Luis. At the time of my visit, he was intensely worried about the draft. As the son of *desaparecidos*, he was not required to serve (owing to a law passed under Alfonsín) but had to appear and submit his documents for review. The prospect of an interview with the army was making him a nervous wreck.

"You should know," Negrita said, sharply, "I didn't always live like this. But don't think that I'm ashamed; *they're* the ones who should be." For years she had a thriving business, the flower stall at the entrance to the Catholic cemetery. "I couldn't stand it anymore, I was going mad, mad, always hearing her voice. Where did she call me from? There was a military base nearby and all sorts of people came for bouquets. The flowers arrived at about 2 a.m., so they'd be fresh for funerals in the morning. People would come in the middle of the night, I had no idea who was who—spies, military, police. Undercover this or that. Everyday people came to me as they buried their loved ones. But where was my daughter? No one—not the army, the navy, the air force, the police, or government—would say. My writs of habeas corpus I'm sure they tore up. There were soldiers in my daughter's house, but no one had any record of the break-in."

In desperation, Negrita sold her house and flower stand and hired private detectives. She isn't sure how much she spent, probably around $50,000. "They charged by the hour and always in dollars so, with inflation, it got very confusing," she told me. "But whatever they asked for, I paid. I paid everything until eventually I had nothing." She didn't know then that the so-called detectives were really police.

For seventeen years, the military, the police, and the elected provincial government denied any knowledge of the break-in, the kidnap, or the blind couple's fate. Which is odd, since Negrita had testified to the CONADEP, and the border police had long been paying the phone bill at the stolen house. Even during democracy, the neighbors have lived in what may be called occupied territory. When I knocked on the door opposite 2815, a woman eventually answered. Frail and obviously ill, she half hid behind her door and whispered, "I had two babies, and soldiers on my roof for a week. Banging around, pounding with the butts of their rifles. As though to remind us they were there. Across the street there were more of them, always pointing their guns right at us." She would talk only briefly, but as we stood there, we saw an elderly man come down the block, knock on the door of the blind couple's house, look in the window, and then slowly walk away. "See?" the woman rasped. "See? I have to go. Be careful." And she closed her door.

Unless Pinina was alive, the house legally belonged to Iván. But no authority would declare her dead or living. The surest way to recover the house was for Negrita to legally declare that her daughter is deceased. But true to the ethic of the Mothers of the Plaza, she refused. "It's not for me to declare her dead," she wept, "if they killed her, then they have to say so. For me to say she's dead would mean that *I* have killed her."

For years every court rejected Negrita's claims. In March 1993, the Mothers staged a protest in front of the house. In thick black letters, the crowd wrote graffiti on the yellow façade: "Murderers! Robbers! We Want Them Alive!" As soon as the ceremony was over, the army moved in and spray-painted the bright yellow house gunmetal gray. A local senator pressed the case in Parliament, which provoked an extensive judicial review. On June 8, 1994, the court decreed that the Second Army Corps would return the house to its legal owners. In the first week of 1995, the keys were officially surrendered, and ownership reverted to Iván.

There is another, linguistic level to this victory. Negrita insisted to the end that the word for her daughter's official status had to be *ausente*, or "absent." In its Final Report, the departing regime had used *ausente* as a code word to absolve itself of any legal or moral responsibility for their victims whose whereabouts could not be established, or whose remains could not be found. Negrita not only salvaged the word, but endowed it with a potent legal sting.

It took eighteen years, but the neighborhood is no longer occupied. And the stolen house, long called *la casa robada*. will be converted by the family into a public space, a center for reflection, a living symbol of resistance, tenacity, and hard-earned due process.

IN DIFFERENT REGIONS of Argentina there are efforts now to recuperate places that were stolen, rededicate public spaces, and convert death camps into centers that resonate with life. In November 1995, I was told by a well-known architect in Buenos Aires, "La Plata is emerging as the capital of remembrances and commemorations." Days later I went to the city, anxious to visit these sites, which are unprecedented in Argentina.

Established in 1882 to be the capital of Buenos Aires Province, La Plata was born to fame: Every element of the new city was planned by a stellar team of international urbanists and architects. The "city of lindens" has sweeping parks and intimate squares, gold domes and cozy neighborhoods, all on a hospitable village-like scale. "This city is a marvel of rhythm and flow, stimulation and relief," enthused Roberto Saraví, an architect and professor at the university. "They actually calculated the most propitious number of human steps between trees."[77] As a political and commercial center, La Plata has been overtaken by other Argentine cities. But in terms of education, intellectual life, and social movements, La Plata has been historically avant-garde. Its Museum of Natural Sciences is the best in South America, and particularly famous for its dinosaur fossils and stuffed birds (immortalized for English readers by Bruce Chatwin in *In Patagonia*). Argentina's only house by Le Corbusier was commissioned here, by an eccentric doctor who studied bird beaks and adapted them for surgery. The National University of La Plata was known as the Sorbonne of South America. Students from all over Argentina, indeed the continent, were attracted by its rigor and engaged political profile. Logically enough, La Plata was a special target of the repression. Proportionately, it lost more of its younger population (16–27 years) than any other Argentine city. "In 1975 and 1976, you heard gunshots all day long. They kidnapped anyplace. There was no way to lead a normal student or intellectual life," recalled Jorge García, an architect who spent those years in what Argentines call "internal exile," living underground or semiclandestinely.[78] Disappearances at the university were staggeringly high: about 5 percent of the student body in natural sciences; 10 percent in humanities. High school students were endangered as well. La Plata is lamentably famous for the Night of the Pencils—September 16, 1976—when seven adolescents who had mobilized for subsidized student bus fares were kidnapped from their homes. All were brutally tortured; only one, Pablo Díaz, survived.[79]

Argentina's first public space dedicated to the *desaparecidos* was created here, at the National University's School of Architecture and Urban Planning. It came about in a deeply personal way, and the effect has been unexpectedly intense and wide-reaching. The process was begun and guided by Daniel Betti and Julio Pueyo, graduates from the late 1960s and early 1970s. Today they work together in Buenos Aires but, like virtually everyone who studied in La Plata, remain passionately tied to the city, which is an hour away. Our meeting took place in Buenos Aires, but every time they referred to La Plata, they said "here," as opposed to "there." They are walking encyclopedias of the city's history.

"Architecture was the vanguard of this highly politicized university," recalled Betti.[80] "Design, building, urban planning were associated with progressive social change. In fact, architecture was the context, the frame, within which social issues were contextualized and discussed. The faculty, and so naturally the students, always had projects in the neighborhoods. There was a rare fluidity, none of the traditional separation between the cutting edge of our discipline and the disadvantaged."

"So you see," Pueyo added quietly, "it wasn't by accident that 40 percent of our classmates were killed by the Triple A [Argentine Anti-Communist Alliance]. *Forty percent.*" Both Betti and Pueyo fled La Plata during the Dirty War. Pueyo spent those years in internal exile; Betti lived in Venezuela until the restoration of democracy in 1983. "Returning to the school was devastating," recalled Betti. "We walked the grounds in a state of shock—at every corner, every column, every tree, we would remember friends who had been murdered, disappeared. We felt a terrible need to do something, but it wasn't the moment. The general public response to what happened here was silence. And that persisted for half a generation. Our impetus was the twentieth anniversary of the first classmate murdered by the Triple A." Carlos de la Riva—"Fabiolo," as he was known—was a close friend of Betti and Pueyo. On November 3, 1974, the charismatic, politically active, father of two young children was riddled with over a hundred bullets by the Triple A, which then dumped his body in a park. Approximately 100 students and faculty from the School were assassinated or disappeared.

"Fabiolo was much beloved," said Betti, "so the idea of a commemoration in his spirit for all of the missing, including those who died in exile, struck a nerve, a need, in many, many people. As architects, we had a natural impulse to build something. Remembrance must happen deep inside each one of us in a very personal process, but it must also happen in our physical environment. You cannot talk about 'social' on one side and 'space' on the other. It's a dialectic, in which the two must have equal weight."

Pueyo continued, "So we formed the Architects Network and announced a competition, which culminated in record time. Normally these things take a year or more; ours was done in two months. And we had over ninety project proposals, which was way beyond the twenty or so we expected." In their excitement, Betti and Pueyo started speaking at once. "We got proposals from former classmates as far away as Sweden and Brazil, who'd left during the repression and never returned. Architects work in teams, and over 500 individuals participated, including some students—so you see the *urgency* the project engendered. This may be the first project in the history of Argentina for which there was no difficulty in raising money. I don't care if it sounds old-fashioned," Betti smiled, "this is a project of the people."

"The process itself was important for the whole community," said Pueyo, "and inspired unplanned reparations. An extraordinary aspect of the school was that it was totally open, there was no separation either from the streets or the woods. One of the shocks we had upon our return was to see the barriers, fences, and walls the junta had erected. The place was liter-ally imprisoned. Spontaneously, in 1994, a group of students got together and tore down one of the military's major walls."

In homage to Fabiolo, the winners of the competition—Roberto Saraví, Jorge García, and their partner Daniel Delpino—were announced on November 3, 1994, at a public ceremony, which included an exhibit of all of the entrants' renderings and models. The competition was judged by a blue-ribbon jury composed of architects and a representative from the local Madres de Plaza de Mayo.

"We contacted the families of every individual being commemorated—also a most difficult job—and asked for photos," recounted Betti, "no IDs, nothing official, we wanted pictures that resonated with life. The walls surrounding the architects' displays were covered with these photographs, all carefully labeled with dates and names. We felt it crucial to represent them as specific, fully identified human beings. To take them out of the mythical realm of *desaparecidos*, and plant them firmly in reality, within the embrace of human history. There was a young woman who'd lost both her parents, and at the exhibit she saw for the first time a picture of herself with her father."

Recalled Betti, "The day was almost unbearably intense in its combi-nation of grief, creativity, and reunion. I had so despaired of this history being lost."

For me, watching the video of the ceremony, perhaps the most moving aspect of this gathering was its tenderness. Twenty-seven sons and daugh-ters of these murdered or missing architects were present at the ceremony announcing the winning design, including Fabiolo's wife and son, who had been brought from Mexico. "It was the first time we were meeting most of these children," said Betti. "It was lovely and at the same time very hard. Some of them are the spitting image of their parents, of our friends." Seated before projections of their photos, Fabiolo's wife read the complete list of missing classmates; at each name the crowd shouted "Present!" Then the children walked to the podium, each one announcing, "I am the son [or daughter] of. . ."

The image of these adolescents arm in arm belied the isolation in which most of them have lived, the anxiety regarding their special history, their unresolved mourning for parents many of them barely knew. "For the first time," wept one young woman, "I can say—publicly, not just in my family—that I am proud of my father, proud to be his daughter." Tall, lanky, loose-limbed Joaquín de la Riva, Fabiolo's son, said, in his Mexican accent, "I feel my father all around me, for the first time, I really have a sense of Fabiolo *alive.*" One daughter provoked laughter when she announced, "I finally got to see the tables on which my father made his speeches!" Struggling against tears, another daughter described her parents' kidnap that she witnessed as a toddler: "The police took all the adults, leaving just me and my little sisters. 'Now that you know what we're capable of,' threatened the cop, 'you'll never tell.' But we have told, we tell it a lot, and we are never going to stop!"

It was also the first time the young people were meeting each other, and this was critical. A son from Córdoba began by thanking the Grandmothers of the Plaza de Mayo "for giving us the truth of our history." He then symbolically accepted the torch for his own generation, inviting all the children of the disappeared to make contact. "In the spirit of our parents, who gave their lives for a better world, we are uniquely prepared to help each other."

Having finally been brought together, the architects' twenty-seven children were not prepared to separate. When after the ceremony they asked to stay on together in La Plata, Betti arranged for them to spend four days at the nearby country house of a good friend. The adolescents vowed to search out and gather in their peers, and planned a communal camping trip for Holy Week 1995. There, in the hills of Córdoba, seventy young people founded HIJOS, the first national network of children whose parents were disappeared, assassinated, or who died in exile. In Spanish *hijos* means "children"; the acronym stands for Hijos por la Indentidad y la Justicia y contra el Olvido y el Silencio ("Children for Identity and Justice and Against Forgetting and Silence").

The monument had already proved transforming. Its creators, Saraví and García, have a joint architectural practice in La Plata. Both teach at the school from which they were graduated, Saraví in 1970, García in 1972. Saraví began here in 1962; both men suffered during Onganía's crackdown in the late 1960s. During the last dictatorship, Saraví was hunted by the police; by happenstance he didn't come home the night the dragnet closed his street. After that, he lived clandestinely in Buenos Aires. García lived in the countryside, where he formed a "micro-environment" with a small group of trusted friends. They are soulful, scholarly, and quietly intense, my gentle hosts on a brilliantly sunny day.

"We did not want to make a monument like those to which we're historically accustomed in the West. We did not want to make an object of contemplation, where the viewer looks up, passive and silent, at a massive form on a pedestal," explained Saraví. "Nor did we want the monument itself to be isolated, a thing alone." "What we did want," said García, "was a place for the hopes and concerns and anxieties of the coming generations who will—we hope—build on the model of social commitment that has always been a part of this school. The repression made for rupture; this is about continuity."

They have brought me to the school's historic green patio, the geographic heart of the place, where students have traditionally met, marched, and held outdoor classes. Situated in the very center is the living monument to their friends. It is an amphitheater spiraling downward into the ground where it culminates in a hollow. In the center of the hollow is a young linden, the city's signature tree, known for its vigorous growth and luxuriant crown. In time, those who come to gather here will be enfolded in the linden's shade.

This is a piece that invites, indeed impels, procession. Starting at the top, you slowly follow the spiral down. The stairs (seats) are smoothly, but irregularly paved with broken bricks, a material reference to the dead and missing architects. At perfectly placed intervals in the broken bricks are shining strips of black granite incised with a victim's name. The names appear in the order of their murder or disappearance, and so Fabiolo (Carlos de la Riva) is first. "The downward spiral going into the earth is like a whirlpool," said García, "but then you get to the bottom and it begets life, hope, the tree. The tree is one level lower than the last name."

The experience of this place is profound. The procession of names is devastating; you are beckoned, and can only follow. And yet there is absolutely nothing morbid or nostalgic here. The formal grace, integrity of materials, and simple open structure extend their welcome. The monument itself is alive; it literally grows. As I talked with the architects, students came to study and visit on the steps. "A magnet" said the gratified architects, "is what this place should be."

Saraví and García were anxious to show me what they insist is the first remembrance made here. During the repression, they explained, the police would come looking for any information that would help them "suck up" "subversives." The secretary in the office stole all the student photos she could find, took them home, and hid them in her house. When the dictatorship ended, and she could learn who was missing, she made a framed little mural from these photos and put it on the wall in the student café. "Alas," said Saraví, "it's incomplete. Only forty of our missing are there. But it was still the first remembrance, and that secretary risked her life to have the means for its creation."

The linden-tree monument was inaugurated on September 14, 1995. "That's our date now," said Saraví, "we've made a change in the academic calendar." The announcement ceremony of the year before had yielded information on nine more classmates, bringing the documented total of the dead and missing to ninety-eight. This process in La Plata has opened a new era for the way that memories of the Dirty War are handled all over Argentina. At the insistence of the architects, the construction site was kept open. Even as the work went on, the spot became a place to meet. Funds were raised to bring all of the victims' parents and children who lacked the means to attend the inauguration. Again, merely locating the families was complicated, given that many had moved or were living abroad. But now there was some momentum, and it was easier than the year before. All over the city, people opened their homes to the architects' families.

By all accounts the most important aspect of the ceremony centered again on the architects' children. Over the previous year, they had indeed begun to organize. This time many more of the architects' children were present. "Of course we wanted them to speak, to participate in whatever way they wished," Betti told me. "We set a time to meet shortly before the inauguration so they could let us know what they had decided. But none of them showed up. We had no idea what to expect. Later, during the ceremony, I had the microphone and called for the children. And for the longest time they didn't appear. Then, finally, they filed in, one by one, individually identified themselves, lit a torch, then walked to their place by their parent's name. The sight was overwhelming. Their growth over the previous year was extraordinary. Where earlier some of them could only cry, here they were highly articulate and, even in their sadness, strong."

Juan Andrés Sala, the son of architect Néstor Carlos ("Flaco") Sala, killed in the 1976 massacre at Margarita Belén, told me that for him the inauguration of the monument finally closed his cycle of grief. Two months after the dedication, we talked at his family's apartment in the Belgrano section of Buenos Aires.[81] Nineteen-year-old Juan Andrés—tall, thin, with large brown eyes and straight, longish light-brown hair—looks unnervingly like his father's pictures. "For me, mourning really began at the first ceremony in November 1994. It felt like my father's funeral, and there I was, feeling obligated to say goodbye to a person I'd never known." Juan Andrés was born in captivity, and insists that he retains consciousness of having been tortured in the womb. (Juan André's mother was offered a choice between rape or the *picana*, an act of participation she refused to accept.) Until the age of six months, Juan Andrés lived in jail—with long stretches of solitary confinement—with his mother, Mirta Clara, a public health psychologist who spent eight years as a political prisoner for "illicit association" with her activist husband. Until he was nearly ten, Juan

Andrés lived with his paternal grandparents, but rarely saw his sister who, for complicated family reasons, lived with their mother's parents. Though ultimately successful, the reconstitution of the nuclear family was traumatic. With the release of many political prisoners in 1983, Juan Andrés was sought out by his father's close surviving friends. They had promised Flaco to tell the boy that his father managed to see him once, through the bars on his window. He was a newborn, held tightly in his mother's arms, as the two were being moved to another jail. "I knew he was overjoyed to have a son; at times I could almost feel my father's gaze. I also knew my father had climbed on a table and made a speech shortly before they were taken away. He knew they were going to kill him. 'Many of us are going to die, but some will survive. Please, *compañeros*, tell our children we were trying to leave them a better world.'" Juan Andrés also knew that his father had tried desperately to protect his pregnant wife, and that he never once "cracked" over many days of physical torture. "So I thought that I had it all 'in order,'" recounted Juan Andrés "and went to La Plata in 1994 feeling clear and pretty calm. But when I got there I fell apart. It was too intense, too much of a shock. All those photos of dead people, I couldn't breathe. I guess, though, that's what I must have needed. Because for the whole year afterward, I rethought my life, what it meant to search for 'one's place in the world.'" He changed his concentration from economics to political science and hopes one day to help forge a "decent" government. "At the inauguration of the monument," he continued, "I felt like I had returned to my brothers and sisters, that we had created a big family. *That*, more than anything, helped resolve my grief."

Exactly one month after the dedication of the completed monument, HIJOS reunited. Their organization was growing. In La Plata, HIJOS operates from a residential house, refurbished pro bono by local builders and architects. By June 1996, there were over 500 HIJOS in a national network that is highly visible and active.

In La Plata, the Architects Network has also thrived and is expanding the scope of its reparations. In the works is the construction of a university-wide student dining hall. In the early 1970s, the Triple A exploded a bomb in the student dining hall, a symbolic warning, in the middle of the night. Famous for its terrible food, this dining hall was nonetheless the heart of the university, where everyone connected. The price of a meal was the same as a ride on the bus. Every province had a separate table for its newspapers. "No matter from how far you'd come," said Betti, "you could always read your hometown news." The junta physically destroyed what the Triple A had symbolically wrecked. Within days of their coup, they reduced the former dining hall to a vacant lot. For over twenty years, the National University of La Plata has lacked a central student dining hall. But that is slated to change. There are also plans for a square dedicated to the Mothers of the Plaza de Mayo and for a number of streets to be renamed. "This whole country was built by generals," said Saraví, "but that, we're determined to prove, is a thing of the past."

Across town was another place I was anxious to see on this visit in November 1995: the university's School of Social Work, located now in a former army base that had served as a secret detention center.[82] Like most new visitors, I arrived with some trepidation. The turreted complex is traditionally colonial in style. The entry was built as a fortress-like gate; within, the white, arcaded buildings surround a central patio. Semitropical, the gardens are wild and ragged, out of control. The place is at once dilapidated, partly collapsed, yet pulsing with color and energy. The effect is immediate and astounding: On every whitewashed wall the students have painted murals, poetry, and quotations ("No one shall be forced to obey an immoral law"). The broken bricks of the central courtyard are stenciled with the signature white kerchiefs of the Mothers. Running the length of an exterior wall is a chain of full-length silhouettes representing the missing.

"We didn't choose to come here," stressed Susana Malacalza, the school's director. Wearing jeans, an embroidered vest, and silver jewelry, Malacalza is attractive and dynamic. She looks younger than her years, moves quickly, and talks precisely. Now in her late forties, she'd been forced into exile and returned from Mexico only with the advent of democracy. For her, personally, the adjustment has been hard; her brother and sister-in-law were last seen in this place. "It was apparently a transit center," she said. "They didn't keep people very long. The neighbors pretty much knew what was happening. On the day of our dedication, a woman who lives on the street brought photos of how the place looked then." She walks me across the courtyard into a large lecture hall, behind which are the bars and other remains of the secret cells.

"The army left it in terrible shape," Malacalza complained, "they took everything they could—doors, faucets, flooring, all kinds of architectural details." Many of the walls have holes; some of the former barracks are missing walls.

Desperately cramped, the university bought the base from the army two years ago. The original plan was to raze the buildings and start new. But the funds never materialized and are no longer really expected.

"The students transformed this place," Malacalza said proudly, "they have made it their own." The library is named for the School of Social

Work's first *desaparecida*. A plaque inside lists them all. More than a few students are the children of *desaparecidos*. It was the first school to decide that no classes would ever be held on March 24, the anniversary of the Dirty War coup.

"But we gather on that day," emphasized Inés Pallavicini, a student who as the daughter of political militants grew up in foreign exile. "My father never recovered from the failure of their project, he never stopped feeling persecuted. Shortly after returning to Argentina, he took his life. In my mind I know that he was a suicide, but in my heart I know they killed him." A short, blonde, muscular woman in her early twenties, Inés speaks frankly and with little embellishment. It was she, not I, who initiated our interview, which included her younger sister, Lucía, and their friend Anita, the daughter of a *desaparecido*. "We have to make March 24 *our* anniversary, to commemorate our own knowledge and awareness. It's essential to come together, with survivors, the Mothers, activists, and scholars. Each year, it's different," Inés reflected, "and that, too, is important, it says something about where we are in relation to that history, which is *our* history."

On March 24, 1995, HIJOS of La Plata had covered the patriotic monuments in the Plaza San Martín and Plaza Italia—the city's two main squares—with black cloth. "We declared it a Day of National Disgrace," said the three young women, talking all at once. "We did the wrapping in the middle of the night, climbing up on the horse, draping the fabric, taping it to the stone. The newspaper vendor on the corner was our 'lookout' for the police." Reflected Anita, the quietest of the three, "I kept thinking of the cadet who was going to have to climb up there the next morning and undo it all. It was very funny, but at the same time it made me wonder what *he* would be thinking. He'd be just our age, after all."

On a warm afternoon late in the spring semester, the classrooms and hallways of the School of Social Work were full of activity. Six hundred students are pursuing degrees. "They spend a lot of time in the barrios on the outskirts of La Plata," said Malacalza. "They're very committed and most arrive with solid prior experience." Academically, the move has galvanized the School of Social Work. In conjunction with the Catholic University of Brazil, it is starting a four-year doctoral exchange program. There is also a new program in mental health. Shortly before we met, Malacalza was abroad, working on the model for a post-doctoral human rights seminar, in cooperation with UNESCO and the National University of Mexico.

Malacalza offered to drive me home to Buenos Aires. While she finished a meeting, I strolled the grounds with Inés, Lucía, and Anita. I was struck by the painterly skill in the murals, the care that was taken with the lettering. As the sun set, some intensely sweet-smelling flowers opened. At twilight, students streamed in for night class and meetings. Small groups were assembling under the arches. The atmosphere was quiet, peaceful, and focused. It was a place I found difficult to leave.

MARCH 24, 1996, MARKED the twentieth anniversary of the coup. For the better part of a generation the anniversaries have rolled around with little public participation. This year, however, was different. A major thrust of the observances involved the taking-back of public space, making visible the history that long was hidden. The push began in late 1995 (high spring in the southern hemisphere) with a vivacious day-long human rights "occupation" of Plaza Las Heras in the Palermo neighborhood of the capital. The Mothers of the Plaza de Mayo—Founding Line garlanded the trees with large photos of their children and set up tables with a selection of their personal items: diplomas and musical instruments; rosaries and yarmulkes; drawings, poetry, postcards, and travel souvenirs. There were soccer balls and tennis rackets, cameras, typewriters, and stethoscopes. Thirty-thousand balloons were released to the sky. "How and when they died is something too many of us still don't know," said Renée Epelbaum, "but no one, no one, shall deny that our children lived. These very particular lives should not be subsumed in any abstract category, even one as legally and morally potent as *desaparecido*. Their disappearance was someone else's crime, not our children's identity."[83]

All over Argentina the last ten days of March were dedicated to commemorations, arts events, and human rights activities. At the culminating march in Buenos Aires, some 100,000 people converged on the Plaza de Mayo (the police figures, always extremely low for such demonstrations, put the numbers at 50,000). None of these massively attended actions was marred by violence. In a gesture that many found insulting, President Menem did not attend a single gathering, but issued a prerecorded five-minute statement, blandly criticizing the lawlessness of the last military regime. "Events have proven me right," declared Menem in a March 24 radio interview during which he was challenged on his pardon of the convicted ex-commanders. "I regret nothing. We had to pacify the country in order to transform it. We have definitely closed the wound."[84]

The President's statement is, of course, absurd. A whole slew of events testifies to his bad faith, and to high anxiety in official circles concerning any kind of popular mobilization. In late February 1996, the focus was again on La Plata, when the police and military violently suppressed a student rally against government plans to end the longstanding tradition of free tuition and open admissions at public institutions of higher learning. Demonstrators were subjected to tear gas, clubbings, and rubber bullets—as seen across the country (and as far away as Miami) on the television news. In what many have described as a "replay" of Dirty War tactics, the streets of La Plata were patrolled by armored trucks and Ford Falcons without license plates. More than 300 students were picked up—many in preemptive police strikes and held without charge on suspicion that they *intended* to participate in the rally. In contrast to the climate of twenty years ago, residents opened their doors to youths running from soldiers and the police. "We had no idea who they were," said one woman. "What difference does it make? They needed protection." A father who went to a police station to inquire after his daughter was summarily taken into custody. Some of the students picked up are children of *desaparecidos*, and were held in some of the same precincts as their parents. Pedro Tello, a member of HIJOS, was arrested for bringing toilet paper to friends being held by the police. Lucía García, also a member of HIJOS, was one of about 100 students guarded by dogs on the interior patio of an infantry base known to have been a detention center. "It was horrible," she said, "to think that our parents might well have been tortured *right there, by the same guys.*[85] The repressive episode culminated in the police beating of the president of the Mothers, Hebe de Bonafini, a native of La Plata who was at the rally to show support for the youths. The image (Fig. 10) in the papers and on television was a shocker: blood oozing from the signature white scarf, a Madre close to seventy, bent under the blow from policemen armed with shields, clubs, and guns, and whose faces are hidden by heavy, dark-visored helmets.

The Minister of the Interior, Carlos Corach, seized on the events in La Plata in an attempt to prohibit all commemorations organized by Bonafini's segment of the Madres and scheduled for March 21-24 in the capital's Plaza de Mayo. The judiciary, specifically Judge Mariano Bergés, immediately ruled against the government on the grounds of constitutionally guaranteed individual rights, including those of free expression and peaceful assembly. He also pointedly reminded Corach that the obligation to ensure the security of all participants rested with the Ministry of the Interior (which has responsibility for the Federal Police).

One popular action, however, *was* derailed, at the site of the camp known as Olympus (El Olimpo). The Buenos Aires City Council had recently approved a proposal to convert the building into a living museum of memory, to be named El Museo Nunca Más, conforming to UNESCO

FIGURE 10. At a March 2, 1996, demonstration for increased government spending on higher education, the Provincial Police bloody the head of Hebe de Bonafini, president of the Mothers of the Plaza de Mayo. (Photo credit: Associated Press)

guidelines developed in relation to earlier installations in (among other places) Hiroshima, Nagasaki, and Auschwitz. "Our objective is to convert a sinister place devoted to the systematic production of death into an open center for life," I was told by Jorge Tula, one of the councilmen who initiated the project. Having been forced into exile by the repression, Tula spearheaded this work with passion and commitment. "We owe this to our children, to future generations. We see the Nunca Más Museum as a part of our ongoing struggle to cement pluralism, democracy, and creativity in public life. And to accomplish this, we must document our painful history and cultivate collective memory, in a place that is open and freely accessible to all."[86] The museum's three main functions will be to "collect, research, and disseminate." The documentation center will include the full range of print, graphic, and electronic materials. There will also be exhibition, performance, and meeting spaces. The physical conversion will be accomplished with advice from the University of Buenos Aires School of Architecture, the Central Society of (Argentine) Architects, and technical organizations connected to UNESCO. The final design will be selected in a juried competition.

Though the vote in the council was nearly unanimously in favor, the process had been long and complicated, overlapping with—and further stimulated by—the confessions of Scilingo. Every potential crack in party façades of unity was exposed. The conflicts in Menem's Peronist Party spanned the political spectrum. Included in the project's initiators and supporters are former political prisoners, and relatives and friends of *desaparecidos*. Other Peronists told the press they could go along "provided the project was moderate, without allusions to present-day questions, like the [president's] pardon."[87] The vociferous opponent on the party's right was Francisco Siracusano, who has been in public life for as long as anyone can remember. An elderly godfather-type, he shouted at me from behind an enormous desk decorated with a multitude of national flags and two remarkable cigarette lighters: one in the shape of a grenade, the other in the form of a revolver. Two elderly guards had ushered me through a small maze to Siracusano's inner office, and remained posted in the door at my back for the duration of the interview. "And all those killed by the guerrillas? Don't they get a museum?" he bellowed. The point of a government-subsidized center against a history of state terrorism was lost on him.[88]

Another delicate point involved the selection of the site. Of the camp locations remaining intact, only two, Olympus and the Navy Mechanics School, were physically and geographically suitable. "We wanted a place whose appropriation would definitively condemn state terrorism," said Tula. "In that sense, I preferred the ESMA. It would have made a ringing statement against the machinations of Massera, the Navy's promotion of known torturers, and the force's censure of Scilingo's revelations. The ESMA is the reigning symbol of that repression, not just here but also abroad. The possibility of actually getting the ESMA seemed so slim, however, that human rights groups feared the attempt could scuttle the project. So we focused on Olympus, and worked to be ready for an announcement ceremony for March 24."

The former "Residence of the Gods," in operation from 1978 to 1979, was located in a trolley depot in the working-class neighborhood of Floresta.[89] A notable feature of the site today is that the trees in front of the building are comparatively low and thin. The reason is that during the World Soccer Championship, police came in and cut down all the trees on the block, to clear the way for barriers and obstructive fencing. "No one dared to ask them why, to ask them anything," recounted a woman from the neighborhood.[90]

If there had to be such a museum. Federal Police Chief Adrián Pelacchi also favored locating it at the ESMA. The building that had housed Olympus was currently operating under his control, as the Department of Automobile Maintenance and Verification. "After all," he complained, "the police was controlled by the military then. The Argentine Federal Police, like any other police or security institution, acts within the legal limits in force in a given country at a given moment, without questioning whether those limits are legitimate or illegitimate."[91] It is, of course, that unquestioning mode of behavior that the museum seeks to address.

When, shortly before March 24, a group from the leftist Frepaso party announced plans to paint a mural on an exterior wall of the former camp. Federal Police Chief Pelacchi threatened to resign. "The force sees this as a provocation," he told the press, "I'm getting a lot of pressure from within." He allowed that he didn't oppose a symbolic mural, but asked that it be done elsewhere, for example, on municipal bill-boards. For their part, Frepaso was accommodating. If the police weren't going to let them near the building, well, then, they would paint the sidewalk.[92]

During the Twentieth Anniversary, the streets of Buenos Aires visibly belonged to the people. At 3:10 A.M., the exact hour of the "Gentlemen's Coup," HIJOS began a torchlight march to the Federal Court where they delivered 100 writs of habeas corpus. Bonafini's group of Mothers symbolically occupied the immaculately white Cabildo, the country's first seat of government, situated just outside the Plaza de Mayo. Participating in all the events in Buenos Aires was twenty-one-year-old Mariela Gal, a university student concentrating in history and the stepdaughter of Mario Villani. For Mariela, "The marches were beautiful and horrible, moving and hallucinatory all at once."[93]

The length of the Avenida de Mayo was lined with the canvases of forty artists, who had labored for months to construct what they called a "Bridge of Remembrance." Each painting measured four by two meters. Mounted on specially constructed lighted posts ("to illuminate memory") the large works cast an extraordinary power, especially at night. Official excuses to the contrary, the "Bridge of Memory" was no accidental casualty. When by prior agreement the artists arrived to claim their works—at 3 A.M., March 26—they learned that their canvases had already been taken down by municipal employees and trucked to the city's dump. "City workers had got the order to 'clean up the Avenue,'" said Viviana Ponieman, the artist who arranged the exhibit, with funding from the Congressional Workers Union. "The Twentieth Anniversary was barely over, but to look at the Avenida de Mayo, you would never know that anything special had happened there. All traces of the mobilization were gone, we could say *disappeared*." The artists immediately drove out to the dump to recover their paintings. However, by the time they arrived, their works had been already compacted, along with four tons of other garbage, the weight of the city's usual daily haul. "We went tramping through these stinking mountains of trash, here and there you could pick out the remnants of flowers and food,

FIGURE 11. Procession of former *desaparecidos* and political prisoners on the 10th anniversary of the Dirty War coup, March 24, 1986. (Photo © Rafael Wollman)

but of our paintings, there wasn't a trace."[94] The violation of these individual artists is outrageous; the link to past definitions of "filth" and "cleansing" chillingly clear.

Predictably enough, some former members of the regime also seized the occasion to speak out. Ex-commander Emilio Massera held that "the so-called victims had brought it on themselves." Videla's former press secretary declared, "I was, am, and will always be, a man of the Process."[95] However, the vast majority of those men were silent and kept out of sight.

Porteños forge on, claiming their history as a means to make permanent geographic changes in their capital. On March 25, 1996, in the picturesque district of San Telmo, a small square was dedicated to the combatant writer and journalist Rodolfo Walsh, murdered by the regime nineteen years before.[96] On April 30, a street was named for Azucena Villaflor de Devincenti, the founding president of the Mothers of the Plaza de Mayo.[97] It was fifty-three-year-old Azucena who had the idea of marching in the Plaza, "of knocking on Videla's door." She was kidnapped from her home on December 10, 1977, and is believed to have perished in the ESMA. Azucena's street is in the renovated port district of Puerto Madero, a newly chic pedestrian mall full of restaurants, galleries, and cafés. The City Council also voted to rename the Sancti Spiritu Passage in memory of the "Palotine Martyrs," five priests massacred in their rectory on July 4,1976.[98]

Around the country other ordinances have been enacted to protect and preserve communal space. Several municipalities have officially declared personas non grata the ex-commanders and other known repressors.

On May 20, 1996, a highly unusual Catholic mass was celebrated, in memory of all the missing. Until then, such masses were almost exclusively the province of FAMUS, the now-defunct, arch-conservative Relatives and Friends of Those Killed by Subversion. Especially significant was the ceremony's location in the Santa Cruz Church, the site of Astiz's notorious sting of December 8,1977.[99] Those attending the mass more than took back a violated space; one could say they reconsecrated the sanctuary.

FOR THESE TRANSFORMATIONS to even begin, it took the better part of a generation. Given the extent of the trauma, this is hardly surprising. In one of our many conversations, Susana Barros recalled the first time that surviving *desaparecidos* and political prisoners identified themselves in a mass demonstration. It was at the annual March of Resistance in 1986, and the group of survivors wore white plastic masks that covered all of their faces (except for their eyes) and most of their heads (see Fig. 11). Appearing out of the darkness, they were an unnerving sight. "People wept," recalled Susana, "many of them reached out to touch, embrace us, as we walked by. Others stared, I think they were unable to speak. For us, too, it was very hard, wearing the mask gave you an involuntary sense memory of being in *capucha*." After the procession the group sat down, perfectly still, to publicly evoke that image. Some of the survivors wore handcuffs and shackles, though Susana did not, finding that too upsetting. "I've often thought about the power of those masks," she reflected. "We knew that it would be very dramatic, would symbolize clearly our apartness. But the masks also gave us some psychic protection which, speaking for myself, I know I needed. And maybe some of the onlookers needed it, too."

The Dirty War occurred, at least in part, because Argentines were too terrorized to look each other in the face.

Having looked away, or looked blindly on, during public abductions like Susana's, many understandably resisted commemorating that history in communal space. The very concept of communal space has had to be relearned. And while the transformation is new, it appears to be authentic. In Rosario, 2815 Santiago Street is open to everyone, and it is no longer known as the House of the Blind.

6

"The Scilingo Effect"

The Past Is a Predator

The Navy Mechanics School turned me into a criminal, used me, and then threw me away. Why should I be complicit in their cover up?
—(Retired) Captain Adolfo Scilingo, March 1995

What Scilingo showed me was that in the deepest recesses of my spirit, I still hoped my children and grandchild were alive. Hope was my secret, even from myself. It was terrible to discover and, I have to admit, terrible to let it go.
—Laura Bonaparte, June 1995 (Mother of the Plaza de Mayo—Founding Line)

JUST AS MANY ARGENTINES WERE BEGINNING TO REGAIN A SENSE OF communal space, their environment was violated in a new and shocking way. Beginning on March 2, 1995, when Retired Navy Captain Adolfo Scilingo (Fig. 12) publicly confessed to participating in two of the weekly "death flights" that were a hallmark of the Dirty War, the Argentine media gained a harrowing new, though small, cast of characters. Testifying that death-flight duty was rotated to virtually all naval officers, Scilingo is the first military man to sue his superiors for lying about their leadership in the atrocity. In Scilingo's wake, a half-dozen other ex-military men directly involved in kidnapping, torture, and murder in the secret camps also came forward and were featured, day after day, on radio and television, in newspapers and magazines. They included a down-at-the-heels former sergeant at once sympathetic to the victims and awed by his superiors' license to

FIGURE 12. Adolfo Francisco Scilingo, who publicly admitted that while stationed at the Navy Mechanics School in 1977, he participated in two death flights, throwing a total of thirty living, but drugged, *desaparecidos* from navy airplanes into the Atlantic Ocean. (Photo credit: Courtesy of TELAM)

kill, the ex-director of La Perla currently freelancing for Federal Intelligence, the unrepentant Julián the Turk, and "Dr. Death," an obstetrician/ gynecologist who tortured and sold babies as a member of the Buenos Aires Provincial Police. Not one to be kept from the limelight, Massera loudly blamed the victims, who, he insisted, "knew the risks." For months, *porteños* starting their day with the radio were stunned to consciousness by the voices of these men in their bedrooms, in their kitchens, in their cars. "The past is a predator," goes an Argentine adage, and for many it is literally true.

The accounts of Scilingo and the other enforcers, all immune from prosecution because of the Punto Final and Due Obedience laws, set off a dramatic chain of reactions, throwing into relief not just the day-to-day methods of the repression but also the wide spectrum of *internal* factors that enabled it to function: Arguably as important as ideology and the will to power were corruption, opportunism, and hapless confusion. Even more acutely, the stories of these men showed the legal and moral contradictions of Argentine democracy. In this newly divisive, daily unfolding politics of the Dirty War, every institution had its schisms. There have been unprecedented admissions of wrongdoing by the heads of the army and air force, protests from the reactionary sectors of the military, and conflicting messages from the navy, the government, the police, and the Catholic Church. Even human rights groups have disagreed on how best to define, confront, and manage what they call "the Scilingo effect." For some, this "Scilingo moment" represents a potential aperture, and they are pressing the military (and Menem as commander in chief) for reliable lists of how, when, and by whom their loved ones were killed. Other groups refuse to have any dialogue at all with the military. In some circles, there is resistance to letting go of the mythic discourse of the missing, as though to disappear were transcendent, to be murdered banal. Yet others have dismissed the whole fracas as a *"desaparecido* show" dragged out by a cynical press.

"Still and all," said Emilio Mignone, cofounder of CELS (Center for Legal and Social Studies) and father of a *desaparecida*, "the society was forced to confront its own denial, its tacit approval during those years of clandestine crimes. Public reaction was comparatively subdued during the trial of the ex-commanders because the proceedings were not allowed to be televised. In our day and age people need to see faces. It's the only way for them to realize that that nice-looking, well-dressed, articulate Mr. Scilingo, that gentleman who could be your next-door neighbor, is the very embodiment of the Process, the very horror itself, and here he is addressing you in your living room night after night."[1]

This saga began on evening television on March 2, 1995, when Horacio Verbitsky, Argentina's premier investigative journalist, was a guest on *Hora Clave* ("Critical Hour"), the most influential news show in the country. In a rigorous, carefully framed delivery, Verbitsky played tape recordings from nearly a year's worth of closely guarded interviews with Scilingo. The following day, in *Página 12*, the morning paper for which he works, Verbitsky published "The Final Solution," the first part of a series based on Scilingo's tortuous confessions. (Verbitsky also gathered this work into a book, *El Vuelo* ("The Flight"), which became an immediate best-seller.[2]) The following Thursday, March 9, Scilingo himself appeared on *Hora Clave*, ratifying Verbitsky's tapes and filling out some of the details of his horrific story. The man who admitted to throwing thirty living individuals out of airplanes into the sea was impeccably groomed, wearing a suit by Christian Dior, and highly articulate. Dark hair combed back off his forehead, a neatly trimmed moustache, the body language of a man who is educated and socially adept.

In 1976, Scilingo was a junior officer in his late twenties, clearly destined for an elite career. He requested to be sent to the ESMA, "to serve with the saviors of the Nation." At the time, "[he] believed what [they] repeated everyday, 'that the only good guerrilla was a dead guerrilla.'"[3] Before receiving his chosen assignment, Scilingo was stationed at the Puerto Belgrano base in Bahía Blanca. As he tells it, "Vice Admiral Luis María Mendía [then Chief of Naval Operations] got us together in the cinema at the base and explained that, given the circumstances, certain instruments to be used against the enemy would be out of the ordinary. Since colonial times, he said, armies had distinguished themselves by their uniforms, but that had changed. Now we too would go without uniforms, so as to mask our presence among civilians. With regard to the subversives who had been condemned to death, Mendía told us they 'would fly,' and that the ecclesiastic authorities had assured him that this was a Christian, basically nonviolent form of death." If anyone had problems with this he could be assigned elsewhere, allowed the Chief of Naval Operations.

"I," said Scilingo, "had no argument. I imagined that they had studied everything very carefully. We were all convinced it was more humane." The group's questions and discomfort derived from the prospect of dressing as civilians; being out of uniform didn't feel right. But they would adjust; this was, after all, an unprecedented struggle.[4] Scilingo's understanding was at this point abstract; he had no idea what, concretely, this struggle entailed. A few days after arriving at the ESMA (where he was in charge of the auto shop) Scilingo went upstairs to repair a ventilator and accidentally ended up in *capucha*, an area in which he was not allowed. "I opened a door and out came a young woman in an advanced state of pregnancy, dressed in a nightgown, slippers, and robe. She stopped in front of me, looked at me with sad eyes, then continued on to the bathroom. There were other pregnant women in that room. . . . It was unnerving to see future mothers in these circumstances, in spite of the hatred I felt for subversives. . . . This was the war I had asked to fight, but did it have to be like this? . . . It was a scene out of the Middle Ages. . . . There were prisoners of various ages . . . most of them were pestilent . . . trembling. You could hear moaning. Some of them were praying. . . . The air was suffocating. . . . You could feel their terror, as they tried to adjust their leg irons, so they wouldn't rub against the open wounds on their ankles."[5]

Scilingo declared that virtually every officer took part in the flights, which were considered "a form of communion," "a supreme act we did for the country."[6] High-ranking officers and "special invitees" accompanied the flights to lend cachet and give encouragement. He calculated that during his two years at the ESMA (1976–77), "a hundred Wednesdays, between 1500 and 2000 people" were thrown into the sea.[7]

Scilingo was tapped twice, in April and June of 1977, by then Captain Adolfo Mario Arduino, who was later promoted to Vice Admiral and Chief of Naval Operations. Prior to "transfer," Scilingo recounted, the prisoners selected "to fly" were called by their numbers, ordered to form a line and march—shuffle, really—in leg irons to the basement where, the brass explained, they were being flown to a recuperation camp in the south, and would now be getting "vaccinations." Whereupon a physician administered the first dose of a tranquilizer (sodium pentothal) dubbed by the force as Pen-Naval. "It made them drowsy," Scilingo recounted, "and we had to help them to the plane. Once onboard, a physician administered a second shot to knock the prisoners out. The doctors moved back to the cabin so as not to violate their Hippocratic oath," Scilingo glossed, without irony. "Once the prisoners were asleep—this is very morbid," he allowed, "we undressed them, and two of us would drag one prisoner down the aisle and then push him out into the sky. . . ." Scilingo shoved thirty individuals to their deaths: thirteen on the first flight, seventeen on the second. Among them was a sixty-five-year-old man, a sixteen-year-old boy, and two pregnant women in their early twenties. On his first flight, Scilingo slipped and nearly fell out of the plane with a prisoner who was struggling and would not let go. He survived only because a comrade grabbed him and pulled him back. "Its' a recurring nightmare," he testified, "one I'll have for the rest of my life." He is still tormented by "the heavy scrape and jangle of [the prisoners'] chains and shackles . . . the clothing left strewn on the floor of the plane after the 'cargo' was dropped." On the return flight no one said a word; back at the ESMA, Scilingo drank himself into a long, deep sleep and then went to confession, where he was immediately absolved. "It was a Christian form of death," the priest assured him and, bastardizing a parable from Matthew 13:24, explained that subversives were the weeds sown by the enemy among the wheat. The tares had to be burned, so the wheat could be gathered into the barn. "And that," says Scilingo, "is how we were taught to save Western, Christian civilization from the Red terror."[8]

Appearing on the same *Hora Clave* as Scilingo was Vicente Massot, Menem's former Vice Minister of Defense, and a close friend of the ex-director of the ESMA. Admiral Rubén Jacinto Chamorro, whom he used regularly to visit at the camp. Massot "counterbalanced" Scilingo by justifying the repression in rhetoric that came straight from the Dirty War.[9]

President Menem's first reaction was terse and dismissive: "Scilingo is a crook. He is rubbing salt on old wounds." To prove his point Menem had Scilingo arrested for having written a series of bad checks in 1991. Scilingo's real crime, it would seem, is breaking the pact of silence. The head of the joint chiefs of staff, Mario Candído Díaz, immediately buttressed Menem's attack: "[This retired captain] has lost all his virtues as an officer and a gentleman." Indeed, because Menem ordered the navy to strip Scilingo of his rank, the chief of staff, Admiral Enrique Molina Pico, could say, "I don't need to discuss Scilingo. He is no longer part of the force." To an incredulous Mike Wallace on 60 *Minutes*, Menem held firm: "Now I ask: What is the reason to go back to a past that leads nowhere?"[10] Among those responding to Menem were the governments of France, Brazil, Spain, Sweden, and Italy, all of which reopened cases on citizens murdered or disappeared by the last Argentine repression.

For survivors of the torture centers and for relatives of *desaparecidos*, the presence of these men has been a torment that is almost beyond words. Psychologist Laura Bonaparte lost seven members of her immediate family; both a Mother and Grandmother of the Plaza de Mayo, she has raised Ugo, the surviving son of her missing younger daughter, Irene. "This will sound strange," Laura told me, "but my first reaction was bafflement. I was truly *perplexed*. I mean, I have known for years how and when they killed my husband, my older daughter and her husband. I helped identify their remains, was present when they opened the mass grave. I never did learn the exact fate of my younger daughter and her husband, or my son Victor and his wife, but I believed that I understood they were dead, that I was beyond self-delusion. What Scilingo showed me was that in the deepest recesses of my spirit, I still hoped, Hope was my secret, even from myself. It was terrible to discover and, I have to admit, terrible to let it go."[11] In Buenos Aires, families and friends of *desaparecidos* gathered for a kind of funeral, dropping flowers into the high brown waters of the Río de la Plata. Yet the president continued, cruelly, to insist: "The Argentine people are tired of hearing about the Dirty War."[12]

Many survivors I spoke with are frankly embittered. "In terms of the information, Scilingo hasn't said anything new," stressed Osvaldo Barros, speaking for the Association of Ex-Detainees and Desaparecidos. "Numerous witnesses talked about transfers and death flights at the trial of the juntas. The calls, the line-ups, the clothes—but not the people—that reappeared in the camp. For years no one wanted to hear it from us, and now all of a sudden—because of Scilingo?!—the flights are news." (Even *Nunca Más*, whose redactors had spent a year listening to testimony, introduced the subject of death flights with, "This is scarcely credible, but is mentioned by many witnesses.") "Our society harbored all kinds of suspicions about the victims, but immediately gives credence now to the perpetrators. Why?" lamented Barros, "*why?*"[13]

IT WAS SCILINGO'S WIFE, Marcela, who first spoke openly of the death flights and, she insists, no one ever disbelieved, judged, or aggressed her. "I talked about the flights with absolutely anyone," Marcela told me, unblinkingly, as we sat in her living room in November 1995.[14] It was a bright afternoon in late spring, the windows to the terrace were open; on tape, her energetic voice is ringed, unnervingly, with birdsong. "I started [talking] in 1986, or even before. I never hid this, it never occurred to me to worry if the person had missing relatives or anything. I needed to unburden myself. It was *my* problem, and that's how I talked about it. With whom? Well, the children were little, so with other mothers at school, or with cousins, including those who'd been involved in subversion. I told our story without any inhibition—except, of course, to friends whose husbands were in the navy. Everyone, but everyone, understood," she insisted, with a grateful smile. "They understood not only me, but my husband. No one ever said, 'He's a murderer.' Never. Ever. No one. And I've spoken with many, many people."

To Marcela Vallés de Scilingo, the pretty, blonde, vivacious daughter of a civil engineer, who abandoned university studies in agronomy to become an exemplary navy wife, the flights were a terrible *domestic* problem. Since about 1980, her husband had been drinking heavily. "But in the force, you know, there's a lot of drinking, and so I didn't give it a lot of importance." Toward the end of the regime Scilingo was posted, prestigiously, to the Casa Rosada where his duties included receiving foreign dignitaries, among them Alexander Haig.[15] As the departing junta was preparing its Final Report, Scilingo suggested respectfully (and fruitlessly) that they publish a list of the dead. Over the transition to democracy, Scilingo grew so withdrawn as to become estranged from their four children; then, for reasons Marcela didn't understand, he was suddenly denied promotion; in 1986, he insisted on leaving the force after twenty-four years, with less than two years left to be vested for his pension. Among the other things Marcela didn't know was that her husband used to haunt the rounds of the Mothers of the Plaza de Mayo, confused by his guilty compulsion, unable to give up the indoctrination that these women were surrounded by "subversives." Marcela learned about the death flights gradually, beginning in 1985. "He kept having these nightmares of falling out of a plane."

Her first reaction was, "Well, it didn't happen yesterday. I mean, seven years had passed. At that moment, I thought it was right, if they told him

to do it, there was a reason." She reassured him, told him that he had fulfilled his orders. "At the time, there were stories about one officer—a single
officer—who refused and was considered a traitor by everyone else." She
was referring to Captain Jorge Felix Búsico, who testified to the CONADEP
and whose signed declarations appear in 'Nunca Más.[16] "To refuse at that
time was considered insane," she stressed. "And I repeat, civilians approved.
It was war. Adolfo's big concern was that civilians wouldn't understand.
The first person he told—I believe about six years later, or a year before
telling me—was an older cousin, a civilian, who totally agreed, told him
he'd done right. This was with hindsight, after the trials and everything.
Even the church—the priest who baptized our youngest child, gave her
First Communion—absolved, even praised, Adolfo. My husband thought
something was wrong with him. All his friends were handling it, keeping it
in, why couldn't he? He was in very bad shape."

In July 1984, the anguished Scilingo had requested to postpone an
exam he was scheduled to take for entrance to the War College. His request
was denied and, after he passed the test with high marks, his superiors
wanted to know why he had felt he was unprepared. He explained that he
was troubled by his participation in "the war against subversion," and specifically by the flights, which had left him with recurrent nightmares. His
superiors suggested he be seen by a psychiatrist. Days later, on October 7,
1985, he received notice that he was "definitively unsuitable for leadership
functions" and would not be promoted. Scilingo immediately appealed,
citing his long record of exemplary service and assuring his superiors that
his "problem with the flights" was "personal" and had been "overcome."
He got a reprieve in the form of a notice that he was "temporarily unsuitable for leadership functions." According to the navy medical exam,
Scilingo had "no incapacitating psychiatric illness or anomaly," which
confused him even more. In any case, it was clear that his career was ruined.

Husband and wife lived through these days, which coincided with the
trials of the ex-commanders (April to December 1985), as though on different tracks. To Marcela, the trials were "a political show. We believed
that we had won the war against subversion. That it was necessary to do so.
If you're asking me, 'So you never wondered how many missing there
really were?' then I'll tell you: I didn't ask myself until many years later.
When I saw my husband going from bad to worse." Her husband, who like
Videla had developed an ulcer, was secretly devastated by the posture of
the chiefs, who blamed their subordinates for whatever "errors or excesses
might have been committed." When the ex-commanders were convicted,
Scilingo railed inwardly: "I was wrong ever to have trusted them. . . . Had

I killed thirty people by mistake?"[17] They were making us responsible for thousands of *desaparecidos*, he raged, when there was no such thing. These people were dead, not missing. Shortly after the end of the trials, Scilingo separated from the force.

"Here we were, supposed to be living 'civilly,'" Marcela said, ironically, "but my husband didn't adapt to civilian life. We had horrible economic problems, in fact we eventually lost everything—our house, our furniture, my inheritance. He came to Buenos Aires, I lived in Bahía Blanca with my mother-in-law because, really, I didn't have a peso. I didn't know exactly what he was doing here, though it seemed he was involved with some pretty marginal individuals." Some of them were men he knew from his days in the navy. He might have left the force but emotionally and socially he couldn't escape that world. Scilingo was in such bad shape that he couldn't sleep without sedatives and ended some binges passed out on a park bench. What sanity he was able to retain he credits to Marcela. In the late 1980s he started a videoclub business, which was an immediate roaring success. Riding high, he founded the first video cable business in his native Bahía Blanca, basically a company town for the navy. One of his partners in this enterprise was the man who in 1976 had encouraged him to apply for the ESMA and who still played golf with one of Scilingo's ex-superiors there. Close contact with this man further undid Scilingo, who lost control of the business and ended up bouncing a series of checks that he says he later covered. Along the way a car he bought from an old Federal Police friend turned out to have been stolen, and Scilingo is sure he was framed.[18] Not long afterward, he paid for some videos with checks from a business account he learned afterward no longer existed; here, too, the sum was minor—less than a hundred dollars—and he insists that he paid off the debt. He was charged, but whether or not there was intention to defraud is unclear. In May 1995, it was these minor infractions, and not his thirty murders, that Menem seized on to put the talkative Scilingo in prison.

A crucial turning point for Scilingo had come in December 1990, when Menem pardoned the convicted ex-commanders. Scilingo was literally sickened by Videla's gloating upon his release from prison: "We should be thanked for saving the Nation from chaos and the menace of subversion." Scilingo wrote Videla a registered letter (dated February 26, 1991), detailing his own death-flight experiences:

> Personally I never got over the shock of fulfilling that order . . . and I thought that I would find in you [a man] to take public responsibility for those events.

But concerning the subject of the missing, you said: There are subversives living under assumed names, others died in combat and were buried as NN [No Name] and also we must allow for certain excesses committed by subordinates. Where does that leave me? Do you really believe that the weekly transfers were the result of unplanned excesses?

... Let us put an end to the cynicism. Let us tell the truth. Provide a list of the dead, even though you shirked the responsibility for signing their execution order. . . .

The sentence you served was unjust, but it was signed by a president ordering the trial, your conviction was signed by the Prosecutor, your sentence signed by the judges. Right or wrong, everyone showed their face. . . .

My lawyers advise me to keep this matter private. But if you wish to maintain your position, you will assume your responsibility to publish THE TRUTH.

Videla certainly got the letter—Scilingo has the signed receipt—but never replied. But the navy sent a old friend of Scilingo's to ask him: Was he looking for money? "Don't get involved in this," Scilingo warned. Where-upon Scilingo was called in by Admiral Fausto López (who today has a high-ranking job in internal security): "You need to be careful, think of your family. If you keep this up, you could lose your health insurance."[19] Scilingo ignored the warning. On March 4, 1991, he wrote to then Navy Chief of Staff, Admiral D. Jorge Osvaldo Ferrer. Again, there was a signed receipt and no response. In August, Scilingo wrote once more to the admiral, and that letter too went unanswered.

On August 27, 1991, the irate Scilingo sent a letter to President Menem, along with a copy of all his previous correspondence. Again there was no response, but Menem read the letter and wrote a note to Brigadier Andrés Antonietti, the naval representative in the Casa Rosada: "Stop this mad-man. Take care of this yourselves."[20] How does Scilingo know? Marcela was called in by Antonietti and saw the note stapled to her husband's letter.

Among Scilingo's bizarre suggestions in these letters was that he him-self go to France to testify on behalf of Captain Alfredo Astiz, who was being tried in absentia for the kidnap and murder of Alice Domon (Sister Caty) and Léonie Duquet. Scilingo's rationale? Astiz was following orders, and should not be made a scapegoat for the sins of his superiors. The theme became Scilingo's "magnificent obsession." In 1994, this very sub-ject caused an unprecedented scandal in the Argentine Senate, when two navy torturers came up for promotion. The protagonists were two old friends of Scilingo. Had it not been for them, Scilingo's story might never have seen the light of day.

IN ARGENTINA, the promotions of military officers must be approved by the Senate. The procedure is as follows: The force submits a list to the Executive branch which then passes it, entire or in part, to the legislature. From 1853 (when the Argentine Constitution was ratified) until 1877, the Senate's deliberations were public. In 1877 the system was changed owing to political machinations so that, until 1992, these deliberations were conducted in closed session. With the restoration of democracy in 1983, military promotions became an especially sore and delicate point, as known participants in the repression kept coming up for advancement. The decisive case occurred in 1990, and was initiated by President Menem.

On Friday, July 13, of that year, the Senate obliged Menem by voting in secret session to promote Lieutenant Colonel Guillermo Antonio Minicucci to the rank of full Colonel.[21] During the dictatorship, Minicucci was director of two clandestine torture centers, El Banco and El Olimpo. It was he who named the latter camp, which had this sign over the main torture chamber: "Welcome to the Olympus of the Gods. Signed: The Centurions." Before he was freed on Due Obedience, Minicucci was in preventive custody, having been charged with 105 criminal acts. Minicucci had been decorated by Massera "for his heroic combat against bands of subversive delinquents." His promotion had been delayed owing to a lawsuit over Mrs. Minicucci's credit card abuses. The colonel's "honor" was restored, but it was the last time that such a whitewash would happen in secret. An outraged opposition senator (Adolfo Gass, from Alfonsín's Radical Party) spearheaded a project to have promotions debated out in the open. The change was voted in and incorporated into the Senate's rules in 1992.

If the protocol had not been changed, Scilingo's friends, Captains Antonio Pernías and Juan Carlos Rolón, would have been quietly granted promotions. "The Rolóns lived next door to us," Marcela told me, "the Pernías family lived in the house behind us. They never talked about any of that [the workings of the repression]. Never. We've known Rolón for years, we don't see him now of course, but my husband is certain that he never killed anyone. As for torture, it happened only once. Navy officers didn't torture. It was mostly police who did that."

Her information is incorrect. Scilingo himself may have been unaware of the scope and ferocity of his friends' activities, but about these men there are reams of survivor testimony. Free on the Due Obedience law, Pernías—an intelligence officer, one of whose aliases was "Rat"—was a brutal torturer. Perhaps his greatest claim to nefarious fame lay with his "scientific research" on poison darts. As he told some prisoners in the ESMA, he brought the poison back from the United States with the idea of using it to facilitate kidnaps. He thought that eventually it could also be used to assassinate populist leaders in the exterior. In order to arrive at the proper dosage, Pernías selected from *capucha* Daniel Schapira, who, after a series of "experiments," was eventually transferred. In December 1977, the captain took part in the sting at the Santa Cruz Church. Later, working out of Massera's Pilot Center in Paris, Pernías (presenting himself as "Alberto Escudero") infiltrated the organizations of Argentine exiles.[22] Rolón, a Punto Final beneficiary, was less zealous as an enforcer, though he was decorated in 1978 for "valor in combat," a reference, he told the Senate, to his antisubversive activities.

Neither Pernías nor Rolón denied before the Senate that the navy tortured. They were in fact the first military men on active duty to officially admit to having tortured. Pernías called it "the hidden weapon in a war without rules." Rolón, who has a Master's degree in International Relations and drew in his testimony on Spanish literary critic Ortega y Gasset, was less forthcoming with details. He stressed that the orders (to torture) "were wrong," but handed down by "officers who had been promoted by the Senate to the rank of Admiral." Still, he argued, erroneously, "we cannot forget that Argentina had the largest urban guerrilla movement in the history of the world." Rolón's most valuable statement was that the navy rotated task force duty to virtually all of its officers, "[that] no one was left on the margin."[23]

Even before the deliberations began, it was clear that these men would not be promoted. And so before the storm erupted, their superiors jumped ship. Menem (who had distractedly signed the promotion order not knowing anything about Pernías and Rolón) arranged to go to Tunis to greet the arrival of the battleship *libertad* ("Liberty"). Navy chief Admiral Molina Pico joined Menem for these festivities. The assistant navy chief traveled to Paris for a maritime trade fair.[24] Pernías and Rolón appeared before the Senate not only unaccompanied by the brass, but, so as not to unduly provoke the senators, dressed as civilians. To Scilingo, they appeared abandoned and naked and that, more than anything, seemed unjust.

Not long after the proceedings Scilingo was walking through a passage in the subway where, by chance, he espied Horacio Verbitsky. "I was in the

ESMA," he said, "I want to talk to you." Verbitsky at first misunderstood. "No," Scilingo corrected him, "I'm a friend of Rolón." And so the two embarked on a process that was for both men difficult, frustrating, and painful. There is a kind of poetic justice in Scilingo finding Verbitsky, for it was he who, in December 1976, wrote the first report on the ESMA and the death flights, based on survivor testimony, for ANCLA (Latin American Clandestine News Agency). Verbitsky's whole journalistic career has been devoted to exposing, documenting, and analyzing the dynamics of Argentine repression. A Peronist in his early twenties, Verbitsky was a member of the Montoneros from 1973 until mid-1977, when he left because of disagreements with the leadership over the organization's decision to operate clandestinely underground, and the use of violence as a means for political change. In 1973–74, as editorial chief of the Peronist daily *Notícias*, Verbitsky—together with Rodolfo Walsh and several others later murdered by the regime—had organized the dissemination of reports on the state's human rights violations. This was also his job in the Montoneros. After leaving the organization, Verbitsky remained in Argentina, writing for ANCLA, which was founded by Rodolfo Walsh. Verbitsky's work didn't change: He still arranged for the international circulation of news that was being censored domestically.[25] "So there he was," said Verbitsky, referring to Scilingo, "confessing to someone who just by chance had not been his victim."

Scilingo's original motives were, in Verbitsky's view, "narrow and cheap." Caught in the spider web of military logic, Scilingo was seeking to defend Pernías and Rolón. Why should they be denied promotion, he argued, when their superiors had sailed right through? Subordinates were taking the fall for their leaders and that, asserted Scilingo, was a violation of military ethics. Over the course of the interviews, and particularly once he appeared in public, Scilingo's mindset started to change. "We should all be in prison," he said, three weeks after appearing on *Hora Clave*. Scilingo's coming to consciousness was at once appalling and lacerating to watch, and appeared to surprise Scilingo more than anyone. "It was as though he was hearing himself for the first time," said Rosita Lerner, "it was terrible—terrible and complicated for us to watch him weep."[26]

Marcela was totally supportive of these interviews with Verbitsky. She had been urging her husband for several years to speak out. "You know," she said with amusement, "one of the first reactions of the navy was not 'Why did Adolfo talk?' but 'Why did he talk to Verbitsky?' He is still Enemy No. 1. They will never, ever forgive him. After the third or fourth interview, Adolfo came home and said, 'I can't believe I'm telling it all to my old *enemy.*' Which gave me the chance to say, or perhaps to realize myself, '*Those* enemies don't exist anymore. Everyone made mistakes, it's better to talk.' For us and our family, the process was extremely important. It helped me to understand him, helped him to understand me. Over the years, I had explained a lot of it to our children. They needed explanations for the chaos of our life, the behavior of their father. I mean, for years he barely spoke to them. On March 1, the night before Verbitsky first appeared on *Hora Clave*, I gathered everyone in the living room, and said, 'I want them to hear it from you.' And Adolfo told them. That was the turning point in our family. In spite of everything that's happened, our children say, 'We've gotten back our father.' His speaking out has made them very proud."

Did she never consider leaving him?

"Never."

Does she consider him a murderer?

"He *is* a murderer. That is his cross."

Does she believe that he has truly assumed this cross?

"Absolutely. How could he not? He will carry this burden until he dies. The thrust of his life is to repent. . . ."

I am astonished by her clarity, faith, and religious coherence. Has their Church not betrayed them?

"Yes. Had Adolfo missed mass he would not so easily have been forgiven. But that was certain priests, not the whole Church." If it weren't for her faith in God, Marcela says, neither she nor her family would have survived.

The Scilingos' life is fraught with such seemingly impossible contradictions. Scilingo's recently deceased sister was involved with ERP. "My poor mother-in-law," said Marcela, "was caught in the middle." Marcela too has a cousin who had a tangential relation to one of the leftist groups. At university, Marcela had friends on the left, though she was "basically on the right." The way she thought about it then was that, "As people they are fine, I respect them for taking risks for their beliefs; ideologically, they are the enemy. For me there was nothing personal. Of course," she rushed to add, "I see it very differently now."

The family's relation to the navy is no less curious. In early March— after Verbitsky but before Scilingo appeared on *Hora Clave*—the ex-captain got anonymous calls, presumably from the force, accusing him of being a "traitor." Others, say Marcela, called to encourage him. Scilingo's surviving sister, who lives in the navy town of Bahía Blanca, found the tires of her car slashed. Over June and July, 1995, the family received three death threats from the former ESMA Task Force, one of which said, "Menem locked you up, we'll bury you." None of Marcela's navy friends will speak to her. "They refuse to confront the whole issue of the flights, the fact that their husbands committed murder. The wives are *at least* as closed as their husbands, maybe more." Yet Marcela's sister is married to a retired navy man—in fact Marcela watched the first *Hora Clave* in their home. However, the husband and wife retired to their bedroom to watch the broadcast alone, leaving Marcela in the living room to watch with the children.

"Even though my husband is in jail, and we're totally broke—the stories about the million dollars from Hollywood are lies—this has all been for the good," Marcela says assuredly. "Our children's [parochial] school has been very understanding about tuition, which we haven't been able to pay. Adolfo no longer drinks or takes sedatives. He has written a book, in which he names *many* names, including civilians who took part in the flights. After Adolfo was on TV, people stopped me on the street to give encouragement. 'Keep going, señora, have courage. We'll get to the truth.' Things like that. People I don't even know, but, like me, out walking their dogs."

About two months before we met, Marcela went to the house of the Mothers of the Plaza de Mayo because her husband thought that some of his memories might be useful. She just appeared, without calling for an appointment. "This was Hebe de Bonafini's group, and they treated me as though I were . . . I don't know, there was such hatred, such rancor. My husband spoke out because he has a conscience, because he is sorry. To them, I was just 'the wife of that killer Scilingo.'" In contrast, Marcela said, the Grandmothers were gentle, understanding, and appreciative of whatever bits of information she could offer.

Marcela believes that she has gained deep insights into the wounds left by her country's recent history. She has begun to break through the military mindset and culture, though she is not as liberated as she seems to think. At times she reminded me of a bird pecking through the eggshell that protected her world. Toward the end of our three-hour conversation, she mused, "As I've been typing my husband's manuscript, I've been wondering, 'Where was I all those years?' I imagine that a lot of mothers are wondering the same thing, thinking their children were innocent. . . ."

"Wait a minute," I broke in. "Innocent or no, they were killed in the most bestial way."

"Yes."

"Without having been tried, or even charged."

"Yes."

"Just moments ago, talking about your husband, you complained that there was no presumed innocence in Argentina. What about the presumed innocence of the missing?"

"Of course a lot of innocents died, I'm not saying otherwise. It would have been better to recuperate them. That would have been normal, logical, humane. Not to have killed them the way they did. At least they could have learned."

"Learned what? And with or without kidnapping?"

"What do you mean?"

"You were saying it would have been better to recuperate them in a camp in the south. The question is about kidnapping as a method, as opposed to legal arrest."

"No, no. Arrested, legally. That's what I meant."

For a moment she is quiet.

"I understand the Mothers," Marcela insists, her blue eyes opened wide and unabashedly meeting mine. "I bear them no rancor. I can put myself in their place. If they had killed a child of mine, innocent or no.... I understand, I do."

But does she, really? Can anyone else *truly* feel what a mother like Sara Steimberg feels?

ON THE MORNING of April 25, 1995 Sara Steimberg was in the kitchen of her suburban home, listening as usual to Radio Mitre, a major commercial station. She was alone, tuned in as always to the talk show hosted by Néstor Ibarra, a famous and well regarded journalist. Some months earlier, Ibarra had gotten in touch with Sara and her husband, Jaime (see Fig. 13), after a cashiered army sergeant appeared at the station claiming to have information on a group of *desaparecidos*, including the couple's son, Luis Pablo, who disappeared from within the army while doing his obligatory miliary service. To his parents, who since 1976 have pressured the government, sued the army, and helped found an organization for relatives of the missing, ex-sergeant Victor Ibáñez offered nothing they didn't already know. For them, as for so many, the missing piece is their child's ultimate fate: When, where, by whom was Pablo murdered, and where are his remains?

As she went about her normal kitchen chores, Sara was astounded to hear Ibarra announce that he had Ibáñez in the studio and was about to put him on the air.[27] For ten years, said the forty-four-year-old Ibáñez, he has suffered "a profound depression caused by [his] role in the war against subversion," and that this "sickness" was the reason the army threw him out. His purpose in speaking out, he said, was to make the

FIGURE 13. Sara and Jaime Steimberg standing before the Argentine Congress holding a photo of their son, Luis Pablo. (Photo credit: Cristina Fraire, September 1995)

army furnish lists of the individuals it killed. He himself did not torture, he insisted, but he saw a lot of torture. ("I swear I never even asked them questions.") Even so, he cannot understand that *no one* should be subjected to such abuse. Rather he is obsessed with "vindicating the victims who were innocent, the martyrs" tortured and killed in the Campo de Mayo army base in Buenos Aires. He recalled "long talks [with his charges] about God . . . giving them Christian sustenance" during their ordeal. Enraged, Sara was reaching to turn off the radio when Ibáñez admitted to helping load prisoners onto airplanes and throwing them into the sea. He said he took part in so many flights that he soon "lost count." Though her whole body was shaking, Sara managed to dial the station and keep listening as Ibáñez played a tortuous game of cat-and-mouse: naming names, then falling silent on their ultimate fate, pleading memory lapse and misery, and begging for mercy. "The torment of my life is that I cannot say who was good and who was bad." Quiet, intense, and extremely shrewd, Ibarra bore down and convinced Ibáñez to admit that some of the *same* people he wants now to "vindicate" were on flights that he himself crewed or helped facilitate. As Ibáñez squirms and resists, Ibarra brings back the case, previously raised by the ex-sergeant, of fourteen-year-old Floreal Avellaneda, whose leg had been partially chewed off by concentration camp dogs. "I don't want to tread on territory that is too sensitive, too painful for you, or to be truculent," Ibarra says slowly and deliberately, "but I remember that his was one of the bodies that washed up in Uruguay." When Ibáñez pleads ignorance, Ibarra calmly continues, "He was fourteen years old and, if I'm right, this was the case of the child who died under brutal torture and, by the signs on his body, he had also been impaled. Do you know what *impaled* means?" Ibáñez gasps audibly but says nothing. "You do know, don't you," says Ibarra and when Ibáñez insists that he does not, Ibarra supplies the definition and adds without skipping a beat, "That fourteen-year-old child, you know they *transferred* him. We have a call now from Sara Steimberg. You remember the name Steimberg, don't you?"

Ibáñez admits with a single wooden syllable that he does.

Sara's voice is thick with tears and rage and horror, but she insists that the journalist press her case.

For close to thirty excruciating minutes, Ibáñez continues to squirm, to insist that he too is a victim. He says the "señora must be nice to me, I am so repentant, so Christian."

"Don't talk to me!" shouts Sara, "talk to Ibarra!"

Little by little, Ibáñez cracks, gives in. Finally he says, "Your son was thrown into the sea. Forgive me, señora, forgive me."

"Were you on the flight?" Ibarra wants to know.

"I don't, I don't remember, Ibarra, I really don't...."

"Do you feel like a murderer?"

"No."

"*No*?"

"With my fight to vindicate the innocent, no. No."

Sara's sobs rip through you as you listen to the tape. When she is able to speak, she stammers, "I am feeling all the pain in the world." And so, at that moment, are we.

Porteños can tell you exactly where they were and what they were doing at the time of this broadcast. "I was trimming the ficus," "I was making the bed," "I was alone in my darkroom." As they recount *their* stories of listening to Ibáñez, people cling to these details, repeat these signs of 'normality,' in a state of shock. And, indeed, shears were let go, sheets left hanging, prints ignored in their bath.

The station found no holes or contradictions in Ibáñez's story. Yet Ibarra says that he is "not totally certain" that Ibáñez himself threw prisoners out of airplanes. He may have been more a witness than a direct participant. Graciela Fernández Meijide earlier had told me the same thing, in stronger terms: "About the flights, I believe that he lied. His rank was too low for him to have been selected for a flight. They tapped officers for the most part, individuals with a high level of commitment to the force. Still, being in Campo de Mayo, Ibáñez certainly saw things, knew things. As a jailer there, he *was* a participant. I think that the intense activity generated by Scilingo made him competitive. And then there were all those stories about the money Scilingo had made." Fernández Meijide was in charge of testimony for the CONADEP, and personally interviewed the dozen or so "repentant" enforcers who came forward in 1983–84. "Lying was a trait they had in common," she said, "also a need to be in the limelight, and to get revenge on the institution they felt betrayed them. Virtually all of these men had separated from their force, in fact most of them were in jail for stealing more than their 'fair share' of the war booty. They were so intent on peddling testimony (in exchange for immunity from prosecution or leniency in sentencing) that they'd get together in their cells and concoct stories, taking an element from this one's experience, another detail from someone else. It was hair-raising. They were profoundly, essentially criminal."[28]

Ibáñez does not really fit that mold. Ibarra told me that he never asked for money. "He would not accept so much as a coffee—all he would drink was water." And though he lived well outside the capital, in Buenos Aires Province, he only once accepted cab fare home. To Ibarra, the ex-jailer was plainly tormented by a guilty conscience, perhaps as much for what he did *not* do as for what he did. Both on and off the air, Ibarra had pressed Sara Steinberg: "Does your mother's intuition say he's telling the truth [about the flights]?" Sara's reply was always "Yes."

About six weeks after the broadcast, I talked with Sara in a bar near the Congress.[29] She did an unnerving imitation of Ibáñez, perfectly capturing his whining, wheedling, downtrodden tone. But every time she quoted him, she slightly, but critically, misquoted him. "I threw your son into the sea," she told me he said. Yet his actual words were impersonal, indirect: "Your son was thrown into the sea." Though he asked her forgiveness, he would not state that he was on the plane. It may be that Sara's intuition is correct. It could also be that after two decades of being lied to, she *needs* to believe Ibáñez. Who can say which is better? Which is worse? How even to distinguish such fine gradations of horror?

"For eighteen years, we searched for our son. So that part of our struggle is over. This brings relief," Sara told me through tears, "a *terrible* relief." After the show she pulled herself together and took a train to Buenos Aires to organize with other relatives of the missing. "I couldn't stay home and just cry, the fight is for *all* of the families, all of the *desaparecidos.*" A waiter—not the one who brought our food—hovers so close to our table, I finally ask him what it is that he needs. A lot of waiters in this neighborhood are former bodyguards to generals and presidents, and known to be spies. They are blatant, and this one simply shrugs, moves off and watches us from a corner. Every day for the last week, Sara tells me, she has received menacing phone calls. She will not back down, but she is unsettled. It's an old story in Argentina—a voice from out of nowhere to punish you for having been punished.

OVER THE YEARS such threats and surveillance have added to the anguish of concentration camp survivors. For them, "the Scilingo moment" has been like a nightmare that will not let go. Mario Villani had crossed paths several times with Julián the Turk before they "met" again on May 1, 1995, on national television.[30] Villani was taped separately, but viewers—and he himself—later saw a split screen with the guests and journalist "together," or "jumped" back and forth among the torturer, Villani, and Ana Maria Careaga, another of his victims. "The norm was to kill everyone," said Julián, looking straight at the camera, "and anyone kidnapped was tortured." He conceded that "torture didn't always work, it left people too destroyed" to give any information. Contradicting much survivor testimony, Julián maintained that he himself "tortured on very few occasions." We cut to a close-up on Mario Villani:

> They had left the door open . . . and there was Julián standing over a prisoner they had naked, laid out on his belly, with his legs hanging down over the end of the table. Julián was torturing this man with an electric cable which he had shorn of its insulation and charged to 220 volts. It seems this wasn't enough for Julián for he then inserted a stick into the man's anus and then tortured him some more with the cable. As the man's body writhed and jolted, the stick tore apart his intestines, and he died.

Equally as devastating is the look on Mario's face, a combination of aftershock and willed composure. As he told me later, "It's not that I remember these things. I relive them."

Survivors were hit again with the forced intimacy of the concentration camp. "I hear that voice, see those gestures and expressions, and it all comes rushing back," said Mario. Mónica Brull—blind, pregnant, and sent by Julián to be raped as well as tortured—had made legal history during the CONADEP by identifying Julián's sidekick "Colores" by the sound of his voice. "That had never been done before in Argentina," she told me, "but after what I'd been through with him there was no way I could miss. He was furious." Mónica says that in spite of her best efforts to control it, the Channel 13 broadcast stirred up intense curiosity about Julián. "My husband told me that he is missing several teeth. I can't help but wonder what happened to him. It's not that 'I care' or am 'concerned,' but I still want to know, and this bothers me. It means there's still this involuntary connection. It's not surprising," she said with a sudden gesture, "he was *right here*, after all. That's right, Colores and one they called Juan Carlos used to come to this house and check on me. My father was an importer of candy, and they used to ask for cartons of the stuff, which of course they received. Julián came too, out of his mind to know how much money my father had paid Soler for my release. It was Soler who brought my baby son to my mother. [Soler was Federal Police Officer Carlos Augusto Rolón.] The Turk was feeling cheated, left out. He sat right there on that couch, having a fit: 'That son of a bitch,' he kept raving about Soler. It was quite a scene," Mónica said, laughing, a little wildly, "I mean, my parents, their nice living room, and the torturer Julián the Turk."[31]

Dr. Jekyll and Mr. Hyde is how some survivors have described Julián. After Mónica returned from the "operating room," Julián brought her pastry. Viewers got a sense of his chameleon nature, and the rage behind it, in his stunning physical transformation on television. Two days before the air date of May 1, Julián realized that in spite of its ambiguous promises, Channel 13 was not in fact going to pay him. Enraged by the station's newspaper ads for their upcoming "exclusive" with him, Julián went to the state-run ATC, and sold them an advance scoop. "It happened while I was there," said Mario. "I had just watched Channel 13's unedited tapes with Julián and, just as we began my interview, Colores called." "Colores" was the alias of red-headed Juan Antonio Del Cerro, who also benefited from Due Obedience. A torturer in four concentration camps—Club Atlético, El Banco, Olympus, and the ESMA—Colores kidnapped over sixty individuals, most of whom remain missing. He boasted to prisoners of having invented a *picana* that would leave their flesh unmarked.[32] "Well, Colores," Mario continued, "was Channel 13's original contact with Julián, who apparently doesn't have a phone. In fact the first time Julián went to the station, Colores accompanied him. But Colores didn't want to talk. He has a job, a family: 'I don't want to be involved in this,' he said, oozing respectability. Even as Colores was talking by phone to the journalists at Channel 13, Julián was making his deal with ATC."

By all accounts, including that of Julián's boyhood friend and apparent manager Raúl Aguiar, the state-run station paid him. They also dressed him up and had him coiffed. On ATC, Julián appeared clean-shaven, wearing a dark suit, and had his hair slicked back with a shiny gel. Thus accoutered, he was grandiloquent: "What I did I did for my Fatherland, my faith, and my religion. Of course I would do it again." He also insisted, as though righting a longstanding wrong, that "Hebe de Bonafini's children are alive and living in Spain." Immediately following, on the independent Channel 13, he was nearly unrecognizable (see Fig. 14). In his own grubby turtleneck, with a beard, and his hair falling into his face, his level of diction was lower, brutish.

When I met Julián, on June 30, 1995, he looked exactly as he did on Channel 13, minus the beard, and with a burgundy windbreaker he never unzipped. It is early evening and we are in the rundown bar he stipulated, on the corner of Salta and San Juan. He lives in a neighboring hotel, supported by a Brazilian prostitute, whose young daughter he is said to adore.

"I can tell just by the title of your book that you misunderstand me," says Julián, mistakenly, as we sit down. "I am not repentant. I'm no crybaby

FIGURE 14. Julio Simón, the torturer known as Julián the Turk, as he appeared on Channel 13, May 1, 1995. (Photo: Courtesy of *Página 12*)

like that sorry Scilingo. That drunkard Ibáñez. This was a war to save the Nation from the terrorist hordes. Look, torture is eternal. It has always existed and always will. It is an essential part of the human being."

In terms of his appearance, there is nothing that sets Julián apart from any of the other men in this seedy old café. His behavior, however, is agitated, though no one seems to notice. We have been brought together by Raúl Aguiar, a former boxer and bodyguard to Lorenzo Miguel, a right-wing Peronist labor leader with longstanding ties to the military.[33] Julián says the program on Channel 13 was "distorted. Not one innocent person passed through my hands." He holds out his hands, which are large and muscular, with trunk-like fingers, and not entirely clean. What about the man with the stick in his bowels? He waves this away. The pregnant blind woman tortured and raped at his command? For some reason this gets to him, he denies ever having tortured "cripples." But the testimony of Mónica Brull (see Fig. 15) is corroborated and air-tight: She, her then husband, and their whole circle of handicapped friends were kidnapped, tortured, and subjected (by Julián) to mock executions. Their "subversive" activity? Before the coup, they had spearheaded legislation (passed unanimously by the Senate in 1975) to protect the handicapped

FIGURE 15. Mónica Brull, who was tortured by Julián the Turk. (Photo credit: Cristina Fraire, September 1995)

from labor discrimination. "Ask Julián about Claudia Victoria Poblete," Brull had pressed me, referring to the baby of her missing best friend, Gertrudis Hlaczik, kidnapped together with her child by Colores. Brull, who lost the son that she was carrying, believes that Claudia Victoria was sold and that Julián was in on the deal. Julián insisted that he knew nothing about this child, but assured me that his "archives [were] extensive." Here Aguiar joined in, touting the "high value" of these archives, suggesting that Julián and he himself be "considered," especially after "the ill treatment by Channel 13."

"I was the Quixote in all of this," lamented Aguiar, who wears dark-tinted glasses even at night, and apparently never read Cervantes. I'd made clear from the outset that money was out of the question. Nevertheless Julián, having complained that "you don't get much time on TV," agreed to a second interview and photo session. He said he would bring his "archives," which they plainly hoped I would buy.

As we discussed the arrangements for our never-to-be-completed second interview, I suggested we meet at El Foro, a well-known café amid bookstores and theaters, and one block from the courts.

"No!" cried Julián, "it's full of lawyers!"

"What's it to you?" I replied. "You're covered by Due Obedience."

He looked stricken, drew back, insisted we meet someplace else.

"Okay," I said, "then where?" Julián opened his mouth, but said nothing. For the first time his eyes darted to the tables around us. It was Raúl who settled the time and place. I watched Julián, studied his face. This large man, notorious for his bestial acts of violence, was frightened of no more than being recognized. I left him sitting in his neighborhood bar, still nervously looking around.

Clearly that anxiety passed. Weeks later I was told by Mario Villani that he was just out shopping, and whom should he see? Julián the Turk, striding through the old Jewish district, buying things for the little girl riding gaily on his shoulders.

CAPTAIN HECTOR VERGEZ is yet another beneficiary of Due Obedience. Former director of the death camp known as La Perla, he came out about two weeks after Scilingo, suggesting that for the sake of "national reconciliation" the military provide a comprehensive list of the missing. ("What we need are lists of the perpetrators," say the Mothers of the Plaza de Mayo.) Clearly motivated by the rumors that Scilingo had got a million dollars from Hollywood, he tried to sell his information to various human rights organizations and then to a left-leaning senator. His asking price, which no one paid, was $30,000. Rejected, he approached the more welcoming Federal Intelligence Services (SIDE). In spite of—or owing to?—his documented Nazi connections, Vergez was engaged to work on the official investigation of the 1994 bombing of the Jewish community center in which 86 people were killed and over 200 wounded. As reported in the Argentine press, Vergez's role in this operation, internationally criticized for ineptitude and lack of will, has been to deflect attention *away* from any Argentine suspects.[34]

Vergez amassed a fortune from the families of his victims, including that of Patricia Astelarra, who was five months pregnant at the time she was kidnapped and who gave birth to her son in captivity. In 1976, he interrogated her night after night, held her for ransom, and then got $10,000 from her family for her release. Until 1983, he followed and threatened her. "He wanted badly to kill me," Patricia recalled, "but we have relatives in the army."[35]

Patricia's speech is intense and rapid-fire. Her voice is clear, low-pitched, and strong. "My first reaction when all of a sudden he was featured in the news was to fall apart. I felt totally done in. My second reaction was to denounce him. Vergez wasn't just anyone. He tortured with incredible ferocity. One of his hobbies was simulated executions. Real ones, too. People need to know just who this character is. So I too spoke out. My third reaction was, 'Maybe there's hope, maybe we'll finally find out what happened to my brother.'" A twenty-four-year-old doctor who worked in a public clinic, Patricia's brother, Santiago, was kidnapped from his home by a military commando and never seen again. "It's been terrible," she allows, her words coming more slowly now. "I see that face and all the images, all the nightmares come flooding back. Vergez bragged about his exploits. He inspired incredible fear."

As we talk, Pablo, who was born in captivity in late 1976, sits listening, quiet and intent. "I've heard the story before," he says, "but there's always something new that comes out."

His mother, a sociologist now in her late forties, was working in the early 1970s for the Ministry of Education, in Córdoba. An activist in the Peronist Youth (and then in the political wing of Montoneros), Patricia had for years done social work in the shantytowns. In Córdoba, she reminded me, the repression started well before the coup, with the Comando Libertador de América (Commando for the Liberation of America). Vergez was one of the original members of that organization, which was the local branch of López Rega's Triple A. "Even more than the Triple A," she said, "the Commando was violently anti-Semitic, and included former Nazis in its ranks. "They kidnapped whole families, stormed factories, dragged away high school students. In Córdoba there was popular resistance, a part of the story that somehow has been forgotten. There were relatives' committees, street protests, work stoppages in important factories, including Renault. I think that's why the crackdown after the coup was so merciless. After the military takeover, Vergez [an army captain] was put in charge of La Perla. With a lawyer friend—who by 1984 was in the Congress—Vergez also had a thriving store in downtown Córdoba, where they sold furniture and housewares stolen from the prisoners in La Perla. From us, they stole everything, absolutely everything we owned," said Patricia, half smiling at her son.

"This whole thing has become a show," said Pablo, "It makes me want to leave Argentina. At first, like my mother said, it gave us hope. But now I don't know. I'm very angry. What my parents went through, how I was born. My uncle was my godfather, but I never got to know him. Vergez, Julián, Ibáñez—all these guys are incredibly morbid. But people were riveted. And then, as with any other show, they move on. Will anything change? It's been what, three months since Scilingo? Already, I sense interest slowing down."

"That," stressed Patricia, "is why we need the lists of what, specifically, happened to whom. We need that measure of relief. This 'Scilingo moment' has been horrific," she said softly, locking eyes with her son. "May it not be for nothing."

WITHIN DAYS OF Scilingo's first television appearance, the government and a consortium of human rights groups got embroiled in what the headlines called the Battle Over the Lists. As commander in chief, President Menem was asked to require each branch of the military to provide its list of individuals executed during the dictatorship. The only response the groups got to their letter was that no government functionary would receive them. Horacio Méndez Carrera, the Argentine lawyer retained by the French government to represent the families of Léonie Duquet and Alice Domon (Sister Caty), made a separate appeal through the Federal Court to the navy. (It has been said that the two women were referred to as "The Flying Nuns" by repressors in the ESMA.) After several weeks of domestic and international pressure, the Federal Appeals Court ordered Menem, Minister of Defense Oscar Camilión, and the commander in chief of the navy to provide the information. Two days later, the Minister of Defense—who was Ambassador to Brazil under Videla, special adviser to Viola, and, as late as 1981, a fervent denier of the secret detention centers—reported that the only lists extant were those of the CONADEP. The Ministry of Interior supported Defense: "The famous lists of *desaparecidos* never existed, or at least they don't exist now," declared the visibly impatient Minister Carlos Corach.[36] Menem cited the order to "burn all documentation" given to his subordinates by the departing General Reynaldo Benito Bignone, the last de facto president of the Dirty War.

It is true that Bignone gave the order in 1983, but that hardly closes the case. "We proved the existence of those lists," shot back Julio Cesar Strassera, the lead prosecutor at the trial of the ex-commanders.[37] And indeed, in March 1995, the newspapers reprised the sworn testimony of Victor Melchor Basterra and Carlos Muñoz, who ten years earlier had recounted on the stand their ordeal as forced laborers in the ESMA Documentation Section. Basterra, whose four-hour testimony particularly moved Jorge Luis Borges, spent four years in the ESMA, much of it in *capucha*. A graphics worker by profession, Basterra was used by the navy to falsify IDs and take photographs of both detainees and enforcers. From 1980 onward, he managed to hide a great many pictures and documents, which he brought as evidence to the trial.[38] Held in the ESMA from August 1979 until December 1983, Basterra was kept under surveillance until August 1984, or a year and a half into the presidency of Alfonsín. Carlos Muñoz, who was held in the ESMA from November 1978 until February 1980, had no idea that the navy kept such extensive documentation until, as part of his "recuperation process," he was tapped for photography (in which he had experience) and the falsification of documents (for which the navy trained him). Muñoz also transferred to microfilm the files of detainees and *desaparecidos:*

> For each arrival the ESMA opened a numbered file, with the person's background and associations, whatever the person had written or signed [under duress]. . . . One page said where the person had been kidnapped, what organization or political group he belonged to, who had participated in the kidnap operation, the date, and finally, the sentence: T for "transfer" or L for "liberated." I had access to these microfilms in October or November of 1979, after three liberated prisoners [Ana María Martí, María Alicia Milia de Pirles, and Sara Solarz de Osatinsky] testified before the French Assembly. That produced a great commotion in the ESMA . . . and they had me look up their files. So that night I went through four cassettes of microfilm, and for the first time I saw the extent of the killing in the ESMA, because there were approximately

5000 cases, and the names marked with an L [for Liberated] were really very, very few.[39]

Emilio Mignone concurs with Strassera that the original lists are extant, and believes that they might even be in Buenos Aires, in the head-quarters of the Intelligence Services. Others, including Juan Gasparini, a survivor of the ESMA who since his release has researched and written extensively on these issues from Geneva, has long held that the navy's doc-umentation is kept in a numbered vault in Switzerland.[40] It is well known that toward the end of his reign in the junta, Massera, in an overture to the Peronists, advocated publishing the navy's lists, which he kept in his per-sonal computer. Why would he do such a thing? Massera wanted to be elected president after the dictatorship and saw Peronist support as crucial to his success.

But even if no one today can lay hands on the original documentation, many, including Hector Verges, ex-director of La Perla, hold that the lists could be reconstructed by the participants, most of whom would be safe from prosecution under the provisions of the Due Obedience and Punto Final laws. In an apparent effort to stem any such process, in late March 1995, Menem ordered his Under Secretariat of Human Rights to dissemi-nate the government's list of the missing.

A central task of this Under Secretariat is to process information pre-sented by relatives of *desaparecidos*, who, based on a law passed by Con-gress in 1994, are entitled to indemnification. The Under Secretariat also keeps a copy of the CONADEP files. Alicia Pierini, Human Rights Secretary, issued a public disclaimer that the forthcoming lists were not what the human rights organizations were demanding. "What they want can only be gotten from the enforcers," she said. "All we have here are names. If there's time, perhaps we'll add the date of disappearance, but noth-ing else."[41] Pierini was obviously being pressured to get the job over and done with.

The list itself came as yet another ugly insult from the government. Published in the major newspapers on April 1, 1995, it consisted of only 545 names, of which 255 had been publicized in 1992. The remaining 290 came from the Under Secretariat itself, from its interviews with relatives seeking indeminification. The list not only added nothing new—no information was provided on the ultimate fate of the victims—but contained a number of mistakes. One individual was listed as missing, although he was mur-dered by the Triple A before the coup, and his family had received his remains. Several others listed as missing are in fact alive. One of these was history professor Jorge Gilbert: "When I saw my name on that list, the past came crashing down on me," he recounted to *Página* 12. A member of the Peronist University Youth until 1975, Gilbert was kidnapped in La Plata in September 1977. After a month of torture in three different clandestine camps, he was released. Neither he nor his family ever testified before the CONADEP, which suggests that his data were procured directly from the Ministry of Interior. "Before," said Gilbert, "our lives were worth nothing, and now it's clear that we still have little value for the state, which is handling all this with a complete lack of seriousness."[42]

THE MILITARY WAS NOT the only institution that maintained lists of detainees and *desaparecidos*. So did certain clergy. In the days following Scilingo, a number of Catholics came forward, some for the first time, to testify publicly on the ambiguities, contradictions, and outright betrayals they suffered at the hands of clerics whom they had consulted in desperation. The reaction to all of this by the Catholic Church can be fairly described as a prolonged public convulsion.

That church officials kept lists of detainees and *desaparecidos* originally came out during the 1985 trial. Exactly ten years later, that, and other historical currents, washed back over Argentina with the inevitability of an ocean tide. Adults and youth who had not absorbed the information during the trials did so now through the newspapers, radio, and television, all of which featured interviews, round tables, and debates, in which bishops, among others, conflicted openly. According to numerous testimonies, the keeper of the ecclesiastical lists was Monsignor Emilio Grasselli, then secretary to the Military Chaplain. Grasselli's index file—compiled at the request of his immediate superior, Monsignor Adolfo Tortolo, and with the knowledge of Pio Laghi, the Papal Nuncio—consisted of some 2500 names. Clearly these men were apprised of the Wednesday transfers.

One of the stories reprised by the media concerned María Teresa de Garín, who in April 1977 had gone with her husband to Grasselli's office in the military vicarage to ask about their missing son, daughter, and son-in-law. Grasselli had a large staff in a forward office that distributed numbers to all those who had come to see him. When a party's number was called, they were led to the monsignor's study. Flipping through his index file, Grasselli told the Garíns, "Your son Arturo isn't here now, and your daughter and son-in-law are listed only until April 25th."

"What does that mean?" asked the mother.

"That the worst has happened or they have begun to collaborate."[43] That was all Grasselli would offer.

Forty days after *her* son's disappearance, Adelina Burgos de Di Spalatro also went to visit the monsignor. He told her to return the following week. "Grasselli showed us a list of many names," she told the CONADEP. "He told us to look for our son's name. Those names with a cross by them were dead, the others were alive. . . . According to this [our son] was alive. . . ."[44]

Does Grasselli's index file still exist? No one will say.

Grasselli was a man who walked both sides of the line. He was sympathetic, even tender, toward those who, according to the military, "did well" in the so-called process of recuperation. He personally arranged for visas (to Venezuela or Bolivia) for about a dozen prisoners from the ESMA. Among this group was Graciela Daleo, kidnapped from the Acoyte subway station on the morning of October 18, 1977. An important witness at the trial of the ex-commanders, she recounted how on April 20, 1979 (after eighteen months in the ESMA), she was brought to Monsignor Grasselli, who awaited her outside the vicarage in his car. "He had everything ready—passport, visa, tickets bought from a navy account from Aerolíneas Argentinas. We sat there a while and talked about what I had been through in the ESMA, the torture, mistreatment, etc. He told me he knew a lot of things. I asked him then why he didn't speak out, and the monsignor answered, 'Because then I couldn't get you a visa, for example.' That affected me deeply, because I wasn't giving up my visa so that he would testify. . . . I told him that I wanted to make confession, it had been a long time, and since I was starting a whole new period of my life, I wanted to express what I truly felt, which was that I had fulfilled the commandment of Christian charity, had not betrayed a single compañero, had never collaborated with the navy." As they separated, Grasselli blessed and gifted her with a crucifix. "You," he said to the ex-Montonera, "are Christ."[45] As soon as she was safely in exile in Spain, Daleo denounced the ESMA to the United Nations and the major human rights organizations.

For all of his loving behavior toward Daleo, Grasselli did not share her perspective on Christian charity. The parents of *desaparecido* Carlos Oscar Lorenzo recounted this conversation with the Monsignor:

> [He] told us that the young people were in a rehabilitation program in houses that had been set up for that purpose and where they were being well treated. . . .
>
> He told us that Videla was the *charitable soul* who thought up this plan to avoid the loss of intelligent people . . . he said that the

work was carried out with psychologists and sociologists, that there were medical teams to deal with their health, and that for those who could not be recuperated, it was possible that "some pious soul" might give them an injection to make them sleep forever. . . . [emphasis added][46]

The monsignor's own peace of mind seems to have rested on his skill in manipulating the sacred lexicon. Did he honestly think that his translations of "piety," "charity," "soul," and "sleep" would bring consolation to parents like the Lorenzos? It is hard to believe.

Grasselli's sleight-of-hand extended to business. In 1979, he executed what has to be one of the most tainted real-estate transactions in the history of the Catholic Church. This little-known story—about an island called "Silence"—exploded in the press days after Scilingo's first appearance.[47] El Silencio was a bucolic island in the Tigre Delta, a couple of hours from the Argentine capital. Owned since 1975 by the Curia of Buenos Aires, it was where the Archbishop, Juan Carlos Aramburu, relaxed on Sundays. With a small group of bishops, he would go out in the morning, enjoy his *asado* (barbecue), and then return, much relaxed, in the evening. In 1979, with the looming prospect of the OAS fact-finding mission, the navy was feeling nervous. They had to disguise the ESMA, disappear the "recuperating" *desaparecidos*. What could be more discreet than an island named El Silencio? The ESMA Task Force bought El Silencio from Grasselli, in both senses of the word. No name associated with the Church appeared on the documents of sale. Officially listed as seller was Marcelo C. Hernández, who was a prisoner in the ESMA, and whose signature was forged by members of the Task Force. (Grasselli insisted that he never met Hernández, as though it mattered.) Just prior to the arrival of the OAS delegation, a group of prisoners from the ESMA (including Susana and Osvaldo Barros) were transported to this island, where they were held in miserable conditions for a month. After the departure of the OAS team, the prisoners were returned to the ESMA. In mid-March 1995, the reaction of the Church to this report was: silence.

Emboldened by the furor, several families also came forward to testify for the first time against Pio Laghi, who during the dictatorship was the Papal Nuncio. In these accounts (as told to Verbitsky in *Página* 12), Laghi was dishonest and pitiless toward those who sought his help. After two decades, he remains one of the most enigmatic figures of the repression. In his interviews with Argentine radio the Cardinal got tangled in his own web of lies, providing the story that dominated Holy Week of 1995. Even as

he repeatedly denied ever having known anything about the inner workings of the repression, two bishops on another show loudly praised him for
having saved people. Laghi did in fact intervene in some cases, including
that of Jacobo Timerman. But he was always extremely selective; he would
not commit his efforts to known (or suspected) leftists, and never once
spoke publicly against the junta. "His job," said the bishops defending
him, "was to inform the Holy See, not publish in the newspapers. . . . The
Church could have done more," they conceded, "but Laghi was one of
the men who cared most about human rights in the difficult decade of the
1970s." When asked about the recent testimonies, they would say not a
word. "Why," the bishops asked, "do we need to know the whole truth?
For the purpose of conflict or reconciliation?"

Menem too rushed to Laghi's defense. "I read the two bishops' response
and it seems to me excellent," the president told Radio América. "The violent ones should also repent, and there are a lot of those in that morning
paper," he said, referring, slanderously, to *Página 12*. "One of those journalists"—clearly meaning Verbitsky—"was among those who planted
bombs, kidnapped, and siphoned off Argentina's resources. While I," he
said, "was a prisoner for five years, they went around pillaging."[48] With
slander, innuendo, and the revisionist distortion of history, the president
tried to blot out the ethical crisis.

As if this weren't spectacle enough, Emilio Massera—who played tennis every two weeks with the ex-Papal Nuncio—jumped into the fray with
a letter to the biggest news agency in Argentina:

> . . . with reference to the behavior of the ecclesiastic leadership in
> the war against subversion, I want to say emphatically that during
> my tenure as commander in chief, all the Church's authorities,
> and in particular Pio Laghi, for whom I feel profound admiration
> and respect, were always concerned about the so-called *detainees-
> desaparecidos*.[49]

Massera's language was indeed curious: When asked at his trial if he knew
anything about kidnapping, secret detention centers, tortures, and so on,
he had replied without missing a beat: "At no time." He insisted that the
Process was "Western, Humanist, and Christian."

Then yet another widow called Verbitsky, and her damning story ran
the following Sunday, which was Easter. When Ana María Giacobe met
with the Papal Nuncio, he showed her a copious file on her missing husband, the scientist Gustavo Ponce de León Sarrabayrouse. More astonishing to her than the fact that Laghi had such files was that the photographs

and documents within were copies of originals that were taken from the family's home the night of her husband's kidnap, which took place before dawn on August 6, 1976. "How did you come to acquire these photographs?" she asked Laghi, who replied, "That is none of your business."

"It is my right, and my duty to others, to recount this experience," Giacobe affirmed, nineteen years later. The couple and their three daughters were living in Palermo, on the calle Austria near the Avenida Las Heras. Her husband was employed as a computer specialist for Fabricaciones Militares. A dozen men dressed as civilians burst in, locked Giacobe in the bathroom, and twice subjected their eldest, a ten-year-old, to a simulated execution. Giacobe's sister-in-law, a musician who had long lived in Rome, denounced the kidnapping and abuse to the Vatican. Amnesty International adopted the case. And that turned Pio Laghi against the family.

"You," he said, "have been adopted by Amnesty. That proves that you are subversives because Amnesty only adopts subversives."

"No," Giacobe replied, "they adopt nonviolent prisoners of conscience."

"That's a lie," shot back the Pope's representative, "Amnesty only adopts subversives".

Giacobe tried to defuse the situation. "I am desperate about my husband," she pleaded, "and your office has a great deal of power."

"All I can tell you," Laghi repeated, "is that your husband was a subversive and you are too, and I recommend Christian resignation."

"That's not worthy of the robes you wear," Giacobe replied, losing her composure. "You know if my husband is already dead and you won't tell me." She started to scream, "If you were a good Christian you would tell me to have faith, not resignation!"

"Right, so have faith," said the Papal Nuncio, and watched her run crying from the room. Recalled Giacobe, "On the way out, I met two policemen in the doorway. I ran all the way to the corner. Even today, remembering all this makes me tremble."

Before the culmination of Holy Week a third hitherto quiet victim of the Dirty War came forward, to talk about the issue of priests' participation in torture. Speaking from his adopted country of France to Argentine radio, *ex-desaparecido* Zacarías Moutoukias brought to bear his experience with police chaplain Christian Von Wernich:

One needs to be careful about mentioning the names of kidnappers and torturers, and maybe I should not, but . . . the person who, even after all these years, still holds the most horror for me, is a priest. Just before releasing us [from the concentration camp], they let us wash, and the priest was standing behind us talking to the guard. The priest suggested they give us "the machine" one more time, so we wouldn't forget that we had been there. I recognized him later as Father Von Wernich.[50]

Yet another bombshell for the conservative hierarchy was the paschal message delivered by the Archbishop of Viedma, Miguel Hesayne, an unwavering champion of human rights and one of the few bishops who openly confronted the junta and supported the Mothers of the Plaza de Mayo. The message was given on Holy Friday, in the dark hours of the observance of the crucifixion, when the crosses, statues, and holy images in Catholic churches are covered with opaque black cloth. "We lament," said Hesayne, "that repentance has not yet come to those who should be sorry, including [many bishops]." Assuming the sins of his Church, Hesayne went on to speak in the first-person plural. "Official meals were taken with those we were denouncing as torturers. . . . And yet [in 1977 at the Plenary Assembly of the Annual Conference of Bishops] we refused to receive the Mothers of *desaparecidos* who waited outside all day in torrential rain." That, he said, was "a tragic day," not only for the Mothers but also for the Church. Even as the Mothers waited, the bishops ate lunch with the commanders. Hesayne says he still shudders to think of Christ's reaction.[51] Of the scores of bishops gathered that day, only a tiny group—led by Hesayne, Jaime de Nevares (from Neuquén), Jorge Novak (Quilmes), Alberto Devoto (Goya), Vicente Zaspe (Santa Fe)—argued to admit the Mothers. After a volatile debate, these men were voted down.

The Mothers were branded "communists" by, among others, the Papal Nuncio. In 1979, six Mothers traveled to Rome for an audience with Pope John Paul II. They had been led to expect a private meeting, but that was canceled due to Laghi's intervention.[52] So much for the bishops' reports-to-the-Holy-See line of defense for the ex-ambassador from the Vatican.

In a separate statement Hesayne expressed gratitude to Zacarías Moutoukias, and announced that he would raise the issue of his testimony at the Conference of Bishops in early May. "It has always worried me that certain men of the Church have not understood that torture is never humane or Christian. This is a subject we need to discuss at the upcoming conference." Needless to say, not all of the bishop's peers agreed. If Moutoukias's testimony can be proved—and he is but one of numerous witnesses against Von Wernich—then Hesayne says the penalty is clear: Any cleric who tortures must be removed from his office. As several other bishops observed, it is well and timely to revisit the subject of ex-communication, since the threat was used to silence priests who objected to a theology of terror.

"Reconciliation does not mean covering [history] with a blanket of oblivion," declared Hesayne. "Reconciliation means truth, justice, and love. Justice without love can degenerate into vengeance. We need to know the truth for medicinal reasons, so that what happened during the Process will never happen again."[53] Hesayne, Novak, Justo Laguna, and several other bishops urged their "Brothers in the Church" to come forward if they had information "that could help relieve the anguish of the families of *desaparecidos*."

A corrective was also administered to Menem: "The position of the president that enforcers like Scilingo should simply 'confess to their priests' is wrong," stressed Hesayne, the always candid Bishop of Viedma. "It is not Christian, it is not part of the doctrine of this Church. In order to properly repent, he who has sinned against the public must make public repara-tion."[54] Because they had not done so, the ex-commanders were forbidden to receive communion in his diocese. "To violate a person is to violate God," Hesayne emphasized. "For those men to receive the Holy Host would be a public sacrilege."[55]

The Conference of Bishops announced that on May 17 it would release an official document responding to the content, character, and ramifica-tions of the testimonies going back to Scilingo. But as that date approached, the institution was still wracked with conflict. The May deadline was canceled. According to some, a report would come out in December. Announcing the delay was the Archbishop of Buenos Aires, Antonio Quarracino. Appointed to that job two days before the promotion of Colonel Minicucci, Quarracino has longstanding ties to Los Carapintada ("the painted faces"), a reactionary fringe of the military. At his press con-ference on April 29, Argentina's highest-ranking Catholic cleric would not say when the response from his institution might be expected. Rather, he insisted that "in order to examine its conscience, the Church would need time and serenity."[56]

As IT TURNED OUT, the most stunning, profound, and important institu-tional response was provoked by the hapless ex-Sergeant Ibáñez. Though much less articulate than Scilingo, Ibáñez was able to identify some of the victims in his charge. To his everlasting credit, the army Chief of Staff, General Martín Balza, realized that he had been given a great opportunity. About ten hours after Ibáñez spoke on the radio, Balza went on national

television and in seven minutes overturned half a century of Argentine
military discourse.

Facing the camera straight on, Balza spoke simply and fluidly, from a
text notably lacking in marshal tones. He leaned slightly forward over his
eight pages, in a posture at once dignified, sad, and forthcoming:

> With this difficult and dramatic message to the Argentine
> community we hope to begin a painful dialogue about the past, a
> dialogue which has yet to be sustained and which has hovered like
> a ghost in the collective consciousness, inevitably returning, as in
> these days, from the shadows where it used to hide. . . .
>
> Every people—even the most cultured—has in its history
> periods that are hard, dark, almost inexplicable. We are no
> exception . . . A history of battle among Argentines, of fratricide,
> has made for victims and victimizers recurrently trading roles
> from epoch to epoch. . . .
>
> This spiral of violence created an unprecedented crisis in our
> young country. The armed forces, and specifically the army, the
> branch for which I am empowered to speak, *believed erroneously
> that the body politic lacked the necessary antibodies* to confront the
> situation, and once again took power, abandoning the road to
> constitutional legitimacy.
>
> *This error led to . . . illegitimate means of obtaining information,
> including the suppression of life.* . . . Again I wish to repeat: *The ends
> never justify the means.* . . .
>
> To be just we must recognize that in this conflict among
> Argentines *almost all us are guilty, by commission or omission, by
> our presence or our absence, by recommending or passively allowing
> it to happen.* . .. Even though we might wish to deposit the guilt
> with a few, in truth the guilt resides in the collective unconscious
> of the entire nation. . . .
>
> It will take generations to heal this loss, to arrive at the right
> road to sincere reconciliation.
>
> For this my words are not enough, words are not enough, all I
> can offer is my respect, silence before your pain, and my
> commitment to try with all my strength to build a future that will
> not repeat the past. [emphasis in original]

Although Balza reiterated that the army had no official lists of the missing,
he nonetheless invited his subordinates to offer whatever information or
testimony they could, with his "asssurance of complete confidentiality."

He then, as head of the institution, would distribute the information. This, he had the humility to say, "was but a small first step in what had to be a long road."

Balza's most important statement was yet to come:

Without looking for innovative expressions, but calling upon old military rules, once more I give this order to the Argentine army, and in the presence of all of Argentine society: *No one is obliged to obey an immoral order or one that violates military laws or rules. Whoever does so shall . . . be severely sanctioned.*

Let me say, clearly, and without euphemism:
It is a crime to violate the national Constitution;
It is a crime to give an immoral order;
It is a crime to execute an immoral order;
It is a crime to employ unjust, immoral means to accomplish even a legitimate objective. [emphasis in original]

When constitutional order is in danger, Balza stressed, "the armed forces are *not* the country's only solution." He then catalogued a host of civilian resources, including labor unions, universities, and political and cultural organizations. As he approached his conclusion, he declared:

We must forever abandon arrogance and apocalyptic visions, we must accept dissent and sovereign will. . . . *If we do not complete our mourning and close the wounds, we will have no future. . . .*

In these crucial hours for our society, I want to tell you that *in my capacity of army chief . . . I assume our part of the responsibility for the errors in that fight between Argentines* which again today has so upset us.[57] [emphasis in original]

Balza's speech was remarkable as well for what it did not say: There was no mention of "the fight against subversion"; no pleading for "excesses" the army "might have committed"; no disparagement of the ex-Sergeant Ibáñez, or anyone else for that matter.

The general was suddenly a star. The public response to the speech was so broadly and warmly supportive that Menem immediately announced he had ordered Balza to give it, which the latter just as quickly denied. (Balza informed the government beforehand, but the initiative was his.)[58] The general does have his skeptics, who are "waiting to see" whether his impressive language will bear results. Others, including Martín Abregú, executive director of CELS, expressed concern that "once again, essential questions of public life are being settled by an army chief and that, in a country like Argentina, is serious."[59] In a gauge of just how odd such politics can be, Balza's harshest critics come from opposite ends of the spectrum: Augusto Pinochet, for one, who sent word of his disapproval from Chile, and Hebe de Bonafini, who called the general "a great hypocrite," characterizing the whole business of Ibáñez's confession and Balza's response as part of Menem's political maneuvering. In a statement that upset the Mothers of the Plaza-Founding Line and other major human rights groups, Bonafini also disaparaged Sara Steimberg, as "the mother they went looking for who would respond [the way they wanted]. Hatred," said Bonafini, "is a necessary emotion."[60] Weighing in on the side of Pinochet were seventy retired Argentine generals who published a protest in the conservative daily *La Natión*.

In truth Balza's speech was not totally a product of the "Scilingo moment" or a hasty response to Ibáñez. (Although he did reportedly say to his colonels, "A sergeant cannot be allowed to manage the army.") Much of the text the general delivered on April 25, 1995, he had pronounced as early as 1992 within the army. That civilians as a whole were astonished is one more indication of the chasm between the military and the rest of Argentine society.

Addressing the graduating class of the Military College in December 1993, Balza emphasized repeatedly the importance of ethics, truth, and morality in the chain of command. There was no such thing, he stated, as Due Obedience in the face of an immoral order. He reminded the graduating cadets that their right to bear arms is legitimized by the Constitution they are sworn to protect; that they may use their weapons only under the conditions enumerated in the Constitution; and that the only legitimate government is that which rises from the sovereign will of the people who freely elect their representatives. The following year, on the occasion of Army Day (May 29, 1994), the general declared: "Esprit de corps is not complicity, nor a blanket of silence, nor the acceptance of lies or crimes."[61]

The speech of April 25, 1995, unleashed what journalists started calling "the Balza effect." Forty-eight hours after the general's television appearance, two more repentant participants in the Dirty War spoke out. Ex-gendarme Federico Talavera had been assigned to Campo de Mayo and to Olympus. His testimony, though nervous and distraught, was solid. It was corroborated by declarations made years ago to the CONADEP, which specifically mention Talavera.[62] As he said on television, his job at Olympus was to drive the prisoners slated to "fly" to the El Palomar Air Force Base. Like Scilingo, he is ravaged by images: The first time he saw torture, it involved specially trained dogs. On one of the flights, he said, there was a woman eight and a half months pregnant. Her name, he remembered, was Vaccaro. "It was terrible," he said brokenly, "she was hours away from giving birth." The dates and information agree with the CONADEP, according to which Marta Vaccaro was kidnapped with her husband, Hernando Dería, on November 28, 1978. Members of the National Political Secretariat of the Montoneros, the couple was taken from their home in Buenos Aires by the First Army Corps. Marta was due to give birth in late December. That much was known. The new information is this: On the sixth of that month, she was thrown from a plane.

The same day (April 27), Luis Muñoz, an ex-conscript, spoke on Radio Continental. (He is not to be confused with *ex-desaparecido* Carlos Muñoz.) Luis Muñoz said that while stationed at the Cavalry School, his job was to hand carry to the Commando of Military Institutes the list of individuals kidnapped that day. "Everything was very well organized," Muñoz affirmed. "[The chiefs] say the lists can't be constructed, but they know we kept lists for everything we did every single day." He planned to talk with his former comrades and urge them to testify for Balza. Given his strong feelings, why did he not come forward before? "I was afraid," he said, "that they would make me disappear."

The "Balza effect" had the commanders of the navy and air force cornered. They had no choice but to respond and did so, on May 3, 1995, with pomp, circumstance, and lots of press. In comparison with Balza's institutional apology, pundits called the other two statements "decaffein-ated" or "lite" (depending on the newspaper). AIR FORCE COMMANDER Juan Paulik admitted that "in the fight against terrorism there were pro-cedural errors [that led to] horrors." He reminded the audience that in 1986, when the Head of the Joint Chiefs was the air force's Teodoro Waldner, Waldner had acknowledged the "illegality" of the last regime. Paulik also legitimately reminded the public that the leadership of his force had been overhauled with the advent of democracy. He echoed Balza's conviction that the military must be subordinate to the Constitu-tion, and expressed "his profound sorrow for those who lost their loved ones in the fratricide." But Paulik "balanced" these strong points by also saying, "The armed institutions were one factor among many in the diz-zying escalation of violence . . . and it would be inappropriate to try the military again, alone, out of context."[63]

The anticipatory tension was much higher for the navy. Its role in the repression was greater than that of the air force; it has a large number of Dirty War enforcers who are not only still on active duty, but who have risen steadily through the ranks; and the institution was still trying to scuttle Scilingo. Still, parts of Admiral Enrique Molina Pico's message were ringingly impressive:

> What is society asking of us at this time? An acknowledgment. What is an acknowledgment? If it means public humiliation, an acceptance of culpability that will serve to defeat us in the future— if that is what acknowledgment means, then no. What we must do is to acknowledge the truth, the whole truth. End this entrenched war of lies: That the armed forces did not undertake a war to exterminate innocents. That we fought according to the rules of legitimate war. The reality is otherwise. We acted without having our Constitution in effect, without respect for the law, and in defiance of the rules of war. The institutions involved bear historical guilt to those they are sworn to protect. [W]e repudiate those actions and are working to prevent their recurrence.

But the admiral also embarked on a tortuous defense of Due Obedience. Guilt, he said, should not be levied at:

> The men who fought the enemy, [the men] whose fears and euphorias I shared. In the midst of hatred and the violence of war, the majority of these men loyally fulfilled plans and orders, in the belief that the cause they were fighting for was just.

He then conflated juridical truth with political expedience. "The Executive power handed down a law; the Congress voted to approve it; and the Judiciary ratified it. The whole institutional process worked, and the navy must obey the juridical truth."[64]

On May 4, the day after the navy's institutional apology, Scilingo was arrested for his spate of bad checks some four years before. The day after that, the admiral confirmed on the radio that Alfredo Astiz, the notorious infiltrator of the Mothers, "had all the moral qualities to be an officer of the navy."[65] As though it were necessary, the admiral reminded his interviewer that Astiz had been absolved under Due Obedience. Would Astiz be referred to the Senate for promotion? Time, he said, would tell. In the ensuing uproar, Menem, who initially backed Molina Pico, affirmed that "Astiz is a good officer," and complained of the "injustice" to which "members of the armed forces are unfairly subjected."[66]

The French government was enraged: The ambassador called the eventuality of the captain's promotion "shocking and shameful." Another high-ranking official warned: "France does not forget." Nor do we, declared

Sweden's ambassador, whose country has sued Astiz for killing a young Swedish national.

It is Astiz (now forty-four) who expresses surprise at the range of opinion against him: "I wasn't a torturer," he says. "I did intelligence."[67] The disingenuous captain is splitting hairs: He knew very well what happened in the ESMA; he helped decide who would be "sucked up" there; and, by numerous accounts, he brought in hundreds of so-called subversives.

And if, strictly speaking, Astiz did not torture, he did murder the sixteen-year-old Swedish-Argentine Dagmar Hagelin. As it turned out, by mistake. On January 26, 1977, the task force headed by Astiz kidnapped Norma Susana Burgos, a friend of Hagelin. They then staked out her house for the rest of the night, awaiting the arrival of another woman, María Antonia Berger, who was expected early the next morning. At about 8:30 A.M., Dagmar Hagelin—a tall blond like María Antonia Berger—came walking toward Burgos's house to say goodbye to her friend before summer vacation. When suddenly Hagelin found herself surrounded, she panicked and ran away. Astiz and some others gave chase and when the girl was about thirty meters ahead of them, Astiz knelt down on the sidewalk, took aim with his pistol, and shot the girl in the back. According to survivor testimony, Hagelin was in the ESMA, incontinent, half-paralyzed, and unable to speak; she was then sent to a navy hospital in Mar del Plata, where the distraught Astiz went to ask her forgiveness.[68] Hagelin's father had reported her kidnapping the day after it happened, and Sweden immediately tried to rescue the girl. But the Argentine navy decided that Dagmar was too handicapped to be released To avoid being incriminated by her injuries, the navy killed her.

In spite of these scandals, Astiz won a military promotion in 1987. In 1992, he was promoted again. He is said to be not just coddled, but revered, within the navy; younger officers reputedly look up to him; older ones defer, as though to a superior of extremely high rank. Astiz has been described as a "gentleman sailor"; unlike many of his superiors, he never stole a cent from a single detainee. The Blond Angel personifies the totalizing concept of Due Obedience, which the navy has yet to let go. Many in the force also feel that Astiz is a scapegoat, a star-crossed victim: Who was to know that his particular cases would cause an international problem?

What really bothers Astiz is that he hasn't been able to travel. Because France and Sweden still have open cases against him, he would immediately be arrested by Interpol. But "Alfredito" is highly mobile within Argentina. He appears frequently in the press, photographed while skiing or beachcombing or dancing with teenage girls in the trendy clubs he favors in Buenos Aires. As one girl told the weekly *Noticias* (on condition that they not print her name), "Alfredo is like radar for pretty women . . . he has this innate charm, this special way of handling them, girls die for him."[69] (Did she hear what she was saying?) Astiz is often pictured holding a glass of Coca Cola. Parents say they approve of him because "he doesn't drink." Outside these rarefied circles, Astiz is a most despised symbol of the Dirty War. As the "Scilingo effect" continued to unfold, the Blond Angel would be subjected to a series of surprisingly nasty encounters.

And in the 1995 world of French diplomacy, the Argentine Admiral Molina Pico was all but *fini*. Any doubts about this were dispelled when he was excluded from the guest list to the embassy's bash for Bastille Day. It reportedly took desperate maneuvering at the highest levels of Argentine government to break the impasse. Voilá! headlined the always irreverent *Página 12*: "Liberté Fraternité Invité!!!"[70]

The admiral's reception at the hands of his hosts was proper but reserved. As soon as he arrived, Argentine human rights leaders pointedly left. No one in the resplendent salon would let him forget that in the City of Light, his *protégé* is a convicted killer.[71]

MEANWHILE BALZA'S STAR shone ever more brightly. On June 8, which in Argentina is Journalists Day, he again stunned the public by offering a large reception for invited members of the civilian press. As if that were not enough, he requested a moment of silence for the ninety-three reporters disappeared or murdered during the last dictatorship. A trumpeter then played taps. Raising his glass in tribute to these fallen men and women, the army chief reminded the guests that two of the country's founding fathers, Manuel Belgrano (1770–1820) and Mariano Moreno (1779-1811), were both journalists as well as military leaders.[72] "We all wept," I was told by a friend who was there. I couldn't help but ask if this strong reaction wasn't due in part to the element of surprise. "Absolutely," he replied, "we were totally unprepared."

According to a survey by the pollsters Germano and Giacobbe, between March and May 1995 Balza was one of the most frequently mentioned names in Argentine print media. In a little less than three months, the general appeared 3,018 times in newspapers and magazines; Scilingo, in comparison, trailed with 1,894 appearances. The word most often used to describe the army chief was *inédito*—"unprecedented." I was anxious to meet this general who was reputed to love French poetry and Impressionist painting; who stood on line with everyone else to get into the movies;

who, as Artillery Commander in the Malvinas campaign, marched in front of his men and fired a cannon with his own hands until the very end; who in 1990 as Assistant Army Chief climbed into a tank to put down a rebellion by the reactionary Carapintadas; who in 1994 invited Anatoly Karpov to army headquarters for a game of chess.

Martín Balza was born in 1934 in the province of Buenos Aires to a Basque mother and a French father with Slavic forbears. After his father's early death, Balza was educated through a series of scholarships. He graduated from the Military Academy in 1955 and from the Superior War College in 1963; in 1967, he was named a U.N. Observer of the Six Day War; from 1976 to 1978, he arranged with the army to teach in the Superior War College in Lima, Peru. He then returned to the School of Artillery at the Campo de Mayo Army Base in Buenos Aires, where he remained until the Malvinas debacle of 1982. His company shot down the first British war plane, for which he won a medal of honor. Balza wears thirty-two medals and decorations. Among his awards are the French Légion d'Honneur (at which ceremony he is said to have sung all the words of "La Marseillaise") and the U.S. Legion of Merit.

"Is he a genius?" I asked Retired Colonel Horacio Ballester, a founder of CEMIDA (Military Center for Argentine Democracy).[73] Ballester is about ten years older than Balza and their careers overlapped. They seem to share many of the same ideas, yet their respective experiences in the force contrast. Ballester's democratic (and Peronist) tendencies had caused him a lot of difficulty in the army. "I was subjected to judicial abuse—court-martialed, denied promotions, demoted, imprisoned, numerous times, without just cause," he volunteered. He entered and left the force during military dictatorships. In the years between 1943, when he joined, and 1971, when he left, only three out of twelve governments were elected (General Perón, 1946–55; Arturo Frondizi, 1958–62; Arturo Illia, 1962–63). In 1971, during the dictatorship of General Lanusse, Ballester was one of a highly prestigious group of colonels that rose up against the de facto president for the cause of free democratic elections. The uprising was quashed, the colonels were cashiered, and immediately thereafter they founded CEMIDA, an unprecedented military human rights group. Even after he was retired from the army, Ballester still suffered persecution. Not long after his separation, Perón invited him to Madrid, where he had spent most of his exile. "I represented our delegation precisely because I was no longer in the army, and so was free to travel without having to ask permission. Perón sent the tickets for a Portuguese flight. I boarded, they closed the doors, but the flight didn't take off.

Finally the Federal Police came on and kidnapped me from the plane on the pretext that I had no authorization to leave the country. The excuse was illegal, and, since we were in a foreign aircraft, we were not even officially in Argentina. They didn't torture me, but they did keep me in solitary for a week."

The founding members of CEMIDA, colonels Augusto Rattenbach, José Luis García, and Carlos Gazcón and the late General Ernesto López Meyer, are military scholars, writers, and activists. They all have similar stories, often involving kangaroo courts and years in prison without having been charged. After leaving the force, they edited a magazine called *Estrategia* and worked for the restoration of constitutional government. When Perón returned for a second term, Ballester was put in charge of the commercialization of meat, a very important job in Argentina. With the coup of 1976, he was fired and put in prison. Ballester was a valuable witness at the trial of the ex-commanders, during which someone put a bomb in the offices of CEMIDA. He tells me that CEMIDA member Colonel Juan Jaime Cesio "is the only military man who remains unpardoned for his 'offenses' during the Dirty War. His crime—for which he was jailed, cashiered, and stripped of his rank—was supporting the Mothers of the Plaza de Mayo. All things considered," he says, "we're lucky. Because, as you know, they *disappeared* officers as well as conscripts. And before that, in the '50s and '60s, a lot of dissenters got shot."

He returns to my question, which he answers with one of his characterically precise paragraphs. "Balza is certainly not a genius. In fact, he was not a particularly distinguished student. He is neither a savior nor a criminal. He is a good soldier. He came up through the ranks by never stepping out of line. He knows how to lead his troops. He saw that [after Ibáñez] there could be a flood of declarations, making the force impossible to govern. So he opted to anticipate the flood. He did two vital things: He acknowledged the history—which no one else in his position had ever done—and he kept the army governable. At this point we should support him. It looks like a door is starting to open. As he himself said, it's a beginning, not the end. Of course history will be the final judge—of his results, by-products, and intentions."

In 1987, the four founding colonels of CEMIDA published a book whose title, translated, is "The Argentine Armed Forces: The Necessary Change." Because these men are separated from the army it is hard to measure their influence within it. But among scholars and the international human rights community, their work is held in high esteem and their main points certainly appear to have resonated with Balza:

To our comrades: May you *never again* execute a coup d'état;

To our compatriots: May you *never again* give consensus to a coup d'état;

To everyone: May sectorial interests *never again* predominate over the genuine benefit of the Nation, [emphasis in original]

In the words of the CEMIDA authors, we also find:

The military cannot operate from an ideology at odds with that of the country, nor can it impose its ideology. . . . The ideology of the the military should *be a direct reflection of the country's political model.* . . . The armed forces should *accompany—neither precede nor twist*—the country's political processes, [emphasis in original][74]

In other respects, CEMIDA may still be ahead of the progressive chief of the army. In 1987, these authors held that "the truth, however burdensome it might be, must be brought to light. All the pain, blood, and misunderstandings generated by the recent past must be put to use for the benefit of present and future generations." Regarding the full disclosure of historical truth, Balza has not used imperative constructions. It is true that according to Argentine civilian law, no one can be required to testify against himself It is also true that because Due Obedience and Punto Final are still on the books, with very few exceptions no one can be prosecuted.

I ask Ballester if he thinks that Balza truly hopes that his invitation will engender a series of declarations. "Might he be offering a space knowing that the gesture itself would likely put the brake on confessions?"

"I don't think that he is offering a space," Ballester replied. "I think that he—as the force's chief—may well believe that his acknowledgment substitutes for individual testimonies. If we've heard it from a general, do we need to hear it from a sergeant? If that's what's happening, it would be contemptible, but it would still be a useful first step. We need to take advantage of whatever opening seems to present Itself."

"To achieve what?"

"Justice."

"And what does that mean, concretely?"

"That we find out who the enforcers were. That we know the history, so we don't repeat it."

"It looks like the system won't allow it."

"Then we expose the contradictions in the system."

Horacio Verbitsky has covered Balza for a number of years now. I asked him: "Is the general way out in front of his institution, or does he arise from, represent, an emerging army culture?" To my surprise, Verbitsky laughed. "García Márquez told of a man who sold turtles, toy turtles that moved. And they were so realistic, that a man passing by asked, 'Are they plastic or are they alive?' And the vendor said, 'Both!' But seriously," Verbitsky went on, "as a soldier his performance has been exceptional. At the same time, as chief, the reforms and speeches he's made have been accepted without the slightest objection from those inside the army, on active duty. And those reforms definitely mark a rupture with the past. Something else to bear in mind: Since the Malvinas his behavior has been absolutely coherent. No trace of opportunism, speculation, or ambiguity. We can't forget that much of what happens will depend on society. Not only on Balza, the armed forces, the administration. The society as a whole must affirm these changes, demand that they be realized. I do think that there is an interesting, promising harmonization between the changes going on within the army and those happening in society."

I ask if he thinks that Balza might really be trying to contain a potential flood of testimonies.

"I don't think so," Verbitsky replied, "it wouldn't work. I think we'll see more testimonies. What I do think is that Balza didn't want to be left on the sidelines." He fell silent for a moment. "What is possible is that the government thought that if the Joint Chiefs made institutional statements, then that would discourage, subsume, individual confessions. To put the lid on testimonies for a few weeks until after the [upcoming parliamentary] elections, yes, the administration would definitely prefer that. But it won't last forever. It can't."

"Could the promise of anonymity be seen as the continuation of the old solidarity pact?"

Verbitsky pauses. "Yes," he says slowly, "that is a reasonable reading. It's not the only interpretation, but I would not discount it. Though I think it would be more a side effect than a direct objective or goal. A by-product."

"Confidentiality could also produce more information."

"Time will tell. It's possible that as we speak they're taking testimony and that the information will be released. If they come back and say, 'No one knows anything,' at that point we can be more critical."[75]

Mignone essentially agrees with Verbitsky, and adds this: "What Balza wants is to *save* the army. The way to do it is to change the army, break with the old Prussian model, and integrate the force into society. The military has made a mess of it every time they've taken over the government. So that era is over for them. Finished. Balza's thinking is very intelligent. To continue to defend the indefensible is *not* the way to enhance the army's prestige. Here is an interesting anecdote: As you know, Alfonsín was the first to require military graduates and those being promoted to swear to defend the Constitution. They used to swear to defend the *patria*. Well, just two weeks ago, a man being promoted to major refused to make the pledge. So Balza cashiered him. Because you cannot defend the nation without defending the Constitution."

Everyone I consulted about the army chief concurred on one vital point: He is, as they say, "unstained by the blood of the repression." Balza is surrounded by a close-knit, well-educated, cosmopolitan group of colonels (one is a graduate of the Sorbonne). They treated me with extraordinary cordiality and efficiency. My main contact was Colonel Mario Crethién, who, in spite of my demurrals, kept offering a chauffeur to drive me to the general. (I won this point, and arrived by cab.) Our appointment was originally scheduled for June 12, but had to be postponed because of a bomb found hanging in a tree outside army headquarters. It turned out to be an amateurish affair, but it was enough to have the block sealed off for the rest of the day. The next morning the general left for an inspection of troops in Bosnia. (It was he who convinced Menem that Argentina should participate in the peacekeeping effort in the former Yugoslavia.) In the back and forth of scheduling, Mario Crethién called so many times that once when I picked up, he said jokingly, "Margarita, its your colonel." Our meeting finally took place on July 3, 1995. I was unprepared for the warmth and informality that seemed to reign within army headquarters, located in the hideously looming and martial Edificio Libertador. Balza himself came down to greet me and then he, Colonel Crethién, and I rode up to his office in the elevator. The general knew everyone we happened to meet, not only the officers, but also support staff.

Balza indeed lit up at the mention of French poetry. "I can still remember by heart whole works by Paul Verlaine," he said proudly. "What you learn at seventeen, eighteen, twenty, stays with you, it's 'engraved.'" Balza is extremely tall (about six foot five) and strongly built. He towers over me, and at this point in our conversation, he seemed to be handling himself with some delicacy, so as not to emphasize the great difference in our statures. "I am not the only one around here who loves French painting and poetry," he says. "If you could spend some days conversing with our officers, I think you would get a lot of surprises. How they think, how sensitive they are. The Military Academy requires those aptitudes, instills these values and sensibilities. I remember that the first cut-off in the entrance exam (which I took in 1951) was literature; if you were not well read, you were immediately disqualified from the other parts of the test. Also on the entrance exam were music and mathematics. So as to have soldiers who were both sensitive and precise. Our cadets have a full humanistic education. They study Kant, who says: 'Man is an end in himself, and never a means for the ends of others.' Our context is the whole Judeo-Christian ethic—and I'm not talking in religious terms, but referring to that essential respect for human beings, loving one's neighbor as oneself. In order to maintain the level of discipline required in the military, one needs a great deal of sensitivity. One leads through example; one leads through love. And those who obey must feel that."

It was indeed a beautiful, and surprising, speech. But I had to observe that those precepts seemed at odds with his institution's history. And he omitted to mention that the Doctrine of National Security was for decades a central part of the military curriculum.

Before I could elaborate the query, the general sharply cut in: "I don't know of any army in the world that doesn't have some bad memories. Not one. If you do, I'd like to hear it."

"I don't," I said, which seemed to calm him. It is a fact that Balza has done much to modernize the education his cadets receive, to bring it closer to what civilians study. To that end, their program must now be approved by the Ministry of Education. Among the recent additions to the curriculum are human rights and military sociology. "The intellectual separation [from civilians] during these formative years is very unhealthy," says the army chief "The military must arise from the people. How can it do so, if it lives and learns as though in a world apart?" Balza has also introduced women into the Argentine army, and effected a smooth transition to an all-volunteer force. Confronted with steep cuts in military expenditures, he reacted with unparalleled grace: "In common with with the rest of the Nation, we too must assume budgetary restrictions. . . . The interests of the Nation have priority, then those of the army, and then those of the [force's] members."[76]

I communicated Ballester's assessment that Balza had made a positive rupture with the history of Argentine military culture. ("Your superior is always right, the more so when he is wrong," the retired colonel had summarized.) Balza responded by emphasizing the continuity represented by his speech of April 25. "It was not a personal statement, but a response to cultural developments within the force. I could not have made that speech, or any of the ones leading up to it, without the full support of the army, without those concepts and feelings being shared." He stressed that his explication of Due Obedience derives from military, not civilian, law. "It is in the Handbook of Command. Before becoming Chief I was in the army for forty-four years. Never once did I receive an immoral order. And if I had I never would have carried it out. Because that is beyond the margin of military law."

Certainly, though, he knew that others around him in Campo de Mayo were giving and receiving immoral orders?

"No," he says shortly, leaning back and sitting straighter.

"But there was a concentration camp within Campo de Mayo."

He coughs. "As you very well know, the fight against subversion was very compartmentalized, it wasn't the whole army."

"But given your rank—"

"I was a lieutenant colonel. I was not a general."

"Let's be clear. No one has accused you of any atrocities, you are widely described as 'untainted,' and it's one of the reasons I wished to speak with you."

"There were many army men who battled subversion completely within military rules and regulations, for instance in Tucumán in 1975 and early 1976 [when the leftist ERP was defeated]. Those men have nothing to be ashamed of."

"But by 1978 there were many reports in the international press, as well as here to some limited extent, about the missing, about the camps. Even if you saw nothing, you must have heard something."

"It's one thing to hear things in the news . . . but, it's like certain political goings on, you hear things, read things, but—"

"You didn't take seriously the *New York Times*, the *London Times, El País?*"

"I don't have time to read those newspapers, I don't—"

"Even on such important subjects?"

"I'm interested in the news produced by the papers of my own country, which of course cover international news. I do read the *Buenos Aires Herald*. the editorials, mostly, which are translated. I don't think anyone really has the time to read lots of newspapers."

"But if you were reading, even sporadically, the *Buenos Aires Herald*, they were covering these issues. Jacobo Timerman, for example, published lists of the missing. What use did you make of this information?"

He coughs again. "You know, it is hard to analyze a political situation twenty years later. The information that comes in the news is useful, of course, but it goes only so far. I repeat," he says sternly, "I never saw any action committed in my units that fell outside the law. Never once under my responsibility."

I have no reason to doubt him on this point, and tell him so. Though I have no proof to the contrary, I find the rest of his denial hard to believe. "Was there terror as well within the force?"

"No. What do you mean? I want to be sure I understand."

"The question is straightforward. Illegal actions *were* committed under the orders of other officers. That can create fear. Was there a way to combat those actions, resist that way of thinking and operating, sow the seeds of a different behavior?"

"At no time were those [illegal] things, that climate, generalized throughout the army. If you think so, you are wrong."

"Okay, accepting that, you still knew these things were happening."

"No. No."

"If you have always been opposed to military coups, how could you remain in a force that has carried out so many?"

"Right." He has clearly expected this question. "Many were opposed. I'm not the only one." He calls in three of his colonels. "She wants to know why, if we oppose military takeovers, we didn't leave the army." As if on cue, they look at each other and gently laugh. "Because if we had left we would have lost the opportunity to transform certain aspects of the culture—like the integration of the force with democratic institutions. Perhaps our reforms are in themselves a judgment, a prosecution of the force."

I take his point. "But, honestly, I have trouble understanding how a person with a fundamentally democratic nature could have stayed in the army during the Process."

The general says nothing.

"You were holding out hope?"

"Of course we held out hope. I think we all know that it takes time to transform an institution, a society. You have to do this from within the institution."

I suggest we return to his speech, which many, myself included, have praised. "But some things could be debated," I suggest. "I, for example, question the statement that, 'the guilt resides in the collective unconscious of the entire Nation.' After all, it wasn't everyone who kidnapped, tortured, killed, threw living people into the sea. . . . I think we should mark a difference between—"

Once more he cuts me off. "Read it to me again." I do. "You have not lived long enough in this country, you have not experienced a military coup. The history is clear. Going back to 1930, all of our coups had the participation, complicity, call it what you will, of the civilian population. If there had not been that civilian participation, the Process would not have happened."

There is truth to what he says, but his statement is too broad, too pat. The whole point of the Process was that its workings were clandestine.

Three days before our meeting, another ex-sergeant, Pedro Caraballo, had come forward to testify about the trafficking of newborns in the concentration camp run out of Campo de Mayo. Caraballo was stationed there from 1976-1983; Balza from 1978–1982. "As you know, the Lawyers Association of Buenos Aires is reopening the case on babies stolen from Campo de Mayo. Is that an important development for the force?"

"No. [Baby trafficking] is a civilian crime and should be handled in civilian courts. Caraballo doesn't belong to the army. He was in the force for a couple of years three decades ago. [While in Campo de Mayo] he was with the National Gendarme."

"But he was apparently a witness to goings-on within the army."

"But not as part of the army."

"Some have said that what you really want is to put a brake on the testimonies." I say this very respectfully.

It infuriates him. "Do you believe that?"

"It's my job to ask you that question."

"And it's my job to ask if you believe it."

There is a heated pause. "Then believe what you like."

"I'm asking because I don't want to believe it."

"Then why are you asking? I don't understand."

"Because I want to hear your answer."

Again there is a pause.

"Your offer of anonymity could be seen as the continuation of the solidarity pact, the pact of silence. How do you respond?" I asked.

"Everyone can interpret my words as they wish. I know what I meant. If some *bastard* way of thinking wants to twist the ethical content of my message, then so be it."

"I understand that no one can be obliged to incriminate himself. But without violating that precept, or asking them to incriminate others, could you not order your men to provide the information they might have on the victims?"

"No," the general continued more evenly, "I can only appeal to the conscience of these individuals, their own willingness to come forward. And I am committed to releasing whatever information that might yield."

"Is the process working?"

"Well, obviously, I cannot comment publicly, because it's confidential."

"I'm not asking for names, only if there's been some movement, *movimiento de conciencia*."

"*There's always mavimiento de conciencia. Always.*"

"You believe then that the force will survive the confessions of Ibáñez and—"

"I don't understand."

"Because these confessions substantiate a very dark and bloody past."

"Yes."

"Inhuman."

"Yes."

"And in the wake of all that it might well be hard to carry on."

"We will carry on. That dark past—like the dark pasts of other countries—has been totally overcome."

"Totally?"

"Totally. Within the force I command. And within the country, I think. Certainly you appreciate the respect of this force for democracy."

"I do."

"And the respect of the Argentine people for its armed forces. Everywhere in the country I see profound respect and affection for the army. You can see it at any parade."

"There is also suspicion," I venture, "and fear."

"On the part of whom?"

"I for one know many people who are afraid of the armed forces."

"I don't agree. I don't know anyone who is afraid of the armed forces. That someone could be afraid of the armed forces in the Republic of Argentina, there I think you're wrong. But that's just my opinion."

"I do think that you personally engender a great deal of respect. But in view of the history of this institution, not just 1976 to 1983, but—"

"—1976 to 1983," the general breaks in, "is not the whole history of this country."

"That's what I'm saying. The whole history has engendered a certain amount of apprehension."

He pauses. "That's one opinion," he says, and calls in his colonels for the ceremonies of my departure.

General Balza has arranged two gifts for me. He extends a jeweler's box holding a brooch with the army shield. "I was going to pin it on her," he joked to his colonels, "but I don't know about this one, if she'd want to wear it." He placed the box in my hand. He also gave me a ceramic boot with a broken toe, the symbolism of which still eludes me (and everyone I've asked).

I am still puzzled by the general's volatility, by his quickness to perceive insult where none was intended. Not one of my questions was in any way a trap; all of my questions were in fact transparent. Balza is, perhaps, unaccustomed to being challenged. Maybe the way he's been lionized led me to expect more openness than is realistic in a man of his position. May what the general says be true, that he is not "singular'" but representative of the increasingly humanistic culture of the Argentine army.

In the year and a half since our conversation, Balza's public comments and behavior have been at one with his famous speech of April 25,1995. Yet at this writing no one separated from the army has followed ex-sergeant Caraballo with new testimony on the atrocities of the Dirty War. Nor has Balza's invitation to his active subordinates yielded anything new.

As always, the Grandmothers of the Plaza de Mayo were working quietly behind the scenes. They have estimated that over 500 babies disappeared during the dictatorship; of 220 documented cases, only 56 of those children have been located. For seventeen years, maternal and paternal relatives searched for Carlos D'Elía-Casco, both of whose parents are missing. The families were virtually certain that in 1978, Carlos was sold to a navy couple unable to have children of their own. In 1988, the Grandmothers of the Plaza de Mayo, using genetic tests, established the boy's identity to within a probability of 99.99 percent. After seven more years of scrupulous legal work, in late June 1995 an Argentine Federal Judge arranged a meeting of the biological relatives and ordered the arrest of the adoptive parents and the obstetrician who had sold them the baby.

The doctor in question is police physician Jorge Antonio Bergés, known as "Dr. Death" or "the Argentine Mengele." Convicted in 1986 on numerous counts of torture, then released on Due Obedience the following year, Bergés had been living quietly in the province of Buenos Aires where he ran a private women's health clinic. The plaque at the entrance to his building lists the following specialties: Gynecology, Obesity, Liposuction, Cellulitis, and Esthetic and Reconstructive Surgery.

Suddenly in June 1995 Bergés was again important news, as the first official to be charged with baby trafficking, a crime that falls outside the Punto Final and Due Obedience laws. He is known to have supervised the births of numerous pregnant *desaparecidas*, one reason his case is so important. Another is that he was still on the payroll of the Buenos Aires Provincial Police, who, in this most recent ordeal, did their utmost to protect him.

Day after day as the case developed, the media recapitulated the doctor's history through interviews with witnessed and victims. Jacobo Timerman recalled Bergés as an "implacable torturer, incredibly cynical and nasty. 'It's over for today,' he'd croon, 'let's calm down, let's rest up for

torture tomorrow.' No one was despised more than Bergés. Always impeccable, his coat spotless, you could see that he took pleasure in his 'work.'"
Indeed the color photos in popular magazines like *Noticias* showed Bergés
to be dapper: dark hair cut close to his head, a neatly trimmed moustache,
excellent posture in the brilliant white coat of his profession. Timerman
crossed paths with Bergés in two camps in Buenos Aires Province: "His job
was to keep a check on my heart so I wouldn't die. I'm glad they've got
him, I'm sure that many of us will celebrate."[77]

Another survivor who has repeatedly testified against the doctor is
Adriana Calvo de Laborde, a physicist who was forced to give birth handcuffed and shackled in a speeding truck. "After they got me to hospital,"
she recounted, "Bergés yanked the placenta out of me and threw it on the
floor. He then forced me to clean the room, naked, while he insulted me
with all sorts of obscenities." In sworn testimony, Calvo de Laborde has
affirmed that Bergés had "a side business, which consisted of selling babies
born in captivity."[78]

A fellow physician, Justo Horacio Blanco, also declared against Bergés,
concerning the falsification of birth records at a public hospital and the
disappearance of a young mother and her premature daughter. During
Bergés's 1986 trial, Dr. Blanco received death threats and a bomb was set in
his car. "They so terrorized a delivery nurse who worked with me that
when she got to the stand she said she couldn't remember anything." A
psychiatrist who declared was also threatened by Bergés, who parked outside his house for hours on end and sat there, laughing. Withal Bergés was
convicted. When he was released in 1987, he set to harassing the local medical circle which had ousted him. He also went to work on the College of
Physicians so that they would not suspend his license. "They hid behind
Due Obedience," said Dr. Blanco, "but that law didn't address his violation of the Hippocratic Oath."[79]

In June 1995, the adoptive parents went to jail to await trial, but
Bergés—who was still drawing a salary from the Buenos Aires Provincial Police—fled, vanished. And though the police said they "searched
his house and everything," for over three months they were unable to
find him. In late September 1995 the Court of Appeals canceled the war-
rant for his arrest. Bergés reappeared, paying the bail he owed not with
the 40,000 pesos that had been set, but with a piece of borrowed furniture. "This is beyond irregular," said legal experts. Though Bergés signed
the birth certificate of this child of *desaparecidos* last seen in a concentration camp, his lawyer cynically insisted to the media that "this could
happen to any obstetrician who delivers a baby that is later adopted." In

November 1995, this case against Bergés was dropped by a Federal Court, which cited the statute of limitation. Whereupon the Buenos Aires Provincial Police Chief announced that Bergés, who had been granted a paid leave of absence, would be reintegrated into the force at full salary. (The Ministry of the Interior, which is responsible for the Federal Police, quickly contradicted that announcement.) As 1995 drew to a close, Bergés was charged by a different court for having sold another baby. Because this case was first instigated in the early 1980s, there was hope in Argentine legal circles; at least the statute of limitations wasn't going to be a factor. What eventually happened to Bergés is beyond strange; it is absolutely bizarre.

On April 4, 1996, the infamous doctor was shot numerous times as he and his wife were walking their dog near their home in Quilmes, a suburb of Buenos Aires. The assailants were careful not to harm his wife, and later burned the car in which they escaped. The profusely bleeding Bergés (whose body was perforated by over twenty entry and exit wounds) was refused treatment at two hospitals before he was finally admitted to the Naval Hospital in the capital. Claiming responsibility for the attack was a group of which no one had previously heard: the Organización Revolucionaria del Pueblo (ORP, "People's Revolutionary Organization"). The name is an obvious play on Ejército Revolutionario del Pueblo (ERP, "Peoples Revolutionary Army"), a bona fide leftist guerrilla group operative in the early '70s (and defeated by the army in Tucumán in 1975). The statements of ORP were tailor-made for a right-wing crackdown: "The country should be on guard. We will be active until the *next* March 24 anniversary." The group followed up with a phone threat to Bergés's family: "Thirty thousand disappeared. We will kill two for each one you killed. Nobody will be left alive." A bomb—safely retrieved and later detonated by the police—was found outside the hospital wher e Bergés lay gravely wounded. Other bombs were set in banks, but caused no human injury.

In spite of their efforts to have Bergés brought to trial, every human rights group in Argentina condemned the attack, which he seemed unlikely to survive. And no group opposing the former regime has ever used such language, which is a clear echo of the "ten of yours for every one of ours" declarations of the old Dirty Warriors. Three weeks after the attack, Argentines got to hear and see ORP on television (on *Hora Clave*). In what has to be one of the oddest shows ever broadcast in Argentina, two high-ranking members of ORP appeared in a video, seated with their arms resting on a table, their heads and faces shrouded by heavy black hoods. On the wall behind them was a large flag painted with a star. Wearing sports shirts, and with pads of notes before them, they sat side by side, at right angles to the Uruguayan reporter asking them questions. When they replied, their voices were slightly muffled by their hoods. They came across as crude, primitive, and puzzling. As a journalist friend of mine put it, "[they're] like twelve-year-olds who insist they're Marxists before they've even read Marx." Many got the impression these fellows were trying to imitate leftists.

Just who is ORP? Prevailing journalistic opinion (including *La Nación* and *Clarín*, neither of which is particularly left-leaning) is that ORP rose up from the fringes of the police or secret services. Agents provocateurs. Why would they shoot Bergés? The doctor's appeals and possibilities for legal maneuverings are exhausted; ethics aside, politically he's a hard figure to digest, let alone defend. With overwhelming odds that he would eventually be tried and convicted, it is plausible that reactionary forces in the police and military would "sacrifice" him and, in the process, give themselves an excuse to flex some muscle. It may also be simpler and less political, a settling of accounts between rival factions.[80]

Four days after Bergés was shot, there began a wave of threats against some thirty journalists, actors, writers, and activists. The first and most serious incident was a physical attack against the popular cartoonist for *La Nación*, "Nik," (Cristián Dzwonik), who was assaulted, robbed, and held captive for a while in a car. The week before, Nik had participated in a television news show during which the military regime was roundly criticized. Yet the list of those being menaced by ORP was incoherent and contradictory: On the one hand it included figures like Magdalena Ruiz Guiñazú, pioneering reporter, member of the Argentine National Commission on the Disappeared and an important witness at the 1985 trials; on the other, it includes Bernardo Neustadt, a politically conservative television journalist who was a prominent apologist for the military regime. One can confidently say that no group opposing the last repression would wish to harm Nik, Ruiz Guiñazú, or other human rights proponents. President Menem insisted that withal "security in Argentina is guaranteed." The Interior Minister tried to downplay the phone threats by suggesting they are unrelated to ORP, merely the activities of "an individual with too much time on his hands."[81]

"Every day things get stranger here," I was told by a seasoned photojournalist who lived semi-clandestinely in Argentina during the last regime and who asked to remain anonymous. "Reporters and other activists are being threatened. Weird, frightening things are going on, and its all so sinister, hard to pin down. I'm getting feelings of déjá vu."

A writer in her early thirties was calmer: "Certainly there is concern. We are very alert and watchful. But if what they're trying to do is create widespread panic, or paralysis, they've failed."

Was ORP serious about killing Bergés? It is hard to know. In any case. Dr. Death survives. On June 12, 1996, he left the hospital and is being cared for at an undisclosed facility until he is able to return home.

"THE MOST IMPORTANT aspect of this whole 'Scilingo moment' is that it was inevitable," insists Emilio Mignone. "You know, as far back as 1977, I was saying privately, 'They have killed twenty or thirty thousand people; how can they not be aware that it will come back and hit the country like a boomerang? From the standpoint of history, of sociology, it has to happen. Societies *need* to know. That's what this is all about.'"

It is June 1995 and we are sitting in the Mignones' living room, which is full of books, newspapers, magazines, and pamphlets. During the repression there was a constant stream of people into this apartment, as Mignone was one of the few lawyers willing to handle writs of habeas corpus. He did hundreds, perhaps over a thousand. "What was terrible," said Señora Chela Mignone, "was that we could never express what we really felt. People were so desperate. To say in a meeting of the Mothers, for example, that I believed our children were dead would have been a taken as a betrayal."

Through their activities in the Permanent Assembly for Human Rights and progressive church groups, the Mignones had uncommon access to information. "By 1977," said Emilio, "I calculated that 5000 to 6000 individuals had 'disappeared.' If they were in a detention center, say in the south, they would need 20,000 to take care of them. In Argentina, with that many people directly involved, plus their families and friends, you could never keep it secret. So very quickly," he says mournfully, "I concluded that they had all been murdered."

Chela gives me a photograph of their daughter, Mónica, who was twenty-four at the time of her disappearance. She is looking straight at the camera with a serious smile; her long straight dark hair hangs down over one shoulder. A Catholic lay teacher, Mónica had worked for years in shantytowns, in Patagonia, and in the Bajo Flores district of the capital. The members of her group "fell" separately, but on or about the same day, May 14, 1976. All were held in the ESMA, as the family knows from two priests who were eventually released. The Mignones have made a little booklet with excerpts of Mónica's letters from Belén, a *villa miseria* where she lived and worked:

When it's cold, here its even colder. And when it's hot, it's even hotter than in other parts of Buenos Aires. But on Saturday afternoons everyone gathers in the street. Children play and listen to music . . . they come running to hang on my neck and give me a kiss. . . .

Belén changes with the weather. You can feel the sadness when it's cloudy or rainy, and people can't go out except to work. . . . You see people with buckets trying to get the water out of their houses, they have to put jars and bowls everywhere.

In the *villa* everyone knows his neighbor. Everyone looks out for the children. When someone is sick, people take care. The grocer understands that these people are terribly exploited and can't always pay.

The police appear out of nowhere, all of a sudden. One day they gave me a fright. Oscar said they were going to shake down the grocer. He said it's always been that way. If the grocer refuses, they arrest him for "running numbers."

So many things happen like that. But the people who live here are fated not to be heard. The Law gives no shelter here. It protects only the rich.

"They killed her because she was too good," says Mignone, simply. "And not only our Mónica. Such kindness incited their hatred."

Like thousands of families, the Mignones do not know precisely how or when their daughter died, the circumstances of her captivity. They seized "the Scilingo moment" to sue the government on the principle that this lack of information is unnatural, indefensible.

"How can you argue *against* a family's right to know what happened to their loved ones?" Emilio asks me, rhetorically. In April 1995, after the fiasco with the lists, Mignone and a team of attorneys from CELS initiated a different legal tack. The public dissemination of a master list is not the only way to determine the fate of the missing, they argue; families could be informed individually. The case is based on purely humanitarian grounds: "the inalienable right to the truth, the obligation to respect the body, and the right to mourn the dead." The suit also cites the right to definitively establish the identity of the children born in captivity. The CELS case is founded on principles laid down in international human rights conventions ratified by Argentina and by revisions made to the Argentine Constitution in 1994. Specifically, the case cites Article 33, which affirms "the sovereignty of the people" and Article 75, clause 22, which stipulates that international human rights treaties and the rulings of the Inter-American Court of the OAS hold precedence over Argentine domestic law. In 1979, the OAS specifically charged Argentina "to give detailed information on the situation of the missing." In 1988, the Inter-American Court heard a case on a forced disappearance in Honduras, but its ruling applied to all member nations of the OAS: "The State is obliged to investigate every situation in which human rights protected by [the San José Convention] have been violated. . . . This investigation must be undertaken with seriousness and not as a simple formality, doomed beforehand to be unsuccessful." In addition to legal sources, the CELS argument brings to bear world history and literature as support for the essential human need for funeral rites: the burial ceremonies developed by the Neanderthals; Sophocles's *Antigone* (a work frequently adapted by Latin American playwrights in the 1970s and early 1980s); and Philippe Ariés's *Death in the West*, which argues that funerals are the one sacred rite common to Judaism, Christianity, and Islam, and the one observance that binds atheists, agnostics, and believers.

There is yet another essential layer to the CELS argument. As Mignone explained, "The constant [in all of this] is the institutional cover-up, official deceit, the organized denial of the crime. Denial is essential to the system. Otherwise it wouldn't work. That's why we need the full truth about the disappearances, even though prosecution is no longer possible. Uncovering what happened implies dismantling the means by which such crimes are committed. And that is crucial for the future."

How did the federal judges react to these compelling arguments? "They explicitly acknowledged the rights to know and mourn," Mignone told me, "and that is extremely important. In fact, it was a first for our courts. They then ordered the president, as commander in chief, to require the navy to solicit the information from its members. The navy came back and once again said that there was no information. That was a predictable setback," Mignone conceded, "but we've lodged an appeal, and are studying other means to achieve the same ends, including a bicameral parliamentary commission."

The appeal decision was, to say the least, disappointing: The court froze all investigations into the disappeared. Again the law cited was Due Obedience, which prohibits the courts from ordering the military to testify. Only the president is thus empowered, but Menem refused the court's request that he do so. Amnesty International, Human Rights Watch, and other groups have also been working intensely.

The Due Obedience law is a double-edged sword. On the one hand, without its protection, it is hard to believe that Scilingo and the others would have come forward. So one can argue that the law has helped to elicit information. At the same time the law has been interpreted too broadly by conservative courts. "Nothing in the legislation explicitly limits investigations," says Mignone and every other legal expert I have consulted. But since there is zeal in certain parts of society to unmask and prosecute the enforcers, the courts have played it safe.

International human rights organizations have always disapproved of Argentina's Due Obedience law, because it violates (among other things) the precedents laid down at the Nuremburg trials of the Nazis. Yet the great majority of Argentine legal scholars hold that the law would be extremely hard, if not impossible, to repeal. For one thing, the process by which it came into being was totally legitimate. It was drafted by experts, ratified by the Congress, then signed by Alfonsín according to the rules of republican government. But, as Mignone tells me, this is not the only consideration. A person cannot be tried twice for the same crime if he was absolved the first time around. Nor can a person be tried under a law that is harsher than the one under which he was originally convicted.

According to Mignone there remain two alternatives, both, in his view, highly theoretical. The Due Obedience and Punto Final laws could be declared null and void. "It's exactly what the Congress did with the self-amnesty law laid down by the junta just before it left power. Think of it like this," he says. "It's analogous to the Church's annulment of a marriage. It doesn't divorce the couple, it just decrees that the marriage never took place. The second option is to have forced disappearance declared a crime against humanity, in which case there would be no statute of limitations and the trials could take place anywhere in the world. Certainly it would be complicated legally," concedes Mignone, "but the overwhelming obstacles are political. No party is going to go out on a limb for this; at this point, they could never get a majority in Congress." The Congress is overwhelmingly in line with Menem. In fact, by themselves the Peronists are a quorum. Business can be conducted without the presence of a single representative from the opposition.

Alicia Pierini, appointed by Menem to direct the Under Secretariat for Human Rights, bristled when I asked her view of the so-called Scilingo effect. Did she foresee any legal ramifications? "Every institution bears responsibility for what happened," she said vehemently. "Where were the judges? Where . . . ? What were they doing while citizens were being kidnapped? For that matter, where were the politicians? journalists? hospital staffs? A number of sectors have yet to make their autocriticisms. I think that everyone over the age of fifty should say where they were during those years, what they were doing. But if we prosecute these crimes by the penal code, it will never end. We'll have 500,000 people in jail. And nothing but rancor to show for it. Our goal is to heal the institutions; you don't do that by dissolving them."[82]

Pierini spends much of her time taking testimony from the relatives of *desaparecidos*, who are entitled to indemnifications. "We have to stop this talk of the missing," she says firmly, "these individuals are dead. What we need to know is what happened to them, not the persons who did it."

A former Peronist activist who is now part of a highly ambiguous administration, Pierini's job is not without contradictions. She believes that the so-called Scilingo effect was created by the press. "I'm working for history, not a particular contemporary moment. This particular moment impedes, rather than facilitates my work. Because with fifty journalists at my door, I can't receive the individuals who need to see me."

Scilingo, she says, has added "absolutely nothing new." But Ibáñez did, I counter. How is identifying the perpetrators at odds with constructing the history of the Dirty War?

"I have always believed that society is interested in knowing the truth, the historic truth," Pierini insists. "But historic truth is not a matter of first and last names. It's as absurd as knowing who was the first soldier to land at Normandy Beach. Or who pushed the button for the atomic bomb that destroyed Hiroshima. The important fact is that Hiroshima was bombed because of a decision by a major power. It is the institutional action that counts. Particularly now, with the armed forces making institutional apologies. Balza's line transforms the institution. It's no longer the same."

She sits back, clearly frustrated and weary. "I have had this argument with so many of my friends. As I always tell them, the commission of aberrant actions was part of an *institutional* plan. If you're talking about state terrorism, you can't also talk about individuals. Does it matter if it was Juan Pérez or Pedro García? Or Scilingo, for that matter?"

Her version of "historical truth," I say, seems abstract. Particularly since numerous enforcers have risen in institutions like the navy.

"Those of us who were involved in the conflicts of the '70s have no desire to go back," she says, alluding to her own activism. "We are building peace, not looking to fill the jails. Collisions will get us nowhere."

Pierini's stress on "avoiding collisions" reveals the continuing anxiety in Argentina not only about the last repression, but about difference itself. The courts are an arena where differences should be aired and adjudicated, but the judiciary, for much of the country's history, has been captive to one or another administration or regime. With the exception of a few judges, the courts have not seemed to mind being on the sidelines of the controversy provoked by Scilingo. Many believe that this very marginality poses a danger to the courts, and to civil cohesiveness as well.

"At the trial of the juntas, I felt that I was contributing to a whole process," said Mario Villani, "an institutional process that would help lay the foundation for a healthier, more humane, orderly society. The 'Scilingo moment' has been different. On the one hand, it's good that the information should come out. On the other, Due Obedience augments a general sense of impotence. Knowledge by itself will not bring justice. It is precisely knowledge without justice that leads to distrust in the courts and the whole legal system. Ultimately its alienating, atomizing, because there is no communal forum for justice. The media cannot, must not be allowed to step into that breach. If the main thing people derive from this moment is the consciousness of impunity, the spectacle of impunity, then *ciao*, it's all over."

Popular disgust has certainly been a major element in the Scilingo effect. Though of course they count, social sanctions are insufficient, and their spontaneity can be worrisome. The pardoned ex-commanders, hunkered down among their cronies, have been insulted when they appear in public. Massera was heckled out of a restaurant in the posh Uruguayan resort of Punta del Este and declared persona non grata in the Argentine city of Río Cuarto. For the first time since the restoration of democracy, direct participants in the repression have been physically attacked. Both incidents, which occurred in the space of a month (September—October 1995), involved Astiz. The first assault was in the ski resort of San Carlos de Bariloche. Astiz and a female companion were waiting for the bus to take them to slopes, when the Blond Angel was recognized by a former detainee in the camp called Vesuvius. "All I could see were [the Mothers'] white kerchiefs," said the assailant, Alfredo Chávez, a witness at the trial of the ex-commanders. "Son of a bitch! Killer of adolescents!" he yelled, and punched Astiz in the nose. Navy chief Molina Pico was enraged at the "personal aggression." Encouraged by the force, Astiz filed suit. For counsel he retained Pedro Bianchi, the lawyer who was defending Erich Priebke, the Nazi who, until his extradition, lived close to the Bariloche ski resort.[83] The next attack took place in greater Buenos Aires; the assailants this time were two brothers, age nineteen and twenty, taking their dog to the vet. Both boys work, go to university, and live at home with their parents. En route, a car pulled in front of them, blocking their way. From behind his window, the driver, Astiz, taunted the boys with an obscene gesture. The captain was recognized by the younger brother. Though this attack was worse, neither Astiz nor the navy reported it to the police. No one came to the captain's defense as the brothers pulled him from his car, hit him so hard in the mouth his dental plate popped out, then bashed in the hood of his vehicle. "Good boys! Kill him!" yelled a woman through the open window of a bus.[84] Such incidents, although understandable and cathartic, do not serve the greater interests of Argentine society. They arise from a sense of impotent rage, are criminal acts, and could invite reprisals. The boys' father, a devoutly religious man, did not defend his sons' behavior, but offered an explanation that struck a chord with many parents with whom I spoke: "This is what happens after you're obliged to tell your children that justice here doesn't function as it should, that the courts refused to castigate the most horrendous crimes of a horrendous dictatorship."[85] In other words, Argentine justice is not merely corrupt, but corrupting.

It is not just those outside the system who believe this. Dr. Juan José Prado, professor of constitutional law and president of the Buenos Aires Lawyers Association, put it bluntly: "The administration of justice does not exist here. Neither for the poor nor for the rich. What is institutionalized is impunity for those who exercise power."[86] I had come to discuss the lawsuit he and Congressman Alfredo Bravo had recently filed against Julio Simón (Julián the Turk). The charge derives from Article 213 of the penal code, according to which unrepentant boasting about a proven crime is itself a punishable offense. Prado argued that the statements Julián made on television constitute what in Spanish is called *apología del crimen*. Among the evidence they cite are the following statements: "I acted . . . to stop the murderous horde being sent to us from abroad," "In some cases torture had negative results, because the prisoner ended up too destroyed," and "I would do it all over again." Prado said that according to the penal code, the case is airtight, and that Julián should get four years in prison. An aggravating factor is that Simón was not a "freelance," but a member of the Federal Police. However, Prado was certain that they would lose. "They haven't exactly been zealous to convict these guys, have they?"

What, then, is the point of bringing suit?

"To bring the evidence before the court. To add to the store of primary documentation. To *peacefully* protest and accuse. To exercise the levers of democracy. So that when my grandchildren ask me what I did with my life, I can tell them: In the '70s, I did writs of habeas corpus; and in the '80s and '90s, I kept up the fight."

Predictably enough, Prado lost. ATC. the state-run television station that by all accounts paid Julián, refused to submit its tapes. For "lack of evidence," the judge dismissed the case.

THIS NARRATIVE DRAWS to a close in October 1997 with some good news, some bad news, and some other news that is hard to decipher. *Nunca Más* is now required reading in Argentine high schools; *Página 12* began publishing weekly installments of this seminal work, starting on Bastille Day 1995. Every Friday, readers of the paper received a small booklet illustrated by León Ferrari, a prestigious artist and father of a *desaparecida*. The facsimiles immediately became collectors' items, especially among adolescents.

The navy did not pursue a promotion for Captain Astiz. Moreover, the Blond Angel was forced into early retirement, in September 1996. The official story is that Astiz himself requested to be retired but, owing to diplomatic pressure, the captain did not have a choice. Within the navy there was a contained protest on his behalf, staged by approximately fifty officers, sympathizers with Massera, who added his booming voice to the chorus of support. Navy chief Molina Pico once again expressed the institution's "total support" for Astiz, whom he said "ennobled himself by requesting retirement."[87]

Molina Pico and Lieutenant General Mario Candído Díaz, who, as Head of the Joint Chiefs publicly praised "the fallen and the veterans in the war against subversion," were themselves pushed into retirement by Menem, who clearly prefers to be identified with Balza.[88]

The Argentine courts reopened the case on Dagmar Hagelin, another sign of the importance of international pressure, and the continued efforts of groups like Amnesty International and Human Rights Watch. In an effort to encourage testimony, the Federal Court has offered anonymity to all those who have information that might be helpful. Spain has intensified its investigation on the disappearance during the last regime of 266 Spanish citizens (38 native-born, the rest being children of Spaniards with double nationality). The case has garnered a great deal of coverage in Spain, not just in the print media, but with documentaries on prime-time television as well. The legal team, headed by the young dynamic Judge Baltasar Garzón, has traveled widely to gather testimony and made the dramatic announcement that it intends to extradite a number of Argentine military officers, including ex-commander Emilio Massera. The extradition order is made possible by the U.N. Convention on the Prevention and Punishment of Genocide, which holds that the crime of genocide has no statute of limitations and that the perpetrators may be tried in any country bringing charges. (It is the reason that Nazis, for example, are still being prosecuted.) Even though Argentina signed that convention and is bound to uphold it by Article 75, clause 22, of its own Constitution, the process is likely to be complicated, taking as long as two years by the estimate of Emilio Mignone. Even then, he says, political machinations could prevent the extraditions. The Spanish government, working together with various nongovernmental agencies, insists that it will not be deterred.[89] Italy also presses forward with its investigation into the disappearance of 617 of its nationals in Argentina during the Dirty War. There too the media have galvanized popular support, particularly among the younger generation for whom much of the history was news.

For the first time ever, a U.S. court tried a foreign country, namely Argentina, for abuses committed on its own soil. José Siderman, a Jew who emigrated to Argentina in 1941, prospered in his new country, so much so that he aroused anti-Semitic envy. He was kidnapped on the night of the coup, brutally tortured, and abused for being Jewish. He was illegally divested of property and assets totaling over $25 million. Siderman, now eighty-five, took U.S. citizenship in 1984. The Argentine government erroneously charged Siderman with fraud and issued an international warrant for his arrest. Because the Argentine government brought suit here under false pretenses, it became vulnerable to prosecution. After an odyssey of twenty years, Siderman finally won a settlement from Argentina, which was forced to admit that it had abused, tortured, and defrauded him. The decision is a human rights milestone.[90]

In Buenos Aires, Congressman Alfredo Bravo—who with Prado tried to prosecute Julián the Turk—brought before the lower house of Parliament a proposal to overturn the Punto Final and Due Obedience laws. Did it succeed? As everyone knew, it was doomed for the short term, but the gesture is important, and may be the first step in a long, eventually fruitful process.[91]

The Argentine Judiciary made an institutional apology for its shortcomings during the dictatorship. So too did Nehemías Resnizky, the former head of the DAIA.[92]

In September 1996, the Grandmothers of the Plaza de Mayo announced that they had uncovered thirty-six new cases of babies born in captivity and never returned to their biological relatives. With a total of 300 documented but unsolved cases, they are now bringing suit against a group of generals for the systematic robbery of children, rather than proceeding, as they did in the past, strictly case-by-case. Even though some of these men were earlier pardoned under Due Obedience and Punto Final, they have no immunity from prosecution now for baby trafficking.[93]

In October 1996, in a hearing held in Washington, D.C., by the Inter-American Human Rights Commission of the OAS, Argentina acceded to relatives' demands to investigate the cases of *desaparecidos* from the ESMA. To be conducted under the auspices of a Truth Commission, the investigations are intended to yield information, not result in prosecutions.

On the other side of the register, the long-awaited statement from the Catholic Church—finally released on April 27, 1996—came as an anticlimax. A number of prominent bishops held that the promised "examination of conscience" never took place. The closest the document comes to an institutional apology is to regret that "their actions on behalf of human rights were insufficient." At the same time the authors expressed regret that "there were Catholics who justified and participated in guerrilla activity inspired by the Marxist doctrine. . . ."[94]

On July 3, 1995, Retired General Antonio Domingo Bussi was elected governor of the province of Tucumán. During the last dictatorship, the army designated Bussi to be governor of the "garden province" of Tucumán. They wanted a strongman there, where ERP had fallen to the army in 1975, and where the sugar cane fields were "breeding ground for subversion." As military *interventor* Bussi oversaw two secret detention centers. He was later made commander of the entire Zone 3, which comprised the central northwest provinces: Córdoba, Mendoza, Catamarca, San Luis, San Juan, Salta, La Rioja, Jujuy, Tucumán, and Santiago del Estero. Bussi was responsible for at least 600 cases of forced disappearance. As a consequence of the Punto Final law, the Supreme Court dropped the charges against him in June 1988. Owing to his rank, Bussi is *not* covered by Due Obedience. Shortly before the vote, human rights groups organized a symbolic public trial, which he dismissed as "a purely psychological action." The day after he was elected, Bussi referred back to the dictatorship. "I cannot repent," he said. "It would be like repenting for having been born, for having lived, and triumphed honestly against subversive aggression." Running on an "order and security" platform, Bussi won a four-party race with nearly 45 percent of the vote.[95]

When the Buenos Aires City Council voted almost unanimously to declare the ex-commanders of the last regime personae non gratae, Menem exploded. In a radio interview just before Menem called Pinochet to wish him a happy birthday, the president denigrated the project as "pointless, a return to a past that we must not repeat." He took issue with the "biased view of history" represented by the vote, insisting that the Dirty War was begun by the leftist opposition. What about them? he asked. Shouldn't they be personae non gratae? Menem seems incapable of comprehending the desire to *separate* from the rest of society the perpetrators of state terrorism.[96]

Ibáñez has disappeared from sight. Verges has been extremely quiet. "Colores" finally agreed be interviewed on television, where he defended the "scientific" value of torture.[97]

Has the Scilingo effect brought an end to the discourse of *desapareci-dos*? The Steimbergs believe they know what ultimately happened to their son. The Vaccaros now know what happened to their pregnant daughter. The suspicions of many others have been confirmed. But the newly corroborated information does nothing to negate the lived experience of having a loved one simply vanish; of having to bear up under the rage, scorn, and indifference of public officials; of seeing the masterminds of the genocide pardoned, and their minions free to prosper. Sara and Jaime Steimberg can say definitively that Pablo is dead; but for eighteen years, their son was *missing*. We must remember that the Steimbergs are the exception; the vast majority of these families are still being denied their "right to know."

For Hebe de Bonafini, "Our children are neither dead nor missing. They are *alive*. They are with us in all that we do. They inspire us, give us strength and clarity. We gave birth to these children, yet it is they who continue to give us life. Their fight for justice will impassion the coming generations."

H.I.J.O.S. continues to be active, but since their candelight vigil on the 20th Anniversary of the coup, they have been menaced repeatedly. Over the last six months, about a dozen members have been threatened, followed by cars, and publicly harassed. On the fourth day after Bergés was shot, five HIJOS got menacing calls within the space of hours. The phone threats are particularly unnerving, since the voice on the other end often asks for the child's missing parent, or says, "Your grandma is going to be wearing a white kerchief, *for you*." After a series of such calls, by men and women, Lucía Herrera's apartment was entered with a skeleton key and robbed while she slept. Fourteen-year-old Luciano Angelini was kidnapped by a group of hooded, heavily armed men who held him for forty-five minutes in a white car that belongs to the Buenos Aires Provincial Police. "The car was out of service," said a government official, "so we can't identify who made the attack." HIJOS refuses to be intimidated, and insisted on a meeting with the Minister of the Interior, who is ultimately responsible for the police.[98]

In mid-May 1996, investigations into an arms scandal that led to the resignation two months later of the Minister of Defense uncovered a little-known fact: The current Policy Director of the Defense Ministry was in charge of three Dirty War concentration camps—El Sheraton, El Banco, and El Vesubio. Retired Brigadier General Antonio Fichera ran a particularly sinister program in the Sheraton, much like the ESMA's fish tank, except without survivors. After all his selected prisoners were transferred in mid-1978, Fichera moved on to the General Secretariat of the presidency, where he served under both Videla and Viola. When democracy was restored, he was teaching at the Superior War College. In 1985, the Senate approved his promotion to brigadier general, in spite of the detailed documentation presented by the legal team of CELS. Pressured by the army, the senators affirmed that they had found the CELS evidence "insufficient." In any case, Fichera would eventually be covered by the Punto Final and Due Obedience laws. He retired from the force in 1987, after his ill-advised participation in an uprising with the reactionary Carapintadas. As a civilian, he started a public relations firm. By the time Menem was president, the Ministry of Defense was one of Fichera's clients. He won the Policy Director job in 1992; at this writing, he holds the position still.[99]

Ten days after Fichera came to light, yet another ex-enforcer in officialdom was identified by serendipity. Once again the irony of the situation bears out the maxim—so apt in Argentina—that truth is stranger than fiction. On May 27, *La Nación* ran a photograph accompanying an article on the opening of the Federal Police's new Center for Victims of Sexual Violence. This new facility, intended to serve women who have been raped or abused, is part of the larger Victims Orientation Center, whose director, Commissioner Ricardo Scifo Módica, was pictured with the story. Mario Villani happened to see the piece, and immediately recognized the Commissioner as *"Alacrán" ("Scorpion")* his *nom de guerre*. As Mario told *La Nación*, "Without a doubt, that's Scorpion. I saw him in Club Atlético, El Banco, and El Olimpo. As far as I know he did not participate in interrogations. He was what they called an 'operative' [a kidnapper]. I remember him perfectly."[100] As the week unfolded, other survivors came forward and also identified Scorpion. Ana Maria Careaga and Susana Caride did so openly; several others were too afraid to let the media publish their names. Scifo Módica continued to receive his victims of violence; Alicia Pierini, Menem's Secretary for Human Rights, said, "This is not my concern, it's a matter for the Federal Police."[101] Her statement does little to encourage trust: In fact, the original accusation against Scifo Módica was made during the CONADEP, all of whose files are in Pierini's custody. (Scifo Módica was first fingered by "Colores," who was trying to make a deal for himself.) Moreover, the Undersecretariat for Human Rights is under the auspices of the Ministry of the Interior, which is responsible for the Federal Police. When pressed as to why she as the government's highest appointee in human rights wasn't listening to survivor testimony, she replied, "That isn't proof." The Federal Police chief refused to answer any questions. (Scifo Módica also maintained his silence, after initially denying that he was Scorpion.) Only when a group of senators demanded a report from the government did Pierini belatedly admit that she "should have taken the question more seriously," and that "it would be a gesture of reconciliation to have Scifo Módica moved to a different position." She did not say that he should be fired, only that he be given a less sensitive job. The police chief defended his man, saying that "as a young officer he had fulfilled his professional obligations faithfully and with rectitude during a difficult time" (i.e., the Dirty War).[102] Predictably enough, he blamed the current situation on the press: "We cannot allow unimpeachable young officers from those times to be exposed to public opinion as though they were real repressors." He also praised his more recent performance, insisting that since 1991, when Scifo Módica was put in charge of the Victims Orientation Center, he has "performed brilliantly in service of the community."[103] In the midst of the uproar, Scifo Módica suddenly left on vacation.

In the Scorpion story a number of issues come into play. Once again, ad nauseum, we see the continued power of ex-repressors. It strains credulity that a Dirty Warrior could be charged with taking reports on police brutality, but that is indeed one of the functions of the Victims Orientation Center. Year after year, Amnesty International has cited Argentina for the brutality and quick trigger of its police, who are guilty of "extrajudicial executions" as well as disappearances. The most recent report is no exception. Once more we see official refusal to take responsibility. Interior Minister Carlos Corach insisted that "the government had nothing to do" with Scifo Módica's appointment and that the accusations against the Commissioner "must have escaped them." He tried finally to dismiss the whole incident by saying that it "arose from without the government." "That's an insult to the intelligence of the Argentine people," Mario Villani declared in the press. "The state should indeed be responsible for the hiring of its personnel." Human rights groups are not—and do not wish to be considered—hunters of past enforcers, or of anyone else for that matter. "Such investigations are the responsibility of the courts, but they do nothing," said Ana María Careaga, repeating the classical Argentine lament.[104]

On June 27, 1996, the Mothers made their 1000th march around the Plaza de Mayo. They are undeniably old women now, virtually all of them in their seventies and eighties. Not a few walk with some difficulty, their feet swollen in support shoes, their ankles covered by socks over thick stockings. Yet still these aged women in their embroidered white kerchiefs exude the strength and purpose of a sacred mission. Every time I have been with a Mother in the moment she pauses, silently, holding the white cloth in front of her before putting it on, I am reminded of the blessing of humility, thanks, and awe that precedes the donning of the *tallit*, or Jewish prayer shawl. In all the world there is no more eloquent symbol than the Mothers of the prophetic power of maternal love.

July 9 is the Argentine Independence Day; tradition calls for the president to stride from the Casa Rosada across the Plaza de Mayo to Metropolitan Cathedral for the solemn "Te Deum." In 1996, the Mothers took up places inside the sanctuary the night before. Their idea was to have a day of prayer and fasting for the cause of "dignified work for all." (This was also a pointed criticism of Menem's economics of austerity, which has spiked unemployment, eroded middle-class security, and disproportionately victimized the poor.) They arrived singly, one by one occupying the first row of pews, normally reserved for the president. Fourteen Mothers sat in the cold and dark, until the priest custodian of the cathedral discovered them: "Get out," he said, "this is my house."

"We thought it was God's house," replied Hebe de Bonafini.

They stayed through the night without heat, light, or access to a bathroom. The next morning, by order of a federal judge, the Mothers were forcibly removed for "violation of private property." The cathedral, they were told, belonged not to God or to the faithful, but to the curia. In anticipation of the eviction, the blocks around the cathedral were closed. To keep the tension at a minimum, the Mothers were taken by female police (two or three for each Mother); two by two, they were driven away, in ambulances rather than police cars; the vehicles then went to different hospitals. The last thing the government wanted was for the entire group to end up together in a public place. Supporters of the Mothers in the Plaza, including about thirty members of HIJOS, were roughed up by the SWAT teams, which came equipped with dogs. The Mothers' photographer got his camera smashed. The Interior Minister defended the eviction: "In places devoted to worship," he said sanctimoniously, "there must be no disturbance."[105]

But there has been no end of disturbance for the Argentine government. On April 3, 1997, two highly regarded Spanish journalists reported in a Madrid daily that the mystery of the missing archives of the last dictatorship may soon be solved.[106] According to the sources, in late 1983 (just before Alfonsín took office), the documentation kept by the ESMA was flown from Buenos Aires to Madrid where the Spanish secret services photocopied the archive. One set was allegedly sent to Switzerland, where it has been kept ever since in a major bank. (The other sets have yet to be located, but they are not, according to Spanish authorities, in any of its own government or intelligence facilities.) On June 12, it was reported that the Spanish legal team, aided by Swiss officials, turned up another potentially important discovery: One hundred top military officers from the last regime—including the ex-commanders and numerous directors of concentration camps—were found to have numbered accounts and safety deposit boxes in Swiss banks.[107] These accounts and strongboxes are being embargoed with the expectation that they may hold secret documents, and/or stolen jewelry, currency, and property titles. In both cases, the Argentine government pledged its full cooperation.

At the same time the administration took some dramatic steps to counteract the potency and prestige of these findings. On June 18, 1997, the Argentine Senate began debating the military promotion of yet two other ex-repressors of the Dirty War: Lieutenant Colonel Carlos Enrique Villanueva, who in 1978–79 was director of La Perla concentration camp, and Lieutenant Ernesto Guillermo Barreiro, a well-documented kidnapper, extortionist, and torturer. The candidacies of Villanueva and Barreiro were put forward by President Menem and Army Chief of Staff General Martín Balza, who insisted that these officers "were never prosecuted for any wrongdoing." What they disingenuously omitted is that they escaped being charged owing to Punto Final. Menem's posture is consistent with his past. But Balza's stance is to many sorely disappointing. Particularly galling—and damaging to Balza's image—is the fact that Villanueva was due for promotion in March 1995, but Balza chose to table the nomination, owing to "the controversy provoked by Scilingo." It is all but certain that these promotions will be voted down, since a number of ranking senators have declared for the record that the body "will not swallow this latest insult."[108]

Adolfo Scilingo served nearly two years on check-kiting charges that were finally declared null and void. He left La Plata penitentiary on June 17, 1997, still resolved that the full truth about the *desaparecidos* should come out.[109] He has testified in the cases of the French nuns and Dagmar Hagelin, and offered an explanation for the missing ESMA archives. Scilingo may well know something on this issue: He is reported to be one of the military men found to have a secret bank account and strongbox in Switzerland.

The very day Scilingo was released, it was reported that Alfredo Astiz, who was supposedly forced to retire, has in fact been working for Naval Intelligence. At first, Menem (though he is commander in chief)

296 A LEXICON OF TERROR

sidestepped the matter, saying only that "it was the navy's affair." The highest-ranking admiral blamed ex-head of the force Molina Pico. But after yet another diplomatic blow-out with the French, the administration instructed the navy to terminate Astiz's employment. In the course of the scandal, it was revealed that not a few former repressors who could never be promoted by the senate have found safe harbor in Naval Intelligence.[110]

On August 14, 1997, the Mothers of the Plaza reported a break-in at their headquarters near the Congress. Because the robbers took documents, research files, and communication tools—the group's fax machine and the printer on which they produce *Las Madres*, their monthly magazine—it is widely assumed that the intrusion was an officially sanctioned political attack. The Mothers immediately brought the case to the Courts. Three weeks later, the Casa de las Madres was ransacked and robbed yet again.[111]

On September 11, Adolfo Scilingo was kidnapped by four men with police identification who forced him into a car and carved into his face the initials of three well-known journalists to whom he has given extensive interviews: Horacio Verbitsky, Magdalena Ruiz Guiñazú, and Mariano Grondona. "Lay off the subject of the disappeared," they told him, "or we'll rub out the four of you." Scilingo was kidnapped near the Congress while walking to a meeting with his lawyer, whose office is nearby. The subject of that meeting was the ongoing death threats to which Scilingo and his family have been subjected since his release from jail. A day or two earlier, Scilingo's attorney had confidentially—or so he thought—petitioned the Minister of the Interior for an appointment to discuss his client's safety. As soon as the kidnappers got Scilingo in the car, they said, "You wanted a private audience, well, this is it."

Then, using a knife, they carved an "M" into his forehead, a "V" into one cheek, and a "G" into the other. After driving him around for over two hours, they dumped him out, beaten, bloody, and disoriented.

The attack came three days after President Menem unleashed a particularly nasty threat against the press. This time he went so far as to suggest physical violence as a reasonable deterrent against the "unbounded" freedom of "irresponsible" journalists. When asked his reaction to the kidnapping, Menem replied, "I don't trust his type," referring to the victim.[112]

For Scilingo, the incident apparently strengthened his resolve to be of use in the Spanish lawsuit against Argentina. Although warned that Judge Garzón was unlikely to extend immunity from prosecution, Scilingo nonetheless traveled to Madrid to testify for the better part of a week. At one point, proceedings had to be suspended for a day because Scilingo could not stop sobbing. For the crimes he committed in the ESMA, Scilingo was taken into preventive custody on October 7 and installed in Carabanchel prison where, according to Spanish law, he may be held for up to two years until his trial. The judge also has the option to release him. Since his public confession in March 1995, Scilingo has seemed more and more repentant. His wife has said that she believes he is seeking a legitimate, coherent punishment.[113] On the basis of his and other testimony, especially that of survivors who also traveled to Madrid (among them, Mario Villani, Graciela Daleo, and Adriana Calvo de Laborde), Spain has international arrest orders out for ten high-ranking participants in the Dirty War, including Massera and the current head of naval intelligence. Argentina, predictably, is refusing to extradite these men.

But progress has been made on another legal front. Within a week of Scilingo's kidnap, ex-police commissioner Miguel Etchecolatz went on television to promote his new book in which he asserts that had torture been officially sanctioned in the 1970s fewer lives would have been lost. Convicted of ninety-five counts of torture and sentenced to twenty-three years in prison, Etchecolatz was freed under one of Alfonsín's legal loopholes. Etchecolatz appeared on the show with one of his victims, Congressman Alfredo Bravo, whom he verbally abused and slandered. The Permanent Assembly for Human Rights brought suit for *apología del crimen*, the same charge brought unsuccessfully in 1995 against Julián the Turk. Etchecolatz was placed under house arrest for a period of twenty days.[114] A small, indeed pitiful, sentence considering the crime, but it represents an improvement over the last time this legal tactic was used.

Life for many in Argentina still means constant vigilance; an impending sense of disaster, carnal knowledge of fear. A sense that history never moves on, but circles, raven-like, round and round. Yet as the testimonies in this book make clear, the most castigated Argentines manage to maintain deep reserves of courage, clarity, and tenderness. If indeed "the past is a predator," there is popular volition to meet the danger at its source, by exposing and resisting the entrenched politics of impunity and amnesia.

Epilogue

DECEMBER 2009: FULL SPRING IN THE SOUTHERN HEMISPHERE. BUENOS Aires is bright and clear in the lavender glow of the jacaranda; balconies overflow with geraniums and clematis, freesia and roses, kiosks on most every corner offer jasmine, so even the newspapers smell sweet. The news itself is a heady mixture: ex-repressors shuffling handcuffed into courtrooms to stand trial for crimes against humanity; the surviving family of Jorge di Pasquale, a labor leader murdered by the last dictatorship, at long last receiving his powdery bones; the Grandmothers recuperating their 100th "grandchild."

But these are not the only headlines. At precisely 11:32 on the morning of Friday, December 11, as the judge opened the long-awaited and much-delayed trial of nineteen ex-repressors of the ESMA, President Cristina Kirchner, traveling in the official helicopter, received a death threat over the supposedly secure radio: *Kill her, kill the bitch*[1] exhorted a deep male voice backed by the official theme music of the last dictatorship. It was not the first such threat to her life; I was told by a high official that Kirchner usually keeps them undisclosed so as not to sow panic, but this one, given the context and technological sophistication, could not be kept under wraps.

Later the same day, as virtually everyone expected, Luciano Benjamín Menéndez, the ex-general formerly in charge of the Third Army Corps, received his third *prisión perpétua* for crimes against humanity committed under his watch. Currently indicted in fifty-eight separate court cases, he always makes a high-flown speech (as is his right) before his sentence is handed down.[2]

His grandiloquence had been much in the air this week. On December 9, even as survivors of the Atlético, Banco, and Olimpo concentration camps gave chilling testimony in federal court, Abel Posse, a writer and career diplomat who served under the dictatorship, was sworn in as Education Minister of Buenos Aires City. In his acceptance, Posse quoted Menéndez. With Mauricio Macri, the tough-guy mayor who appointed him, at his side, Posse declared that the officers on trial should all be granted amnesty ("it's nothing but politics"); that the trials in process should immediately stop; that the societal conflicts over what happened during the dictatorship should be decreed over and done; that the numbers of the missing were vastly inflated, and that too was nothing but politics. Warming to the themes of his office, he stated that the purpose of education is to suppress adolescent tendencies toward delinquency and "trotsko-leninism." Because adolescents who commit crimes "effectively lose the defense of youth," he would lower to 13 or 14 the age at which minors should be tried as adults, and advocated the creation of special "recuperation colonies," another echo from dark times past.[3] As though to return the courtesy, Menéndez quoted Posse as he glorified once again "the war to save the Nation." We could not help but remember that a key witness during Menéndez's second trial was found dead in mysterious circumstances—a sharp blow to the chest being called a suicide—and that Jorge Julio López, a 77-year-old witness in a 2006 trial in La Plata went missing soon after he testified, the first *desaparecido* of the democracy.

The decade closed on yet another alarming incident. On the sunny late afternoon of December 30, two men broke into the office of the Secretary of Human Rights for the Province of Buenos Aires, assaulting and tying up seven employees, including 80-year-old Secretary Sara Derotier de Cobacho, a distinguished former congresswoman who has served on numerous international rights commissions. Brandishing guns, the assailants demanded the combination to the safe, from which they extracted some 11,000 pesos put aside for administrative expenses connected to the trials. They also left with Cobacho's laptop, which contained files for those prosecutions. The computer was soon returned, scrubbed clean of its contents, except for the photo of infantry officer Juan Perizotti, who in 1976 had tortured Cobacho during her illegal detention in the province of Santa Fe. She had been detained on the day of the coup; over the next two years, her two sons, two sons-in-law, and a daughter-in-law would all be murdered or disappeared. "They knew exactly what they were looking for," Cobacho said of the incident. "These are events in which the past and present come together."[4]

Day after day events were full of stark reminders that history is an ongoing argument, and that the disentangling of past and present is yet a challenge full of drama. While there is no serious fear of a military coup, no one denies that the armed forces, police, security, and some civilian sectors harbor the odd "dinosaur" leftover from the dictatorship, as well as younger adherents to the far right. Individuals within the forces are believed to represent less risk; nostalgic retirees and bitter ex-soldiers or police are considered much more dangerous. It is widely believed that Jorge Julio López was murdered by a few ex-cops, who got cover from a police force whose major interest was to protect itself from being investigated.

The past is a predator is a theme of the first edition of this book, which ended on a moment that was dreadful, dramatic, and riveting. Torturers, including the notorious Julián the Turk, not only went about their lives with impunity but vaunted their crimes in the major media. While historians will continue to debate whether Due Obedience and Punto Final were necessary to keep the military at bay, no one denies the high costs and moral compromises that underlay the democratic recovery. And yet, over the last ten tumultuous years, democracy has established tough roots and continues, however imperfectly, to spread its canopy.

Twelve days after his swearing in, Posse was forced, by the peaceful popular revolt led by teachers, to resign. "Macri Queda *DesPosseído*," (Macri Is Dis*Posse*ssed) ran one headline. Within a week Cobacho's assailant was identified as a disaffected ex-policeman; he awaits trial in preventive prison.

At this writing, 634 military and police are on trial for crimes against humanity; 73 have been convicted and sentenced; seven have been acquitted. Counting convictions for baby stealing, the figure reaches above 90. Including those who have been indicted or identified for eventual indictment, the number rises to over 1,000 in various stages of prosecution. In just 2009, there were ten major trials, with 31 convictions.[5] These figures are quick to write and quicker to read, but it must be emphasized: the nullification of legal impunity has been grindingly long, hard, and gradual.

It was only in 1998, after seventeen years of democracy, that relatives of *desaparecidos* were granted the official "right to truth and information" about their missing loved ones—the manner of their presumed death, identification of those responsible, and the disposition of their remains. *Caso Urteaga* had to go all the way to the Supreme Court, whose unanimous decision (in which the justices were obliged to note that the laws of

Due Obedience and Punto Final were still in force) would nonetheless have far-reaching implications. The same year, Congress derogated those laws, a highly significant political act, but one that lacked the import of case law. There ensued a series of highly publicized *juicios para la verdad*, or "truth trials," in which survivors, witnesses, and relatives gave sworn testimony. In spite of the Supreme Court ruling, the military was not forthcoming with information. Critics of the "truth trials" called them depressing, useless, and nothing more—or less—than political spectacles. Even those who participated felt torn. As I was told by one survivor, "It was like being caught in a web. On the one hand, you bear witness, which is an act of strength and integrity; on the other, you are always conscious that you are doing so in a climate of judicial impotence." Yet and still, the "truth trials" provided infrastructure for the expanded gathering, corroboration, and conservation of testimony, some of which was new, and it would all would prove useful years later. For those not yet born or too young to remember the 1985 trial of the ex-commanders, these events offered living history, at once intimate and collective, a way to situate themselves with regard to what they knew, thought they knew, or had never considered. This is not to suggest that they constituted a vast generational change in public consciousness; for all their painful drama, the public summoning of courage and composure, they were but one more incremental development in a long and taxing struggle.

Having been pardoned in 1991 by President Menem, Videla and Massera were enjoying life at home; photographs showed them playing with their grandchildren. In 1998, they were arrested for the kidnap of babies born in captivity (a crime for which there had never been amnesty). For the next five years, Videla would fight back, arguing that the seven hundred cases for which he was convicted in the 1985 trial constituted a totalizing *cosa juzgada* and that, as a result, he could not be accused of any other crime that took place from 1976 to 1983. Finally, on August 21, 2003, the Supreme Court clarified matters by upholding the classic definition of *cosa juzgada*: a case in which the same defendant is accused [again] of the same crime against the same victim for the same reason. Videla lost on every aspect of his argument, but had dragged his twisted reasoning up the entire judicial ladder, adding insult to unspeakable injury.

Even in the economic unraveling that began in 1999, the struggle against impunity did not get lost. In early 2001, the laws of Due Obedience and Punto Final were declared by a federal judge to be unconstitutional, as "disguised amnesties" of the Gentlemen of the Coup, who had violated

Article 29 with their violent takeover of the government.[6] The ruling animated other courts, in Buenos Aires, La Plata, Salta, and Chaco, to do likewise, opening the way for eventual trials in these locations.

But then the economy totally collapsed; between December 10, 1999 and January 2, 2000, Argentina had five presidents, one of whom held office for a single day. By early 2002, 52 percent of Argentines were living below the poverty line; 20 percent could not afford sufficient food.[7] Argentines at all levels were living by their wits—improvising, bartering, and inventing ways to survive that did not involve cash. The value of the peso had sunk like lead, and anyway bank accounts were frozen. Neighborhood groups *(asambleas populares)* stepped into the breach, organizing cooperatives for the distribution of food, essential services, and political action. Some say those days of mutual aid and the *cacerolazo*, the spontaneous banging of pots and pans as a form of political protest, helped enlarge a sense that "human rights" were not restricted to the torture of times past; they could be marshaled, now, by parents unable to provide for their children.

Haunting the scene, like a rabid political ghost, was Carlos Menem, grasping for a return to power. When it was clear he would lose in a runoff, he withdrew and, on May 25, 2003, Néstor Kirchner was elected to the presidency on a rights platform that emphasized dignity, equal access to opportunity, and "an end to impunity." At his inauguration Kirchner, who has said that as young man he belonged to the then-proscribed Peronist Youth, quoted at length from Martin Luther King's *"Tengo un sueño"* ("I Have a Dream . . ."). In his first speech before Congress, which he reprised at the United Nations, President Kirchner declared, "We are all sons and daughters of the Mothers and Grandmothers of the Plaza de Mayo," acknowledging them as *the ultimate moral reserve* of Argentine society at a time when ethics were violated as a matter of policy. The phrasing was highly deliberate, *ultimate moral reserve* being the traditional self-description of the armed forces, which have had to relinquish the epithet since they must now swear their primary allegiance to the Constitution. Kirchner immediately retired officers from all three forces whose reputations were stained during the Dirty War and removed Supreme Court Justices who had been appointed during the dictatorship.

As for Due Obedience and Punto Final, he sent Congress a bill for their repeal and never let up on the pressure. On August 3, 2003 the lower house passed the measure; on the August 21, the senate did likewise. On

June 14, 2005, the Supreme Court declared the laws null and void, making possible the trials of ex-repressors in the entire chain of command.

Julián the Turk often said he wanted to go down in history. So it is a gratifying irony: he provided the case whose ruling dislodged the laws that for so long had protected him.

Shortly before meeting with him in 1998, I was pressed, by Mónica Brull, "Ask him about Claudia Victoria Poblete," referring to the baby of her missing best friend, Gertrudis ("Trudi") Hlaczik. Julián hated my questions about this group, whose "crime" was spearheading legislation (passed unanimously by the Senate in 1975) to protect the handicapped from job discrimination. Trudi and her six-month-old daughter were kidnapped on November 28, 1978; her husband and the baby's father, José Liborio Poblete, was kidnapped, by the same crew, later the same day. Mónica and six-month-old Pablo were captured on December 7, 1978. The whole group ended up in the camp known as Olympus.

"I never tortured cripples," Julián insisted in our interview, although he did, with special zeal. He personally brutalized Mónica, who is blind, and who at the time of her capture, was five months pregnant. Julián commanded his underlings to rape her, as a consequence of which she miscarried. According to Mónica and other witnesses, Julián had special torments for José who had lost his legs in a train accident; and for his wife, Trudi, who was also confined to a wheelchair. A Chilean lathe operator, José had come to Argentina for rehabilitation. He and Trudi met as members of the Peronist Front for the Handicapped. Trudi and José were *transferred*; witnesses saw his wheelchair lying on its side near the airstrip. When I asked Julián about the infant, he professed to know nothing but then tried to sell me his "archives," touting their "extremely high value."

Sitting together last December in her comfortable home, Mónica and I recalled how impossible it had seemed that this emblematic sadist would ever be tried. "'Soler' [Oscar Augusto Rolón] brought my baby son, Pablo, to my mother. Julián said he'd had Claudia sent to her grandmother as well, but 'maybe the messenger lost the address.' I always thought Julián sold Trudi's baby to 'Colores' [redheaded Juan Antonio Cerro] who had seven blond daughters. They were the ones who kidnapped us, so it seemed logical."

The Poblete family came to accept that José and Trudi were dead but never flagged in their efforts to find Claudia. However, Trudi's mother, who as late as 1980 kept hoping, trying to believe her daughter was alive, committed suicide in 1981. "It was terrible, more than terrible," said Mónica. "She was eaten alive, consumed with impotent rage, desperation.

I think, I know she resented me, hated that somehow I was there and Trudi was not—we had been so close as to be almost inseparable and then to be separated *like that* . . ."

For a long moment she says nothing. It turns out that Claudia and my son Pablo both studied engineering, at the same university, although they never met. She did systems, and my son industrial engineering.

"What's odd, she continues, is that the adoptive couple— Lieutenant Colonel Ceferino Landa and Mercedes Beatriz Moreira, who knew very well where the baby had come from—had already been identified by Abuelas, but on suspicion of having a different child. So when they ran the DNA, the results were unexpected; the child they actually found was Claudia Victoria, who had lived as the Landa's daughter for over twenty years. It was all very difficult; I think she had had some doubts—she'd seen pictures of herself as a baby, but never photos of her mother pregnant, things like that—but then the Landas had raised her lovingly, doted on her, with aunts and uncles who adored her as the only child of a couple who couldn't have kids. They got a light sentence—the father had house arrest owing to his age—but still. One day to the next, a person's whole life story changes."

Claudia Victoria Poblete recuperated her biological identity in February 2000. Her photo on the website of the Abuelas de Plaza de Mayo shows a young woman with a calm smile, looking steadily at the camera: "Recovering my identity has meant a new beginning for me, one with clarity, and without lies. Finding my past has enabled me to plan for my future without old fears, it is such a relief to know that there are no longer any black holes in my history."[8]

Mónica expresses great sadness that she and Claudia have not become close. "How could it not be complicated for her? But I am here for her, always. And here's another coincidence: Claudia's husband is somehow related to my very dear elementary school teacher, who tells me she has re-created her life, of course after a great deal of pain and grief. I'm told she has a daughter, Guadeloupe, which makes me very happy. Yes. I will always be here for Claudia, and have done my best to let her know that."

Mónica testified against Julián (Cerro would die in the interim) in the case that exposed what the attorneys called "the schizophrenia" of Alfonsín's laws. Carolina Varsky, who handled the matter as a lawyer for

CELS [Center for Legal and Social Studies] explained that the laws permitted the prosecution of the baby's kidnappers but not the mother's, even though they were kidnapped on the same day, by the exact same individuals. Varsky remembers the stakes as being very high. "There was a lot of international attention: Was Argentina capable of prosecuting such crimes? Would we honor the treaties we had signed? Would we continue to be a case study for impunity? It was very intense."

After five months of study, on March 6, 2001, Judge Gabriel Cavallo, accepted the CELS argument, declaring Due Obedience and Punto Final unconstitutional. "So this was a landmark," said Varsky, "we prosecuted both the appropriation of the child and the disappearance/torture of the parents. Julio Simón was convicted and sentenced to twenty-five years, the maximum under the penal code. Cavallo's ruling was just for this case. There were more legal hoops to go through." The Solicitor General ruled in favor of Cavallo's ruling in August 2002; but then the army started putting pressure on the courts; even so, Congress derogated in 2003 and then when the Supreme Court declared the laws unconstitutional in 2005, *that* finally annulled them. It did not happen all at once. But what did happen was that Cavallo, after listening to the horrendous testimony about Gertrudis Hlazcik and José Poblete, ordered the investigation of all the other events he had heard about. "If a judge doesn't do this," Varsky stressed, "then the cases just sit there. You need a specific imputation, concrete charges against a particular person. So Julio Simón will be tried again and again and again."[9]

Monica affirmed, "I'll testify as many times as they need me. I've already been called, am only waiting for the date."

Mónica is referring to the trial known as "ABO," its initials standing in for The Athletic Club, the Bank, and Olympus (el Atlético, el Banco, el Olimpo). Seventeen men, including Julio Simón, are accused of the forced disappearance, torture, and murder of 181 victims in these camps, which functioned serially as one unit. As in all of the trials, this figure represents far fewer than the actual number of victims, witnesses having been murdered, evidence having been destroyed. This trial, which opened on November 24, 2009, is being heard in Federal Court No. 5, and since December, has been sharing the room with the ESMA trial. ABO meets Mondays and Tuesdays; ESMA on Thursdays and Fridays; they alternate Wednesdays.

The federal courthouse is located on the Avenida Commodoro Py, directly across the street from the Edificio Libertad, which houses the Navy

High Command. Libertad is a severe and looming building at the top of a high broad flight of stairs; a huge anchor is sunk in the ground near the flagpole. About a hundred yards away, Naval Air has an outpost on the turnoff called Antarctic Avenue (Avenida Antártica). The bus stops on both sides of the street are full of sailors, officers, and civilians who work for the Navy. Behind the courthouse is the shabby, teeming Retiro train station; traffic races anarchically around the small circular green. On the other side of the green is the Plaza Hotel, in whose bar the coups of the 1960s and 1970s were arranged over drinks among the brass and well-connected civilians.

There is a general shabbiness in dim hallways, the elevators groan and climb slowly, descend in fits and starts. It is not unusual to see defendants and guards, handcuffed together, shuffling into public bathrooms.

Courtroom No. 5 is in the basement. Recently redone, it is modern and well lit, its walls and tables are fashioned of amber-toned wood; the chairs are grey with black backs. Although security is remarkably lax, entry into the courtroom is carefully monitored so that victims and their families should not cross paths with the supporters of the defendants. There had been incidents of witnesses being taunted and physically aggressed by the wives of the men who had tortured them. Mothers of the Plaza have been screamed at and spit on. As a member of the press, I had to sit in the balcony, behind a wall of bulletproof glass, with the wives, daughters, sons, fathers, and colleagues of the nineteen men charged with atrocities. After a long delay engineered by the defense, the accused enter the courtroom through a narrow door, each one hand-cuffed to a guard. They walk slowly and awkwardly; we can hear the metallic rasp. Ex-members of the infamous Task Force 3.3.2, they are among the biggest names in the business of the Dirty War and include: Acosta (the "Tiger" in charge of Navy intelligence, who liked to go dancing with the women he tortured); Astiz ("The Blond Angel"); Cavallo ("Serpico"); Capdevila ("Tomy," a doctor who attended *desaparecidas* as they gave birth and then trafficked their babies); Pernías ("Rat"); Rolón ("The Boy" in charge of kidnaps); and Scheller ("The Nazi"). There is also Adolfo Donda, who arranged the kidnap of his brother and sister-in-law, played cards in the next room while they were being tortured, personally approved their *transfer*, and stole their newborn daughter, passing her on to ex-prefect Juan Antonio Azic.[10] The recipient of two baby girls born in captivity to different young mothers, Azic is not in court; he is detained in hospital, having grievously wounded himself trying to commit suicide.

The naval wives and daughters lean out over the balcony, calling names and blowing kisses.

"Alfredito! Alfredito!" they call to Astiz, assuring each other he looks "divine."

"My husband is still a looker," brags one woman.

"Papá has an *excellent* mind," says the daughter of Oscar Montes, "He won't miss a *trick*." A former vice admiral, he was minister of foreign relations during the 1978 World Cup. While not charged with hands-on torture, he is accused of giving the orders, of having ultimate authority for the missions and the overall plan. Today he is a frail-looking old man who looks small in his wheelchair; still he is impeccably dressed, in a gray slacks, black blazer, blue shirt and dark tie. Sentenced in an earlier case, Montes has been serving his time under house arrest. "I'm afraid he may be cold, does he look cold?" his daughter asks the woman next to her. She takes a woolen scarf from her bag and holds it out over the balcony.

These naval women are a stylish lot—tanned, mostly blond, with sporty haircuts, and contemporary eyewear. Montes's daughter wears a white patent-leather raincoat. They have a country club look about them and treat this balcony as if it were their own, by right.

The defendants, most of whom wear dark suits, look up and wave. Rolón tosses his head of wavy white hair and winks as though it were all a minor annoyance. Astiz, who has been treated for kidney cancer, looks puffy, slovenly, and sour. He wears grubby jeans, a limp white polo shirt under an old navy blue sweater, white socks, and scuffed-up brown shoes. Which is not to say he is passive: the Blond Angel carries a book that has been causing a scandal—*Volver a matar*, by the philo-Nazi Juan B. Yofre, a member of the ultra-secret Chamber of Terror, organized in the early 1970s to eliminate subversion. The title may be translated as *Back for the Kill*. The next time this trial is convened, Astiz is wearing the same clothes but carrying a copy of Kafka's *The Trial*.

This case is referred to as the "ESMA Mega-Trial," even though it is limited to crimes committed in 1977. Elements of this case were ready for court early in the new democracy but got shut down in 1987 by Due Obedience and Punto Final. For the purposes of this trial, five separate cases have been conjoined: "Testimonios A" has the largest number of victims and nine accused; "Testimonios B," with thirteen accused, focuses on Astiz's "sting" in the Santa Cruz Church that resulted in the disappearance of two French nuns, three founding Madres de Plaza de Mayo, and several of their supporters; "Testimonios C" charges eleven men in the murder of writer Rodolfo Walsh. There are two other cases, "Donda" and

FIGURE 16. This photo was taken on the first day of the ESMA Mega-Trial. Six of the accused, from left to right: Raul Scheller (partly obscured), aka "The Nazi," Juan Carlos Rolón ("Rat"), Ricardo Miguel Cavallo ("Serpico"), Jorge Eduardo Acosta ("Tiger"), Carlos Capdevila ("Tomy"); and Adolfo Donda. (Photo courtesy of TELAM)

"Montes y Capdevila," with one and two defendants, respectively, on the trafficking of babies born in the ESMA. It is fair to say that no one is really happy with this structure. Survivors and witnesses will have to testify repeatedly in just this one prosecution, since the trials within the Mega-Trial overlap (see Fig. 16).

Carolina Varsky, who is prosecuting part of the case for CELS, explained, "The court should have given greater thought to an overall prosecution strategy well suited to the way the repression was organized on the ground. Instead the judge decided to go year by year, so we will have ESMA 1976, ESMA 1978, and so on. But we need larger swaths of time, especially given that some 5,000 people passed through that place, and some of them were there for years."

Horacio Méndez Carreras—patrician, formidable, and highly respected—is prosecuting the mass kidnap that took place on December 8, 1977, in the Santa Cruz Church ("Testimonios B"). On that day, the Madres de Plaza de Mayo had organized a meeting to collect funds to publish the names of their missing loved ones, in *La Nación*, on December 10, International Human Rights Day. Astiz, who had infiltrated the Madres, by posing as the brother of a *desaparecido*, organized a sting in which twelve individuals (including three founding Madres) were disappeared.

> Horacio and I meet for a late dinner after a very long day in court.[11]
>
> Of course structure is a problem. The procedural code we have is antiquated, developed for chicken rustling, if you will. It wasn't conceived for crimes of this magnitude, let alone for crimes against humanity. Outdated procedural codes can easily lead to injustice—illogical rules of evidence, untenable standards of proof, a basic ill fit between the crimes and the trial's forms.
>
> But the structural point here is that all these cases are paradigmatic. ESMA itself is the Argentine Auschwitz. Rodolfo Walsh was one of our most brilliant and courageous *engagé* writers, a national treasure. The operation in the Santa Cruz church was the largest group kidnapping carried out by Task Force 3.3.2, and it was against defenseless civilians. The disappearance of the nuns—Alice Domon and Léonie Duquet—makes the trial International.

And there the case comes full circle to the far interior of Argentina, to Goya, where Alice Domon worked the earth with the Ligas Agrarias, struggled with the peasants led by Sergio Tomasella, a key witness in this trial (see chapter 4).

Horacio, who formerly headed the Human Rights Section at the Ministry of Foreign Relations, took the case in 1984, at the request of the French government. "I am a lawyer for the facts. But if anyone had told me then that it would take a quarter of a century to get to court . . ." He lets the sentence trail. I know the case has obsessed him, caused upheaval in his personal life, and brought real sacrifice.

> But turn the page? Move on? It's not possible. Each of the figures in Santa Cruz church was emblematic—each was on a quest, a Crusade to find information about their loved ones. They were not *militantes*. Their connections were not political or ideological, they were blood ties. Think of a lion, take her cub; a cow, take her calf; or a sheep, take her lamb;—the mother will react with rage and desperation. Fence her in and when she gets out many days later the first thing she does is go looking for her young. Desperate. Unstoppable. If an animal does this, what about a human being? This is not 'political.' It is much deeper. A healthy society cannot be created based on the enforced, willing, or passive relinquishment to criminals—*to state terrorists*—of our defenseless dead.

In an Argentine trial, proceedings begin with the reading of the accusation. It is an old, even archaic form, never intended to go on for hours on end, over the course of days and weeks. But that is exactly what is happening here. Every instance of every crime is recited; graphic testimony is read out; corroborations are patiently assembled. Most of the testimony was familiar to me. Even so, it was astonishing to sit there listening to what I already knew. The Secretary of the Court read clearly and calmly, like the educated gentleman he apparently was; his tone never faltered; his breath never failed. And yet for the better part of five hours he enunciated the unspeakable. The judges followed along, occasionally marking their copies of the text. The prosecutors sat in a collective knot of tension. There was not much movement from the accused; the defense seemed to rest.

The balcony was a whole other story. The Secretary read from the testimony of Osvaldo Barros, who was kidnapped by Donda, "there were five or six torturers in the room, each one applying charges of 220 volts . . ."

"*Por favor,*" groaned the defendants' women.

The word "torture" elicited a collective rolling of eyes, a batting of the air as though at flies. "Violations of personal security" brought forth, "*Y la nuestra?!*" (What about *our* security?) *Capucha* had them patting their heads. And then they would get bored, leaf through the papers, pass around candies. As their husbands were described committing acts of kidnap, torture, death flights, and rape, they smirked and riffled through their purses. The admiral's daughter—María Alejandra Montes de Howard—nibbled from a sizable plastic bag of brightly colored M & M's.

"*Picana, picana, picana,*" yawned one woman, nestling into the corner of her chair for a conspicuous nap.

Listening to the testimony of Osvaldo and Susana Barros, Graciela Daleo, and Carlos Muñoz, I watch Donda's wife, who has come to court with a tote bag full of magazines. Tanned, her neat blond bob set off with casual bangs and wire glasses, she wears black cigarette pants, a beige blazer, sandals, and small gold-hoop earrings.

"And then 'Gerónimo,' that would be Donda . . . he and Capdevila tortured Thelma again, with even more intensity . . ."

As we break for the lunch recess, I ask Señora Donda if it is hard to listen to such things.

"No!" she says, looking me straight in the eye. "No, it isn't. I know my husband. After forty years of marriage, I know who he is."

María Alejandra Montes de Howard steps in, "Do *you* know anyone who's been married that long? It says a lot about a person." And then they turned their backs, chatted with the guard, and walked out of the courtroom.

Later in the day, this entire group of women would explode. As the judge closed the afternoon's proceedings, and H.I.J.O.S. sent up their signature chant for justice, the naval women threw themselves at the chest-high bullet-proof barrier, shrieking, *"Terroristas! Terroristas!"* The judge's calls for order were not as assertive as one might have expected. Perhaps the better part of wisdom was to let everyone vent for a few moments? Things quickly quieted down, but exits from the courtroom were strictly controlled: not until the witnesses and victims' relatives had cleared the area were those in the balcony permitted to file out. The incident had evidently been anticipated, for in the final fifteen minutes of the proceedings, the number of guards in the balcony quietly increased, with at least one in each corner, and two manning the door. Even as they tried to contain the outburst, they soothed the women, their words and gestures full of deference.

The men in the balcony were much quieter. Several were courtly, suggesting seats with better sightlines than those reserved for the press, reminding me not to forget the jacket I had draped on the back of my chair. One older man has been particularly attentive; he is elegant in a fine woolen cape over a fine dark suit. He is perfectly bald, wears perfectly round glasses, and uses a brass-tipped, highly polished, dark wooden cane. He is fair, delicately flushed, and has eyes that nearly match the loden color of his cape. He has come to the trial from the middle of Buenos Aires province, where he lives on his *estancia*.

"The military never should have taken over," he volunteers. "When it comes to governing, they're morons, if you'll excuse the expression."

He asks if I would like to hear more. I would, and do.

"And *who ever* had the idea of putting such a pair as Videla and Massera *in charge*? Civilians burned down the country and then went into exile. They only came back after the nightmare was over. I lived through it, they did not.

"But this," he gestures to indicate the court, "is also politics gone awry. The defendants are political prisoners. Some have been held for years in so-called 'preventive prison.' This country was *at war*. If the military are to be tried, what about the guerrillas? These trials keep the war going. We should all be trying to live in peace, in *concord*. I presented a petition to the Supreme Court," he tells me, "but here we are." He shrugs, with a sad smile.

He is here on behalf of his son, Ricardo Miguel Cavallo ("Serpico"), who waged a long, ferocious battle to have the charges thrown out. A beneficiary of Due Obedience and Punto Final, he might never have been arrested had he not been so outrageously corrupt as an executive for the (outrageously corrupt) Mexican consortium that issues auto registrations. Investigative reporting on the Mexican scandal led to evidence that Cavallo had had a role in the Argentine repression. When the Buenos Aires correspondent of *Reforma*, the Mexican daily that broke the story, showed Cavallo's photograph to Mario Villani, he identified him without hesitation. So did four other ESMA survivors: Osvaldo Barros, Victor Basterra, Graciela Daleo, and Juan Gasparini.

Cavallo was arrested and detained in Mexico on August 24, 2000, at the request of Baltazar Garzón, and extradited to Spain, where he was charged with genocide and terrorism. Mexico thus became the first Latin American country to extradite a person charged with crimes against humanity. After the amnesty laws were annulled, Spain extradited him to Argentina to stand trial for atrocities committed at the ESMA.

Cavallo *padre* is quietly eager to talk. "If my son is guilty, then he should go to jail and serve his sentence. But 'guilt' during war is very hard to define, let alone prove. And these so-called 'crimes against humanity'—they are a foreign invention. War is the crime against humanity. We should leave it at that, and resolve to live in peace."

His arguments deserve a response. His analysis of the run-up to the coup is superficial. That the country was "at war" implies symmetry. The armed Left had been routed in 1975, the year prior to the coup.[12] The "subversive threat" was a pretext for the radical reorganization of Argentina's economy, concentrating wealth, resources, housing, healthcare, and education as a "privilege" for those who "loved the dictatorship in the deepest chambers of their heart." As for prosecuting guerrillas who had placed bombs in the early 1970s, the vast majority of those individuals were killed in the immediate aftermath by military and police. They could have been charged and tried —should have been—but were instead "eliminated." There is also an essential difference in the definitions of their respective crimes: the armed Left were not state actors; they did not have a systematic plan for massive repression; there are statutes of limitation for the kidnaps, extortions, robberies, and murders they committed (another reason to have moved quickly on prosecutions). The ESMA trial (like those concerning ABO, Plan Condor, La Perla, Vesubio, Campo de Mayo, the five separate army corps) are directed at *crimes against humanity* (as defined by a host of international rights treaties and conventions) committed by state actors, and as such have no statute of limitation. As to the argument that the trials depend on "imported law," Carolina Varsky points out that torture, kidnapping, baby stealing, and murder are separately delineated in the Argentine penal code. "They were crimes when they were committed, they are crimes now. This not an 'exotic' invention from abroad."

When I ask about some defendants having had long periods of preventive prison, Varsky expresses concern. "As a human rights organization, CELS doesn't want anyone to be held for an inordinately long time. Our system allows for three years—two years, plus one if the case has been unable to move to trial. There have been problems. For the massive appropriation of minors, Acosta was arrested in 1999 or 2000. It's bad, which is a major reason we want these trials to be accelerated."

Méndez Carreras strikes a different note.

> Preventive prison works very well for them. These are five-star jails—white pavilions, rolling lawns, tennis, golf, swimming pools. They themselves have engineered this; their lawyers file endless procedural appeals, questions, comments, all sorts of hold-ups. . . . Judges have so much discretion that in one recent conviction, preventive prison counted not as two-to-one, but as four-for-one. So do the math: Acosta is sixty-six; even if he gets *prisón perpétua* or twenty-five years, his nine years automatically get converted to eighteen—or fewer—and he's out. In any case, at seventy, he gets house arrest. No, they are playing this both ways: publically protesting that they are 'political prisoners,' and working the system to keep it going. Delayed trials and slow trials are to their advantage. Astiz, who has had serious cancer, keeps changing attorneys precisely to drag things out, to avoid being convicted before he should become too sick, or die. As for the younger, hale and healthy Cavallo, you were there for his latest stunt."

Just after the judge opened the morning's proceedings, the CELS legal team made an objection: Cavallo had not, in fact, been serving his preventive prison. Unbeknownst to the prosecution and perhaps (though perhaps not) to the court, Cavallo had been for the last month in a private room in the Naval Hospital, owing to what he called "lumbralgia."

"This minor backache is their favorite diagnosis," says Méndez Carreras. "It can't be seen on an x-ray, a CT Scan, or an MRI. If you say you have it, who can say you don't? Lumbralgia is a real thing, I've had it myself. At its worst, it lasts maybe five days; and it shouldn't put anyone in the hospital."

The certain whereabouts of the defendants would seem a minimum standard for any trial, let alone one of this magnitude. But the judge merely noted the objection and moved on.

"Every day I expect unpleasant surprises," says Horacio. "When the court asked the navy for Cavallo's files (as proof he had been at the ESMA) those files somehow got lost. They lost them on purpose, of course. The whole file, all of his basic navy records."

The prosecutors eventually prevailed, but the resistance is unlikely to let up.

"There is definitely a wall, but we are perforating that wall in various ways," I was told by Eduardo Luis Duhalde, the distinguished attorney, historian, professor, and since 2003, the Secretary of Human Rights. Forced into exile in 1976 when the Junta issued a decree by which they stripped him of his civil and political rights, ordered his capture, and took control of his material assets, he founded the Argentine Commission on Human Rights (CADHU) to organize international protest against the junta.[13]

"We are constantly investigating, and while the armed forces are not cooperative, the Ministry of Defense (headed by a civilian ex-*militante*, Nilda Garré, appointed by President Kirchner) collaborates with us on everything. The records pertaining directly to state terrorism were removed from the country before the dictatorship finally fell. I don't believe they destroyed anything. Now and again a book comes out defending the dictatorship and one can see that the author had access to information that proves the archives were not destroyed. We, however, do not have access, so we look at complementary records and construct the intersections. Last year, after a great deal of difficulty, we gained access to the secret bulletins of the three forces. Again, there was no mention of illegal operations, but there are records of decorations, personnel movements, and special missions. When a military officer in a certain period of time received a one hundred percent salary increase for "having served on dangerous missions," we know that he either participated in the Task Forces, or infiltrated civilian groups. We look at citations "for bravery in battle"—if it was before the Malvinas war, then where did he fight? Day by day we are digging into materials that give us clues that are more than clues. We have been able to identify the members of Battalion 601—the intelligence service that was the hard nucleus of the repression—who operated not only here, but also in Nicaragua, Salvador, Honduras, Guatemala, as part of the Condor Plan [see Fig. 17]. The de-classification of CIA documents—thanks to the untiring efforts of the National Security Archive—has been of enormous help."[14]

The Ministry has been "instrumental," to quote Méndez Carreras, in tracing and retrieving fugitives hiding abroad. "They have a whole budget dedicated to this purpose; it is organized as part of their essential function." Human Rights is part of the Ministry of Justice and Security, a Kirchner innovation that no doubt has facilitated such operations. Duhalde's long international history also comes into play: a Human Rights Consultant to the United Nations, he has served on peace missions in Africa, Chiapas, Nicaragua, Peru, and Colombia.

"The State committed these crimes, and so the State must do everything possible to make amends," Duhalde insists. The Ministry is itself a plaintiff in the ESMA trial and in that of Reynaldo Bignone, the final de facto president of the junta, and five other generals stationed at Campo de Mayo, the seat of the First Army Corps and base of operations for Battalion 601. Campo de Mayo also functioned as an enormous concentration camp, primitive maternity ward, and army headquarters for baby stealing.

FIGURE 17. "Open Sesame" was the password that drivers used to open the metallic sliding door and drop off their [human] "packages." This auto mechanic shop was rented in 1975 by the Triple A (Argentine Anti-Communist Alliance); it was taken over by the Argentine and Uruguayan armies under the Condor Plan. Three hundred persons are known to have passed through Orletti, which also housed auto parts and kidnapped cars. (Photo copyright © by Cristina Fraire, 2009)

This is the second Campo de Mayo trial; the first having ended in September 2009. As the practice was to kill virtually everyone, there are extremely few survivors, but these witnesses have provided corroborating evidence. This trial, restricted to 1976–78, is focused on fifty-six victims. Juan Carlos Scarpati gave one of the earliest accounts of Campo de Mayo. Kidnapped on April 28, 1977, after having been shot eight times, he was tortured even as he lay for twenty days in a coma. As soon as he was able to walk, they took him out of *capucha* and put him to work a few hours a day as a kind of janitor, a job he had to do with his hood pulled up just enough so he could see. By the time he managed to escape in 1979, he calculated that 3,500 people had died in Campo de Mayo, which continued to function for another four years.[15] Scarpati died in 2008, but he was present at this trial through his testimony, along with 130 living witnesses (see Fig. 18).

The first known victim of Campo de Mayo was 14-year-old Floreal Avellaneda. Kidnapped from his family's home with his mother on April 15, 1976, his tortured, bound, partially dismembered body was found one month later floating in Uruguayan waters. His parents, Iris and Floreal Avellaneda, trade unionists, sat in the courtroom among the families of other Campo de Mayo victims. Among the accused were General Fernando Ezequiel Verplaetsen and General Jorge Omar Riveros, the latter convicted in a separate trial, two months earlier, for Floreal's death. Like Julio Simón and hundreds of others, these repressors are likely to be tried in many separate cases. On November 9, 2009, the third day of this second Campo de Mayo trial, the accused continued to exercise their right to silence—all except for Verplaetsen, who when one of the prosecutors said his name, rose and declared, "Here I am, you son of a bitch."[16]

Before the trial got underway, a revealing sideshow unfolded in the search for a fitting courtroom. The trial needed to be held near Campo de Mayo, which is located outside Buenos Aires City, and the federal judges deemed that none of the local courthouses would do. The suburban town of Vicente López offered a space formerly used for recreational soccer. When local shopkeepers protested that the trial would be bad for business, create traffic jams and other disturbances, the trial was eventually moved to another stadium in the neighboring town of San Martín.

The Ministry attorneys have requested the penal code's maximum penalty—twenty-five years—for each of these Campo de Mayo defendants. At age 81, Bignone, who as the regime collapsed ordered the destruction of all military records, is expected to be convicted. But given his age, he will receive no more than house arrest, domestic life with his grandchildren.

FIGURE 18. To date over 600 ex-concentration camps and secret detention centers have been identified. Each one bears at least a plaque; a number now function as living memory sites, administered by the Instituto Espacio para la Memoria <http://www.institutomemoria.org.ar>;, whose director is Ana María Careaga. This is "The Four Columns," of the Navy Mechanics School, Buenos Aires City. On the silhouette: "A secret detention center functioned here," and photos of *desaparecidos*. (Photo copyright © by Cristina Fraire, 2009)

Duhalde concedes frustration but also insists, "The convictions and sentences are inscribed in the judicial record; they become part of our institutional fabric. They are proof of moral protest, of society's judgment against that history."

So justice delayed is not justice denied?

Duhalde, a portly man in his seventies, sighs heavily.

"I prefer justice that comes late to justice that never comes at all. We cannot abandon our debt to this history, our responsibility to prosecute those whose repression still has profound effects for our society. There is yet a black hole in the collective consciousness, there are grave sequelae in our society's mental health. State terrorism didn't only leave grief and pain in the survivors and relatives of *desaparecidos*. We see it in small episodes. Any citizen, even one who "had nothing to do with anything," will tremble if a Ford Falcon races by with its siren going, or if he sees a Ford Falcon with four persons inside. He can't help but remember the nights of the dictatorship. In these recent threats to the president . . . why would they play that music? Because they know it still provokes terror. And that is because justice has not been done."

He lights yet another cigarette. Dignified in a double-breasted suit, he yet bears traces of exhaustion. He works a fourteen-hour day, often flying from province to province. He attends at least part of every major trial.

"The fact is, these are symbolic reparations. How can one really *repair* the damages done by torture, by years in concentration camps, by terror? Of course, we have to enact economic reparations where possible, and institute every sort of acknowledgment of what happened, though this too is symbolic. It is all we have. It is *what* we have. We cannot go back in time."

And yet.

"You can't help but re-live the events as you testify," says Osvaldo Barros, who is both a witness and a plaintiff in the ESMA trial.

"When you go to declare, you are right back where all those things happened. On one level, it's involuntary—the experience is seared into you. But it is also necessary—our greatest fear is that we might forget something we know, something we need to say. It is both an intellectual and a personal challenge—to fully express what happened, and to do it well, cogently. We have been preparing ourselves. Through the Asociación of Ex-Detenidos and Desparecidos, we have psychologists who work with us as a group; and then we work with each witness individually as his or her date comes up. The Secretariat of Human Rights also has a team of psychologists, but we've continued with our own. This is going to be a difficult trial. The defense is playing very rough."[17]

Osvaldo is clearly drained after this first day in court. We had arranged to meet in *Abuela Pan*, a gourmet health-food restaurant in the heart of San Telmo. He is waiting for me on the sidewalk and wears, to my astonishment, a long white apron. He never mentioned that in 2001 he lost his job selling medical equipment. Not long after, he joined with a friend who needed a partner to make the restaurant go. In this old house typical of the *barrio* lived the colorful nineteenth-century writer Fray Mocho. Though still in need of some sprucing up, the place is full of charm, architectural interest, and cultural history. Everything is homemade and artisanal. Even though the restaurant is closed (it only serves lunch), neighbors call and then stop round for soybean patties and other items Osvaldo makes available for takeout. Far from showing his fatigue, Osvaldo welcomes these customers. "I like providing people with food," he says, "I do some of the baking, but we have two chefs for the meals. And I'm fortunate to have an agent who shops the markets at four in the morning." Still he arrives not much later and remains until evening. Since the restoration of democracy, he and Susana have been tireless activists—related not only to their own past experiences in the ESMA but also in a host of neighborhood initiatives that started as reactions to one or another in the unending chain of economic and political crises.

"We were all extremely tense this morning," he allows. "You realize that once again you're going to be in the same room with those monsters. One compañero had such a backache he couldn't walk without a cane."

Susana, who comes in late from her biochemical lab, and Osvaldo are preoccupied with the range of potential hurdles. "The judges closest to the military structured it this way in order to consolidate impunity. They divided this enormous matter into little cases, when in just our part of the five-part 'Mega-Causa,' 250 repressors and nearly 600 missing compañeros were identified with first and last names. Each one documented by eyewitnesses, by survivors, by *us*. The *juez de instrucción*, Sergio Torres, recommended these cases be elevated to trial, but the court declined. In the Donda case, Torres added sixty additional cases and a few new repressors, but again the court declined, arguing it would delay matters."

Susana, who was personally tortured by Donda, listens, nodding and smoking nonstop.

"The fragmentation of the cases doesn't allow for an accurate vision of what really occurred, that it was a massive systematic plan, a genocide." On this point, Osvaldo is insistent to the point of bitterness.

"Genocide" is the term that many Argentine human rights activists, including attorneys and government officials, use to describe the repression. Yet their usage does not conform to the 1948 UN Convention on the Prevention and Punishment of the Crime of Genocide, which delineates "any of the following acts committed with intent to destroy, in whole or in part, a *national, ethnical, racial or religious* [italics added] group, as such: killing members of the group; causing serious bodily or mental harm to members of the group; deliberately inflicting on the group conditions of life calculated to bring about its physical destruction in whole or in part; imposing measures intended to prevent births within the group; forcibly transferring children of the group to another group." Because the Argentine victims were not selected according to the four categories italicized above, many legal scholars hold that genocide did not occur. Others argue that the very definition of genocide needs to be modernized.

Among those who support the charge of genocide is Spanish Magistrate Baltasar Garzón, who called for the extraditions of both Scilingo and Pinochet. A little-known fact is that Pinochet would not have been arrested at that time had the Spanish magistrate not been working to prosecute the Argentine repressors. On the very afternoon that he called for arrest of the Chilean general, Garzón had had to put aside his files on Argentina in order to contact London. For better or worse, he applied his Dirty War template to Chile. Garzón's argument was both based in and went beyond the 1948 UN Convention. For Garzón, the systematic robbery of babies and their gift or sale to "suitable" families constituted "auto-genocide," the term the UN devised to characterize the Khmer Rouge massacres in Cambodia. ("Auto-genocide" pertains to situations when victims and aggressors are of the same group.) Garzón argues that the Argentine regime itself created the profile of the enemy—"the subversive"—and eliminated individuals they believed fit the criteria. As the regime repeatedly stressed, "the repression is directed against a minority we do not consider Argentine." The "subversive" was likened to the Antichrist, the "destroyer of Western, Christian civilization," as well as the *ser nacional* (the collective essence, soul, or consciousness).[18]

For Osvaldo, Susana, and many others, the experience of having been designated an intellectual race apart, bears its own sequelae. I cannot help but wonder if the charge of genocide—an acknowledgment that one suffered as part of a like-minded group—somehow helps to assuage the profound aloneness of being naked, helpless, and strapped down; of being tortured to point of death; of being isolated, blindfolded, and shackled in *capucha*; of listening to the screams of dying compañeros.

"Genocide is how we experienced it," Osvaldo insists. "It is what they perpetrated, and what it felt like. In the quest for justice, that needs to be acknowledged. Otherwise it is a form of still criminalizing an entire political project, which in broad terms was to create a different, better, more human society."

Susana nods. "They massacred the flower of Argentine youth. It was their plan. And society today needs to reflect on that."

They remind me that in the 2006 conviction of Miguel Etchecolatz, ex-chief of the Buenos Aires Provincial Police, the judge noted that while the court could not formally convict him of genocide, since it was not delineated in the Penal Code, "these crimes [kidnap, torture, murder] were committed in the context of the genocide."[19] A similar reference to genocide was made in the 2007 conviction of the German-born police chaplain Christian von Wernich. The trials and convictions of Etchecolatz and von Wernich were the second and third, respectively, after the nullification of Due Obedience and Punto Final, following close upon the trial of Julio Simón (Julián the Turk).

"The Catholic Church never even ex-communicated von Wernich, who was present at torture, and who gave spiritual counseling to the crews on the death flights. That," said Osvaldo, "is a terrible commentary on the Argentine Catholic Church."

I note that during the day's reading of the accusation, they were both quoted numerous times, but always in reference to someone else. "I am both a plaintiff and a witness in 'Testimonios A' and," says Osvaldo, "Susana is in both 'Testimonios A' and 'Donda,' which is a sub-matter of 'A.' We will testify to what happened to us and to others."

Susana continues, "One cannot always testify on one's own behalf. How could I know who tortured me? I was blindfolded. I learned later it was Donda because eyewitnesses made the identification. They have pushed the whole burden on to the victims. There are camps where no one saw anything, where everyone was always hooded or in total isolation. In such instances, how do you prove you were tortured? How do you prove you were killed? Yet that's what they're demanding."

"How," Osvaldo goes on, "do you prove that Capdevila gave the injections of PEN-Naval on the death flights? We know, because guards told us after the fact, but no *compañero* on those planes lived to testify. We *can* prove that Capdevila—known as 'Tomy'—was the attending physician at torture, at Susana's torture, that his role was to say for how much longer it could go on, how much more and she would die."

"Cavallo is another case. We saw him every day, he was our boss in *pecera*. But we did not actually see him in the act of kidnap or torture. Others, however, did. So we help place him at the ESMA; others take the proof a few steps further."

The testimonies get woven together. "But they will try to unravel every little piece," says Susana.

"We saw what we saw," Osvaldo says, softly. "We have done this before." As in the 1985 trial that convicted the ex-commanders.

In this trial, a number of the accused are for all intents and purposes already convicted—Acosta, Astiz, and Donda. So much has been established that it is hard to imagine that they could be acquitted, Osvaldo thinks.

"But there is a problem with officers of lower rank," notes Susana. "In the last trial of the First Army Corps [which ended in late 2009] they acquitted three area chiefs, even though military structure indicated that they had to be at Campo de Mayo. The difficulty was there were no eyewitnesses—at least none that hadn't been killed. The court ruled the evidence 'circumstantial' and therefore exculpatory.'"

Varsky and her team from CELS are appealing the decision.

"It's insane," Osvaldo shakes his head. "José Luis d'Andrea Mohr [a colonel descended from a long line of colonels] made a detailed chart of the armed forces, showing where each rank had responsibility, how the whole repression functioned, laid out every sphere of command."

The late d'Andrea Mohr, one of five colonels cashiered for "democratic tendencies," and outright support of the Madres de Plaza de Mayo, was a key witness in 1985, and in later prosecutions, truth trials, and investigations. He was my undercover bodyguard when I met with Julián the Turk in 1998.

"The chart is unimpeachable, has legal precedence, and yet unless the court admits such organizational charts, many mid-level officers—who both gave and executed atrocious orders—will go free," laments Osvaldo.

What, I ask, in this difficult legal framework, do they really want from these trials?

"We need to know what happened to each and every one of our *desaparecidos*. Perhaps we won't succeed," he allows, "but that's the struggle. If the quote continues below, don't we omit the quotation marks?

"Memory. Truth. Justice."

Memoria. Verdad. Justicia. This is the keynote phrase, emblazoned on the letterhead of the human rights groups, chanted at marches and memorials, inscribed on the façades of the secret detention centers now functioning as "living sites of memory." The meaning of each term in this ringing phrase has been a matter of evolution and debate, not just across ideological divides but also within them. Is societal memory dependent upon consensus? Is "truth" a matter of what a society can tolerate? Is "justice" an abstraction? A Platonic ideal? Or, conversely, a pragmatic accommodation? The ways in which these terms conjugate may be forever difficult to parse. Memory is unstable—elusive, even inaccessible, then suddenly explosive, flooding over with new information.

Commemorations can be a catalyst, as I saw in the garden of the Santa Cruz Church where, each year on December 8, a memorial is held for those caught by the sting in the Sanctuary. This year the ceremonies would have unexpected legal importance, owing to new and surprising testimony. Founded in 1880 by Irish Brothers of the Passion, the church is movingly beautiful, with stained glass from Dublin, ivory-colored stone, and one of the finest organs in Buenos Aires. It has always been known for its open doors to this south-side neighborhood, as a haven for immigrants, for devotion to the poor, its legions of lay workers in the *villas miserias*, and for political courage in times of repression. Events spill out onto the Avenida San Juan; the procession makes the round of the whole neighborhood. At the entrance to the garden on the avenue is a life-size statue of the Virgin—impoverished, pregnant, and with obviously indigenous features. Scrawled on an outer wall on the side street is a black graffito: *Iglesia montonera terrorista* (see Fig. 19).

Survivors have testified to the torture suffered by Esther Ballestrino de Careaga, María Ponce de Bianca, and Azuzena Villaflor, by the two French nuns, and seven other activists, who died when within ten days of their kidnap, they were thrown from navy planes and hit the sea. On December 20, as their bodies started washing up along the shores of Buenos Aires Province, local doctors confirmed the cause of death as "impact against a hard object from a great height." Without further investigation, the remains were shoveled into a mass grave in the General Lavalle Cemetery. The remains would not be identified until 2005. Ana María would finally kneel before her mother's grave—a simple black marker in the garden of

FIGURE 19. Nora de Cortiñas, at left, of the Madres de Plaza de Mayo, in the Santa Cruz Church Sanctuary, December 8, 2009. (Photo copyright © by Cristina Fraire, 2009)

Santa Cruz Church (see Fig. 20). She is buried there with Sister Léonie Duquet, activist Angela Auad, and María Ponce de Bianca. (The ashes of Azucena Villaflor were spread across the Plaza de Mayo.) All afternoon, people came in off the street to offer a prayer at these simple markers, kneeling to touch, even pat, the stone. "I don't necessarily know them," said Ana María, "they are here—in this Garden dedicated to Martyrs for Justice—for reasons of their own."

Implausible though it might be, Astiz ("Judas") had let it be known that at trial he would deny that he was even at the church whose raid he organized, banking on his lawyers' abilities to rattle, cast doubt on the several very elderly witnesses. Speaking for the first time about that night in 1977 was the niece of Angela Auad, who had been taken to the event by her aunt. "We went immediately into exile, and I grew up in Spain," she said. "One of my strongest memories was of the nice young man who put his hands on my shoulders and kept me from getting shoved into a car. 'Not the little girl,' he said, 'not this pretty little girl.' I always thought of him as my savior. Years later, when I saw his picture in the newspaper, I realized: *That was Astiz.* The Blond Angel. Angel of Death." A vigorous, clear-speaking woman in her forties, she is expected to make a fine witness in the courtroom.

FIGURE 20. Ana María Careaga, outside the Santa Cruz Church. (Photo copyright © by Cristina Fraire, 2009)

Three days after the annual March for Resistance (held December 10, International Human Rights Day), I met with Gerardo dell'Oro,[20] whose family story—already twisted by the 1976 disappearance of his sister—was torqued again by the testimony of Jorge Julio López who, it turned out, had shared Patricia's captivity.

The presence of this 77-year-old mason is kept alive in the publications and websites of all the human rights groups. At the March for Resistance, his testimony was played over a loudspeaker in a corner of the Plaza de Mayo:

On [November] 5th, at 11 or 12 in the morning, Patricia Dell'Orto appears with her husband, all tortured, they were tortured for one, two days, with [the rest of] us. What were you doing in the *unidad básica* [basic neighborhood unit]? But they wouldn't say so they kept torturing them. . . . Patricia screamed and so they taped her mouth and hit her and at night they came back and tortured her some more, night and day. Because they wouldn't talk.

[On the night of the 9th] this nasal-sounding guy came in, screaming; first they grabbed us and shoved us all into a cell and Patricia said, "Are you López? If you go to my house don't forget to tell my baby and my parents, tell them where I was."

And then they took Patricia, who screamed, "Don't kill me, don't kill me, take me to a jail, but don't kill me, I want to raise my daughter." And you'll see if one day they find her body, the skull has a hole where the bullet went in, here, and then went out, there.

Pum, another bullet.

Then they came for her husband . . .

And then for another, another shot. . .

López was blond and ruddy, with gray-green eyes. His voice is light timbered and yet insistent. When the judge asks questions about details, López is impatient. He has been clear and precise all the way through, hasn't he? Yes, the judge assures him. Yes, he has.

"López was a very tortured man," Gerardo tells me. "He had made this promise to my sister, but for years and years he kept quiet, he hoarded his memories, *hoarded* them. But I'll get to that."

A photographer for *Clarín*, Gerardo has recently had an exhibition of *Imágenes en la Memoria*, images with text—his own photographs and writings, as well as pages from the notebooks of Jorge Julio López, who was missing for three or four months and then jailed without charges for three years.

Gerardo was 10 when Patricia was taken.

In La Plata, things were rough; there were bombs, loud noises, it was weird but normal to see tanks in the streets. I was aware that my sisters—ages 18, 17, 16—has some political activities. They were in the Peronist Youth and did neighborhood projects. I do remember that when she was kidnapped, we were living just outside the city in a house on a little property—she and her husband came to live with us, I guess because of her advanced pregnancy and the political situation. The kidnapping happened 25 days after my niece was born. It was typical: a dawn *operativo*, we were all there. In context, it was light, no violence, they only took a few things, and they left the baby with us.

Not long after, we left to go stay with aunts and grandparents. And then we moved to Quilmes. But we had this odd situation, a temporal problem, a very dangerous one. We didn't know how to explain the baby, my mother being nearly fifty. So we told everyone that my sister and brother-in-law had gone to Canada and because it was so cold there, they left the baby with us. Even now, I cannot believe we would come up with such a story. One would think that the lie would be ridiculously obvious, but the state of denial in society was so high, so intense, no one pressed us. And I spent most of my later childhood and adolescence trying to avoid the whole subject of how the family was constructed.

Because my mother was caring for her own two kids and Mariana, it was my father who filed the writs of habeas corpus, sought friends of friends with connections in the church, the armed forces, everything. Until the end of the dictatorship we expected them to come back. We'd received word that they were legalized prisoners, At the Disposition of the National Executive Power. By then, of course, they were dead.

Mariana essentially became my sister. She accommodated herself to being my parents' child. For me, grief had the face of my mother. I had been so young when Patricia was taken, with the years she became *my parents' missing daughter*, and then on the next level, *my missing sister*.

I met López for the first time in the late 1990s. The fellow my sister had wanted to be Mariana's godfather, a radio journalist, had returned from exile and let me know he was someone I could turn to if I wanted to know more about my sister. After some time goes by I call him and he says that at the Truth Trial, someone had testified about their *assassination*. This came as a huge shock, but also as a kind of relief, the relief of certainty. So I summoned a family meeting, make the announcement, and what does Mariana say? "I knew that." She had met with her godfather several years before I had. The truly strange thing is that my mother was at this meeting; he told them both. And my mother? She says, "Well, I never heard any such thing."

How do you explain that? Two people get the same information at the same time; one takes it in; the other "buries" it to the point of oblivion.

In 1999, my father goes to testify at the Truth Trial in La Plata. Our information was so sketchy, I don't know how he decided to do this. But he did. The reporters all comment on his fat folding files—that too struck me as weird. All families of *desaparecidos* have these same files, brown with accordion-like pleats. Within a week of my father's testimony, López comes forward and meets with us both. Undercover, if you will, because his wife *hated* what he was doing, wanted him to keep out of it all. So finally he keeps his promise to my sister. And that too came as a shock. We had never thought of her as a mother. We had never thought that in dying, *she* would lose her daughter. She was the one to lose that relationship and it had never occurred to us. I'd gone expecting to hear about . . . what one hears about . . . but this was totally unanticipated, and far worse. Searing.

López had had all this information for years, and it was killing him. He kept these notebooks full of what he knew—scribbled in every direction all over the page; fragments of drawings; isolated features; and the writing so tiny and crabbed it is almost impossible to decipher. When I finally managed, it was too terrible, really unbearable. He'd kept gathering information, talking to people, identifying cops. When the notebooks were called in as testimony, I photographed them so as to have a good record. Things have a way of disappearing in our courts.

In 2006, we were notified that my sister and brother-in-law's cases were being used in the trial of Etchecolatz. [Chief of the Buenos Aires Provincial Police, he ran eight concentration camps.] López was the key witness at this trial, in which 62 were charged. He was last seen on September 18, 2006. He left his house very early, not dressed for court but in a track suit, I think to meet with someone who had promised him information. That was the fatal appointment. It was immediately clear he'd been kidnapped; Mariana's godfather and I went searching all over La Plata, knowing it was futile but unable to sit in court.

But you're right. Jorge Julio López seems to be everywhere. When you see him making that gesture, it's the bullet ripping through my sister's skull.

Gerardo closes his eyes and shudders.
On a day that ABO survivors were testifying in court, I attended a special seminar at the Ministry of Defense. One of only several civilians, I watched as officers in training from the army, navy, and air force entered the large ornate salon. They wore parade-ground uniforms, starched, bright, full of complications—belts and epaulettes, high boots with gaiters, sabers strapped to the hip and extending down below the knee. The women wore pearls in their ears and their hair tucked up into their caps. This was the last of a four-part series on the general theme of the military role in democracy. But the subtext was *Memory Truth Justice*. The invited panelists were: General Martín Balza, who in his familiar excoriation of the conduct of the Malvinas War, found time to dilate on the importance of never giving or executing an immoral order; Eduardo Basualdo, an economist, economic historian, and member of the Board of CELS; Fabián Bosoer, an historian of trade unionism; and Horacio Verbitsky, President of CELS and longtime antagonist of the Argentine armed forces. Balza stressed the need to overcome the "phantasms" of past military failures; the historians seemed to speak as they would to any group of undergraduates; Verbitsky began by expressing surprise that anyone would have him in this particular room, and then recalled having presented the military with 600 writs of habeas corpus, which he supposes they simply shredded. I sat up front with the senior officers (why not) and listened as the room listened with utmost courtesy. When the time came for questions, they were all of a piece: one mid-rank officer after another rose, thanked the panel, and then told of being a child terrified of guerrilla bombings, of being frightened to pass a nursery school lest it explode as he walked by (the armed Left, it need be said, never bombed a nursery school). One after the other told of having an epiphany—he would rise to the occasion of his fear, he would swear to serve, to help protect the beloved nation under siege. Why, they wanted to know, were those who terrorized their childhoods, not on trial? An easy question for Verbitsky. I was struck that the men who rose did not speak of war or battle; but rather of service,

safety, and community. It seemed to me that they were balanced on a cultural edge: they were drawn to the military, even though by the time they entered, it had lost a great deal of prestige and was if anything more isolated than ever from the rest of society. And yet military education since 2003 has been radically reformed to emphasize the soldier-as-uniformed-citizen, with courses in democracy, human rights, and humanitarian law. The first two years of coursework at the academies is identical to that of the national university system. Soldiers now have the same judicial system as civilians, in which there is no death penalty. This generation would seem to be transitional: educated by elders in a chain of command still partially tainted; groomed for an institution with an untenable history; prepared for a mission defined by civilian government. The creation of continuity—arguably important for any institution—is a very tough challenge.

For guidance, Argentina has turned to Germany, whose Prussian Guard was the original model for its own military culture. (Hitler's Praetorian Guard, or SS, would be a later model.) In October 2008, the Ministry of Defense participated in a seminar near Berlin on "Armed Forces in Democracy." A group of officers, military scholars, and experts in human rights studied the ways in which a defeated and disgraced military—Germany's—had reformed and reintegrated itself into civilian society.[21]

Judith Said, Coordinator of the National Memory Archive (part of the Secretariat of Human Rights), works closely with the Ministry of Defense.

"We did a project with Defense on soldiers who disappeared during their obligatory service. It has been tricky confronting officers with our findings; even the younger ones, who might be more open, still have a corporatist orientation. I also coordinate the project on identifying military sites that were used for clandestine detention centers. To date, we have identified over 600 such centers, or 300 more than were known at the time of the CONADEP. Each time we make a positive identification—and this only after extensive physical examinations and corroborated testimony—I meet with the commanding officer of the geographic area. This is not exactly welcome news for them, but many times they want to participate in the ceremony and press conference."[22]

Could that be mere public relations?

"It is public relations. But when I present these findings, I am representing the President of the Nation, and she is the Commander in Chief."

The National Memory Archive has been integral to the trials. It is located in the complex known informally as the ex-ESMA, and officially as the Space for Memory, Promotion and Defense of Human Rights. Created by an act of law in 2004, the complex (still a work in progress) will house the major human rights groups, including the Madres and Abuelas de Plaza de Mayo. There is a cultural center, named for the missing *engagé* writer Haroldo Conti, with exhibition, performance, and seminar spaces; and even though the buildings are not totally renovated, there has been scholarly, arts, and outreach activity (see Figs. 21 and 22). Guided visits— often led by survivors—may be taken of the places that once functioned as *capucha* and *pecera*.[23] The Archive not only houses materials pertaining to 1974–83, it also has the charge to investigate. "That we carry out that mission and do it *here*, at what was formerly 'the Argentine Auschwitz,' is more than a gesture, or a symbol; it is a concrete way of taking back those places of horror, of re-infusing them with purposes at once humane and intellectually rigorous," explains Said, who lost family in the camps of the Dirty War. "We work not only on the last dictatorship, but on every period when rights were violated. We investigate, compile, and organize materials not only about the crimes that were committed but also about society's responses to those events. We look at labor unions, for example, social groups, unofficial as well as official contexts. Memory for us is dynamic; it is action; it is plural, and in a permanent state of energy and evolution."

When I ask Martín Gras, Secretary for the Promotion of Human Rights, about the theme of memory, he startles me by saying, "I don't want to talk about memory."[24] One of about 100 *desaparecidos* to survive the ESMA, he is a witness in the trial. Charged to work with the Ministry of Defense on the development of academic curricula, he works with high-ranking officers every day.

"My work is oriented toward the future. We are in truth beset with threats to our security, the worst of which is inequality. In Buenos Aires, we have 410,000 youths who neither have work nor study. Unemployment remains high. People need to have the hope of bettering themselves, of their children having better lives than they. Ordinary crime has risen sharply. The middle class feels vulnerable, victimized. These are the kinds of situations that encourage the rise of politicians like Macri [the right-wing mayor of Buenos Aires City], when what we need is a better societal sense of human rights. In the old days, the conception was 'security' vs. 'human rights,' or Right vs. Left, if you will. Our job is to inculcate the sense that human rights cover everyone, and that the State must be the

FIGURE 21. The Parque de la Memoria is a 14-hectare sculpture park on the banks of the Plate River in the northernmost section of Buenos Aires City. Intended to be a site for reflection on the recent past, it was inaugurated in 2007, after years of planning and an international sculpture competition, which attracted 665 entries from 44 countries. Twelve were selected; six distinguished Argentine artists were invited to contribute works. *30,000*, by Nicolás Guagnini. Consisting of 25 straight prisms, the image is the face of the artist's missing father. "It is the photo my grandfather used in marches," he has said. The features appear and disappear, depending on where the viewer stands. (Photo copyright © by Cristina Fraire, 2009)

guarantor of security of person, freedom of mind and spirit, the right to hope, to have ambitions, and the societal resources to help one realize those ambitions."

No one I spoke with in the human rights community disagrees.

The Secretariat of Human Rights houses the Institute Against the Discrimination of Persons, the Registry of Abandoned Children, as well as

FIGURE 22. Another sculpture in the Parque de la Memoria is *Reconstruction of the Portrait Pablo Miguez*, by Claudia Fontes. The artist tried to capture the signature stance of this fourteen-year-old *desaparecido*. The oxidized sculpture is made to float at varying depths according to the river's waves and currents, and to dip according to the wind. (Photo copyright © by Cristina Fraire, 2009)

departments on public health, mental health, and labor. When Duhalde was appointed in 2003, Human Rights had a small basement office. There are now over 600 professional employees in two modernized buildings. "This is not about territory," Duhalde stresses. "We must be present in the infrastructure of the State. If human rights are to be guaranteed, they cannot exist or not exist at the whim of a particular administration. Governments will come and go; the protection of human rights—the development of the very concept—needs to be permanent."

I remark that I have been impressed that the civil institutions are being re-invigorated by some of the most castigated Argentines—ex-political prisoners, *ex-desaparecidos*, relatives of the missing, former exiles who have leadership positions in government, NGOs, universities and research organizations, as well as certain sectors of the press.

"Some of us have been granted a second chance," says Gras, "a second life even. It has not been easy. But I think the project was always to build a better society—we can argue about methods and the finer points of

FIGURE 23. Neighborhood associations started the *baldosa* movement, in which plaques are placed to mark where *desaparecidos* lived, worked, or studied. When these are vandalized, they are repaired or replaced in public actions. This baldosa is located in the neighborhood of San Cristóbal, Buenos Aires City, on Avenida San Juan. (Photo copyright © by Cristina Fraire, 2009)

ideology—but yes, the effort has been conscious, perhaps even unconscious, and above all tenacious."

There is widespread agreement that H.I.J.O.S. [Sons and Daughters of the Disappeared] is the most important political/human rights group to have emerged in the new democracy (see Figs. 23 and 24). Their *escraches*—communal marches to the homes of known repressors, whose outer walls are spray painted with *Asesino, Violador, Raptor de niños*—have had a simple message: We know who you are and you cannot live among us as a normal citizen. A society that for years evaded the question, "What have you done with our children?" was forced a generation later to confront

FIGURE 24. A pioneering investigative reporter and founder of *Prensa Latina*, a left-wing press service, Rodolfo Walsh was murdered on March 25, 1977, by members of Task Group 3.3.2, in the Plaza Constitución. His remains, which were identified by *ex-desaparecidos*, have never been returned to his family. The Plazoleta Rodolfo Walsh, pictured here, was instigated by H.I.J.O.S. (Sons and Daughters of the Disappeared) and dedicated in 2005. (Photo copyright © by Cristina Fraire, 2009)

those who demanded answers about their missing, massacred parents. The *escrache*—which translated crudely-- means "to be outed." But the word has come to signify much more—a communal demand for transparency, justice, and solidarity. It is a word that overflows with energy—a fitting lesson to the old from the young.

Gras insists, "The most remarkable thing in our democracy is what has *not* happened: there has not been a single instance of a survivor or relative of a *desaparecido* taking justice into his own hands. *Not one instance in over thirty years.*"

Which brings us round again to Jorge Julio López.

And to the work of Gerardo dell'Oro. His images are quiet, intimate, black-and-white. His parents, Mariana, his sisters and brother-in-law. There are pages from Jorge Julio López. There is a series on trees, begun during the Truth Trials in 1999.

I remember how during our visit he quoted from a poem at once lyrical, political, and a statement of plain fact:

Existe la creencia de que los árboles respiran el aliento de las personas que habitan las ciudades enterradas.[25]

"There is a belief that trees breathe the breath of those who inhabit graveyards."

It is an Argentine double helix of a wish—a peaceful home for the dead, who are sheltered by a living canopy.

Notes

PREFACE

1. The figure given by the Mothers of the Plaza de Mayo, 30,000, has the greatest currency in Argentine human rights circles. According to *Le Monde* July 27, 1979), Argentine courts rejected over 20,000 writs of habeas corpus between 1977 and 1979. See Alvaro Abós, *El carnívoro* (Buenos Aires: Editorial Legasa, 1985), 92.

2. Lorenzo Miguel has been particularly vociferous on this point. As head of the "62 Organizations," a major Peronist labor confederation, Miguel was held prisoner with Menem on the *Treinta y tres orientales,* a naval ship moored in Buenos Aires Harbor.

3. Griselda Gambaro, *Information for Foreigners and Other Plays.* edited, translated, and introduced by Marguerite Feitlowitz, afterword by Diana Taylor (Evanston: Northwestern University Press, 1992.)

4. *Nunca Más: The Report of the Argentine National Commission on the Disappeared* (New York: Farrar Straus Giroux and London: Index on Censorship, 1986). Published in Spanish in 1984.

INTRODUCTION : THE GENTLEMEN'S COUP

1. See my "Dance of Death: Eduardo Pavlovsky's *Paso de dos,*" an essay accompanied by interviews with the artists. *The Drama Review* 35, no. 2 (Summer 1991): 60–73. The play's title translates *as pas de deux.*

2. The Mothers' national base of operations is the Casa de las Madres, located near the Congress in the heart of Buenos Aires. All of the provinces and most major cities in Argentina have a local branch of the Mothers. In 1986, internal disagreements impelled about a dozen Mothers, most of whom were among the originators of the organization, to form their own group, the Mothers of the Plaza de Mayo—Founding Line. Among the

members of this latter group—which has a completely egalitarian structure—are María Adela Antokoletz, Laura Bonaparte, Nora de Cortiñas, Renée Epelbaum, Matilde Mellibovsky, and Chela Mignone. The president of the other group of Mothers is Hebe de Bonafini. Among the subjects on which the two groups have conflicting views are exhumations of cadavers and government indemnifications to survivors and their relatives, both of which Bonafini strongly opposes. "We will not be contented with a bag of bones," Bonafini has railed, when asked about exhumations of mass graves. She has referred to indemnifications as "blood money," a position that many *ex-desaparecidos* find insulting and cruel. Bonafini's group maintains its profile as the radical opposition to whatever party might be in power; the Mothers of the Plaza—Founding Line agitate from within the system, consulting the Congress on new and pending legislation, working on behalf of political candidates, and so on. On issues where the two groups agree, they work together.

3. One of the most puzzling aspects of this controversy had to do with the stellar artistic team, particularly director Laura Yusem, author/actor Eduardo Pavlovsky, and Susana Evans, all long active in human rights. During the last dictatorship, Pavlovsky, also a well-known psychiatrist, escaped a heavily armed military commando by jumping out the window of his office, and then fleeing to Spain. Ideologically, he is a pacifist; as an artist he displays an obsessive need not only to write but to act the role of torturers, in an increasingly graphic way.

4. For an excellent study of Perón, see Juan José Sebreli's *Los Deseos imaginarios del peronismo* (Buenos Aires: Editorial Legasa, 1983).

5. Alain Rouquié, *Pouvoir militaire el société politique en république Argentine* (Paris: Presses de la Fondation Nationale des Sciences Politiques, 1978). On the subject of Uriburu, see Introduction, 176–206, chap. 5, and 694–96.

6. Ibid., 655.

7. As her husband's vice president, Isabel Perón assumed the presidency on the death of Juan Domingo Perón, July 1, 1974. The latter was president of Argentina from 1946 to 1955 and 1973 to 1974.

8. Decree No. 261, signed by Isabel Perón on February 5, 1975, charged the commander in chief of the army with the *"erradicación de elementos subversivos."* The decree gave the army operational control of the Federal Police and the Provincial Police of Tucumán (a stronghold for the ERP, the leftist People's Revolutionary Army). Decrees 2770, 2771, and 2772, signed on October 6, 1975, extended army control over all Provincial and Federal Police in the entire territory of Argentina. Signed by acting president Italo Luder during Isabel Perón's extended sick leave (strongly encouraged by the military), these decrees also provided for the creation of a Defense Counsel and a Council for Internal Security to aid in the planning and coordination of the "eradication of subversive elements." See Daniel Frontalini and Maria Cristina Caiati, *El Mito de la guerra sucia* (Buenos Aires: CELS, 1984), 74.

9. See Frontalini and Caiati, *El Mito,* 72. These numbers for leftist guerrillas were confirmed for me in an interview I did in September 1990 with a former Montonero who for a time managed the group's weapons. At his request, I omit the name of this interviewee, who lived clandestinely as a Montonero and later left the group as a dissident. In its

lying Final Report (May 1983) the junta declared victory over "25,000 subversives, 15,000 of whom were armed combatants."

Prudencio García, in *El Drama de la autonomía militar* (Madrid: Alianza Editorial, 1996), 53–54, gives the complete breakdown of deaths caused by leftist guerrillas: The Buenos Aires Provincial Police suffered 141 assassinations; the Federal Police 119; Córdoba Provincial Police 48; Santa Fe Provincial Police 35. Among the military, the army lost 105; the navy, 19; air force, 10; and gendarmes, 9. García's numbers come from the junta.

10. Videla made this declaration in Montevideo at the Eleventh Conference of Latin American Armies. Quoted in *Clarín*, Argentina's largest-circulation daily, on October 24, 1975.

11. David Rock, *Argentina 1516–1987: From Spanish Colonization to Alfonsín* (Berkeley: Univ. of California Press, 1987), 365.

12. He would later regret this remark. In the late 1970s Borges disappointed many in the literary and international human rights communities for his reluctance to actively protest the regime. (Borges and his aristocratic family were wary of democracy and bitterly anti-Peronist. In the late 1940s, Perón's government transferred the poet from his job at the National Library and reassigned him to inspecting poultry.) However in September 1980, Borges gave an interview in Italy in which he said, "People have come to see me, one woman whose daughter has been missing for four years. For a while now I have been receiving letters in which people tell me such things. . . . If crimes have been committed it is necessary to investigate. They say that the number of victims has been exaggerated, but one case is enough; Cain slew Abel only once; Christ only once was crucified." Originally quoted in the Italian weekly *Panorama* (September 15, 1980); reprinted in Oscar Troncoso, *El Proceso de reorganización nacional, vol 4: Cronología y documentación* (Buenos Aires: Centro Editor de América Latina, 1992), p. 120.

In mid-1985 Borges went one day to watch the trial of the ex-commanders, saying afterward, "Massera [ex-commander of the Navy] is a murderer, one of the most sinister individuals in this country." In the same interview he lamented, "It will be difficult to get justice because there are too many individuals involved. That's why it seems to me important that you put out this newspaper [devoted exclusively to the trial], because people forget quickly. This is a defect that is very Argentine." *El Diario del Juicio*, no. 10, July 30, 1985, p. 208.

13. Timerman was the founding editor of, among other publications, the renowned daily *La Opinión*. The quotes appeared there on March 26 and 27, 1976. In the early '70s, Timerman wrote numerous editorials against the armed left, and received death threats from them in reply. Of course in time he would come to abhor the military dictatorship, which kidnapped, tortured, and illegally detained him for over two years (April 1977–September 1979). See his important memoir, *Prisoner Without a Name, Cell Without a Number* (London: Weidenfeld & Nicolson and New York: Alfred A. Knopf, 1981). It appeared in Spanish under the tittle *Preso sin nombre, celda sin número* (1980).

14. From his interview with *Extra*, forty-eight hours after the coup. Paladino was asked, "What happened on March 24, what is going to happen now?" In Spanish, his complete sentence (which I compressed) reads, *"Y en este caso las Fuerzas Armadas no han hecho más que aceptar* [emphasis in original] *un pedido general, tácito y/o expreso de la*

ciudadanía, para, con su intervención, encarar una crisis de supervivencia de la Nación que las instituciones formales y las organizaciones civiles demostraron ser incapaces e impotentes para resolver." See Troncoso, *El Proceso, vol. 1* (Buenos Aires: Centro Editor de America Latina, 1984), 114–16.

15. *Nunca Más,* 443.

16. Ibid, 444.

17. Ibid. Distributed in Argentina as War Office Bulletin No. 3411, September 10, 1964.

18. At a meeting in Argentina of the Western Hemisphere defense ministers, U.S. Defense Secretary William Perry vowed that the U.S. army would never again train Latin American soldiers in the tactics of terror. Perry's comments, reported by Reuters, are found in the *Boston Globe,* October 9, 1996, p. A5.

19. Congressman Joseph P. Kennedy II has for years worked to get the SOA closed. He has proposed a bill to transform the SOA into the United States Academy for Democracy and Civil—Military Relations, which would have an emphasis on human rights. For sending me excerpts of the manual and other documentation, I thank Suzy Glucksman, Kennedy's legislative assistant in Washington, D.C. The Congressman's Boston office was also extremely helpful. I got no help from the SOA itself. My call of September 10, 1996, was referred to one Captain McGiver, who identified himself as the new Public Relations Director. He promised to call me back with further information about the manuals on Friday, September 13, but he never did.

20. SOA Study Manual, "Handling of Sources," 1989, 4.

21. SOA Study Manual, "Counter intelligence," 1991, 263.

22. Ibid.

23. SOA Study Manual, "Handling of Sources," 14.

24. Testimony of Graciela Geuna. My thanks to CELS for providing me with this document.

25. Patricia Astelarra and Gustavo Contemponi, *Sobrevivientes de la Perla* (Buenos Aires: El Cid Editor, 1984), 30, 32, 34, 47.

26. See Rita Maran, *Torture: The Role of Idealogy in the French–Algerian War* (New York: Praeger, 1989), 49.

27. Ibid., 52.

28. Interview with *La Prensa,* a major daily, on January 4, 1981. Also in Frontalini and Caiati, *El Mito,* 31–32.

29. See Ricardo Rodríguez Molas, *Historia de la tortura y el orden represivo en la Argentina* (Buenos Aires: Editorial Universitaria de Buenos Aires, 1984), 97–99.

30. Ibid., 128. Sàbato used *El Mundo argentino,* the magazine he edited, as a forum. When he was persecuted for this action, the Argentine Society of Writers refused even to make a statement in his defense.

31. All quotes come from the *Documento final de la junta militar sobre la guerra contra la subversión y el terrorismo,* published in its entirety in all the major dailies. My copy ran as a "Suplemento Especial" in *Convicción,* April 29, 1983.

32. See, for example, Emilio Fermín Mignone, Cynthia Estlund, and Samuel Issacharoff, "Dictatorship on Trial: Prosecution of Human Rights Violations in Argentina," *Yale*

Journal of International Law, 10 (Fall 1984): 118–50. See also the reply by Carlos Santiago Nino, ibid. 11 (Fall 1985): 217–30.

33. See *Culpables para la sociedad, impunes por la ley* (Buenos Aires: CELS, 1988). The Punto Final is usually translated as the Full Stop law.

34. I interviewed the late Professor Nino on March 11, 1993, at the Yale Law School, where he was teaching a two-month seminar on human rights law. A legal philosopher, he was on the permanent faculty of the Law School of the University of Buenos Aires. As support for his statement that Argentina was "not an essentially violent country," he offered its comparably low murder rate, and the fact that not one civilian has tried to assassinate or physically injure any individual involved in the repression. Professor Nino died of a heart attack in August 1993.

35. Quoted in *Mother Jones*, February 1985.

36. I am not implying that every *individual* was complicit.

37. Interview with the author. May 14, 1990. Camilión did not at that time occupy a government post. He had run, unsuccessfully, for the Chamber of Deputies, on the slogan he repeated to me. His position on the importance of "forgetting" has, if anything, hardened.

38. See *Página 12*, July 2, 1993.

39. See Noga Tarnapolsky "Murdering Memory in Argentina," *New York Times* editorial, December 12, 1994. Tarnapolsky is Daniel's cousin and the Jerusalem correspondent for *The Forward*.

40. The family asked that I alter this name.

41. Interview with "Federico T.," Buenos Aires, July 1992.

CHAPTER 1. A LEXICON OF TERROR

1. Videla's widely disseminated statement on the two-month anniversary of the coup, May 24, 1976. Quote reproduced in Troncoso, *El Proceso*, vol. 1, 29.

2. From "La Postergación de un destino" ("Postponing Destiny"), a speech Massera made to the navy at the end of 1976. Collected in Emilio Massera, *El Camino a la democracia* (Buenos Aires: El Cid Editor, 1979).

3. I interviewed Epelbaum regularly from mid-1990 until the end of 1995. This quote is from our first interview, July 12, 1990.

4. See Troncoso, *El Proceso*, vol. 1, 107–113.

5. The Alberte story is recounted by Miguel Bonasso, "Respuesta de ultratumba," *Página 12*, April 4, 1996, p. 8. Alberte's letter goes on much longer, cataloguing a century of Argentine military violence, particularly against workers. Bonasso resurrected this incident in the context of a current scandal: The chairman of the joint chiefs. Lieutenant General Mario Candido Díaz, had days before praised "the fallen and the veterans of the fight against subversion" and "categorically rejected the protest commemorations" during the 20th Anniversary of the coup. Alberte's murdered colleague was Máximo Augusto Altieri; the young man's body was found in the cemetery of Avellaneda, a city just outside the capital. Neither President Menem nor Defense Minister Oscar Camilión offered a reaction

to Diaz's speech, in spite of calls from human rights groups that he be reprimanded, or at the very least rebutted.

6. Troncoso, *El Proceso*, vol. 1, 111. From Article 1 of the Acta Fijando el Propósito y los Objetivos Básicos para el Proceso de Reorganización Nacional: ". . . *a fin de asegurar la posterior instauración de una democracia republicana, representante y federal*" [emphasis in original]. And from Article 2.1, "*Concreción de una soberanía política basada en el accionar de instituciones constitucionales revitalizadas. . . .*"

7. "Sin ira y sin odio" ("Without ire or hate"), editorial in *La Prensa*, March 25, 1976. The paper's style can be described as "intellectual": references to antiquity abound; philosophers, historians, and literary figures are also mentioned frequently. *La Prensa* of those years is in all things anti-Peronist. It considered that movement to be the source of virtually all the country's ills.

8. *Para Tí*, April 12, 1976.

9. Videla's speech was covered in all the media. My copy is from *La Prensa*, March 27, 1976.

10. *La Nación*, March 29, 1976.

11. Viola made this statement on May 29, 1979. In Abós, *El Poder carnívoro*, 31.

12. "Se abatió en Buenos Aires a 12 terroristas," *La Prensa*, January 6, 1977, pp. 1–2.

13. Quoted originally in *La Nación* on January 22, 1976. See also Frontalini and Caiati, *El Mito*, 23.

14. Nicolaides was interviewed by *La Razón* on June 6, 1976. Quoted in Frontalini and Caiati, *El Mito*, 22.

15. From "El Rol de los empresarios y de las fuerzas armadas en el momento actual"("The Role of Businessmen and the Armed Forces at the Present Moment"), a speech he gave in 1976. Collected in Massera, *El Camino*, 41–45, esp. 44–45. The admiral was a master at manipulating hypocrisy. The quote in the body of the text is from a speech he gave to an audience of businessmen: Early on, he imputed their drive to generate wealth to their sense of "the common good, social responsibility." Making clear that he was merely *reminding* his audience, Massera stressed that "a government is not, cannot be, a technostructure. . . . It should use its technostructure to solve mechanical problems, but without ever abdicating its metaphysical principles. . . . Which is why the government knows that man does not live by bread alone." He went on to say that "reeducation" was needed in all productive sectors of society, "because the Republic needed everyone . . . and no one has the right to fall short of the exigencies of the moment."

16. From Videla's press conference with British journalists, in *La Nación*, December 18, 1977, pp. 1 and 18.

17. *La Prensa* (August 16, 1977) ran its article on Feced's speech under the following headline: "Con los subversivos sólo con el plomo dialogaremos" ("With Subversives We'll Dialogue Only With Lead"). The ceremony, full of pomp and circumstance, was attended by a host of luminaries, including the provincial governor (Vice Admiral Jorge Aníbal Desimoni), the provincial police chief (Colonel Alberto Ramírez), and the second-in-command of the Second Army Corps (General Jorge Aníbal Ferrero).

18. In this statement to cadets on April 23, 1976, Bignone warned that "the military and police uniforms were attractive targets to those who were anti-fatherland, to these agents of the antichrist. You young Argentines who, despite the risk wear the uniform, must assume your full responsibilities, must know how to respond each time circumstances demand it of you."

19. Horacio Verbitsky, ed., *La Prensa clandestina* (Buenos Aires: Ediciones de la Urraca, 1985), 50. This volume is a compilation of the news reports done by ANCLA, the underground agency founded by the pioneering writer/journalist Rodolfo Walsh, who was murdered by the state in 1977. During its short lifetime ANCLA was one of the best—perhaps the best—sources of information on the Argentine situation. Its contributors included reporters who could not bring to their own publications the stories they passed on to ANCLA. Many reports in the international press originated with ANCLA.

20. Ibid., 56.

21. "Los Muertos por la patria," in Massera, *El Camino*, 15–18.

22. Ibid., 49–50.

23. Ibid., 43–44.

24. Ibid., 49–50.

25. From "Creemos" ("We Believe"), ibid., 63.

26. See *La Nación* and *Clarín*, December 18, 1977.

27. Videla's statement of November 12, 1978, is cited in Abós, *El Poder carnívoro*, 66.

28. Videla, July 29, 1979. In ibid., 67.

29. The date of this famous declaration is December 19, 1979. In ibid., 53.

30. Videla's U.S. television appearance was September 14, 1977. See Troncoso, *El Proceso*, vol. 2: 63–64.

31. I visited with Fanny and José Bendersky at their home in Buenos Aires on July 12, 1992. They kindly gave me copies of the letters from MIT and Senator Kennedy.

32. In Troncoso, *El Proceso*, vol. 2: 68.

33. Videla's statement to journalists on April 12, 1976 is cited in Troncoso, *El Proceso* vol. 1: 17.

34. Ibid., 23–24.

35. Ibid., 88. Originally a radio broadcast.

36. "The Quiet and Subtle Cyclone," in Massera, *El Camino*, 51. The speech was made on Navy Day (May 3), 1977.

37. From "Dissentir en paz," ("Dissenting in Peace"), in Massera, *El Camino*, 102. The text is not dated, but the speech was given to CARBAP, an agribusiness association that was objecting to having to pay certain taxes. Massera's aim was, of course, to get their compliance.

38. From "The Quiet and Subtle Cyclone," in ibid., 51.

39. Massera, May 5, 1977. In Troncoso, *El Proceso*, vol. 2:14.

40. This information comes from Federal Police Inspector Rodolfo Peregrino Fernández, who was himself an adviser to Harguindeguy from April 1976 until January 1977. I am grateful to the Permanent Assembly for Human Rights (APDH) in Buenos Aires for providing me with a copy of the testimony he made before the Argentine Commission

for Human Rights on October 8, 1983. Peregrino Fernández opposed the methods of the de facto government, was forced from the police on trumped-up charges of fraud, and left the country in fear for his life in 1980. The two Nazi ideologues were Alberto Villar, who, as Federal Police Chief organized the precursor of the lethal Triple A (Argentine Anti-Communist Alliance), and Federal Police Commander Jorge Mario Veyra. Peregrino Fernández asserts that even though Harguindeguy was supposed to keep track of the detentions, the volume and intensity of operations overwhelmed the ministry's capabilities, and they really had no idea how many people had been taken. Regarding the minister's own kidnapping ring, Peregrino Fernández said this: "[He] had personal and direct responsibility in every aspect of the clandestine repression through the formation of an operations brigade . . . devoted to illegal acts, such as the kidnap of persons whose political activity was of direct interest to the Minister, or who constituted special cases that had to be handled within the realm of the [Ministry]. The brigade was headed by [among others] Federal Police Officer Juan Carlos Falcón, alias "Kung Fu," [and] Inspector Norberto Cajal, alias "Beto" [a nickname suggesting *betonero*, "cement mixer"]. . . . When the risk outstripped the capacity of this group, they got assistance from the Director of Federal Security, Police Commissioner Juan Carlos Lapouyole." All three of these men were beneficiaries of the Punto Final law: Falcón also served at the camp called El Olimpo; Cajal, a member of Task Force 2, was a kidnapping specialist; Lapouyole (known as "El Francés," or "The Frenchman") ran the concentration camp in the headquarters of Federal Security.

41. From statements made on August 21, 1976, in the northwestern city of Salta. Cited in Troncoso, *El Proceso*, vol. 1: 60.

42. Ibid., 75. Harguindeguy said this in Tucumán on October 11, 1976.

43. Harguindeguy gave this warning in the northeastern city of Posadas on July 15, 1977. See Troncoso, *El Proceso*, vol. 2: 45.

44. Cited in "Informe *de* EE.UU sobre Argentina: El Mundial en una cárcel," *Cambio 16*, January 2, 1978, pp. 38–40.

45. In Troncoso, *El Proceso*, vol. 2: 117.

46. Feced, *La Prensa*, August 16, 1977.

47. Widely disseminated statement from May 1976.

48. Viola, in an interview with *La Razón*, May 29, 1979.

49. Videla, October 24, 1977. In Abós, *El Poder carnívoro*, 63.

50. Clausewitz (1780–1831), the Prussian general and writer who greatly influenced Perón, held that "war is the continuation of politics by other means." Clausewitz founded the Military Academy in Berlin. Perón reversed the Prussian's formulation: "Politics is the continuation of war by other means."

51. Menéndez, May 9, 1978. In Troncoso, *El Proceso*, vol. 2: 123.

52. Harguindeguy, September 13, 1977. In ibid., 63.

53. Sebreli, *Deseos*, 189. Perón's "lower forms of the species" is a clear echo of the Nazis. The Dirty War juntas generally avoided such references to evolution and modern biology, which they associated with "subversion," in favor of a "metaphysical" idiom.

54. From a speech given at the John F. Kennedy University in Buenos Aires, in Massera, *El Camino*, 121.

55. From a speech delivered on December 12, 1979. In Troncoso, H *Proceso*, vol. 4: 24.

56. From "Postponing Destiny," in Massera, *El Camino*, 22.

57. See Sebreli, *Deseos*, 33. The hospital in question is El Hospital Ramos *Mejía*, located at Urquiza 556, opposite Commissary No. 8.

58. From "Derecho al mar" ("The Right to the Sea"), in Massera, *El Camino*, 38.

59. This statement was made at an air force ceremony on May 27, 1977. In Troncoso, *El Proceso*, vol. 2: 28–29.

60. From Videla's press conference at the airport in Iguazú, on August 12, 1976. In Troncoso, *El Proceso*, vol. 1: 56. When Anmesty International delegates went to Argentina in 1977 for a one-week fact-finding mission, the junta intensified its operations, kidnapping 400 Argentines during those seven days.

61. The Archbishop made this statement on May 13, 1979.

62. Videla, June 26, 1978. In Troncoso, *El Proceso*, vol. 2: 133.

63. See Prudencio García, *El Drama*, 475–77. This section is filled out from my conversations with Argentines who were parents and students during the regime.

64. Massera, *El Camino*, 88.

65. From "Venimos a traer el mar a los Andes" ("We Come to Bring the Sea to the Andes"), speech given in Salta to inaugurate the first Naval Lyceum for women. In Massera, *El Camino*, 54–55.

66. *Para Tí*, November 20, 1978. For a more linguistically technical study of *Para Tí* from 1976 to 1984, see María Magdalena Chirico, "El Proyecto autoritario y la prensa para la mujer: Un ejemplo de discurso intermediario," in *El Discurso político: Lenguajes y acontecimientos* (Buenos Aires: Hachette, 1987), 55–85. Oscar Landi (also a contributor to the volume) mentioned Chirico's work to me in mid-1990; at that point, however, my research emphasis lay elsewhere. By the time I consulted this fine article, in early 1994, I had finished my own examination of *Para Tí*.

67. *Para Tí*, November 20, 1978.

68. Ibid.

69. Ibid., May 22, 1978. The text uses the folksy *feria* as a synonym for market, reinforcing its exhortation that the magazine's readers be modern, sophisticated: "*Usted no puede refugiarse en el simple: 'A mí lo único que me importa es cómo aumentaron los precios en la feria.'*"

70. Ibid., November 20, 1978.

71. Ibid., September 24, 1979. Editorial signed by Lucrezia Gordilloy and Augustín Bottinelli, editorial directors.

72. The interview appeared on September 3, just three days before the arrival of the OAS delegation, which stayed until September 21.

73. See Troncoso, *El Proceso*, vol. 1: 25–26. The PR convention opened on April 18, 1976.

74. From a phone interview with Emmanuel on September 27, 1996. Emmanuel also said that he thought the trials of the ex-commanders were "legitimate," that "Harguindeguy was a thug," that "things got out of control." When I asked his reaction to Adolfo Scilingo's confession about his participation in the Navy's death flights (see Chapter 6),

346   NOTES TO PAGES 49–56

Emmanuel surprised me by saying, "What people do to each other almost defies belief. As we speak, people are probably being thrown out of planes over Palestine, Iraq, Burundi. Nothing astonishes me anymore." Yet he continued to insist that the way to address the human tendency to violence was through a free-market global economy.

75. My quotes from the BM report in this section are taken from two sources: Andrea Fishman and Richard Alan White, "The Selling of Argentina: Madison Ave. Packages Repression," *Los Angeles Times,* June 11, 1978, and R. Scott Greathead, "Truth in Argentina," *New York Times* editorial. May 11, 1995, p. A29. Fishman was Southern California coordinator of Amnesty International; White a professor of Latin American Studies at California State University, Los Angeles. Amnesty International obtained a copy of the report in 1978, a year after it received the Nobel Peace Prize. This is a well-balanced article, which emphasizes that Burson Marsteller was acting totally within U.S. law. BM is cited (among other agencies) as evidence in a larger argument: "In a society based on free enterprise, businesses such as Burson Marsteller and other international public relations agencies cannot be condemned merely for seeking a profit. On the other hand, the United States long ago recognized that the drive for profit cannot go entirely unrestrained. Thus, America has enacted laws requiring 'truth in advertising.' If Madison Ave. is prohibited from making false claims on behalf of a mouthwash, why should its advocacy of a foreign government's interests not be subjected to careful legal scrutiny?" Whitehead, a member of the board of directors of the Lawyers Committee for Human Rights, was writing in the wake of the confessions of Scilingo et al.(see Chapter 6). He addressed the history of pardons that has allowed perpetrators of the Dirty War to avoid accounting for the missing, and urged President Menem to repeal the Punto Final and Due Obedience laws.

76. I am grateful to Juan Mandelbaum for providing me with a copy of this supplement, as well as that which appeared in *Business Week* on July 14, 1980.

77. Emmanuel told me that he had never heard of Saint Jean. When I asked him about Stanley Ross, he replied, "Doesn't ring a bell. Not even a faint gong. Do you mean Bobby Roth?" It appears that "Stanley Ross" is a fiction. Bobby Roth, Emmanuel told me, was "a prolific, pro-military writer, an attorney who taught at the University of Buenos Aires." Going on Emmanuel's comment, it would seem that Professor Roth did some writing directly for the regime. U.S. readers were deceived yet again: Not even the captions in this supplement were reliable.

78. From my interview with Susana and Osvaldo Barros on August 13, 1990.

79. For Cabezas's trial testimony, see *El Diario del Juicio,* no. 10, June 30, 1985, pp. 230–31, and no. 25, November 12, 1985, pp. 465–73. The entire Atlántida publishing group, which owned *Somos* and *Gente,* as well as *Para Ti,* was coopted by the regime, as its magazines clearly demonstrate. In 1984, *Somos* ran two articles on "rehabilitation camps for subversives" described as providing a "familial atmosphere" and staffed by lawyers, priests, doctors, and psychologists. The pieces on these non-existent facilities were accompanied by trumped up–photographs.

80. From our interview of July 6, 1990.

81. From his speech of May 29, 1979. In Argentina, May 29 is Army Day.

82. This secret manual was unearthed by the American Association of Jurists, Argentine Branch, which published excerpts in *Juicio a los militares: Documentos secretos, decretos, leyes, jurisprudencia* (Buenos Aires: Associación Americana de Juristas, 1988), 16. I was reminded of these orders by Juan Gelman's eloquent column in *Página 12*, November 22, 1995.

83. See *Nunca Más*, 164.

84. *Testimonio sobre campos secretos de detención en Argentina*, (Buenos Aires: Amnesty International, 1980), 25–28. Oscar Alfredo González ("X–15") and Horacio Guillermo Cid de la Paz ("X–86") managed to escaped from detention on February 18, 1979. González had been held over a period of fifteen months in two camps; Cid de la Paz spent over two years in a total of four camps.

85. See *Nunca Más*, 222.

86. Ibid., 167.

87. Ibid., 130.

88. Ibid, 57.

89. González and Cid de la Paz, *Testimonio*, 20.

90. *Nunca Más*, 129. See also Muñoz's extensive trial testimony in *El Diario del Juicio*, no. 24, November 5, 1985, pp. 452–64.

91. *Nunca Más, 164.*

92. González and Cid de la Paz, *Testimonio*, 5.

93. See *Nunca Más*, 30.

94. Trial testimony of Graciela Beatriz Daleo, in *El Diario del Juicio*, no. 22, October 22, 1985, pp. 421–31, esp. 423.

95. González and Cid de la Paz, *Testimonio*, 5, 20.

96. Ibid., 26.

97. *Nunca Más*, 162–63.

98. Ibid., 39.

99. Gras's testimony before CELS runs to forty pages. The passage quoted here is found on p. 4. He was kidnapped on January 14, 1977, and held in the ESMA until 1979. He was a former professor at the National University of Tucumán and served the Municipality and Province of Tucumán in various official capacities. Under the military dictatorship of Alejandro Lanusse, he was arrested for being a Peronist activist on August 18, 1971, and then amnestied on May 26, 1973. (The Peronist Party was then proscribed.) After his release from the ESMA, he was granted refugee status in Spain, under the provisions of the Geneva Convention of 1951.

100. González and Cid de la Paz reproduce a "work card" in *Testimonio*, 5.

101. *Nunca Más, 31.*

102. Jean Améry, *At the Mind's Limits* (Bloomington: Indiana University Press, 1980), 28–34.

103. See Michel Foucault, *Discipline and Punish* (New York: Vintage Books, 1979). 29–30.

CHAPTER 2. NIGHT AND FOG

1. Born in 1930, Carlos Mujica dropped his law studies in 1951 in order to enter the seminary of Villa Devoto, where he was ordained. In 1959, he left the capital to spend a year in the remote rural north of Santa Fe province. Upon his return to Buenos Aires, he founded a cooperative vicariate, Nuestra Señora del Socorro ("Our Lady of Help"), and was a theological advisor at San Salvador University. He is best known for his pioneering work in the Buenos Aires shantytown of Retiro (near the train and bus station of that name). After spending part of 1968 in France, Mujica returned to Buenos Aires where he founded a movement dedicated specifically to work in *villas miserias* (El Equipo Pastoral para Villas de Emergencia). He was also active in the Third World Priests Movement (discussed in Chapter 4).

2. See Astelarra and Contemponi, *Sobrevivientes de la Perla,* 61–62. For more on Astelarra, see Chapter 6.

3. From my interview with Astelarra in Buenos Aires on June 28, 1995. After 1978, there were proportionately more survivors of La Perla; even so, the vast majority of individuals disappeared there were murdered.

4. Astelarra and Contemponi, *Sobrevivientes de la Perla,* 48.

5. Testimony of Graciela Geuna, unpub. ms. p. 33. My thanks to Daniel Frontalini, then of CELS, for providing me with a copy of this important document. Geuna was in La Perla from June 1976 until April 1978. In May 1979 she managed to leave Argentina on a passport taken out under her maiden name. Even though she was warned to "never say a word" about the camp, she testified to human rights groups soon after arriving in Europe. The prisoners made to participate in the Red Cross farce were Piero Di Monte, Liliana Callizo, and Horacio Dottori. Geuna says that Callizo tried to signal the Red Cross delegates that things were not what they seemed, but was unsuccessful as Barreiro never left the room.

6. Astelarra and Contemponi, *Sobrevivientes de la Perla,* 59–60.

7. Ibid., 60.

8. Ibid., 52.

9. Ibid., 83.

10. Testimony of Gracila Geuna, 31.

11. Astelarra and Contemponi, *Sobrevivientes de la Perla,* 35 and 89; Testimony of Graciela Geuna, 49.

12. Testimony of Graciela Geuna, 32. The deceased activist was named Córdoba; his wife was known as Cleo. *La Voz del Interior,* published in the city of Córdoba, is the main daily for the central provinces of Argentina. Although it may lack the clout of papers from the capital, it is nonetheless the main source of news for a great many Argentines.

13. Testimony of Graciela Geuna, 21.

14. I interviewed Benítez at her home on July 6, 1995. For more about her, see Chapter 4.

15. For more on Susana Dillon, see my "A Daughter of the Disappeared," in *Women's Review of Books,* 10, nos. 10–11 (July 1993): 7–8.

16. From my interview with Yamila Grandi in Buenos Aires on July 16, 1993. I interviewed her grandmother, Julia de Grandi, at her home in Paso del Rey, on July 24, 1993.

17. Testimony of Graciela Geuna, 22.

18. I interviewed Norita in her native city in a central province on August 8, 1993. She asked that I not publish her name out of consideration for her children.

19. See Juan Gelman, "Resistencias," *Página* 12, March 20, 1996. Gelman, one of Argentina's most important poets of this century, writes a regular back-cover column for this daily. The two books Paoletti wrote in captivity were *Poemas con Marcel Proust* and *Poemas con Roberto Arlt*.

20. Villani was kidnapped on the morning of November 18, 1977, at the corner of Jujuy and Garay. From that date until December 28, 1977, he was interned at the camp called El Club Atlètico ("The Athletic Club"); from December 28, 1977 until August 1978 he was in El Banco; from August 1978 until the end of January 1979, he was held in Olympus. These concentration camps were located in Buenos Aires, in buildings controlled by the Federal or Provincial Police. From January 1979 until March 1979 he was in the Quilmes Pit in Buenos Aires Province, run by the Provincial Police. From March 1979 until August 1981, Villani was held in the Navy Mechanics School, located in a beautiful building on manicured grounds in the exclusive Palermo section of Buenos Aires.

21. Villani's testimony of May 22, 1985, was covered in the first issue of *El Diario del Juicio*, May 27, 1985.

22. Villani, Lerner, and I did this first interview on October 6, 1990. I interviewed them on every subsequent research trip to Buenos Aires, and periodically by phone until just before this book went to press.

23. Villani was married to another woman during the years he was held captive. He and Lerner got together after his divorce, during the 1985 trial of the ex-commanders.

24. *Quebrado*, literally "broken" or "twisted," was slang for "collaborator." It is a term I normally do not use, as it rings with accusation. None of us can say for sure what we would do under torture or the constant threat of it.

25. "The Electronic Cat" was Carlos Gattoni, an electronics professor at the Navy Mechanics School. The nickname is a play on his surname, which incorporates *gato*, "cat." "If you don't sing, we'll make you dance with Carolina," prisoners were told. Two other variations on the electric prod were also given female names by the male inventors: Susana and Margarita (whose English translation is "daisy"). Daisy was equipped with sharp appurtenances (a Daisy wheel) that bore into the victim's skin.

26. "*¿No estás demasiado ratoneado?*" Covani asked Villani, a reference to a form of torture using rats. After the trial, "No me ratones" came to mean "Don't bother me" in teenage slang.

27. The Miara case is paradigmatic. As this book goes to press, the Reggiardo–Tolosa twins have yet to be restored to their biological relatives. On television and in documentaries, the boys have shown all the signs of Miara's brainwashing.

28. *El Diario Juicio*, no. 20, October 8, 1985, p. 25.

CHAPTER 3. "LIFE HERE IS NORMAL"

1. The dailies that ran the story were *Nuevo Sur,* June 8, 1990, and *Página* 12, June 9, 1990.The strangeness of the space, and its likely past as a secret detention center, was publicized in June 1987 by the Cinematographic Workers Union. At the time, a crew was shooting a movie called *Las Esclavas* ("The Slaves"). The union contacted the Mothers of the Plaza de Mayo, which investigated and then published an article in their monthly publication. *Las Madres.* Luis Moreno Ocampo, associate prosecutor of the ex-commanders, affirmed that the detention center in the basement of the Galerías Pacífico belonged to the First Army Corps and was under the direct responsibility of General Guillermo Suárez Mason, who in mid-1990 was extradited from California to stand trial for thirty-nine homicides committed during the Dirty War. According to Moreno Ocampo, the space belonged to the Railroad Police until 1973 when it came under the control of Federal Coordination (of Intelligence). The man in charge of interrogations was intelligence agent Raúl Guglielminetti, who during the dictatorship went to prison on some twenty-four criminal charges. He was freed on Due Obedience and served in intelligence during the first years of the new democracy. According to several survivor accounts, Carmen Román was disappeared from Galerías Pacífico. Román, a thirty-five-year-old member of the communist party, was kidnapped with six other individuals from the corner of Callao and Sarmiento (downtown Buenos Aires) on May 20, 1977. Among the features that made the space desirable as a detention center were its structure, a two-tiered basement with direct, discreet access to the street, and its accoustics, which blotted out sound.

2. This appointment took place on July 6, 1990.

3. Matilde believes that the kidnap she saw was carried out by the Triple A, or Argentine Anti-Communist Alliance. The Triple A was founded by the fascistic José López-Rega, Isabel Perón's closest advisor.

4. *Nunca Más!* was reclaimed by the Argentine National Commission on the Disappeared (CONADEP) and serves as the title to its massive report.

5. Some of these details are included in the book Matilde was then completing and which would be published about seven months later. I had the honor of reading the manuscript at her dining-room table. Consisting of her conversations with other Mothers of the Plaza, it is entitled *Círculo de amor sobre la muerte* (Buenos Aires: Ediciones del Pensamiento Nacional, 1990).

6. "L'Immigration juive" ("The Jewish Immigration") appeared on August 22, 1881, as an editorial in *L'Union française.* Quoted in Robert Weisbrot's *The Jews of Argentina* (Philadelphia: Jewish Publication Society, 1979), 45.

7. Interview with Santiago, September 8, 1990.

8. President Hipólito Yrigoyen, a beloved figure of democracy in Argentina, was brutally overthrown by General José Felix Uriburu, who ruled for the next two years.

9. Quilmes is an industrial city just outside Buenos Aires.

10. It is a custom among Jews to place a few small rocks on top of the tombstone when visiting a loved one's grave.

11. I was given a copy of this and other confessions by Graciela Fernández Meijide, president of the Asamblea Permanente por los Derechos Humanos (Permanent Assembly for Human Rights) in Buenos Aires. I made the request on September 10, 1990, two days after my conversation with Santiago.

12. I met with Susana Aguad at her office in Buenos Aires on October 1, 1990. I interviewed Raúl Aragón, who was also present for Valdez's testimony, at the Permanent Assembly for Human Rights on September 21, 1990.

13. The general impression among Argentine Jews is that Rubén Beraja, current president of the DAIA, has done much to professionalize the organization.

14. The pogrom, which took place during the second week of January 1919, is known as the Tragic Week *(la semana trágica)*. It was the culminating event in a chain reaction. First the metal workers in Vasena went on strike and, in their anger, vandalized machinery. Factory owners called in the police, who killed one worker and wounded forty. That sparked a nationwide general strike, which brought the economy to a halt. The government's efforts to repress workers coincided with a newspaper campaign against "outside agitators" and a "Bolshevik conspiracy." Police and right-wing agitators set upon Jews with impunity, killing 700, wounding approximately 4000, and vandalizing Jewish neighborhoods, homes, businesses, and synagogues. See Weisbrot, *Jews of Argentina,* 200–201. The definitive book-length study is *La Semana trágica* by Nahum Solominsky (Buenos Aires: Biblioteca Popular Judía, 1971).

15. Interview with Nehemías Resnizky, July 21, 1992, at his law office.

16. Meyer recounted this to me on several occasions. It was also cited in the *New York Times,* November 7, 1992.I interviewed Meyer periodically between 1990 and 1993. He very kindly offered me free access to his extensive files on his years in Argentina.

17. See Ignacio Klich, "Política comunitaria durante las juntas militares argentinas: La DAIA durante el proceso de reorganización nacional," in *El Antisemitismo en la Argentina,* Leonardo Senkman, ed. (Buenos Aires: Centro Editor de América Latina, 1989). Father Weeks's quote appears in a paragraph on the House hearings, p. 285. Klich was the first scholar to study the role of the DAIA during the last dictatorship, and I am pleased to acknowledge my debt to him. His work is based on close scrutiny of key DAIA publications, newspaper accounts, and interviews with non-DAIA figures. He did not interview Resnizky or Gorenstein.

18. I interviewed Rosenthal at his ADL office in New York on August 18, 1992.

19. The most recent book on the subject, Juan Gasparini's *El crimen de Graiver* (Buenos Aires: Ediciones Grupo Zeta, 1990), holds that Graiver did handle investments for the Montoneros (among other clients), and that he was murdered in an airplane accident engineered by the CIA. We may never know for sure, but Gasparini is a recognized expert on the Montoneros, and his hypothesis is credible and well supported.

20. See Introduction, note 13.

21. I am indebted to Klich for this account.

22. I first learned of Resnizky's videotape from Renée Epelbaum in early 1990. The subject routinely came up in conversations with Matilde Mellibovsky, Marcos Weistein, and other parents of Jewish *desaparecidos.* Klich also writes about the incident.

23. This and all other ADL memos cited here were made available to me by Morton Rosenthal.

24. See Senkman, ed., *El Antisemitismo,* Appendix, n. 17.

25. Interview with Gorenstein, Buenos Aires, July 20, 1992.

26. This English translation was circulated by the de facto Argentine government through its foreign embassies.

27. See Edy Kaufman "Jewish Victims of Repression in Argentina Under Military Rule (1976–1983)," *Holocaust and Genocide Studies,* 4, no. 4 (Fall 1989). Also *Nunca Más,* 67–72, 336, 414, 438.

28. The Mishnah, tractate Sanhédrin, chap. 4.

29. Interview with Klimovsky, Buenos Aires, July 23, 1992.

30. See Falcoff, "The Timerman Case," *Commentary,* July 1981, pp. 15–23.

31. Shortly before the "Sirota affair," the democratically elected Argentine president Arturo Frondizi was overthrown by the military. Frondizi's appointed replacement, José-María Guido, gave free rein to fascist anti-Jewish groups like the notorious Tacuara. Guido horrified the more moderate elements in the military, which is why some popular reactions called for a military crackdown.

32. Interview with Timerman, Buenos Aires, July 29, 1992.

33. Timerman's use of the word *Judenrat* is highly provocative and controversial. Strictly speaking, the *Judenrat* were Jewish administrative bodies appointed by, and responsible to, the Germans in Nazi-occupied territory during World War II. The *Judenrat's* assignments included taking censuses of Jews within their jurisdiction, arranging for the evacuation of Jews from ghettos to concentration camps, and making sure that German rules and regulations were obeyed. For an excellent discussion of the *Judenrat,* see Helen Fein, *Accounting for Genocide* (Chicago: Univ. of Chicago Press, 1979), 121–42.

34. Of all the people with whom I spoke (and my sources go beyond those quoted), only Timerman said the DAIA "gave names to the generals." I see no reason to censure Timerman's statement, but emphasize that I have no hard evidence to prove his declaration. Among my sources, the consensus is that the DAIA stopped short of "marking" individuals for kidnap.

35. No group has come forward to claim responsibility for the embassy bombing of March 17, 1992, which is highly unusual. Because two policemen walked off their beat exactly five minutes before the explosion, it is believed that the bombing was realized with Argentine help.

CHAPTER 4. THE LAND MOURNETH

1. *Tribunal permanente de los pueblos contra la impunidad en américa latina,* "Sesión argentina" (Buenos Aires: Servicio Paz y Justicia de Argentina, 1990), 2.

2. Dr. Carlos Zamorano provides an excellent brief analytic history of the pardons in *INDULTO: La Perversa impunidad* (Buenos Aires: Liga Argentina por los Derechos del Hombre, November 1989).

3. Under the name of "Gustavo Niño," Astiz had presented himself to the Mothers as the brother of a *desaparecido*. He often appeared with a young woman, a prisoner from the ESMA whom he introduced as his sister. (This survivor, Silvia Labeyru, later testified against Astiz.) The Mothers worried intensely about "Gustavo." Azucena Villaflor, the first president of the Mothers, was especially fond of "Gustavo," and told him that he could stay at her house whenever he wanted. He was furious not to find her that day at the Santa Cruz Church (she was meeting for the same purpose with another group in the apartment of Emilio and Chela Mignone). Two days later, Azucena was kidnapped from her home and disappeared from the ESMA. Today, Astiz is called "Judas" by the Mothers, because he indicated, by a kiss, which women his colleagues were to kidnap and take to the ESMA. The two Mothers taken from the church were Esther Balestrino de Careaga, Ana María Careaga's mother, and Mary Ponce. See Chapter 6 for more on Astiz.

4. This seems to be an allusion to Joel 2, v. 10: "The field is wasted, the land mourneth; for the corn is wasted: the new wine is dried up, the oil languisheth." Sergio knew "the land mourneth" was Biblical but couldn't exactly place its source.

5. Francisco Ferrara, *Qué son las ligas agrarias: Historia y documentos de las organizaciones campesinas del nordeste argentino* (Buenos Aires: Siglo Veinteuno Editores, 1971), 388. This is, as far as I know, the only history of the Agrarian Leagues and covers the movement in the provinces of the Chaco, Formosa, Misiones, Santa Fe, and Corrientes. According to Ferrara, the total number of participants in the Agrarian Leagues was 45,000, the figure normally mentioned to me in interviews.

6. Ibid., 388.

7. Ibid.

8. Onganía sought to revise Argentina's economy according to the model of the Brazilian generals who seized power there in 1964: The main obstacles to prosperity were considered to be inflation, unions, and political parties. Although inflation in Argentina did get lowered and industrial growth had an impressive spurt, these gains were not reflected in popular wage gains. Nor was that really the intention in this project whose aim was to strengthen the economy beginning at the top.

9. Ibid., 37–38.

10. Sergio's statistics coincide with Ferrara's, *Qué son las ligas agrarias,* 436.

11. Ibid., 393.

12. Morello's statement is quoted in ibid., 42–43.

13. Ibid., 386.

14. Ibid., 406.

15. While living in exile in Mexico in 1979, Sergio wrote a detailed testimony on the regimen in prison, providing invaluable information on a number of other detainees. I draw in this narrative from both our series of interviews and his written testimony, which is unpublished. I have one copy; another is now in the archives of CELS.

16. In his written testimony, Sergio misremembered the date, which he located in September 1976. The date in the body of this text is the correct one. For further information on the Massacre of Margarita Belén, see also *El Diario Juicio,* no. 12, August 12, 1985. On this subject I learned a great deal from a long interview with Mirta Clara, whose husband,

Horacio Sala, was murdered at Margarita Belén. Upon her own release from prison, Clara did an extensive investigation of the incident and together with other surviving relatives, brought the case to the courts. See also Chapter 6.

17. Interview with Sister Anne Marie and Sister Marta, Perugorría, July 6, 1995.

18. I stayed for two days with the Olivo family in July 1995.

19. *Paz y justicia.* May—July 1990, p. 20 (back cover).

20. Pope John XXIII stunned many in the hierarchy with two encyclicals, "Mater et Magistra" ("Christianity and Social Progress"), May 15, 1961 and "Pacem in Terris" ("Peace on Earth"), April 11, 1963, which had dramatic resonance, particularly in Latin America.

21. Excellent sources on this movement are Domingo A. Bresci's *Movimiento de sacerdotes para el tercer mundo* (Buenos Aires: Centro Salessiano de Estudios San Juan Bosco/Centro Nazaret, 1994); Alfred T. Hennelly, S.J.'s *Liberation Theology: A Documentary History* (Maryknoll: Orbis Books, 1990); and Ferrara, *Qué son las ligas agrarias,* introduction.

22. Interview with Torres, at his rectory, Itatí, July 7, 1995.

23. Interview with Arroyo, at his home, Goya, July 4, 1995.

24. Bishops Miguel Hesayne of Viedma, Jorge Novak of Quilmes (both in the Province of Buenos Aires), and the late Jaime de Nevares of Neuquén (Province of Rio Negro) were all indefatigable opponents of the last military regime. The surviving Bishops Hesayne and Novak continue to be active and important champions of human rights. For more on these men, see Chapter 6.

25. This letter, written jointly by the Regional Coordinators on July 31, 1969, is quoted in Bresci, *Movimento de sarcerdotes,* 86–88.

26. *Paz y justicia,* back cover. From a Pastoral Letter dated November 29, 1968.

27. See Bresci, *Movimento de sarcerdotes, 61.*

28. Arroyo is at once a deeply rooted country priest and active internationally. He has joint projects and coordinates exchanges with progressive church groups and foundations in Europe. During my first visit he was hosting a group from Austria; just prior to my second, he had returned from a tour he had arranged for a gifted local young musician.

29. See Hennelly, *Liberation Theology,* 12–13.

30. Bresci, *Movimento de sarcerdotes,* 137.

31. *Taxes (impuestos)* appeared in a special section called "Difficult Words" in the League Bulletin of July 1972. See Ferrara, *Qué son las ligas agrarias,* 432.

32. For a detailed account of Scilingo, see Chapter 6.

33. Interview with Benítez, Perugorría, July 6, 1995. For more on her, see Chapter 2.

34. I wish to thank Rogelio Tomasella for his generous interview of July 6, 1995. Space considerations here did not permit me to quote from it but I will make the transcript available for any researchers who might wish to consult it.

35. Interview with Señora Gómez, Goya, July 3, 1995. See also *Nunca Más,* 175 and 381.

36. Interview with Carmen C. and the Puntín family, Perugorría, July 6, 1995.

37. Interview, Goya, August 6, 1993.

38. Interview, Goya, July 7, 1995.

39. See Calvin Sims, "Argentine Military for Rent; Turns Swords into Tin Cups," *New York Times,* January 29, 1996, p. A1.

CHAPTER 5. THE HOUSE OF THE BLIND

1. Details of her kidnap and disappearance are culled from my first interview with Barros, Buenos Aires, August 13, 1990. She was reminded of the weather because our meeting took place on a similarly warm evening of early spring.

2. Barros recalls the car being a Renault 12. It was waiting a block away, near the Castro Barros subway stop. The drive to the Navy Mechanics School would have taken about twenty minutes.

3. As far as Susana, the CONADEP, and I know, Susana's is the only testimony on her kidnap from bus #128.

4. See "Operación Limpieza," *Cambio* 16, no. 329, March 26, 1978, pp. 68–69.

5. Some 80% of the kidnappings documented by the CONADEP took place in front of witnesses; 62% of the missing were kidnapped from their homes; 24.6% were kidnapped in the street; 7% from their place of employment; and 6% from their place of study. See *Nunca Más,* 11.

6. Massera, December 14, 1977. Quoted in Abós, *El Poder carnívoro,* p. 45.

7. See Troncoso, *El Proceso,* vol. 1: 10.

8. Ibid., 11.

9. "Es normal la actividad en todo el país," *La Prensa,* March 26, 1976, p. 1.

10. See *La Prensa,* March 28, 1976, p. 3. The content of the report was in all the print and broadcast media.

11. Jacobo Timerman, "Reflexión," *La Opinión,* March 26, 1976, p. 1.

12. "Hacia una limpieza general," lead editorial in *La Prensa,* April 19, 1976.

13. Raúl Oscar Abdala, "Tras la pesadilla," ibid.

14. Jeane Kirkpatrick was appointed U.S. Ambassador to the United Nations by President Reagan, who reversed his predecessor's arms embargo against Argentina and dismantled many of Carter's human rights policies. Early in Reagan's first administration, Kirkpatrick traveled to Buenos Aires. The Mothers of the Plaza de Mayo requested an interview, but Kirkpatrick summarily declined to meet with them. For a fine discussion on the Carter-Reagan transition, and its effects on U.S. behavior in the United Nations and toward Argentina, see Ian Guest, *Behind the Disappearances: Argentina's Dirty War Against Human Rights and the United Nations* (Philadelphia: Univ. of Pennsylvania Press, 1990).

15. Marie Muller, "Treize alsaciens dans la pampa," *Le Nouvel observateur,* no. 747, March 5–11, 1979. pp. 74–106, esp. 90–91.

16. See Martin Edwin Anderson, *Dossier Secreto* (Boulder: Westview Press, 1993), 219. Anderson's account is based on reporting in the now defunct *Humor,* no. 165, December 1985. Published in Buenos Aires, *Humor* was a progressive, high-profile political/cultural/arts magazine. General Domingo Bussi, the governor of Tucumán province, also "solved" his poverty problem by rounding up shantytown residents and trucking them into the adjacent rural province of the Chaco.

17. Interview with María Claudia A. at a literary conference where she gave a presentation on *Respiración artificial,* by Ricardo Piglia, October 1994.

18. Interview with Raúl T., New York, February 10, 1990.

19. From a letter by Jerónimo José Podestá, ex-Bishop of Avellaneda, published in *Página 12,* March 27, 1996.

20. Quotes are taken from Epstein's internal memo, a copy of which was given to me in August 1992 by Rabbi Morton Rosenthal of the Anti-Defamation League of B'Nai Brith. For more on Epstein, Rosenthal, and the ADL during the years of the dictatorship, see Chapter 3.

21. For obvious reasons, those who had money banked and invested it abroad. By February 1977, the purchasing power of workers' salaries had diminished by a little more than 50% since the coup of March 1976. That same month the Ministry of Economy announced a 120% increase in military salaries. Workers were granted a 20% pay rise, but that did little to offset months of dramatically rising prices: In December 1976 alone, food prices spiked 21%. A lieutenant colonel earned eight times more than a skilled laborer, and fourteen times more than a school principal. See "Aumento con jinetas," *Mensaje* No. 5, ANCLA, February 1977, in *La Prensa clandestina,* Horacio Verbitsky, ed. (Buenos Aires: Ediciones de la Urraca, 1985), 42–43. By 1978, the situation of wage-earners was worse than it had been in fifty years. According to official figures published in *Cambio 16,* no. 340, June 11, 1978, every area of the economy showed serious losses. Total production of wheat (Argentina's major crop) for 1977–78 fell 53% from 1976-77; wheat export was down 13%. An Argentine worker in 1978 was earning one-third the salary of a Spanish worker, and had to contend with higher prices. Foreign debt skyrocketed under the military regime. Just prior to the military takeover the foreign debt was $7,875,000,000; when the military left power the debt was $45,087,000,000. The burden of accumulating interest was staggering. These figures on the foreign debt are cited in Prudencio García, *El Drama de la autonomía militar* (Madrid: Alianza Editorial, 1995), 75. Garda is himself citing Alfredo Eric Calcagno, *La Perversa deuda* (Buenos Aires: Editorial Legasa, 1988), 46.

22. Muller, *Le Nouvel observateur,* March 5–11, 1979, p. 89.

23. James Neilson, "El Horror tolerado," published originally in the *Buenos Aires Herald,* July 6, 1976, collected in his *La Virágine argentina* (Buenos Aires: Ediciones Marymar, 1979), 68–69.

24. For more on Floreal Avellaneda, see Chapter 6.

25. José Solanille was a "Witness of the Week" at the trial of the ex-commanders. See *El Diario del Juicio,* no.6, July 2, 1985.

26. This second part of Solanille's testimony is quoted in Astelarra and Contemponi, *Sobrevivientes de la Perla,* 8.

27. See Informe No. 1, December 1976, in Verbitsky, ed., *La Prensa clandestina,* 37–38.

28. "Campaña de censura y represión contra el periodismo," August 30, 1977, in ibid., 51–52. This dispatch cites a large number of journalists by name, and mentions a host of magazines forced to close. It synthesizes an important report and anti-censorship statements by ADEPA (Asociación de Entidades Periodísticas Argentinas), the Argentine newspaper and magazine association.

29. These missing journalists are commemorated in *Con vida los queremos,* comp. Buenos Aires Press Association (Asociación de Periodistas de Buenos Aires) (Buenos Aires: Unión de Trabajadores de Prensa de Buenos Aires, 1987). A chapter is dedicated to each journalist; in addition to a biographical and professional narrative, there are testimonies, photographs, drawings, and manuscript excerpts.

30. See "Testimonios de una masacre," in *Camino* 16, no. 305, October 16, 1977, pp. 55–56.

31. "Secreto: Los Archivos de la repressión cultural," *Clarín,* March 24, 1996, sec. 2. This excellent supplement includes archival materials on the cultural repression, including the Operation Clarity list of individuals with "ideologically unfavorable backgrounds," and interviews with censured artists and intellectuals. There is also a statement by Colonel Agustín Valladares (Videla's former press secretary), who, though he refused to be interviewed about the publication of these documents, nonetheless insisted, "I have a clear conscience. I lived happily all these years, I was never accused by any court of any wrongdoing. But I don't want to talk because I am loyal to my force, and if the others aren't talking, why would I, I wasn't first in command. We need to let time pass before we can dialogue." Earlier in the week Valladares had declared, "I was, am, and always will be a man of the Process."

32. "Con Paula Speck, una becaria estadounidense," in *La Prensa,* January 15, 1977, p. 5. Interestingly enough. Speck was doing doctoral research on the secret societies found in the works of Roberto Arlt, Macedonio Fernández, Jorge Luis Borges, and Ernesto Sàbato. Coincidentally, she mentions Sábato's "Report on the Blind" in his novel On *Heroes and Tombs* in which the protagonist is convinced that a secret society of the blind controls the workings of the world.

Notwithstanding the literary "news" in the dailies, one of the earliest public rituals of the regime was an enormous book-burning on April 30, 1976. Ceremoniously presided over by General Luciano Benjamín Menéndez, it took place in the courtyard of an army base in Córdoba province before a full retinue of journalists and government officials. Among the thousands of authors whose books went up in flames were Julio Cortázar, Marcel Proust, Gabriel García Márquez, Pablo Neruda, Karl Marx, Sigmund Freud, Antoine de Saint-Exupéry, Eduardo Galeano, and Paulo Freire. According to Menéndez, these authors — spanning centuries, genres, and a spectrum of disciplines and styles—were all "poison for the national soul of Argentina." Standing near the pyre, Menéndez declared, "Just as this fire now destroys material pernicious to our Christian way of being, so too will be destroyed the enemies of the Argentine soul." Of course, both the act itself and the accompanying rhetoric are patterned on Hitler's famous book-burning in Berlin on May 10, 1933. Menéndez is cited in Prudencio García, *El Drama,* 483. García draws on a report written by Cortázar, Miguel Angel Estrella, Mercedes Sosa, et al. for AIDA, the Asociación Internacional para la Defensa de los Artistas Víctimas de la Represión en el Mundo ("International Association for the Defense of Artists Victimized by Repression Around the World"), published in *Argentina: Cómo matar la cultura* (Madrid: Ed. Revolución, 1981), 254.

33. The lectures Borges gave at the Teatro Colón in 1977 are available in English as *Seven Nights,* trans, by Eliot Weinberger, intro. Alistair Reid (New York: New Directions, 1984).

34. Interview with the author, July 31, 1990.

35. Some policemen later testified about these massacres. Here are two corroborating accounts about Commander Augustín Feced, responsible for the Second Army Corps. According to policeman Héctor Julio Roldán: ". . . they were picked up on the streets on the orders of the Commander. They were made to sit inside a car . . . and Commander Feced dispatched them at point-blank range with a machine gun from another car." According to policeman Carlos Pedro Dawydowyz: "In the year 1977, seven people were taken from the Information Service . . . and transported to Ibarlucea (near Rosario), under the pretext that they were in transit to Coronda. These individuals were not officially registered, they were picked up as leftists. They weren't entered into any admissions book or anything of that kind; they had been picked up two or three days previously. Once in Ibarlucea they were made to get out near the police station, and stand about 150 metres from it. Then they were riddled with bullets. On that occasion it was Feced who presided, yelling at the employees inside the police station, and himself shooting up the whole front of the building with a machine gun to give the impression that there had been an armed attack on it. I was there on that occasion and could see everything that was going on. . . ." Quoted in *Nunca Más*, 183.

Ex-captain Adolfo Scilingo has described Montonera leader Norma Arrostito in 1977 in her tiny cell at the ESMA, surrounded by newspapers that had fallaciously announced her death "in a shootout" on December 2, 1976. With no hope of surviving, Arrostito spent the rest of her life being shuttled between *capucha* and the basement of the ESMA. Considered a major "battle trophy," she was often displayed to prominent military and official visitors. Arrostito requested to be shot, considering that a dignified death, but was killed by lethal injection on January 15, 1978. Adolfo Scilingo, unpublished manuscript, p. 39. A copy of this manuscript, written in jail in 1995–96, was provided to me by Marcela V. de Scilingo in May 1996. Hereafter referred to as Scilingo ms.

36. Interview with Loiácono, Buenos Aires, October 20, 1990.

37. "Argentine Women in Weekly Protest Over Abductions," *New York Times*, September 12, 1977, p. 7.

38. From my interview with Enrique Fernández Meijide, Buenos Aires, September 4, 1990.

39. From my interview with Graciela Fernández Meijide, Buenos Aires, September 12, 1990. See also Noemi Ulla-Hugo Echave, *Después de la noche: Diálogo con Graciela Fernández Meijide* (Buenos Aires: Editorial Contrapunto, 1986), 48–49.

40. Interview with "Soledad B.," August 8, 1993.

41. Menéndez made these statements in the March 15, 1984, issue of *Gente*. Cited in *Nunca Más*, 53.

42. Interviews with Susana Dillon, Rio Cuarto, May 21–25, 1990. Also based on this visit with Susana and her granddaughter is "A Daughter of the Disappeared," *Women's Review of Books* 10, nos. 10–11 (July 1993): 7–8.

43. See *Nunca Más*, 381–382. On August 31, 1984, the CONADEP did an inspection of the secret detention center that had functioned in the Acindar company.

44. From the first of my series of interviews with Ana María Careaga, Buenos Aires, May 15, 1990.

45. Ibid.

46. For more on Dr. Bergés, see Chapter 6.

47. See *Nunca Más*, 382.

48. Bernard-Henry Levy, "Como me echaron del Mundial," in *Cambio 16*, June 11, 1978, pp. 7–9. Lévy's reporting on Argentina was extremely perceptive. He was one of the few who traveled outside of Buenos Aires to the provinces. He recounts an extraordinary experience with a young, rather progressive industrialist who presented Lévy with "the strangest, most unbelievable request": to do a fake interview in which he, the industrialist, would praise the dictatorship. This wasn't for publication, the young industrialist explained, but to keep in the event that something happened to him.

49. See *El Diario del Juicio*, no. 3, June 11, 1985, pp. 74–75; and *Nunca Más*, 140–41.

50. *Nunca Más*, 152.

51. Ibid., 137—38. This was not the first time that an Argentine hospital was implicated in torture. During Perón's first term, communists and other dissidents were routinely brutalized by the Special Section operating out of Police Precinct No. 8. (Urquiza 556), in a bustling central district of Buenos Aires. For treatment following torture, prisoners were sent across the street to the Ramos Mejía public hospital. This too was common knowledge, not just among doctors and nurses, but among patients and the general public as well. See Sebreli, *Los Deseos imaginarios del peronism*, 33.

52. Interview, August 13, 1990.

53. The quote, of course, became famous in Argentina and gave rise to a lot of black humor. Reprised periodically by journalists, Viola's interview was repeated at greater length in *Clarín*, on December 29, 1990, in a section of articles on the pardon, signed by Menem on the 28th.

54. Ranea's photos ran in *Nuevo Sur* on July 6, 1989, and in *Gente* on July 7, 1989. On August 13, the story ran also in New York's largest Spanish-language daily, *El Diario/La Prensa*.

55. Interview with Ranea, Buenos Aires, August 2, 1993.

56. Interview with Epelbaum, Buenos Aires, July 7, 1993.

57. Interview, July 16, 1990.

58. *El Diario/La Prensa* (New York), March 23, 1990, p. 12.

59. Ibid., March 11, 1990, p. 10. As this book goes to press, unemployment in Argentina is about 20 percent.

60. Horacio Vargas, "Temperatura en aumento," *Página 12*, March 9, 1990, pp. 12–13. On this two-page spread there are a number of articles and commentaries on the economic crisis as it was being experienced around the country. Among the complaints was that food relief packages were being funneled to Peronist groups (Menem is a Peronist) and away from other parties and groups. Afraid of being looted, some truckers refused to deliver bread, milk, and eggs to certain neighborhoods. In various provinces, police responded to both peaceful mobilizations and looting with tear gas and rubber bullets.

A searing and beautifully executed report on this period is Tomás Eloy Martinez's "Argentina: Living With Hyperinflation," *The Atlantic*, December 1990, pp. 30–43. See also: Shirley Christian, "Argentina's Military Chiefs Warn of Anarchy" and "Price-Shaken

Argentina Halts the Money Flow," *New York Times*, January 2 and 3, 1990; "Argentine Stocks Fall 53%; Inflation Soars," AP report in ibid., January 9, 1990; Christian, "New Notions on Old Crisis in Argentina" and "Peronist Workers Rebel in Argentina," ibid., February 12 and March 22, 1990.

61. Lucy Liguera, "La Olla está próxima a estallar" ("The Pot Is About to Boil Over"), in *El Diario/La Prensa* (New York), February 25, 1990.

62. "Drástico plan económico con cárcel para quienes evaden el pago de los impuestos" ("Drastic Economic Plan with Prison for Those Who Evade Paying Taxes), in *El Diario/LaPrensa* (New York), March 4, 1990.

63. A small notice appeared in *Página 12*, March 9, 1990, p. 13 (see note 60, above). The auction took place during one of the "hottest" weeks of the crisis.

64. Quoted widely. Front-page headline, *Página 12*, July 10, 1992.

65. See, for example, "El Mundial en una carcel" ("The World Cup in a Jail"), *Cambio 16*, February 19, 1978, pp. 38–40. This article is based in part on a U.S. State Department report that asserted that there were 12,000–17,000 political prisoners at that time in Argentina.

66. Interview, August 13, 1990.

67. The school is located at Azcuenaga 1100. The story was first reported by Nora Veiras on June 13, 1993, in *Página 12*, which also carried her follow-up on the polemic.

68. Front-page story in *Página 12*, March 24, 1995.

69. *Clarín*, April 30, 1995.

70. *Página 12*, October 21, 1995.

71. Dr. Marcelo Marmer, editorial, *Página 12*, October 26, 1995.

72. "Una clase de historia" ("A History Lesson"), *Página 12*, October 22, 1995.

73. Ibid.

74. I visited the house in Rosario several times in August 1993. I met with Alejandra Leoncio de Ravelo, "Negrita," at her home in Santa Fe on August 8, 1993. All of her quotes are taken from our interview. This case was brought into public light through an article by historian/journalist Osvaldo Bayer, "La Mirada de los ciegos" ("The Gaze of the Blind"), *Página 12*, December 1992. I am grateful to Alejandro Fogel for sending me the clipping. A local reporter, Carlos del Frade, picked up the story and provided updates for *Rosario 12* (the local version of the Buenos Aires daily *Página 12*) until it was resolved. A few days before my meeting with Negrita in 1993, Del Frade was obliging enough to give me copies of the two pieces he had written earlier that year. Del Frade's subsequent articles (November 28 and December 30, 1994) were kindly sent to me by Dr. Juan Carlos Adrover, a lawyer who has known Negrita for years and who patiently instructed me in the legal twists and turns of this landmark case.

75. This background information was given to me by Dr. Juan Carlos Adrover, the lawyer who headed the regional branch of the CONADEP.

76. Neither Negrita nor I knew it then, but the couple's employee was named Juan Carlos Amador. According to an article published in *Rosario 12*, March 24, 1996; Amador's death certificate was issued by the police on September 23, 1977, and cited his date of death as September 16, the day after the break-in. The document was signed by Dr. Angel Lungo,

who resigned on March 5, 1983 (early in the new democracy), because of "depression." Amador's body was buried in the cementery known as La Piedad. Nearly nineteen years after the events, this information was brought to light by Juan Carlos Amador's brother, Manuel, and his sister-in-law, Nora, who returned to Argentina from France where they have lived since late 1977. Manuel was kidnapped by police intelligence agents eight months before the assassination of his brother. He learned that his brother had been shot while he himself was in captivity but was, until recently, unable to learn more. See "El Domicilio de la memoria" ("The Home of Remembrance"), *Rosario 12,* March 24, 1996, pp. 6–7. My thanks to Juan Carlos Adrover for sending the clipping.

77. Interview with Saraví, La Plata, November 20, 1995.

78. Interview with García, La Plata, November 20, 1995.

79. The only book-length work on this event is Maria Seoane and Héctor Ruiz Nuñez, *La Noche de los lápices* ("The Night of the Pencils") (Buenos Aires: Editorial Contrapunto, 1986).

80. Interview with Betti and Pueyo, Buenos Aires, November 19, 1995.

81. Interview with Juan Andrés Sala, Buenos Aires, November 19, 1995. By the time Juan Andrés came home, I had spent several hours interviewing his mother, Mirta Clara. For a while the three of us talked together, then Juan Andrés and I talked alone.

82. My visit to the School of Social Work took place on November 20, 1995.

83. Conversation with the author, Buenos Aires, November 18, 1995.

84. As early as March 22, the media were reporting on the contents of Menem's speech.

85. There was extensive coverage in the dailies. The quotes in the body of my text are from *Página 12,* February 25, 1996.

86. Because of our respective travel schedules, Tula and I conducted our interview by fax. I sent him a written set of questions in early November and received his copious response on December 2, 1995. He also provided me with a copy of the formal proposal drawn up and voted on by the City Council. Tula's associate Osvaldo Pedroso was most helpful in all of this. I am also grateful for an interview (November 22, 1995) with Councilman Eduardo Jozami, a cosponsor of the project and former political prisoner. Others who gave me their input were Graciela Fernández Meijide, a supporter of the project in the Congress; and Laura Bonaparte (Mother of the Plaza de Mayo—Founding Line), who brought me to an early organizational meeting attended by representatives from the major human rights groups at the City Council in July 1995.

87. See *Página 12,* September 20, 1995.

88. Interview with Siracusano, Buenos Aires, November 23, 1995.

89. That the space operated as a concentration camp was proven by the subsequent inspection and testimony of survivors, including Mario Villani (Chapters 2 and 6) and Mónica Brull (Chapter 6), who accompanied the CONADEP team to the site in 1984.

90. Ernesto Semán, "En el Olimpo," *Página 12,* September 17, 1995, p. 12.

91. See *Página 12,* March 21, 1996.

92. Ernesto Semán, "Si pintan el Olimpo me tengo que ir" ("If They Paint Olympus, I'll Have to Go"), *Página 12,* March 22, 1996, p. 2.

93. Personal communication.

94. Ponieman's quotes are from our phone interview of August 30, 1996. See also *Página 12,* March 27 and 28, 1996.

95. Quoted in *Clarín,* March 24, 1996, Sec. 2, p. 6.

96. See *Página 12,* March 26, 1996, p. 6.

97. There are two pieces in *Página 12,* April 30, 1996: Santiago Rodríguez, "Las Locas de la Plaza," p. 9; and "Presente," a personal reminiscence by Nora de Cortiñas, cofounder, Mothers of the Plaza de Mayo, and Cofounder and member, Mothers of the Plaza de Mayo—Founding Line.

98. Notice in *Página 12,* May 21, 1996.

99. See *Clarín,* May 19, 1996, p. 14.

CHAPTER 6. "THE SCILINGO EFFECT"

1. Interview with the Mignones, Buenos Aires, June 20, 1995.

2. Horacio Verbitsky, *El Vuelo* (Buenos Aires: Planeta—Espejo de la Argentina, 1995). English-language reporters who covered Scilingo's testimony include Stephen Brown, whose dispatches for Reuters began on March 3; Calvin Sims, of the *New York Times,* whose major articles appeared on March 13, 30, and April 5; and Pablo Escobar, who wrote a long piece for the *Washington post* on April 3, 1995. In Spain, *E Pais, ABC,* and *La Vanguardia* gave extensive coverage to the appearances of Scilingo, Vergés, Simón, et al. The week after I completed this chapter, Verbitsky's book appeared in English: *The Flight: Confessions of an Argentine Dirty Warrior,* trans. Esther Allen (1996). My references to Verbitsky's book correspond to the Argentine edition, and all translations from this work are mine.

3. Scilingo ms., 8.

4. The quotes in this paragraph are taken from "La Solución final," the first installment of Verbitsky's series on Scilingo, *Página 12,* March 3, 1995, pp. 2–3, and from Verbitsky, *El Vuelo,* 25–26.

5. Scilingo ms., 37.

6. Quote taken from Verbitsky, "La Solución final," p. 2.

7. Ibid.

8. The quotes in this paragraph are taken from Scilingo ms., 240, and from Verbitsky's "La Solución final," *Página 12,* March 3 and 10, 1995.

9. The statements Massot made on *Hora Clave* were quoted the following day in "Para salvar a la nación," *Página 12,* March 10, 1995, p. 3.

10. Mike Wallace interviewed the Scilingos and President Menem in Buenos Aires. "Tales from the Dirty War" aired on CBS on 60 *Minutes* on April 2, 1995.

11. Interview, Buenos Aires, June 14, 1995.

12. Menem's déclaration was made on March 28, 1995, on Radio 99.9 (which broadcasts to the Argentine capital). He also took the opportunity to again blame the media for "keeping this horrible memory alive." Quoted by Calvin Sims, "Argentine President Discourages New Revelations on 'Dirty War,'" *New York Times,* March 30, 1995, p. A10.

13. Conversation with Susana and Osvaldo Barros, Buenos Aires, June 16, 1995. The quote from *Nunca Más* appears on p. 211.

14. Interview with Marcela V. de Scilingo, Buenos Aires, November 22, 1995.

15. A photograph of Scilingo greeting Alexander Haig was published in *Página 12*, March 3, 1995. Scilingo, then a Navy captain, was part of the navy advisory council at the Casa Rosada; Haig was U.S. Secretary of State. The photo was taken in 1982 during the Malvinas (Falklands) war.

16. Búsico's testimony appears in *Nunca Más*, 125.

17. Scilingo's account of his difficulties within the force in 1984–85 is found in Scilingo ms., 97–99.

18. Ibid., 113.

19. Verbitsky, "La Solución final," *Página 12*, March 3, 1995.

20. This quote is taken from Verbitsky, *El Vuelo.* 43. In the Appendix to this volume, Verbitsky reproduces Scilingo's letters to his naval superiors, to Videla, and to Menem. Also included are Scilingo's formal request to postpone his exam for the War College, the navy's responses, and the psychiatric report on the then-captain.

21. For an essay on the context surrounding Minicucci's promotion, see my "Buenos Aires 1990: The First Two Weeks of July," in *Exquisite Corpse*, no. 34 (Jan.–Feb. 1992): 34–36.

22. For more on Pernías and Rolón, see María Teresa Piñero, ed., *Culpables para la sociedad, impunes por la ley* (Buenos Aires: CELS, 1988), pp. 25–26; and Ana María Martí, María Alicia Milia de Pirles, and Sara Solarz de Osatinsky, *ESMA: "Traslados": Testimonio de tres liberadas* (Buenos Aires: Grandmothers of the Plaza de Mayo, Relatives of Detainees—Desaparecidos for Political Reasons, and Mothers of the Plaza de Mayo—Founding Line, 1995). These three women first testified before the Human Rights Commission of the French Parliament in October 1979. They were released from the ESMA in late 1978/early 1979. Their account of Pernías's experiments on Daniel Schapira and his ambitions for his poison darts is found on p. 37; see also pp. 57—58 for Pernías's activities in Paris. Pernías was also named in *Nunca Más* and mentioned by various survivors at the trial of the ex-commanders.

23. Quotes taken from Senate testimony are found in Verbitsky, *El Vuelo*, 176. Verbitsky's appendix features some twenty pages of Rolón and Pernías's examination by the Senate.

24. Ibid., 20–21.

25. Responding to attacks by Menem—"I can forgive the military, but not Verbitsky, never Verbitsky"—the journalist wrote an article, which included excerpts from an interview he gave to Radio Continental, about his political coming-of-age and past relationship with the Montoneros. The piece ran in *Página 12*, May 4, 1995, and comprised all of p. 4. Menem's ire with Verbitsky centers on the journalist's inveterate reporting on corruption in the administration, which culminated in the book *Robo para la Corona* ("Robbery for the Crown"). When Menem sued Verbitsky for libel, the latter brought his case to the Inter-American Human Rights Tribunal of the OAS, where he was acquitted of all charges.

26. Interview with Lerner and Mario Villani, Buenos Aires, June 24, 1995.

27. My thanks go to Néstor Ibarra for his interview, June 15, 1995, and to Radio Mitre's technical director Hugo Ferrer for providing me with a tape of the April 25 broadcast. Ibarra mentioned other cases on which Ibáñez provided corroborated information, including that of Cecilia Viñas, the missing daughter of the prominent writer David Viñas. Ibáñez remembered that Cecilia's dog, "Loca," was with her in the camp; after kidnapping the young woman the task force returned to her home to pick up the dog.

28. Interview with Graciela Fernández Meijide at her office in the Congress on June 14, 1995. In earlier interviews, as far back as 1990, we also discussed her work with the CONADEP.

29. Interview with Sara Steimberg, Buenos Aires, June 22, 1995.

30. For showing me tapes of the program and for putting me in touch with Julián's contact Raúl Aguiar, and with Mónica Brull, I am grateful to the team at "TeleNoche," Channel 13, especially Eduardo Cura, director of research, and Luis Otero, executive editor and on-air interviewer.

31. Interview with Brull, Buenos Aires, July 26, 1995.

32. For more on "Colores," see *Culpables para la sociedad, impunes por la ley,* 19–20.

33. Lorenzo Miguel was head of the "62 Organizations," the political wing of the Peronist labor consortium. During the dictatorship he was imprisoned on the same navy ship as Menem in Buenos Aires harbor. In June 1983, it was disclosed in the press that Miguel had made a secret pact with then military commander-in-chief General Christino Nicolaides, according to which the military would help the Peronists in the upcoming elections if they in turn closed investigations into the *desaparecidos.* These reports were used to advantage by Alfonsín (of the centrist Unión Cívica Radical, or Radical Party) in his race against Peronist Italo Luder. The reports are credible, given the sources, and since it was Luder who, during Isabelita's absence in 1975, signed the laws that dictated "the eradication of subversion."

34. This story was cracked by Raúl Kollmann, Román Lejtman, and Gabriel Pasquini of *Página 12,* which ran their series on July 11, 13, and 14, 1995. After a year of having no arrests in the AMIA explosion, a married couple, Carlos Alberto Telleldín and Ana Boragni, were detained on suspicion of having sold the vehicle used in the bombing of the Jewish center. It was also known that Telleldín had a habit of doing business with disreputable members of the Provincial Police, and that the car in question passed through the hands of two police officers. Vergez got involved through personal connections: Telleldín's late father, the virulently anti-Semitic Police Chief of Córdoba from 1974 until 1976, was his intimate friend. Vergez was engaged by the SIDE (Federal Intelligence Services) to encourage him to "identify" from a photograph two Brazilians of Lebanese origin as the real purchasers of the vehicle. On the basis of his statement, these individuals were extradited from Asunción, but as no hard evidence could be found, they had to be released, to the international embarrassment of Argentina. In the face of rumors that he had paid Telleldín for his statements, Vergez admitted to the press that he had been allotted two million dollars by the SIDE to "help the case develop." In mid-July 1996, two years after the bombing, eighteen members of the Buenos Aires Provincial Police were arrested for their connections to the destruction of the Jewish community center. The case is not yet closed, but a resolution is

finally in sight. See *Clarín*, July 14, 1996, pp. 2–6 (front-page lead), and Raúl Kollmann, "Más vale tarde que nunca," *Página 12*, July 14, 1996, pp. 23 (front-page lead), and "Los Culpables del dolor," *Página 12*, July 18, 1996, pp. 2–5 (front-page lead).

35. Interview with Astelarra, Buenos Aires, June 28, 1995.

36. Corach's quote appeared on March 22, 1995, in *Página 12, La Nación, Clarín*, and all major radio and television stations.

37. Strassera was interviewed by Rubén Levenberg, *Página 12*, March 22, 1995, p. 2.

38. Basterra's trial testimony is found in *El Diario del Juicio*, no. 10, July 30, 1985, pp. 2–3. On the cover are reproductions of photos he took and/or developed in the ESMA, as well as two falsified documents used by navy staff. He was designated "Witness of the Week" by this weekly newspaper on the trial. Borges attended the trial the day Basterra declared, and his response is found in ibid., 208.

39. Muñoz's extensive trial testimony is found in ibid., back cover, and in ibid., no. 24, November 5, 1985, pp. 452–64.

40. Juan Gasparini, *La Pista suiza* ("The Swiss Trail") (Buenos Aires: Ed. Legasa, 1986).

41. "Después de Scilingo: Una gambeta," *Página 12*, March 26, 1995, p. 9.

42. See Horacio Verbitsky, "Quiero decir que estoy vivo," *Página 12*, April 5, 1995, p. 2.

43. See Miguel Bonasso, "El Fichero de Grasselli," *Página 12*, May 2, 1995, p. 8; and *Nunca Más*, 250. The first and still most complete single-volume work on the conduct of the Catholic Church during the repression is Emilio F. Mignone's *Iglesia y dictadura: El Papel di la iglesia a la luz de sus relaciones con el régimen militar* (Buenos Aires: Ediciones del Pensamiento Nacional, 1986).

44. *Nunca Más*, 251.

45. Daleo's trial testimony is found in *El Diario del Juicio*, no. 22, October 22, 1985, pp. 421–30.

46. *Nunca Más*, 250–51.

47. Horacio Verbitsky, "El Silencio," *Página 12*, March 12, 1995, pp. 2–3.

48. The text of Menem's support of Laghi and declarations against Verbitsky were distributed to the print media by the official news agency Telam. The president made these comments on April 10, 1995; they appeared in print the following day.

49. Massera was quoted widely in the print and broadcast media, including in Horacio Verbitsky, "Laghi estaba preocupado," *Página 12*, April 2, 1995, pp. 2–3.

50. Moutoukias spoke on the radio via telephone with journalist Nelson Castro, The story was then elaborated by *Página 12*, April 15, 1995, p. 11. For more testimony on police chaplain Christian von Wernich, see *Nunca Más*, 249–50. Von Wernich's declarations at the trial of the ex-commanders are found in *El Diario del Juicio*, no. 3, June 11, 1985, pp. 56–60.

51. Hesayne's paschal address was printed in various dailies. For the quotes printed here, I relied on *Página 12*, April 15, p. 11.

52. This is a well-known story. It was told to me on a number of occasions by Mothers who participated in that trip, including Nora de Cortiñas and Renée Epelbaum. It is reprised in Verbitsky, "Una lluvia de recuerdos," *Página 12*, April 16, 1995, pp. 3–4.

53. *Página 12*, April 15, 1995, p. 11.

54. "Polémica de los santos," *Página 12*, April 18, pp. 8–9.

55. "Los Represores no comulgan en Viedma," *Página 12*, May 6, 1995, p. 4. The bishop's remarks were made in a press conference the day before and were carried by all the major media. Hesayne, in Buenos Aires en route to Rome for a visit with the Pope, took the opportunity to describe as "humane and Christian" the institutional apology of General Martín Balza. For more on Balza, see below.

56. Quarracino's press conference of April 29 was reprised in the major dailies the following day.

57. For the complete text of Balza's speech, I relied on *Clarín*, April 26, 1995. Long excerpts were carried in all the dailies.

58. Balza had insisted on this in the press and repeated it to me during our interview, July 3, 1995.

59. Report on CELS in Washington in *Página 12*, March 18, 1995, p. 2. Speaking in the U.S. capital, Abregu was generally supportive of Balza, citing the "historical importance" of his speech, but lamented that it was not the president who had taken the initiative. It was, he said, "proof that democratic institutions in Argentina do not function as they should, and have a long way to go in this regard."

60. Bonafini made these comments in Spain during an interview with the Madrid daily *El País* on April 27, 1995. The story was reprised the following day in *Página 12*, p. 4.

61. Quotes from these speeches are taken from the complete texts provided to me by General Balza.

62. Corroborating Talavera's testimony are the declarations made to the CONADEP on June 18, 1984, by Omar Eduardo Torres, of the National Gendarmes. The salient points were enumerated by Andrea Rodríguez, "La CONADEP confirma la denuncia," *Página 12*, April 28, 1995, pp. 2–3.

63. Paulik gave a preview of his speech on the radio on May 2; the text he delivered on May 3 was reprised by the dailies the next day.

64. Molina Pico's text was also reprised in the dailies on May 4.

65. The admiral's praise of Astiz, made to Nelson Castro on Radio Del Plata on May 5, was printed the next day in *Página 12*, p. 3.

66. Menem's comments, originally made on the radio, were reprinted in *Página 12*, June 6, 1995, p. 9.

67. Quoted by Dario Gallo, "Alfredo Astiz: La Condena del pasado," in *Notícias*. June 18, 1995, pp. 36–41. Accompanying the article are color photos of Astiz in a disco, walking with a friend in the street, in the Georgian Islands, etc. Also pictured is then Minister of Defense Oscar Camilión, suntanned and relaxed in Paris, who said that it was "premature to consider a promotion for Astiz." In an attempt to distance himself from the scandal, Camilión said the matter was "more in the realm of diplomacy than Defense."

68. For more on Hagelin, see *El Diario del Juicio*, no. 18, September 24, 1985, pp. 403–8 (testimony of Ragnar Hagelin, the girl's father), and no. 26, November 19, 1985, p. 480 (testimony of Norma Susana Burgos); and *Nunca Más*, 383–85.

69. *Notícias*. June 18, 1995, p. 39.

70. Page-one banner headline. *Página 12,* July 14, 1995.

71. See María O'Donnell, "Y comieron perdices," in *Página 12,* July 15, 1995, pp. 4–5. When Molina Pico arrived, representatives from the major Argentine human rights organizations pointedly left the French embassy. (These groups included Mothers of the Plaza de Mayo—Founding Line, CELS, Permanent Assembly for Human Rights, and Relatives of Detainees-Desaparecidos for Political Reasons).

72. "Minuto de silencio por los periodistas," in *Clarín,* June 9, 1995, pp. 18–19.

73. Interview with Retired Colonel Ballester, Buenos Aires, June 19, 1995.

74. I have taken this quotation from García, *El Drama,* 389. García cites Augusto B. Rattenbach, Horacio P. Ballester, José L. Garcia, and Carlos M. Gascón, *Fuerzas armadas argentina: El Cambio necesario* (Buenos Aires: Editorial Galerna, 1987), 11.

75. Interview with Verbitsky, June 21, 1995.

76. Interview with Balza by Prudencio García, quoted in García, *El Drama,* 559.

77. Jacobo Timerman, "Torturador implacable," part of a special feature on Bergés in *Notícias,* June 25, 1995, p. 40.

78. Calvo de Laborde has made this declaration repeatedly in sworn testimony since the days of the CONADEP.

79. Quotes taken from Dario Gallo, "Bergés: Primeros auxilios en el infierno," in *Notícias,* June 25, 1995, pp. 39–41.

80. I followed the Bergés/ORP story through telephone conversations with various individuals in Buenos Aires. I relied also on articles in *Clarín:* "El Ejército no dejó que internen a Bergés en el Hospital Militar," April 7, 1996, p. 18; "Entrevista exclusiva con el Ministro del Interior: Hay pistas firmes sobre los atacantes de Bergés," April 14, 1996, pp. 2–5; "Bergés: Confianza del gobierno," April 19, 1996, p. 9; and "Ofrecieron custodia a Alfonsín," April 28, 1996, p. 12; in *Noticias:* Edi Zunino, "Benzi: El Dueño del misterio," April 29, 1996, pp. 32–36; and in *Página 12,* "El Caso Bergés: Detrás de las balas," lead story by Jorge Cicuttín; accompanying contributions by Martín Granovsky and Gabriela Cerruti, and a round-up of statements by prominent human rights activists, April 6, 1996, pp. 1–4; "Se agrava el estado de salud de Bergés," April 10, 1996, p. 12; "De las palabras a los hechos" and Román Lejtman,"Sospechas en el gabinete," Alberto Dearriba, "Raro como perro verde," and "De Cheek a las Madres: Condenas con distinto color," April 12, 1996; pp. 2 and 4; Ernesto Semán and Andrés Klipphan, "Un acto de servicio," and "Era más un buchón que un arrepentido" (no byline), April 14, 1996, pp. 2–3; "El Juego del desconfío," April 16, 1996, p. 7; "Detienen a unhombre que llamó a la casa de Bergés," April 19, 1996, p. 10; "La ORP en penumbras," April 26, 1996, pp. 2–3; "Es apología del delito," April 27, 1996, p. 2; Esteban Schmidt, "Una estupidez absurda," April 28, 1996, p. 15.

81. Alberto Dearriba, "Una voz en el teléfono," accompanied by shorter, unsigned focus pieces on specific aspects of the story, *Página 12,* April 11, 1996, pp. 2–3; "La Oposición pide explicaciones," *Clarín,* April 14, 1996, p. 4. Also, telephone interviews with various sources in Buenos Aires.

82. Interview with Pierini at her office in Buenos Aires, June 23, 1995.

83. These events received wide coverage in the media. I relied especially on *Clarín,* September 3 and 24; and *Página 12,* September 3, 16, 19, 22, 1995.

84. See Luis Bruschstein, "El Angel de la muerte viene golpeado," in *Página 12*, October 6, 1995, pp. 2–3.

85. Ibid, 2.

86. Interview with Dr. Juan José Prado, Buenos Aires, June 23, 1995.

87. See "El Disgusto por el retiro de Astiz estaría inflado por el 'masserismo,'" *Página 12*, December 7, 1995; and "Astiz suma medallas," ibid., December 8, 1995.

88. For more on General Cándido Diaz's speech and the reaction, see "Rechazo esas-voces," *Página 12*, April 3, 1996, pp. 10—11; and "Olímpica gambeta del gobierno," "Una ola derepudio," and "El Frepaso pide una sanción," *Página 12*, April 4, 1996, pp. 8–9. The administration tried to sidestep the issue with ambiguous statements; only Alicia Pierini (Undersecretary for Human Rights) dissented, saying that it was "a step backward compared with the institutional auto criticism formulated by General Balza." Progressive politicians and human rights figures of course repudiated the speech. On October 11, 1996, Díaz and the heads of the navy (Molina Pico) and air force (Juan Paulik) were forced to resign. President Menem's gesture was clearly intended to communicate that he stands firmly behind Balza. See Calvin Sims, "Argentina's Military Reshuffle Makes It Clear President Is Boss," *New York Times*, October 12, 1996, p. 5.

89. See "Pérez Esquivel declaró en Madrid por los españoles desaparecidos," *Página 12*, June 18, 1996; "Luz verde en Madrid," *Página 12*, July 3, 1996; "España y Francia no olvidan" *Página 12*, July 4, 1996; "Strassera se ofrece," *Clarín*, July 5, 1996; Silvana Boschi, "Cuentas que siguen pendientes," *Clarín*, July 7, 1996, p. 10; "Un camino complicado," *Página 12*, July 9, 1996;"Madrid investigará," *Página 12*, July 12, 1996.

90. The Siderman story was superbly reported by Tim Golden of *New York Times*. See his articles of September 2, 4, and 14, 1996. I thank him for sending me the court documents on this extraordinary case, and hope that he will continue to write about the Siderman family.

91. Telephone interview with Rubén Levemberg, who is on Congressman Bravo's staff, August 5, 1996; see also "Las Leyes de la impunidad," *Página 12*, June 12, 1996.

92. Resnizky's apology came during an interview with Raúl Kollmann, "Cometimos errores y hoy pido perdón," in *Página 12*, December 15, 1996, pp. 9–10.

93. See "Hijos de desaparecidos: Otros 36," in *Clarín*, September 8, 1996, p. 8; and "Podemos lograr una condena," in *Página 12*, December 31, 1996.

94. The quote is taken from Sergio Rubín, "Derechos humanos: La Iglesia dice que lo que hizo fue insuficiente," in *Clarín* April 28, 1996, pp. 2–4. See also *Página 12*, which ran various articles on April 27 and 28.

95. Bussi's statement was printed in *Página 12*, July 4, 1995, p. 2. This issue of the paper ran several articles on the election, which got intense national coverage. See also *Clarín*, July 2–4, 1995.

96. Alberto Dearriba, "No sirve para nada," *Página 12*, November 25, 1995, pp. 4–5.

97. In connection with the prosecutions by the Spanish government, Juan Antonio del Cerro ("Colores") appeared on a Barcelona television show *(Investigación)*. See "A las ocho de la noche, por tevé, una de terror," in *Página 12*, December 3, 1996.

98. *Página 12:* "H.I.J.O.S. Denuncia Amenazas," paid advertisement, April 10, 1996, p. 10; Andrea Rodríguez, "Los Desconocidos de siempre," April 19, 1996; "Contra HIJOS: De la

amenaza, al hecho," April 25, 1996; "Víctimas de amenazas, los HIJOS le reclamaron al ministro Corach," May 21, 1996.

99. Miguel Bonasso, "No te olvides el nombre de Fichera" and "Un represor asesora en Defensa," *Página 12*, May 19, 1996, pp. 2–3.

100. Rafael Saralegui, Jr., "La Rara Historia de Alacrán y del comisario Scifo Módica" and "El Policía negó la acusación," *La Nación*, July 7, 1996, pp. 19–20.

101. Andrea Rodríguez, "La Vuelta de Alacrán," *Página 12*, July 7, 1996, pp. 12–13.

102. Pierini's backpedaling and Corach's defense of Scifo Módica are found in Andrea Rodríguez, "'Sería un gesto de reconciliación cambiarle el destino' a Alacrán," *Página 12*, July 19, 1996. See also "Piden informes sobre un policía," *Clarín*. July 20, 1996, p. 56.

103. Andrea Rodríguez, "El Ministro necesita que le avisen," *Página 12* July 19, 1996, and Rafael Sarelegui, Jr., "Alacrán fue reconocido por otros sobrevivientes," *La Nación*, July 18, 1996.

104. See note 102 above.

105. See the following articles in *Página 12*: Diego Schurman, "Las Madres esperan a Menem en la catedral," July 9, 1996; Diego Schurman, "A los golpes en la catedral," July 10, pp. 2–4; "Madres en la catedral: Corach ataja una ola de repudio," July 11, 1996; and Hebe de Bonafini, "De quién es la catedral?," July 12, 1996.

106. Manuel Cerdán and Antonio Rubio broke this story on April 3, 1997, in *El Mundo*, a major Madrid daily. The Argentine press immediately reprised the piece through its own correspondents. I relied on the articles in *Página 12*, April 4, 1997, pp. 2 and 3.

107. Juan Gasparini, "Chau secreto bancario," *Página 12*, June 12, 1997. Gasparini is the paper's Geneva correspondent. See aso Luis Vásquez, "Altos militares argentinos alquilaron en Suiza cajas fuertes durante la dictadura," *El País*, June 12, 1997; and Juan Jesús Aznárez," Argentina apoyará las pesquisas sobre las cajas fuertes alquiladas por sus militares en Suiza," *El País*, June 13, 1997.

108. Horacio Verbitsky, "Las Uñas del gato," *Página 12*, June 15, 1997, and "La Inteligencia de un gato," *Página 12*. June 19, 1997. See also "Camino difícil para el Gato con botas," *El País*, June 17, 1997; and Carlos Quiros, "El Senado no quiere sorpresas," *Clarín*, June 18, 1997, and "Un militar, sin ascenso," *Clarín*, June 20, 1997.

109. "Liberaron al ex marino Scilingo," *Clarín*, June 18, 1997.

110. Susana Viau, "Astiz en buena compañía," *Página 12*, June 17, 1997, and "Un ángel servicial," *Página 12*. June 18, 1997. See also "Francia presionó y Astiz volvió a quedar sin trabajo," *Clarín*, June 19, 1997; and Eduardo Febbro, "Sin garantías sobre Asriz," *Página 12*, June 19, 1997. Reporting from Paris, Febbro focused on French diplomatic rage, and quoted one high-level functionary as saying, off the record, "Ces Argentins se foutent de notre gueule" ("These Argentines keep fucking with us").

111. See "Robo en la sede de las Madres," *Clarín*, August 15, 1997; "Robo y destrozos en el local de las Madres," and "Las Madres denuncian a la Corte robo de 'delincuentes oficiales'," *Página 12*, August 15 and 16, 1997.

112. For coverage on Scilingo's kidnapping, see Horacio Verbitsky, "Primeros Palos," and Luis Bruschtein, "Vamos a matar a los cuatro," *Página 12*, September 12, 1997; Calvin Sims, "Vicious Reminder of 70's Atrocities in Argentina," *New York Times*, September 13,

1997, pp. A1 and A4; "El Falcón regresa a las calles pero ahora es blanco," *Página 12*, "September 13, 1997; "Con copia a la Casa Blanca" and "Justicia por propia mano," *Página 12*, September 19, 1997.

According to an Argentine press association, since Menem took office there have been 880 documented cases of physical threats or attacks against reporters. In January 1997, José Luis Cabezas, a journalist reporting on government corruption, was murdered by a task force connected to the police. The Cabezas case has engendered considerable popular mobilization and great concern in human rights circles.

113. For coverage on Scilingo and survivors giving testimony in Madrid, see: "Garzón tiene más pruebas contra Emilio Massera," *Página 12*, September 19, 1997; Juan Carlos Algañaraz," Un juez español detuvo a Scilingo por los crímenes que cometió en la ESMA," "Instalaron al ex marino en una prisión madrileña," and "Piden la captura de Massera y de otros ex jefes militares," *Clarín*, October 8 and 11, 1997; and Horacio Verbitsky, "El vuelo de la muerte," Carla Artes, "Ni olvido ni perdono," José M. Bustamante, "El verdugo y la víctimas," and Juan Ignacio Irigaray, "Mi marido está feliz aunque esté preso, consiquió lo que buscaba," in *El Mundo*, October 12, 1997.

114. Cristian Alarcón, "Elogio al uso de tormentos," Juan Gelmán, "Irresponsabilidades," and Jorge Cadano, "Una historia con picana," *Página 12*, September 16, 1997.

EPILOGUE

1. In Spanish, the threat was even more vulgar and misogynist: *Máten la, la yegua*. *Yegua*, which means "mare," refers, crudely, to women who are powerful and physically large. So objectionable is the term, it is not often used.

2. Menéndez received *prisión perpétua* for atrocities committed at La Perla, on July 24, 2008; for crimes committed in Tucumán, on August 29, 2008; and on December 11, 2009, for crimes committed by the Córdoba Police Information Department, the greatly feared "D2." Fifty-eight cases are pending against the ex-general, who is doing his time in a common jail.

3. The event was covered by all the media. An extended interview with Posse appeared in *Página 12*, December 13, 2009.

4. The quote is from *La Nación*, January 2, 2010. See also *Clarín*, January 3 and 8, 2010; and *Página 12*, January 17, 2010. For Cobacho's bio, see <http://www.sdh.gba.gov.ar/autoridades.htm>.

5. Ministerio Público Fiscal ([Ministry of the Public Prosecutor] October 2009. <http://www.mpf.gov.ar>. See also CELS <http://www.cels.org.ar> and Centro de Información Judicial <http://www.cij.gov.ar>.

6. A superb source on this legal history is *Argentina: Combate a la Impunidad*. Secretaría de Derechos Humanos, Ministerio de Justicia y Derechos Humanos. (Buenos Aires: EUDEBA, 2006). The above paragraphs draw on pp. 13–19.

7. David Rock, "Racking Argentina," *New Left Review*, no. 17 (Sept.–Oct. 2002), pp. 55–86.

8. <http://www.abuelas.org>/ar/material/testimorios/+006.htm.

9. From my interview with Varsky in Buenos Aires, December 16, 2009.

10. Victoria Donda recovered her identity in 2004, by which time she was already active in politics. A Deputy in the lower house, she is the youngest woman ever elected to the Congress. See her *Mi nombre es Victoria: Una lucha por la identidad* (Buenos Aires: Editorial Sudamericana, 2009).

11. From our interview, December 17, 2009.

12. See pp. 3–8 of the present volume.

13. His *El Estado Terrorista Argentina* (1984) was the first analytical history of the period and has since been updated. Eduardo Luis Duhalde is not to be confused with Eduardo Duhalde, a politician of a different stripe, who was president from January 2, 2002 until May 25, 2003.

14. Housed at George Washington University, <http://www.gwu.edu/~nsarchiv>.

15 *Nunca Más*, op. cit., pp. 164, 166.

16. *Página 12*, November 6, 2009.

17. From our interview, December 11, 2009.

18. See my "The Tortured Road to Justice," in *Dissent* (Spring 1999): 33–40; and "The Pinochet Precedent," a three-part series in 2000 for the Crimes of War Project, <http://www.crimesofwar.org/expert/pin-marguerite1.html>.

19. See Werner Pertot, "Delitos cometidos en el marco del genocidio," *Página 12*, September 20, 2006.

20. Gerardo changed his last name from Dell'Orto to Dell'Oro.

21. For an account of this seminar, see Osvaldo Devries, "Las Fuerzas Armadas en la Democracia," in *Revista de la Defensa*, no. 4 (RD4), 144–48.

22. From our interview, December 18, 2009.

23. The law authorizing the creation of the Espacio Para La Memoria, Promoción y Defensa de los Derechos Humanos was passed on March 24, 2004. It has been open to the public since October 1, 2007. Not everyone agreed that the ex-ESMA should be used as a site for human rights: CELS, for example, proposed that the navy continue to function in the renovated space, so that the memory of what it did in the past should never fade; an artists' collective advocated blowing up the four massive columns on the façade of the main building and letting the rest of the complex fall gradually into ruin. Hebe de Bonafini's group of Madres has installed an art gallery and theatre, and will be running a school; the Madres Founding Line will also have youth-oriented activities. Approximately twenty groups will operate in these buildings. See <http://www.derhuman.jus.gov.ar/espacioparalamemoria>.

24. From our interview, December 9, 2009.

25. The line is from Miguel Angel Asturias (1899–1974), Guatemalan poet, novelist, and diplomat.

Selected Bibliography

This book has its origins in testimony, and my greatest debt is to the many individuals I
 interviewed from late 1989 until late 1997. As the dates of these conversations are
 recorded in the notes for each chapter, they are not repeated here.
Specific newspaper reports and magazine and journal articles are listed in the endnotes for
 each chapter, and are likewise omitted here. Similarly omitted, but invaluable, are
 Amnesty International's annual country-by-country human rights analyses and
 periodic crisis reports.

BOOKS

Abós, Alvaro. *El Poder carnívoro.* Buenos Aires: Editorial Legasa, 1985.
Abraham, Tomás. *Historias de la Argentina deseada.* Buenos Aires: Editorial Sudamérica,
 1995.
Abudara, Oscar, et al. *Argentina psicoanálisis represión política.* Buenos Aires: Ediciones
 Kargieman, 1986.
Abuelas de Plaza de Mayo. *Niños desaparecidos en la Argentina entre 1976 y 1983.* Buenos
 Aires: Paz Producciones, 1990.
Aguinis, Marcos. *Un país de novela: Viaja hacia la mentalidad de los argentinos.* Buenos
 Aires: Editorial Planeta, 1988.
Anderson, Martin Edwin. *Dossier Secreto: Argentina's Desaparecidos and the Myth of the
 "Dirty War."* Boulder: Westview Press, 1993.
Arendt, Hannah. *Eichmann in Jerusalem: A Report on the Banality of Evil.* New York:
 Penguin Books, 1977.
Nunca Más: Report of the Argentine National Commission on the Disappeared. New York:
 Farrar Straus Giroux; London: Index on Censorship, 1986. (Originally published in
 Spanish by Editorial Universitaria de Buenos Aires, 1984).

Asociación Americana de Juristas. *Juicios a los militares: Documentos secretos leyes jurisprudencia.* Buenos Aires, 1988.

Asociación Madres de Plaza de Mayo. *Historia de las Madres de Plaza de Mayo.* Buenos Aires: Página/12, 1996.

Asociación de Periodistas de Buenos Aires. *Periodistas desaparecidos: Con vida los queremos.* Buenos Aires: Unión de Trabajadores de Prensa de Buenos Aires, 1987.

Astelarra, Patricia, and Gustavo Contemponi. *Sobrevivientes de la Perla.* Buenos Aires: El Cid Editor, 1984.

Bayer, Osvaldo. *Rebeldía y esperanza: Documentos.* Buenos Aires: Ediciones B., 1993.

Belli, Maria C., et al. *Desde el silencio: Escritos de jóvenes secuestrados–desaparecidos durante la dictadura.* Buenos Aires: Sudamericana-Planeta, 1985.

Bermann, Sylvia, et al. *Efectos psicosociales de la represión política: Sus secuelas en Alemania, Argentinay Uruguay.* Córdoba: Goethe Institut, 1994.

Boccia Paz, Alfredo, et al. *Es mi informe: Los Archivos secretos de la policía de Stroessner.* Asunción: Centro de Documentación y Estudios, 1994.

Bonaparte, Laura. *El Mundo guarda silencio: La Tragedia de Cañuelas.* Buenos Aires: Catálogos Editora, 1993.

Bonasso, Miguel. *Recuerdo de la muerte.* Buenos Aires: Puntosur Editores, 1988.

Botana, Natalio R. *La Libertad política y su historia.* Buenos Aires: Editorial Sudamericana, 1991.

Bresci, Domingo A. *Movimiento de sacerdotes para el tercer mundo.* Buenos Aires: Centro Salessiano de Estudios San Juan Bosco/Centro Nazaret, 1994.

Brown, Cynthia, ed. *With Friends like These: The Americas Watch Report on Human Rights and U.S. policy in Latin America.* New York: Pantheon Books, 1985.

Buda, Blanca, *Cuerpo I—Zona IV: El Infierno de Suárez Mason.* Buenos Aires: Editorial Contrapunto, 1988.

Campra, Rosalba. *América Latina: La Identidad y la máscara.* Mexico City: Siglo Veintiuno Editores, 1987.

Careaga, Ballestrino, et al. *Semillas de vida: Ñemity ra.* Asunción: Comisión de Familiares de Paraguayos Detenidos Desparecidos en la Argentina, 1993.

CELS et al. *Culpables para la sociedad, impunes por la ley.* Buenos Aires: CELS, 1988.

———. *Medios de comunicación, inseguridad ciudadanía y derechos humanos: Documento de trabajo.* Buenos Aires: Centro de Estudios legales y Sociales, CELS, 1992.

Center for the Study of Human Rights, Columbia University. *Twenty-four Human Rights Documents.* New York: Columbia University Press, 1992.

Chomsky, Noam. *Chronicles of Dissent: Interviews with David Barsamian.* Monroe: Common Courage Press, 1992.

Cohen Salama, Mauricio. *Tumbas anónimas: Informe sobre la identificación de restos de víctimas de la represión ilegal.* Buenos Aires: Equipo Argentino de Antropología Forense and Catálogos Editora, 1992.

Corradi, Juan E., et al., eds. *Fear at the Edge: State Terror and Resistance in Latin America.* Berkeley: University of California Press, 1992.

Crasswell, Robert D. *Perón and the Enigmas of Argentina.* New York: W. W. Norton and Co., 1987.

Deutsch, Sandra McGee, and Ronald H. Dolkart. *The Argentine Right: Its History and Intellectual Origins, 1910 to the present*. Wilmington: Scholarly Resource Books, 1993.

Diago, Alejandro. *Hebe de Bonafini: Memoria y esperanza*. Buenos Aires: Ediciones Dialectica, 1988.

Duhalde, Eduardo. *El Estado terrorista argentino*. Buenos Aires: Editorial Argos Vergara, S.A., 1983.

Echagüe, Hernán López. *El Enigma del General Bussi: De la Operación Independencia a la Operación Ritorno*. Buenos Aires: Editorial Sudamericana, 1991.

Eloy Martínez, Tomás. *Lugar común la muerte*. Buenos Aires: Editorial Bruguera, 1983.

———. *La Novela de Perón*. Buenos Aires: Editorial Legasa, 1985.

Faye, J.R *Langages totalitaires*. Paris: Hermann, 1972.

Fein, Helen. *Accounting for Genocide: National Responses and Jewish Victimization During the Holocaust*. Chicago: University of Chicago Press, 1979.

Ferrara, Francisco. *Qué son las ligas agrarias: Historia y documentos de las organizaciones campesinas del Nordeste argentino*. Buenos Aires: Siglo Veinteuno Editores, s.a, 1971.

Forner, Juan Pablo. *Discurso sobre la tortura*. Barcelona: Editorial Crítica, 1990.

Foucault, Michel. *Discipline and Punish: The Birth of the Prison*. New York: Vintage Books, 1979.

Frontalini, Daniel, and María Cristina Caiati. *El Mito de la guerra sucia*. Buenos Aires: Ed. CELS, 1984.

Gabetta, Carlos. *Todos somos subversivos*. Buenos Aires: Editorial Bruguera, 1983.

Gambaro, Griselda. *Dios no nos quiere contentos*. Barcelona: Editorial Lumen, 1979.

———. *Ganarse la muerte*. Buenos Aires: Ediciones de la Flor, 1976.

———. *Teatro,* vols. 1-6. Buenos Aires: Ediciones de la Flor, 1984–96. Comprising plays from the early 1960s until 1994.

García, Alicia S., *La Doctrina de la Seguridad Nacional* Buenos Aires: Centro Editor de América Latina, 1991.

García, Analía, and Marcela Fernández Vidal. *Pirí*. Buenos Aires: Ediciones de la Flor/La Maga/UTPBA, 1995.

García, José María. *Reforma agraria y liberación nacional*. Buenos Aires: Centro Editor de América Latina, S.A., 1987.

García, Prudencio. *El Drama de la autonomía militar*. Madrid: Alianza Editorial, S.A., 1995.

Gasparini, Juan. *El Crimen de Graiver*. Buenos Aires: Ediciones Grupo Zeta, 1990.

———. *Montoneros: Final de cuentas*. Buenos Aires: Editorial Puntosur, 1988.

———. *La Pista Suiza*. Buenos Aires: Editorial Legasa, 1985.

Gelman, Juan. *Interrupciones I/Interrupciones II*. Buenos Aires: Ediciones Libros de Tierra Firma/Ediciones Ultimo Reino, 1988.

Gelman, Juan, and Osvaldo Bayer. *Exilio*. Buenos Aires: Editorial Legasa, 1984.

Gillespie, Richard. *Soldiers of Perón: Argentina's Montoneros*. New York: Oxford University Press, 1982.

Giussani, Pablo. *Los Días de Alfonsín*. Buenos Aires: Editorial Legasa, 1986.

———. *Montoneros: La Soberbia armada*. Buenos Aires: Sudamericana–Planeta, 1987.

Grecco, Jorge, and Gustavo González. *Felices Pascuas!: Los hechos inéditos de la rebelión militar.* Buenos Aires: Grupo Editorial Planeta, 1988.

Guest, Iain. *Behind the Disappearances.* Philadelphia: University of Pernnsylvania Press, 1990.

Guzman Bouvard, Marguerite. *Revolutionizing Motherhood: The Mothers of the Plaza de Mayo.* Wilmington: SR Books, 1994.

Halperin Donghi, Tulio. *El Espejo de la historia: Problemas argentinos y perspectivas hispanoamericanas.* Buenos Aires: Editorial Sudamericana, 1987.

————. *Historia Argentina, vol. 3: De la revolución de independencia a la confederación rosista.* Buenos Aires: Editorial Paidos, 1985.

Hennelly, Alfred T., S.J. *Liberalion Theology: A Documentary History.* Maryknoll. New York: Orbis Books, 1990.

Herrera, Matilde, and Ernesto Tenembaum. *Identidad: Despojo y restitución.* Buenos Aires: Editorial Contrapunto S.A., (n.d.).

Horne, Alistair. *A Savage War for Peace: Algeria 1954–1962.* London: Macmillan, 1977.

Isis International. *La Mujer ausente: Derechos humanos en el mundo.* Santiago de Chile: Isis International, 1991. A collection of essays by Ximena Bunster, Rita Arditti, Brinton Lykes, Amartya Sen, and others.

Izaguirre, Inés. *Los Desaparecidos: Recuperación de una identidad expropriada.* Buenos Aires: Instituto de Investigaciones de la Facultad de Ciencias Sociales, 1992.

Kordon, Diana R., and Lucila I. Edelman. *Efectos psicológicos de la represión política.* Buenos Aires: Sudamericana–Planeta, 1986.

Kovadloff, Santiago. *Argentina–Oscuro país: Ensayos para un tiempo de quebranto.* Buenos Aires: Torres Agüero Editor, 1983.

————. *Por un futuro imperfecto.* Buenos Aires: Botella al Mar, 1987.

Latin American Studies Association. *La Represión en argentina 1973–1974: Documentos.* Mexico City: Universidad Nacional Autònoma de México, 1978.

López Saavedra, Emiliano. *Testigos del proceso militar.* Buenos Aires: Centro Editor de America Latina, 1984.

Martí, Ana María, María Alicia Milia de Pirles, and Sara Solarz de Osatinsky. *ESMA: "Traslados": Testimonio de tres liberadas.* Buenos Aires: Ediciones de Abuelas de Mayo, Familiares de Desaparecidos y Detenidos por Razones Políticas, Madres de Plaza de Mayo Línea Fundadora, 1995.

Maran, Rita. *Torture: The Role of Ideology in the French-Algerian War.* New York: Praeger, 1989.

Massera, Emilio E. *El Camino a la democracia.* Caracas: El Cid Editor, 1979.

Mellibovsky, Matilde. *Círculo de amor sobre la muerte.* Buenos Aires: Ediciones del Pensamiento Nacional, 1990.

Mero, Roberto. *Conversaciones con Juan Gelman: Contraderrota–Montoneros y la revolución perdida.* Buenos Aires: Editorial Contrapunto, 1988.

Mignone, Emilio F. *Iglesia y dictadura: El Papel de la iglesia a la luz de sus relaciones con el régimen militar.* Buenos Aires: Ediciones del Pensamiento Nacional, 1986.

Neilson, James. *La Vorágine Argentina.* Buenos Aires: Ediciones Marymar, 1979.

Organization of American States, Inter-American Commission on Human Rights. *Report on the Situation of Human Rights in Argentina.* Washington, D.C.: General Secretariat, 1980.

Paoletti, Alipio. *Como los Nazis, como en Vietnam: Los Campos de concentración en la Argentina*. Buenos Aires: Edición Cañon Oxidado, 1987.

Partnoy, Alicia. *The Little School: Tales of Disappearance and Survival in Argentina.* Pittsburgh and San Francisco: Cleis Press, 1986.

Pérez, Mariana Eva, and Yamila Grandi. *"Algún día . . . ": Poemas y prosa*. Buenos Aires: Abuelas de Plaza de Mayo, 1990.

Peters, Edward. *Torture*. New York: Basil Blackwell, 1985.

Piglia, Ricardo. *Respiración artificial*. Buenos Aires: Editorial Sudamericana, 1980.

Puget, Janine, and Rene Kaës, eds. *Violencia de estado y psicoanálisis*. Buenos Aires: Asamblea Permanente por los Derechos Humanos, 1991.

Randall, Glenn R., and Ellen L. Lutz. *Serving Survivors of Torture*. Waldorf: American Association for the Advancement of Science, 1991.

Restivo, Néstor, and Camilo Sánchez. *Haroldo Conti, con vida*. Buenos Aires: Editorial Nueva Imagen, 1986.

Rock, David. *Argentina 1516-1987: From the Spanish Colonization to Alfonsín*. Berkeley: University of California Press, 1987.

Rodríguez Molas, Ricardo. *Historia de la tortura y el orden represivo en la Argentina*. Buenos Aires: Editorial Universitaria de Buenos Aires, 1984.

Rouquié, Alain, ed. *Argentina, hoy*. Mexico City: Siglo Veintiuno Editores, S.A., 1982.

———. *Pouvoir militaire~société politique~république Argentine*. Paris: Presses de la Fondation Nationale des Sciences Politiques, 1978.

Scarry, Elaine. *The Body in Pain: The Making and Unmaking of the World*. New York: Oxford University Press, 1985.

Senkman, Leonardo, ed. *El Antisemitismo en la Argentina*. Buenos Aires: Centro Editor de América Latina, 1989.

———. *La Colonización judía*. Buenos Aires: Centro Editor de América Latina, 1984.

———. *El legado del autoritarismo: Derechos humanos y anti~semitismo en la Argentina contemporánea* (edited with Mario Sznajder). Buenos Aires: Grupo Editor Latino-americano; Jerusalem: Harry S. Truman Institute of the Hebrew University of Jerusalem, 1995.

Seoane, María, and Hector Ruiz Nuñez. *La Noche de los Lápices*. Buenos Aires: Editorial Contrapunto, 1986.

Timerman, Jacobo. *Preso sin nombre, celda sin número*. Buenos Aires: El Cid Editor, 1981.

Troncoso, Oscar. *El Proceso de reorganización nacional*, 4 vols. Buenos Aires: Centro Editor de América Latina, 1984, 1985, 1988, 1992.

Uriarte, Claudio. *Almirante cero: Biografía no autorizada de Emilio Eduardo Massera*. Buenos Aires: Planeta–Espejo de la Argentina, 1991.

Verbitsky, Horacio. *Civiles y militares: Memoria secreta de la transición*. Buenos Aires: Editorial Contrapunto 1987.

———. *Ezeiza*. Buenos Aires: Editorial Contrapunto, 1988.

———. *La Posguerra sucia: Un análisis de la transición*. Buenos Aires: Editorial Legasa, 1987.

———. *La Prensa clandestina*. Buenos Aires: Ediciones de la Urraca, 1985.

———. *El Vuelo.* Buenos Aires: Planeta—Espejo de la Argentina, 1995. Engl. Transl. Esther Allen, *The Flight: Confessions of an Argentine Dirty Warrior.* New York: New Press, 1996.

Walsh, Rodolfo. *Operación masacre.* Buenos Aires: Ediciones de la Flor, 1972.

———. *El Violento oficio de escribir.* Buenos Aires: Planeta–Espejo de la Argentina, 1995. An anthology.

Weisbrot, Robert. *The Jews of Argentina.* Philadelphia: Jewish Publication Society, 1979.

SYMPOSIA VOLUMES

Grupo de Iniciativa por una Convención Internacional Sobre la Desaparición Forzada de Personas. *La Desaparición: Crimen contra la humanidad.* Buenos Aires: Asamblea Permanente por los Derechos Humanos, 1987.

La Desaparición forzada como crimen de lesa humanidad. Coloquio de Buenos Aires, October 10-13, 1988. Buenos Aires: Grupo de Iniciativa, 1989.

Mitos viejos, luchas nuevas: Transformación o ruptura de la cotidianidad en la lucha de Madres y Abuelas de Plaza de Mayo?. Conference coordinated by Alicia Moscardi and Piera Oria in August 1986 in Buenos Aires.

NEWSPAPERS AND MAGAZINES

Argentina

Newspapers: *The Buenos Aires Herald, Clarín, El Diario del Juicio, Las Madres, La Nación, Nueva Sión, La Opinión, Página 12, La Prensa, La Voz del Interior;*

Magazines: *Boletín CELS, El Caminante, Crisis, Gente, Humor, La Maga, Notícias, Para Tí, Somos*

Spain

Newspapers: *ABC, El País, La Vanguardia;*

Magazines: *Cambio 16*

France

Newspapers: *Le Monde, Liberation;*

Magazines: *L'Express, Le Nouvel Observateur*

United States

Newspapers: *Boston Globe, New York Times, Washington Post, Los Angeles Times;*

Magazines: *American Voice, Atlantic Monthly, Business Week, The Economist, Harper's, Mother Jones, World Press Review*

Index

J

Jewish colony in Argentina, 108 (*see also* anti-Semitism, during Dirty War dictatorship)

Jews, in Argentina, 113–19, 123, 351*n*13

John Paul II, Pope, 47, 258

John XXIII, Pope, 158, 354*n*20

Jorges, Los, 64

Judenrat's assignments, 352*n*33

juicios para la verdad (Truth Trials), 302

Juliana, Queen, 46

Julián the Turk, 66, 92, 99–100, 198, 226, 244–48, 287, 289, 297, 301, 304, 322–23 (*see also* Simón, Julio)

junta(s), Final Report of, 12, 14, 104, 207, 231

Justo Laguna, Bishop, 259

K

Kandinsky, Wassily, 186

Karpov, Anatoly, 267

Keitel, Marshall, 59

Kennedy, Ted, 46

Khmer Rouge massacres, 321

King, Martin Luther, 115

kinship, 78

Kirchner, Néstor, 303

Kirchner, President Cristina, 299, 315–16

Kirkpatrick, Jeane, 179, 355*n*14

Klimovsky, Gregorio, 124

L

Laghi, Pio, 163

La Matanza, 67, 195

Lambruschini, Armando, 18

La Nación (newspaper), 53, 131, 186, 280, 292, 309

Land, expropriation of, 142

Landa, Lieutenant Colonel Ceferino, 305

language
    as form of torture, 57–71
    unfettering of, 161

Lanusse, Alejandro, 138–39, 141–42, 267, 347*n*99

Lanusse, Pedro, 138

La Opinión (newspaper), 6, 38, 178, 187

La Perla (concentration camp), 37, 62, 66, 74, 75, 79, 177, 226, 295

La Perla (prison camp), 12, 37, 62, 64, 65, 66, 75–76, 79, 177, 184, 191, 248, 250, 313

La Plata, 207–8, 216, 300
    student rally in, 218

La Prensa (newspaper), 24, 27, 177, 178, 186–87, 189, 190, 342*nn*7, 17, 352*n*37

La Razón (newspaper), 176

La Ribera prison, 74

las locas de la Plaza de Mayo, 38–39

Las Madres (magazine), 296

Las Marías (company), 138

latifundistas (large landowners), 132, 137, 142

La Voz del Interior (newspaper), 76, 348*n*12

Lawyers Association of Buenos Aires, 275

League for the Rights of Man, 54

Le Figaro (newspaper), 186

Le Monde (newspaper), 46, 75, 117

Leonera, 64

Lerner, Rosita, 84–100, 102, 237

Levingston, General, 138

Levinson, Burton, 115

Lévy, Bernard-Henri, 194

Liberales party, 143, 161, 170

Liberation Theology, 115, 126–27, 158, 161
    Catholic, 161
    Jewish, 126

Ligas Agrarias. *See* Agrarian Leagues

Liggett and Myers (L&M), 136

linden-tree monument, 212

Loiácono, Guillermo, 187–88

London Times, 273

López, Admiral Fausto, 234

López, Jorge Julio, 300–301, 326–29, 336

López Meyer, Ernesto, 268

López Rega, José, 6, 350*n*3

Lorenzo, Carlos Oscar, 254

Los Angeles Times, 119

Lucía, as collaborator, 90

Luder, Italo, 15, 338*n*8, 364*n*33

Lugones, Leopoldo, 14

lunfardo, 95

L'Unitá (publication), 46

luz verde (green light), 69

M

MacNamara, Robert, 9

Macri, Mauricio, 300–301, 332

Madres de Plaza de Mayo, 3, 210, 308 (*see also* Mothers of the Plaza de Mayo)